The Aesthetics and Politics of Linguistic Borders

This collection showcases a multivalent approach to the study of literary multilingualism, embodied in contemporary Nordic literature. While previous approaches to literary multilingualism have tended to take a textual or authorship focus, this book advocates for a theoretical perspective which reflects the multiplicity of languages in use in contemporary literature emerging from increased globalization and transnational interaction. Drawing on a multimodal range of examples from contemporary Nordic literature, these eighteen chapters illustrate the ways in which multilingualism is dynamic rather than fixed, resulting from the interactions between authors, texts and readers as well as between literary and socio-political institutions. This book highlights the processes by which borders are formed within the production, circulation and reception of literature, and, in turn, the impact of these borders on issues around cultural, linguistic and national belonging. Introducing an innovative approach to the study of multilingualism in literature, this collection will be of particular interest to students and researchers in literary studies, cultural studies and multilingualism.

Heidi Grönstrand is Senior Lecturer at the Department of Slavic and Baltic languages, Finnish, Dutch and German at Stockholm University. She has published on literary multilingualism and language ideologies in a variety of journals and edited books. In 2014–2017, she led the research group Multilingualism in Contemporary Literature in Finland.

Markus Huss is Assistant professor of German at the Department of Slavic and Baltic languages, Finnish, Dutch and German at Stockholm University. He has published on literary multilingualism, intermediality and multimodality, the relationship between historiography and literature, German and Swedish postwar literature and exile literature.

Ralf Kauranen is a sociologist and comics scholar based at the Department of Finnish Literature at the University of Turku. He has written on Finnish comics culture from different perspectives, political cartoons, transnationalism and social class. In 2018–2020 he leads the project Comics and Migration: Belonging, Narration, Activism (migrationcomics.fi).

Routledge Critical Studies in Multilingualism
Edited by Marilyn Martin-Jones, MOSAIC Centre for Research on Multilingualism, University of Birmingham, UK and Joan Pujolar Cos, Universitat Oberta de Catalunya, Spain

14 **Multilingual Brazil**
Resources, Identities and Ideologies in a Globalized World
Edited by Marilda C. Cavalcanti and Terezinha M. Maher

15 **Queer, Latinx, and Bilingual**
Narrative Resources in the Negotiation of Identities
Holly R. Cashman

16 **Language and Culture on the Margins**
Global/Local Interactions
Edited by Sjaak Kroon and Jos Swanenberg

17 **Agency in Language Policy and Planning**
Critical Inquiries
Edited by Jeremie Bouchard and Gregory Paul Glasgow

18 **Researching Agency in Language Policy and Planning**
Edited by Gregory Paul Glasgow and Jeremie Bouchard

19 **Critical Perspectives on Linguistic Fixity and Fluidity**
Languagised Lives
Edited by Jürgen Jaspers and Lian Malai Madsen

20 **Bilingual Parent Participation in a Divided School Community**
Julia Menard-Warwick

21 **The Aesthetics and Politics of Linguistic Borders**
Multilingualism in Northern European Literature
Edited by Heidi Grönstrand, Markus Huss and Ralf Kauranen

For more information about this series, please visit: https://www.routledge.com/Routledge-Critical-Studies-in-Multilingualism/book-series/RCSM09

The Aesthetics and Politics of Linguistic Borders
Multilingualism in Northern European Literature

Edited by
Heidi Grönstrand, Markus Huss
and Ralf Kauranen

LONDON AND NEW YORK

First published 2020 by Routledge

2 Park Square, Milton Park, Abingdon, Oxon, OX14 4RN

605 Third Avenue, New York, NY 10017

Routledge is an imprint of the Taylor & Francis Group, an informa business

First issued in paperback 2020

Copyright © 2020 Taylor & Francis

The right of Heidi Grönstrand, Markus Huss and Ralf Kauranen to be identified as the authors of the editorial material, and of the authors for their individual chapters, has been asserted in accordance with sections 77 and 78 of the Copyright, Designs and Patents Act 1988.

All rights reserved. No part of this book may be reprinted or reproduced or utilized in any form or by any electronic, mechanical, or other means, now known or hereafter invented, including photocopying and recording, or in any information storage or retrieval system, without permission in writing from the publishers.

Notice:
Product or corporate names may be trademarks or registered trademarks, and are used only for identification and explanation without intent to infringe.

Library of Congress Cataloging-in-Publication Data
A catalog record for this title has been requested

ISBN: 978-0-367-20315-3 (hbk)
ISBN: 978-0-367-77675-6 (pbk)

Typeset in Sabon
by codeMantra

Contents

Acknowledgements ix
List of Contributors xi

PART I
Introduction 1

1 Introduction: The Processes and Practices of
  Multilingualism in Literature 3
  RALF KAURANEN, MARKUS HUSS & HEIDI GRÖNSTRAND

PART II
Multilingualism as a Challenge to National Borders 25

2 Follow the Translations! The Transnational
  Circulation of Hassan Blasim's Short Stories 27
  OLLI LÖYTTY

3 Broken Lineages, Impossible Affiliations: The Russian
  Baltic Subject in Andrei Ivanov's "Zola" and
  Peotäis põrmu 48
  ENEKEN LAANES

4 De-bordering Comics Culture: Multilingual Publishing
  in the Finnish Field of Comics 64
  RALF KAURANEN

5 The Multilingual Landscape of Sámi Literature:
  Linguistic and Cultural Border Crossing in the
  Work of Sigbjørn Skåden 87
  KAISA AHVENJÄRVI

vi Contents

6 Kjartan Fløgstad's *Pampa Unión:* A Travel on the
   Border of Languages in Latin America   101
   ANNE KARINE KLEVELAND

7 Humour and Shifting Language Borders in Umayya
   Abu-Hanna's Auto-fictional Novel *Sinut*   114
   HEIDI GRÖNSTRAND

8 An Author's View: To Be a Bridge between Cultures   130
   ZINAIDA LINDÉN

9 The Pilot's Son (Short Story)   139
   ZINAIDA LINDÉN
   TRANSLATED BY ERIC DICKENS

PART III
Multilingualism as Problematization of Language   151

10 Language Play and Politics in Contemporary
   Swedish Hip-Hop   153
   KARIN NYKVIST

11 "Conversations in misspelled English": Partial
   Comprehension and Linguistic Borderlands in Tomas
   Tranströmer's *Östersjöar. En dikt (Baltics)*   176
   MARKUS HUSS

12 Transcending Borders through Multilingual
   Intertextuality in Ville Tietäväinen's Graphic Novel
   Näkymättömät kädet   199
   AURA NIKKILÄ

13 Multilingualism and the Work of Readers: Processes of
   Linguistic Bordering in Three Cases of Contemporary
   Swedish-Language Literature   225
   JULIA TIDIGS

14 "So let me remain a stranger": Multilingualism and
   Biscriptalism in the Works of Finland-Swedish Writer
   Tito Colliander   242
   HELENA BODIN

15 Urbanized Folk Life: Multilingual Slang, Gender and
   New Voices in Finnish Literature   263
   KUKKU MELKAS

16 The Permeable Border: Anxieties of the Mother
   Tongue in Contemporary Nordic Poetry   278
   ELISABETH FRIIS

17 The Small Mysteries of Code-switching: A Practitioner's
   Views on Comics and Multilingualism   300
   INTERVIEW WITH MIKA LIETZÉN BY RALF KAURANEN

18 1917 – Libau (Comics Short Story)   316
   MIKA LIETZÉN

   Index   323

Acknowledgements

This volume is the result of a long cooperation between the authors, who share an interest in examining multilingual practices in contemporary literature and comics. Our discussions, often in various languages, have taken place at conferences and seminars, in informal meetings and in emails and Skype sessions. As always in research, many other people have also been involved in this book project. Many thanks to all those who at different kinds of events, both academic and non-academic, have discussed multilingualism in literature from diverse angles, adding theoretical as well as practical points of view. We especially want to thank our colleagues at the Department of Finnish Literature at the University of Turku for their valuable comments when we presented the first ideas for this book. In the final stage of the project, Olli Löytty, Julia Tidigs and Lasse Vuorsola commented on individual chapters, and we thank them for their careful attention and helpful suggestions.

The starting point of the book project lies in the research project Multilingualism in Contemporary Literature in Finland (2014–2017), funded by the Kone Foundation. We are indebted to the staff at the Kone Foundation for their unswerving support for our ideas. Literature as a Leading Research Area at Stockholm University, which contributed funding to the proofreading costs of this volume, has also made this book possible. We had the privilege of working with Albion M. Butters, who helped us with the English language and revised the final version of the manuscript. While we are grateful to him for his clear-sighted comments and corrections, any remaining mistakes are ours.

We are also thankful to Routledge Critical Studies in Multilingualism for accepting our book in the series, and the editors Marilyn Martin-Jones and Joan Pujolar earn our deepest gratitude for their encouragement throughout the book project. Last, but definitely not least, we would like to thank all of the copyright holders of the texts, images and other works of art cited in this volume for their kind permission to include them.

Contributors

Kaisa Ahvenjärvi, University Teacher of Literature, University of Jyväskylä

Helena Bodin, Professor of Literature, Stockholm University and The Newman Institute, Uppsala

Elisabeth Friis, Senior Lecturer in Comparative Literature, Lund University

Heidi Grönstrand, Senior Lecturer, Stockholm University

Markus Huss, Assistant Professor of German, Stockholm University

Ralf Kauranen, DSocSci., School of History, Culture and Arts Studies, University of Turku

Anne Karine Kleveland, Associate Professor, Norwegian University of Science and Technology

Eneken Laanes, Senior Researcher, Under and Tuglas Literature Centre of the Estonian Academy of Sciences, and Associate Professor, Tallinn University

Mika Lietzén, MA, Comic Artist and Illustrator, Turku

Zinaida Lindén, MA, Author, Åbo and St. Petersburg

Olli Löytty, Associate Professor, School of History, Culture and Arts Studies, University of Turku

Kukku Melkas, Senior Lecturer, School of History, Culture and Arts Studies, University of Turku

Aura Nikkilä, Doctoral Candidate, School of History, Culture and Arts Studies, University of Turku

Karin Nykvist, Associate Professor, Lund University

Julia Tidigs, Postdoctoral researcher, The Society of Swedish Literature in Finland and University of Helsinki

Part I
Introduction

1 Introduction
The Processes and Practices of Multilingualism in Literature

Ralf Kauranen, Markus Huss &
Heidi Grönstrand

Multilingualism is ordinary: in the lives of the majority of humankind, language contact and the use of multiple languages are everyday features. Social interaction, whether it is related to buying groceries, consuming media or maintaining friendships, often entails at least some knowledge of more than one language. Despite the commonness of multilingualism, however, it has historically been and continues to be a contested issue in different fields. One description of this dispute is offered by Yasemin Yildiz's concept of "monolingual paradigm", which describes the monolingualism that emerged in Europe in the 1700s. According to her, monolingualism

> constitutes a key structuring principle that organizes the entire range of modern social life, from the construction of individuals and their proper subjectivities to the formation of disciplines and institutions, as well as of imagined collectives such as cultures and nations.
> (Yildiz 2012, 2)

Language, and the question of different languages' relative positions, has been a central feature in modern nation-state building processes, to which, among other things, education and literature have been harnessed. The idea that a nation's and a culture's literature is best written and represented in one language has prevailed over the last decades. This is certainly true of the Nordic and Scandinavian region as well. Now literary scholars and linguists are paying increasing attention to "literary multilingualism", and it becomes more and more clear that, in literature also, the coincidence of multiple languages is rather mundane. Due to ideological reasons implicated by the monolingual paradigm, however, it has historically been shunned or ignored.

The Aesthetics and Politics of Linguistic Borders: Multilingualism in Northern European Literature takes its point of departure in the multiplicity of languages that prevail in contemporary literature, and it formulates a new theoretical approach to the study of literary multilingualism. The book reflects a continuation of the recent positive attention that has been paid to multilingualism in literature. It demonstrates the highly dynamic and processual nature of multilingualism in contemporary literature, where the phenomenon emerges as a result of interactions between authors, texts and readers, as well as literary and political institutions on different societal levels. In contrast to and as a complement to previous approaches, which, to a large extent, have focussed on multilingualism on the level of the literary text and/or as part of an author's oeuvre, the individual contributions in this volume span different levels of literary multilingualism, driving the perspective on literary multilingualism towards a multilevel analysis.

In order to assess the dynamics of literary multilingualism in this way, we analyse and contextualize the dynamics involved in demarcating and/or dissolving borders between different languages and disparate literatures, sometimes in border and translation studies referred to as a process of *bordering*. These linguistic and literary borders, however, are also connected to border formation processes of other kinds (for instance, the creation (and dissolving) of national borders). The term "bordering" has been widely applied in various disciplines (e.g. in human and political geography, see Houtum et al. 2005). It has been used for analysing and contextualizing border formation in various contexts and focussing on differing types, such as national, cultural, linguistic, symbolic and epistemological borders. The concept of bordering places the analytic focus on how borders are established and manifested in different kinds of practices, in different situations and contexts, in culture and in everyday life at large (e.g. Linde-Laursen 2010, 2; Kiiskinen 2013, 96–97). It also emphasizes the fact that globalization and the movement of people, goods and ideas have given rise to new kinds of borders, border controls and reclamations of space (Houtum et al. 2005, 2), processes with which language questions are also tightly intertwined (Blommaert et al. 2012, 2).

Our approach emphasizes the *practices* and *processes* of demarcating, crossing and dissolving borders connected to language use and literary multilingualism in particular. As history has made evident, borders between languages, linguistic registers, literatures and literary genres, as well as between language and non-language (such as noise), have repeatedly been drawn, muddled and re-drawn in the course of societal, political and cultural changes. Border construction or bordering is a practice that takes place constantly and repeatedly in the literary field and in society at large. It is actively formed in the production, circulation and reception of literature, and it has large-scale effects on the conceptions of literature and its value. The discussion on borders and the concept "bordering" also have a background in translation studies in the work of Naoki Sakai. According to him, translation is not only a means of crossing linguistic and cultural borders, but also a form of bordering, that is, "an act of drawing a border" (2009, 83). In Sakai's view, this is connected to the crucial issue of what languages are. Among others (see Martin-Jones et al. 2015, 10–11), he questions the unity of a language and asks whether languages should rather be compared to water instead of clearly separable and countable entities, such as apples and oranges (Sakai 2009, 73, 84). While languages are contingent and have blurred boundaries, the translation process involved in multilingual literature is precisely a practice that reifies languages and the differences between them.

Borders and the demarcations between different entities imply order. In other words, bordering is also a form of *ordering*. This concept hails from sociology's actor-network theory (Law 1992; Harris 2005; Latour 2005), as it offers an attempt to view social order as a practice and process, as something in the making rather than as a self-evident, stable entity. As borders are created and shifted, different kinds of orders are simultaneously introduced, consolidated and changed. In these ongoing processes, linguistic orders are intermingled with issues concerning nationalism and national orders, literary canonizations, genre conventions and aesthetic values. By including a focus on processes of border and order formation in the study of literary multilingualism, the present volume examines how linguistic orders in the literary field today are intertwined with other cultural, societal and political orders and how literature therefore participates in questioning and forming contemporary notions of cultural, ethnic, linguistic and national belonging. Our aim is to move to a multilevel approach that takes into account how literary multilingualism stems from a dynamic of interactions between authors, texts, readers and society at large. In order to strengthen this approach, the volume also includes contributions from an author and a comics artist active in the Nordic literary field.

Previous Research on Literary Multilingualism

The early 21st century has proved to be a vivid and dynamic period in the research of literary multilingualism. The phenomenon of literary multilingualism, usually defined as literature combining various linguistic registers, codes or languages, has received increased scholarly attention during the last two decades, both among literary scholars and linguists (e.g. Kellman 2000; Schmitz-Emans 2004; Sommer 2004; Wirth-Nesher 2006; Lennon 2010; Domokos & Laakso 2011; Knauth 2011; Englund & Olsson 2013; Tidigs 2014; Gardner-Chloros & Weston 2015; Tidigs & Huss 2017). It is a characteristic of the subject that it has been discussed from various perspectives.

In literary studies, research on multilingual literature has directed attention at authors and texts often falling outside the framework of national literatures, based on a putative natural connection between language and ethno-cultural identity (see, e.g. Yildiz 2012). The boom of interest in literary multilingualism can be understood as a reaction against a long tradition of regarding multilingualism as unimportant, or even as threatening nationhood, "cultural purity" and national loyalty (see, e.g. Tidigs 2014 for discussion). In line with our own wish to discuss literary multilingualism as a multilevel phenomenon, previous research can also be outlined in this way. On one level, literary multilingualism has been regarded as a textual phenomenon. On another level, it has been studied vis-à-vis the author as an intertextual phenomenon manifest in an oeuvre. Third, previous studies of literary multilingualism have proposed views that focus on the literary field or literary world, on local as well as on national and global levels. Obviously, a classification like this is only descriptive on the most general level and neglects the plentiful cross-currents between the levels in each study.

For many literary scholars, sociolinguistics has offered valuable insights into the phenomenon of multilingualism (see Tidigs 2014, 31). An enduring sign of the influence of sociolinguistics is the use of the concept of code-switching, which originally designated language variation in oral discourse, but subsequently has been used for the switching of code in written text as well. While useful for the description of cases of lexical multilingualism or the existence of "foreign" words in a text and linguistic alternations more broadly, some caution is in order when describing multilingualism in terms of code-switching. The term may suggest a clear-cut, detectable border between different "pure" codes (languages, dialects, variants, styles, etc.) that are used in a text. As Julia Tidigs (2014, 48; our translation) notes, this risks "naturalizing a view on languages as precisely separable unities, perhaps with 'natural' borders". At times, a more productive view is to understand textual occurrences of multilingualism as the creation and dissolution of codes rather than as a switch between pre-existing, normative codes (also Blommaert 2010).

While the term "code" superficially or in itself may suggest a form of language that is pure, contained and separate, languages and their borders vis-à-vis other languages are in fact porous, in flux and always conventional, that is, socially grounded one way or the other. Also, each "natural language" can be divided into a number of varieties and resources (sociolects, dialects, professional jargons, media discourses, etc.) based on social groups and spheres of life.

For many scholars who work with intratextual multilingualism, Mikhail Bakhtin's concepts have provided a useful framework for the understanding of language (see, e.g. Lalor 2010). According to Bakhtin, language is embedded in social structure and interaction. He emphasizes the diversity of speech: language is not only stratified into dialects, but various other varieties as well, such as languages belonging to professions, genres, particular generations and so forth. Language is never unitary. Instead, it is permeated with power relations as "[e]very utterance participates in the 'unitary language' (in its centripetal forces and tendencies) and at the same time partakes of social and historical heteroglossia (the centrifugal stratifying forces)" (Bakhtin 1981, 271–272). The dialogic nature and polyphony of language is reflected in literature and, in particular, according to Bakhtin, in the novel, which can present for the reader various perspectives and ways of using languages. Ideally, as literature combines and brings into contact different socially differentiated languages, "[a] dialogical novel reveals and relativises linguistic borders, making discourse travel across them" (Robinson 2011).

The highly political nature of the connections between language and literature is highlighted by Gilles Deleuze and Félix Guattari ([1975] 1986) in their study of Franz Kafka and "minor literature". Alongside Bakhtin, the work of Deleuze and Guattari is often referred to in current research on literary multilingualism. According to them, "A minor literature doesn't come from a minor language; it is rather that which a minority constructs within a major language" (Deleuze & Guattari ([1975] 1986, 16). Minor literature has three characteristics: it is highly deterritorialized, utterly political and collective as enunciation. The first characteristic refers to the language of a minor literature being deterritorialized from the language's dominant territorial connection (in Kafka's case, to Prague German). But, in minor literature, the language is even further deterritorialized in the ("strange and minor") usage of the language. The political dimension refers to the narrow space granted to minor literature. Because of this, every single utterance of it resonates with the broader political and social issues connected to the language of minor literature. Accordingly, minor literature also represents a form of collective enunciation. Minor literature is communal in another sense than major literatures, in which, Deleuze and Guattari suggest, a conception of individuality being disconnected from the collective is a possibility.

The political and collective nature of minor literature is deemed a revolutionary potential by Deleuze and Guattari. They extend this thought: "We might as well say that minor no longer designates specific literatures but the revolutionary conditions for every literature within the heart of what is called great (or established) literature" (Deleuze & Guattari ([1975] 1986, 18). Julia Tidigs draws on Deleuze and Guattari's concepts and views on language as a starting point in her work on literary multilingualism, particularly in terms of the textual effects of literary multilingualism. In her view, the concepts of deterritorialization and reterritorialization implicate a dynamic that makes it impossible to deal with "text", "author" and "world" in terms of coherent, enclosed entities. Literary multilingualism is a unifying – as well as divisive – force (Tidigs 2014, 28–29).

Intertextual multilingualism is a term that has been used in reference to a number of phenomena (for different definitions of the concept, see, e.g. Kremnitz 2004; Knauth 2007; Laakso 2011, cited in Tidigs 2014, 50–51). K. Alfons Knauth (2007, 1) uses it in reference to

> heteroglot works of different authors linked to each other in a specific way (like those of the European and Latin American corpus of Petrarchan poetry) or between the heteroglot works of the same bilingual author (like Samuel Beckett's alternative English and French fiction and drama).

The latter aspect is also covered by literary scholar Steven Kellman's (2000) concepts "translingualism" and "translingual literature", by which he refers to the phenomenon in the Western literary canon where authors, due to colonization, migration and exile, have written in multiple languages, or at least in another language than their primary one. In his research, Kellman has focussed on individual authors such as J. M. Coetzee and Vladimir Nabokov, and their translingual writing. Attention has also been paid to the frictions and intersections between the writer's native language and the acquired one and how an author's exile might result in the creation of the writer's own poetic language (Olsson 2011). This perspective is echoed in the volume *Languages of Exile: Migration and Multilingualism in Twentieth-Century Literature* (Englund & Olsson 2013), which encompasses essays exploring relationships between exile, migration, materiality and different languages. Rather than offering a theoretical scrutiny of literary multilingualism, the chapters investigate specific literary works and how they have been shaped by experiences of expatriation and migration, as well as writing in multiple languages. The study testifies to the important linkages between modernist studies, avant-garde studies and literary multilingualism studies (see Schmitz-Emans 2004; Tidigs 2014, 28). This is perhaps most vividly described in Jesper Olsson's contribution to the volume, outlining the connections between modernist visual poetry of the inter- and post-war period, through the neo-avant-garde of the 1950s and 1960s, to contemporary examples of multilingual sound poetry (Olsson 2013). Olsson draws on Marjorie Perloff's book on the 20th-century avant-garde tradition *Unoriginal Genius: Poetry by Other Means in the New Century* (2010), which also partly addresses the topic of multilingualism in contemporary poetry.

The connection between language and migration is also dealt with in the frame of post-colonial studies, but with a stronger emphasis on power relations and the resilience of colonial structures (e.g. Thiong'o [1986] 1994; Aschcroft et al. 1989). In this context, Ngũgĩ wa Thiong'o's *Decolonising the Mind: The Politics of Language in African Literature* ([1986] 1994) is seminal. Thiong'o emphasizes the importance of disconnecting African literature from the colonial languages of English, French and Portuguese, for in his view, African literature written in African languages is a crucial part of the anti-imperialist struggles of the peoples of Africa. In a Nordic context, colonial power relations have been discussed especially among those researchers who deal with indigenous literatures (e.g. Sámi literature (Hirvonen [1999] 2008)), but the dynamics between the centre and the margins, between majority and minority languages, have also been addressed in relation to immigrant literature and minority literatures, such as Kven literature in northern Norway, Tornedalian Finnish literature in Sweden, and Roma and Greenlandic literature (Gröndahl 2002).

Another broader theoretical trend in disciplines across the humanities and social sciences has been to criticize notions of fixed entities modelled according to nation-states and homogenous national histories and cultures. The interest in "transnational studies" or "cross-border studies", which aim to challenge nationalist paradigms and ideas of separate, clear-cut national literatures and instead focus on the interwoven relationships between individual actors, cultures and literary traditions, has also accentuated the importance of language questions. For example, a question pertaining to the consequences of writing between national paradigms, "bilingually" or "multilingually", has become significant during the last twenty years (see e.g. Seyhan 2001; Pollari et al. 2015). In the introduction to the anthology *Literature, Language, and Multiculturalism in Scandinavia and the Low Countries* (2013), Wolfgang Behschnitt and Magnus Nilsson discuss cultural diversity in literature under the term "multiculturalism". They do not, however, present an understanding of literatures and cultures as homogeneous and clearly delimited entities, as some definitions of the concept suggest, definitions which, in turn, have been criticized in scholarship on the subject (e.g. Gröndahl 2002). Although the focus is on four countries (or regions) – Denmark, Sweden, the Netherlands and Flanders – the local literatures and literary spheres are viewed as entangled with the global. There is also a strong emphasis on language issues: "Multilingual features of the literary text, thus, are both an important aspect of the discursive construction of multicultural literature, and, at the same time, a textual strategy to put into question hegemonic languages and cultures" (Behschnitt & Nilsson 2013, 14). This view echoes an implicit assumption that multiculturalism as a term is not sufficient to encompass the diversity in contemporary literature and the need to deal with literary multilingualism more thoroughly. While multiculturalism for a long time functioned as a concept which was actively used in literary studies as well as in other disciplines when ethnic and cultural diversity was discussed, it has been criticized for not taking into account complex social structures. Satu Gröndahl was one of the first literary scholars to suggest that the diversity of Nordic literature should be addressed by the term multilingualism instead of multiculturalism (Gröndahl 2002, 29–31).

Language has been an important, if not fundamental, element of nation-building. It is not an exaggeration to claim that it has been one of the key elements in the efforts to bring and establish order among people. The assumption of an individual possessing one language, a "mother tongue", through which he or she is organically linked to a particular ethnicity, culture and nation – and national literary tradition – was deeply rooted in the idea of the modern nation all over Europe, including its Northern parts, as well as in North America. In general, all scholars dealing with multilingualism discuss nationalist ideologies and ideas in one way or another. Doris Sommer has in a vivid and thought-provoking style advised and demanded her readers to wake up from the dangerous daydreams of monolingual societies and their imagined coherence. Sommer underlines that monolingualism has proved to be an insufficient frame in literary and cultural studies when dealing with the changing cultural map of languages and literatures (Sommer 2003, 2004, 2007). Moreover, combining this view with a text-oriented and playful approach to multilingualism, she invites her readers "to play bilingual games, even if you don't have much of a second language yet" (Sommer 2003, 2).

Yasemin Yildiz examines the concept of "mother tongue" more closely than many other literary scholars in her study of monolingualism and the imagined coherence of monolingual societies. In her view, it is at the centre of the monolingual paradigm. By framing it thus, she shifts the discussion around the notion of the mother tongue from an individual and private sphere to a public and social sphere. Yildiz points out that the word "mother" in "mother tongue" has strong associations with a maternal, corporeal origin, displaying an affective and corporeal intimacy, and natural kinship. In this way, the word "mother" also demonstrates a static mode of belonging to the national collective, which has implications for literature as well as literary studies. In Yildiz's view,

> The uniqueness and organic nature of language imagined as 'mother tongue' lends its authority to an aesthetics of originality and authenticity; in this light, a writer can become the origin of creative works only with an origin in a mother tongue, itself imagined to originate in a mother.
>
> (Yildiz 2012, 10–14)

This would disavow the possibility of writing in non-native languages or in multiple languages at the same time.

It is evident that literary multilingualism has been approached from multiple angles, including perspectives that foreground the author's biography in creating a multilingual text, as well as more text-centred views in which the interplay between the text and context is addressed in one way or another. As the views on multilingualism have multiplied, theoretical attempts have been made to scrutinize the premises and ideological assumptions underlying the very concepts of "language", "monolingualism" and "multilingualism" (e.g. Sommer 2004; Yildiz 2012; Dembeck & Mein 2014). However, we find it important to analyse the changes that multilingual literature brings to the literary fields more broadly (e.g. to the concept of national literature(s)).

Towards a New Understanding of Literary Multilingualism: Processes and Practices of Border-Making

The perspective of literary multilingualism as processes and practices of border-making or bordering – and the related formation of orders or ordering – rests on one further theoretical foundation. Viewing literary multilingualism as ongoing processes and practices takes its inspiration from the relational ontology of the philosophical and conceptual work done by Deleuze and Guattari ([1975] 1986, [1980] 2005) on a more general level, but also specifically in relation to language and literature. When outlining the principles of a rhizome in the introductory chapter of *A Thousand Plateaus* ([1980] 2005), Deleuze and Guattari start off by discussing their own book. They point out that it is an assemblage and a multiplicity (and a machine); this describes their theoretical perspective, which suggests the question of how assemblages (e.g. a literary work) function in their relations and connections to other assemblages. This abandonment of questions concerning *the meaning* of a literary text is connected to Deleuze and Guattari's critique of linguistic models (associated, e.g. with Noam Chomsky) that advance an understanding of language as a system of order. The following long quote is an apt summary of the rhizome as ontology, as well as how language can be understood within this broader framework:

> Our criticism of these linguistic models is not that they are too abstract but, on the contrary, that they are not abstract enough, that they do not reach the abstract machine that connects a language to the semantic and pragmatic contents of statements, to collective assemblages of enunciation, to a whole micropolitics of the social field. A rhizome ceaselessly establishes connections between semiotic chains, organizations of power, and circumstances relative to the arts, sciences, and social struggles. A semiotic chain is like a tuber agglomerating very diverse acts, not only linguistic, but also perceptive, mimetic, gestural, and cognitive: there is no language in itself, nor are there any linguistic universals, only a throng of dialects, patois, slangs, and specialized languages. There is no ideal speaker-listener, any more than there is a homogeneous linguistic community. Language is, in Weinreich's words, "an essentially

heterogeneous reality." [...] There is no mother tongue, only a power takeover by a dominant language within a political multiplicity. Language stabilizes around a parish, a bishopric, a capital. It forms a bulb. It evolves by subterranean stems and flows, along river valleys or train tracks; it spreads like a patch of oil. [...] It is always possible to break a language down into internal structural elements, an undertaking not fundamentally different from a search for roots. There is always something genealogical about a tree. It is not a method for the people. A method of the rhizome type, on the contrary, can analyze language only by decentering it onto other dimensions and other registers. A language is never closed upon itself, except as a function of impotence.

(Deleuze & Guattari [1980] 2005, 7–8)

For the understanding of literary multilingualism in terms of border and order formation, the above quote brings to the fore a number of relevant points. First, and in accordance with Sakai's view, language is not a unified or clearly demarcated entity separable from other languages. Hence, although literary multilingualism nominally refers to the co-presence of multiple languages, the borders between languages are not clear, but created all along in literary processes.

Second, the multiplicity of the linguistic world (with, e.g. its dialects, etc.) is not simply a question of the existence of various registers. The heterogeneity of language is precisely an effect of languages being defined by their relationships to any kind of other elements of the social and material world. To put it differently and in terms used earlier, language is formed in the processes and practices that form its connections. These dynamics vary from broad processes, such as the ones dubbed as globalization via international migration and national cultural policies, to the material aspects of literary publications and the linguistic resources of individual readers.

Third, one of the aspects that the understanding of language as heterogeneity points to is the multimodality of artistic and literary expression. Literary multilingualism is not only a question of words (in different registers); it is also connected to the visuality of text, the relations between words and other visual elements of literature, the audibility of a text being read (in silence or aloud) and the tactile aspects of, for example, literary works in different translations. A multimodal approach to literary multilingualism allows us to highlight the aural and visual dimensions of the phenomenon, most prevalent in genres and art forms such as sound poetry and comics.

Fourth, the heterogeneity of language also means that "There is no ideal speaker-listener", emphasizing the need for a diversified conception of readers and the multiplicity of linguistic resources – or lack thereof to different degrees – that readers bring to processes and practices of literary multilingualism. The "ideal reader" or "target reader" can no longer easily refer to a community of readers with shared language and nationality, but rather to different groups of readers with various backgrounds. Literary multilingualism highlights this aspect of multiple readerships, but also how different resources on the part of the reader activate a variety of modalities and modes in the reading process (see Tidigs & Huss 2017). Pluralism aside, the target reader can also become a "target of exclusion or confusion", as Doris Sommer (2003, 2) puts it.

Fifth, linguistic stability – a language – in the rhizomatic framework is a question of power, of which the mother tongue constitutes the example par excellence. Our (predominant) conception of linguistic unity as a social fact is maintained and learned in various practices related to language, such as national school systems or literary fields. Literary multilingualism can work in different directions with regard to linguistic stability. On the one hand, it can build bridges and reduce the distance between groups (of readers); on the other hand, it can also create difference between languages and promote hermetic associations.

Sixth, the stabilization of "a dominant language" conceals the multiplicity of linguistic reality, which, however, needs to be brought into play (by "a method of the rhizome type") in order to understand linguistic dominance as well as the phenomenon of so-called multilingualism. Literary multilingualism needs to be seen in terms of the manifold relations which bring it into existence. As a set of practices and processes, literary multilingualism is related to social phenomena on various levels: in relation to the institutional level of a nationally defined (and canonized) literature, in relation to a (dominant) language community, in relation to an author's oeuvre, in relation to various readerships and in relation to the textual level.

The six points presented above offer us a general framework for understanding literary multilingualism as a form of constant and ongoing construction, reconstruction, erasure, delining, and the drawing and redrawing of borders. While literary multilingualism is easily understood as play, creativity, evolutionary or revolutionary renewal, deterritorialization or destabilization of borders of different kinds – in language, in literature and in the world – it is also clear that this liberating potential is not necessarily actualized in all practices of literary multilingualism. De-bordering and reordering may just as well be replaced by a strengthening of borders and orders. The outcomes or functions of literary multilingualism are not always the same, but dependent on the connections created in the various processes and practices.

The Aesthetics and Politics of Linguistic Borders: Multilingualism in Northern European Literature moves between and focusses on different "local" literatures, literary traditions and practices in Northern Europe. While the starting point lies in the literatures of the Nordic countries and Estonia, it is apparent that any kind of frame which stems from a national or even regional discourse is insufficient to examine the literary multilingualism of contemporary literature.

In the volume section "Multilingualism as a challenge to national borders", we examine how literary multilingualism contributes to and is interrelated with borders on the national level. Multilingualism affects the concept of national literatures and the connections between nation, language and literature. This is partly due to increasing migratory movement and the exilic lives led by a large number of people. Another reason is the increasing transnational flow of literatures and other cultural artefacts, whose travel is aided by linguistic resources and limited by linguistic borders.

Nowadays, Arabic is the second most spoken language in Sweden, and there is a growing interest in Arabic literature in the whole Nordic region. The number of Arab authors who live in Europe and North America has increased, and, in the Nordic countries, Arabic literature has been acknowledged on literary festivals and through prizes (Al-Nawas 2017, 11–12). In his chapter "Follow the translations! The transnational circulation of Hassan Blasim's short stories", Olli Löytty focusses on the writer Hassan Blasim, who does not fit into the classification system based on distinctive national literatures. An Iraqi refugee living in Finland, Blasim has been critically acclaimed as one of the most important contemporary authors in Arabic. Löytty focusses on the multilingual routes Blasim's texts have taken in the global literary field and the mechanisms that regulate their circulation across national borders. He illuminates how translations have the potential to dismantle the hierarchies between languages.

In Chapter 3, "Broken lineages, impossible affiliations: The Russian-Baltic subject in Andrei Ivanov's 'Zola' and *Peotäis põrmu*", Eneken Laanes moves the focus to the Estonian literary field. Laanes's chapter deals with questions of multilingualism, transnationalism and the tenaciousness of linguistic borders in post-Soviet Russian Estonian literature, in particular in the work of the transnational author Andrey Ivanov. Laanes discusses the ways in which Ivanov's fiction, written in Russian, and well-received and much-awarded both in Estonia and Russia, has been extremely difficult to classify and has, in the process, called into question the linguistically drawn borders of literary fields and national literatures. In discussing the questions of exile and non-belonging in Ivanov's texts, Laanes draws on Edward Said's reflections on exile, on the crisis of natural filiation and on the position of secular criticism arising from these conditions. She shows that Ivanov rejects the possibility of affiliation because of the ways in which affiliative communities reproduce filiation, instead seeking to carve out in his works of fiction a radical position that would make visible the ordering function of all borders.

Processes and Practices of Multilingualism 15

As perhaps the most vivid example of transnational dynamics in the field of literary multilingualism, contemporary comics and comics culture in the Nordic region offer numerous examples of cross-national practices. In Chapter 4, "De-bordering comics culture: Multilingual publishing in the Finnish field of comics", Ralf Kauranen analyses the practices of multilingual publishing in Finnish comics. He examines their implications for linguistic borders in comics culture on an institutional level and in comics as a multimodal art form, and he suggests a typology of different ways of presenting a comic multilingually. Bi- or multilingual publishing de-borders comics culture and strengthens transnational tendencies, while the practices simultaneously reproduce other borders (e.g. by maintaining English as a lingua franca of comics culture). In relation to the multimodal framework of representation characteristic of comics, Kauranen sheds light on how the connections between verbal and visual are formed in different ways based on the chosen practice of multilingual presentation: these both invite variegated reading paths connected to the linguistic competencies of different reader positions and posit textual elements in different languages in distinct relation to the visuality of the comics page.

The field of Sámi literature is yet another illuminating example of multilingual practices in Nordic literature today, crossing national boundaries. A large part of Sámi literature is nowadays published in one of the nine Sámi languages. Throughout its history, Sámi literature has also been published in Nordic majority languages and multilingualism can be a feature of texts, authors and readers, as well as the Sámi literary field. In her chapter, "The multilingual landscape of Sámi literature: Linguistic and cultural border crossing in the work of Sigbjørn Skåden", Kaisa Ahvenjärvi illuminates the different levels of multilingualism in Sámi literature and analyses the multilingualism of poems by Sigbjørn Skåden, who actively uses and mixes different languages, linguistic registers and multicultural allusions. In her analysis, Ahvenjärvi shows how Skåden dismantles the border between Sámi literature and majority literatures and demonstrates that Sámi poetry is an important part of the Western literary canon.

A common aesthetic feature in the genre of travel literature has been the use of "foreign" and "exotic" words, sometimes serving the purpose of creating titillating levels of foreignness and adventure. Anne Karine Kleveland's chapter "Kjartan Fløgstad's *Pampa Unión*: A travel on the border of languages in Latin America" takes its point of departure in Nordic travel literature with a particular focus on the Norwegian author Kjartan Fløgstad's book *Pampa Unión. Latinamerikanske reiser* (1994 Pampa Unión: Latin American travels). It includes thirty-eight short texts which portray the first-person narrator's encounters with Latin American societies and cultures, peoples and languages in a previously colonized territory. Where the ethnocentric travelogues of past centuries often described an encounter with the exotic Other, Fløgstad's late 20th-century traveller states that *he* is the Other. In Kleveland's reading, *Pampa Unión* turns languages and their borders into the main topic, whereby the protagonist's own language is dislocated from the linguistic centre of the journey. Regardless of Fløgstad's efforts to challenge the colonial power discourses, however, Kleveland demonstrates how the colonial wound often hinders the traveller-narrator from fulfilling this quest.

A different strategy for coping with language borders is presented in Heidi Grönstrand's chapter "Humour and shifting language borders in Umayya Abu-Hanna's auto-fictional novel *Sinut*". Here Grönstrand addresses autobiography as a genre, which has an important role in bringing into discussion issues of changing linguistic borders. Grönstrand looks specifically at the multilingual traits of Abu-Hanna's literary language in *Sinut* (You), a story that portrays the life of Umayya Abu-Hanna, who in the beginning of the 1980s moved from Palestine to Finland. The story foregrounds the narrator-protagonist's efforts to meet the required language standards in Finnish, but the border between her language use and the norm remains sharp. The protagonist's collisions with the language border are, however, addressed with humour. Humour becomes an important means by which a demand for a change of attitudes towards interpretations of questions of language and belonging is signalled. The main language of *Sinut* is Finnish, but by including long passages in English and giving space to the newcomer's language, which is characterized by creativity and innovation, Umayya Abu-Hanna widens the language repertoire of Finnish literature.

In "An author's view: To be a bridge between cultures", Zinaida Lindén reflects upon her own experiences being a bilingual author and self-translator working in Swedish (one of the national languages of Finland, where she mostly lives, spoken by a 5 per cent minority) and Russian (her mother tongue). She considers herself to be somewhat of a bridge between cultures, crossing borders and bringing different people closer to each other. In her contribution, Lindén ponders how her short stories and novels are perceived in Finland (in the Swedish-language press of Finland and in the Finnish press), as well as in Russia. While the same story can be interpreted differently depending on the audience, some things get "lost in translation". Although both versions of her texts are to be considered as originals, Lindén emphasizes that they each create distinct effects and nuances.

Lindén's chapter is followed by her short story "The Pilot's Son" ("En flygares son"; translated by Eric Dickens). It considers questions of national and linguistic borders from the viewpoint of a flight attendant, Henrik Lappalainen (Finland-Swedish forename and Finnish surname, implying trilinguality, with English), who keeps himself aloof from the rest of the cabin crew. The other protagonist is an eight-year-old boy who joins the flight as an unaccompanied minor. The boy is bilingual (Finnish-Russian) but tries to hide his background, trying to come across as an American, as he admires his American father. During the long overseas flight, the flight attendant and the boy get to know each other, and their meeting changes the flight attendant's views on how to connect with people in a fundamental way. "The Pilot's Son" was first published in Swedish in the collection of short stories called *Valenciana* (2016), and it has been translated into Finnish, Danish and Russian.

The concluding volume section, "Multilingualism as problematization of language", deals with borders between languages and the borders of language, especially the different practices in which they are formed and given meaning. The everyday conception of language as a clearly demarcated entity separable from other languages is put under critical scrutiny. Many of the contributions of the section also highlight how literary multilingualism is not only a question of wording, but also connected to the visual and auditory dimensions of a text.

In "Language play and politics in contemporary Swedish hip-hop", Karin Nykvist provides insights into contemporary Swedish hip-hop and its use of multilingualism. In her analysis of Swedish rap poetics, Nykvist shows how hip-hop lyrics turn to multilingual aesthetics in order to destabilize and question ideas of national identity and to deconstruct the monolingual ideals that those ideas are founded on. She demonstrates how the political performance of multilingualism in contemporary hip-hop lyrics disturbs and alters notions of the Swedish language, as well as the idea and ideology of Swedishness itself.

Markus Huss examines the work of the Swedish poet Tomas Tranströmer. The chapter "'Conversations in misspelled English': Partial comprehension and linguistic borderlands in Tomas Tranströmer's *Östersjöar. En dikt (Baltics)*" argues for the need to re-examine canonical works of Nordic literature from the perspective of literary multilingualism, in order to achieve a better historical understanding and aesthetic appreciation of them. Huss also addresses the concept of literary multilingualism itself, calling for an expanded notion that includes multimodal dimensions, such as visual and aural components. Following these two aims, Huss analyses Tranströmer's long poem *Östersjöar. En dikt (Baltics)*, demonstrating how the poem's overarching theme of the border connects to a focus on the acoustic and visual dimensions of language. He underscores the importance of the acoustic sphere of literary multilingualism, which he claims to be a fundamental component of a multidimensional understanding of literary multilingualism.

Aura Nikkilä's chapter "Transcending borders through multilingual intertextuality in Ville Tietäväinen's graphic novel *Näkymättömät kädet*" also brings to the fore the multimodal aspects of multilingualism. The Finnish comics artist Ville Tietäväinen's graphic novel *Näkymättömät kädet* (2011; Invisible hands) tells the story of Rashid, a poor

Moroccan man who illegally crosses the Mediterranean to Spain in search of work and a better life for himself and his family. Tietäväinen's work deals with global inequality, irregular immigration, questions of ethnicity and racism, religion, honour and insanity. This graphic novel of Finnish origin has crossed borders in the form of translations into Swedish, German, French and Arabic, but the original work itself is far from being monolingual. Nikkilä examines how the multimodal, visual-verbal intertextual references that frequently make use of multilingualism transcend both cultural and national borders, as well as the borders of different media. She shows how multilingual elements, such as Spanish and Arabic phrases in the dialogue, Spanish and Finnish song lyrics, and Spanish-language graffiti, make visible and cut through many kinds of borders: geographical, physical and mental, but also the border between the graphic novel and the reader.

The role of the reader in relation to literary multilingualism has, with a few exceptions, seldom been problematized or explored in previous research. Julia Tidigs's chapter "Multilingualism and the work of readers: Processes of linguistic bordering in three cases of contemporary Swedish-language literature" illuminates the role of readers in processes of linguistic bordering in literary texts. Taking as a starting point that borders between languages, as well as the border between multi- and monolingualism, are not a given but, on the contrary, continually constructed, deconstructed and reconstructed, she explores different ways in which contemporary literary texts engage the reader in processes of bordering, where inter- and intralinguistic borders are simultaneously drawn, blurred, and challenged. With examples from contemporary Swedish-language literature from Finland and Sweden (Ralf Andtbacka, Alejandro Leiva Wenger and Aase Berg), including poetry as well as prose, Tidigs shows how different kinds of readers with varying linguistic resources are all a part of the creation of the effects of literary multilingualism. Thus, this chapter demonstrates how contemporary literary multilingualism demands that readers turn from passive "consumers" of multilingual texts into active co-creators of multilingualism, and it reveals how conventional categories of "ideal" versus "linguistically incompetent" readers of multilingual literature have lost relevance with regard to the newest forms of literary multilingualism.

The intriguing multimodal genre of "biscriptalism" is examined in Helena Bodin's chapter "'So let me remain a stranger': Multilingualism and biscriptalism in the works of Finland-Swedish writer Tito Colliander", which also ties into the role of the reader in the construction of literary multilingualism raised in Tidigs's chapter. Bodin treats the Finland-Swedish, polyglot writer Tito Colliander's memoirs, showing how Colliander embodied the three roles of author, translator and stranger in the Orthodox Christian diaspora, in both Finland and Estonia, ever since his decision to become a Russian-Orthodox Christian.

She analyses the use of spoken Russian and Cyrillic script in order to discuss what these devices meant for his poetics and identity, also taking into account religion as an important parameter of diversity in the study of literary multilingualism and translingual life writing. Bodin demonstrates that the experience of translating, mediating and going in-between is crucial to Colliander's life and work: multilingualism and biscriptalism play decisive roles in his diasporic Orthodox Christian identity, but the reader is also invited to continue this task of the translator and to experience the in-betweenness of Colliander's stranger.

In "Urbanized folk life: Multilingual slang, gender and new voices in Finnish literature", Kukku Melkas explores the multi-voiced novel *Wenla Männistö* (2014) by Riina Katajavuori. The novel is based on a Finnish literary classic, Aleksis Kivi's *Seitsemän veljestä* (1870; *Seven Brothers*, 1929). Like its predecessor, the modernized version of the classic relies in its language use on vernacular, folksy and in many ways improper language. In contrast to Kivi's novel, *Wenla Männistö* presents women as the main protagonists, granting them space to be taken seriously and for their voices to be heard. In her analysis, Melkas shows how *Wenla Männistö* attributes a positive value to the language of the young, suburban girl characters. The novel underlines the ways in which language moves and changes in different social and cultural contexts and how language and manners of speaking, power and gender are intertwined in an urban environment.

Elisabeth Friis's "The permeable border: Anxieties of the mother tongue in contemporary Nordic poetry" takes its approach from the concept of the mother tongue, which she demonstrates to be inhabited by ambivalence. Friis argues that this concept functions as a point from which contemporary Nordic poetry can engage in a nuanced and inclusive critique of colonialism, racism, linguistic homogenization and cultural (re-)production in the broadest sense. This critique, in turn, is based on a negotiation of the very nature of linguistic borders. In her analysis of poems by Jessie Kleemann (Greenland), Athena Farrokhzad (Sweden) and Ursula Andkjær Olsen (Denmark), Friis shows how their work reveals what the notion of the mother tongue actually carries along with it in terms of division, confusion, pain and profound ambivalence, and how this, in turn, functions as the point of departure for a critique of society.

The chapter "The small mysteries of code-switching: A practitioner's views on comics and multilingualism" presents an interview (conducted by Ralf Kauranen) with Finnish comics artist, publisher and translator Mika Lietzén. Outside Finland, Lietzén's comics have also been published in, for example, France and Sweden. Discussing the frequent code-switching between languages in these comics, Lietzén and Kauranen come to the conclusion that they often function as small mysteries in the stories while also thematizing language use, intercultural relations and a longing for being elsewhere. Multilingualism is also discussed in relation to Lietzén's working practices. Although most of his comics have first been published in Finnish, Lietzén's working language is usually English. All in all, the interview provides a broad picture of what multilingualism has come to mean in a contemporary comics artist's life and work in the Nordic countries.

The final chapter in this volume is Mika Lietzén's comic "1917 – Libau", which was originally published simultaneously in Finnish and Swedish in a collection of short stories that fictively treat the Finnish Jägers in the early 20th century. These were Finnish men who volunteered to be sent to Germany for military education, some of who were stationed in Libau (in contemporary Latvia) and played a crucial role in the Finnish Civil War in 1918. Lietzén's story depicts this specific form of transnational travel and thematizes the linguistic border crossings it germinated.

Many chapters discuss translation-related issues and often also include translations of literary texts. When available, published English translations have been used; when not, the chapter's author has most often made the translation. Yet there are cases, where we were provided with a sample translation from a professional literary translator. As for quotes from the literary source texts, we have found it crucial to provide the original text in endnotes. The practice of displaying the original work alongside the translation is important in order to acknowledge the linguistic variety of contemporary Northern European literature. This practice is not, however, consistent throughout the book. At times, the original novel or short story has been published later than the translation, and the translation has therefore been considered as the original in the public eye. In some cases, different versions of the original text exist, which complicates the relation between the original and the translation. The literary original discussed in one chapter has turned out to be virtually untranslatable, due to its avant-gardistic multilingual style and the difficulty to actually define its "language" – an equally aesthetic and political statement in itself. Our pragmatic, if inconsistent, approach to these multifaceted issues of translation in the volume does however reflect the numerous ways in which the questions of translation are embedded in contemporary literary multilingualism in Northern European literature.

In a world characterized by complex and overlapping border processes at various levels, it is crucial for literature and language scholars to examine how, why and on what grounds linguistic and aesthetic borders are drawn, muddled and re-drawn. Our aim in this volume has been to outline a new, multilevel approach to the phenomenon of literary multilingualism, with a specific focus on contemporary Northern European literature. Needless to say, our theoretical outline and the individual chapters constitute only the beginning of what we hope to be a continued critical discussion on the subject of literary multilingualism.

Bibliography

Al-Nawas, Ahmed (2017) *A View of the Conditions of Arabic Literature in the Nordic Region: Multilingualism and Diversity as a Resource in the Cultural Field*. Helsinki: Culture for All Service. Accessed December 20, 2017, www.cultureforall.info/doc/research_and_reports/A_View_of_the_Conditions_of_Arabic_Literature_in_the_Nordic_Region.pdf.

Aschcroft, Bill; Griffiths, Gareth & Tiffin, Helen (1989) *The Empire Writes Back: Theory and Practice in Post-colonial Literatures*. London: Routledge.

Bakhtin, Mikhail (1981) *The Dialogic Imagination: Four Essays by M. M. Bakhtin*. Edited by Michael Holquist and translated by Michael Holquist. Austin & London: University of Texas Press.

Behschnitt, Wolfgang & Nilsson, Magnus (2013) "Multicultural Literatures" in a Comparative Perspective. In Wolfgang Behschnitt, Sarah De Mul & Liesbeth Minnaard (eds): *Literature, Language, and Multiculturalism in Scandinavia and the Low Countries*. Amsterdam & New York: Rodopi, 1–15.

Blommaert, Jan (2010) *The Sociolinguistics of Globalization*. Cambridge: Cambridge University Press.

Blommaert, Jan; Leppänen, Sirpa & Spotti, Massimiliano (2012) Endangering Multilingualism. In Jan Blommaert, Sirpa Leppänen, Päivi Pahta & Tiina Räisänen (eds): *Dangerous Multilingualism: Northern Perspectives on Order, Purity and Normality*. New York: Palgrave Macmillan, 1–21.

Deleuze, Gilles & Guattari, Félix ([1975] 1986) *Kafka: Toward a Minor Literature*. Translated by Dana Polan. Minneapolis: University of Minnesota Press.

Deleuze, Gilles & Guattari, Félix ([1980] 2005) *A Thousand Plateaus: Capitalism and Schizophrenia*. Translated by Brian Massumi. Eleventh Printing. Minneapolis: University of Minnesota Press.

Dembeck, Till & Mein, Georg (eds) (2014) *Philologie und Mehrsprachigkeit*. Heidelberg: Universitätsverlag Winter.

Domokos, Johanna & Laakso, Johanna (eds) (2011) *Multilingualism and Multiculturalism in Finno-Ugric Literatures*. Finno-Ugrian Studies in Austria. Wien: LIT.

Englund, Axel & Olsson, Anders (eds) (2013) *Languages of Exile: Migration and Multilingualism in Twentieth-Century Literature*. New York: Peter Lang.

Gardner-Chloros, Penelope & Weston, Daniel (2015) Code-switching and multilingualism in literature. *Language and Literature* 24(3), 182–193.

Gröndahl, Satu (2002) Inledning. Från "mångkulturell" till "mångspråkig" litteratur. In Satu Gröndahl (ed.): *Litteraturens gränsland: Invandrar- och minoritetslitteratur i nordiskt perspektiv*. Uppsala: Centrum för multietnisk forskning, 11–34.

Harris, Jan (2005) The Ordering of Things: Organization in Bruno Latour. *The Sociological Review* 53(Issue supplement s1), 163–177.

Hirvonen, Vuokko ([1999] 2008) *Voices from Sápmi: Sámi Women's Path to Authorship*. Translated by Kaija Anttonen. Guovdageaidnu, Norway: Dat.

van Houtum, Henk; Kramsch, Oliver & Zierhofer, Wolfgang (eds) (2005) *B/ordering Space*. Aldershot: Ashgate.

Kellman, Steven G. (2000) *The Translingual Imagination*. Lincoln: University of Nebraska Press.

Kiiskinen, Karri (2013) *Bordering with Culture(s): Europeanization and Cultural Agency at the External Border of the European Union.* Turku: University of Turku. http://urn.fi/URN:ISBN:978-951-29-5415-5.
Kivi, Aleksis (1929) *Seven Brothers.* Translated by Alex Matson. New York: Coward-McCann.
Knauth, K. Alfons Knauth (2007) Literary Multilingualism I: General Outlines and Western World. In Márcio Seligmann-Silva, Paola Mildonian, Jean-Michel Djian, Djelal Kadir, Lisa Block de Behar, Alfons Knauth & Dolores Romero Lpez (eds): *Comparative Literature: Sharing Knowledges for Preserving Cultural Diversity.* In Encyclopedia of Life Support Systems (EOLSS), Developed under the Auspices of the UNESCO. Oxford, UK: Eolss Publishers. Accessed December 21, 2017, www.eolss.net/ebooks/Sample%20 Chapters/C04/E6-87-07-05.pdf.
Kremnitz, Georg (2004) *Mehrsprachigkeit in der Literatur: Wie Autoren ihre Sprachen wählen: aus der Sicht der Soziologie der Kommunikation.* Wien: Ed. Praesens.
Lalor, Doireann (2010) "The Italianate Irishman": The Role of Italian in Beckett's Intratextual Multilingualism. *Samuel Beckett Today/Aujourd'hui* 22, 51–65.
Latour, Bruno (2005) *Reassembling the Social: An Introduction to Actor-Network-Theory.* New York: Oxford University Press.
Law, John (1992) Notes on the Theory of the Actor-Network: Ordering, Strategy, and Heterogeneity. *Systems Practice* 5(4), 379–393.
Lennon, Brian (2010) *In Babel's Shadow: Multilingual Literatures, Monolingual States.* Minneapolis: University of Minnesota Press.
Linde-Laursen, Anders (2010) *Bordering: Identity Processes Between the National and Personal.* Farnham: Ashgate.
Martin-Jones, Marilyn; Blackledge, Adrian & Creese, Angela (2015) Introduction: A Sociolinguistics of Multilingualism for Our Times. In Marilyn Martin-Jones, Adrian Blackledge & Angela Creese (eds): *The Routledge Handbook of Multilingualism.* London & New York: Routledge, 1–26.
Olsson, Anders (2011) *Ordens asyl: En inledning till den moderna exillitteraturen.* Stockholm: Albert Bonniers förlag.
Olsson, Jesper (2013) Speech Rumblings: Exile, Transnationalism and the Multilingual Space of Sound Poetry. In Axel Englund & Anders Olsson (eds): *Languages of Exile: Migration and Multilingualism in Twentieth-century Literature.* New York: Peter Lang, 183–200.
Perloff, Marjorie (2010) *Unoriginal Genius: Poetry by Other Means in the New Century.* Chicago: The University of Chicago Press.
Pollari, Mikko; Nissilä, Hanna-Leena; Melkas, Kukku; Löytty, Olli; Kauranen, Ralf & Grönstrand, Heidi (2015) National, Transnational and Entangled Literatures: Methodological Considerations Focusing on the Case of Finland. In Ann-Sofie Lönngren, Heidi Grönstrand, Dag Heede & Anne Heith (eds): *Rethinking National Literatures and the Literary Canon in Scandinavia.* Newcastle upon Tyne: Cambridge Scholars Publishing, 2–29.
Robinson, Andrew (2011) In Theory Bakhtin: Dialogism, Polyphony and Heteroglossia. *Ceasefire* July 29, 2011. Accessed November 13, 2017, https://ceasefiremagazine.co.uk/in-theory-bakhtin-1/.
Sakai, Naoki (2009) How Do We Count a Language? Translation and Discontinuity. *Translation Studies* 2(1), 71–88.

Schmitz-Emans, Monika (2004) Literatur und Vielsprachigkeit: Aspekte, Themen, Voraussetzungen. In Monika Schmitz-Emans (ed.): *Literatur und Vielsprachigkeit*. Heidelberg: Synchron, 11–26.

Seyhan, Azade (2001) *Writing Outside the Nation*. Princeton & Oxford: Princeton University Press.

Sommer, Doris (2003) Introduction. In Doris Sommer (ed.): *Bilingual Games: Some Literary Investigations*. New York: Palgrave Macmillan, 1–18.

Sommer, Doris (2004) *Bilingual Aesthetics: A New Sentimental Education*. Durham & London: Duke University Press.

Sommer, Doris (2007) Language, Culture, and Society. In David G. Nicholls (ed.): *Introduction to Scholarship in Modern Languages and Literatures*. Third Edition. New York: The Modern Language Association of America, 3–19.

Thiong'o, Ngũgĩ wa ([1986] 2007) *Decolonising the Mind: The Politics of Language in African Literature*. London: James Currey.

Tidigs, Julia (2014) *Att skriva sig över språkgränserna. Flerspråkighet i Jac. Ahrenbergs och Elmer Diktonius prosa*. Åbo: Åbo Akademi.

Tidigs, Julia & Huss, Markus (2017) The Noise of Multilingualism: Reader Diversity, Linguistic Borders and Literary Multimodality. *Critical Multilingualism Studies* 5(1), 208–235.

Wirth-Nesher, Hana (2006) *Call IT English: The Languages of Jewish American Literature*. Princeton: Princeton University Press.

Yildiz, Yasemin (2012) *Beyond the Mother Tongue: The Postmonolingual Condition*. New York: Fordham University Press.

Part II
Multilingualism as a Challenge to National Borders

2 Follow the Translations! The Transnational Circulation of Hassan Blasim's Short Stories

Olli Löytty

What is the secret of Hassan Blasim's success in the international literary space? That is a blunt but fairly accurate way of expressing the object of interest behind this chapter. By success, I simply mean things like the number of translations and awards as well as visibility in the literary sphere in the countries where his books are published. For a contemporary author writing in Arabic, a language from which there is but a very limited number of translated works of fiction into major European languages, Blasim already has a noteworthy career with more than twenty translations of his books and multiple accolades, such as the International Foreign Fiction Prize he received in 2014.

Coined by Pascale Casanova (2004), *international literary space* is a concept which refers to a global system of literatures that formed around the 16th century, concurrently and analogously with the capitalist system of interlinked national economies. Similarly to the economies of the world system, some of which belong to the ruling core and some of which belong to the dependent periphery, no literature can coherently be studied as a discrete entity. According to Casanova, a core group of European nations – led by France and England – possess large reserves of "literary capital" and therefore dominate the means of cultural legitimation for the countries of the global literary periphery.

During the past century or so, however, the map of global literary power relations has changed, especially with the rise of decolonization and globalization, as writers from nations outside Europe and without previous literary standing have demanded access to literary legitimacy and existence within the indubitably Eurocentric system of literatures. Translation is obviously a key mechanism in that validation. Following the ideas presented by Pierre Bourdieu, Casanova (2004, 133) calls translation "a form of literary recognition" or a type of *consecration*: "Translation is the major prize and weapon in international literary competition." To understand Blasim's position in *world literature* – to use another, much older concept referring to literature as a global system – I will discuss the significance of translations in general and the mechanisms that regulate their circulation in particular. How do Blasim's stories written in Arabic find their translators and publishers in different countries?

In this chapter I will draw from current theoretical discussions concerning multilingualism, transnationalism and translation theory. I will not, however, pay much attention to the contents of Blasim's texts but consider them rather as textual artefacts travelling around the globe in translations. Apart from the written sources, such as reviews and articles, I have interviewed Blasim himself, as well as his publishers across borders, namely, his British, Bulgarian, Finnish, Norwegian and Swedish publishers. The case of Finland, his present country of residence, will be given the most attention. What is the position of writers like Blasim who write in "non-dominant" languages (i.e. not in Finnish or Swedish, the two national languages of the country) in the national literary field of Finland? In addition, as part of the international literary space, the case of Finland reveals some of the mechanisms occurring in the relations between the national and international literary fields, as well as in the global circulation of translations.

The Transnational Biography of an Author

Blasim is a *transnational* writer in many senses of the word. As a point of view, transnationalism draws attention to "sustained linkages and ongoing exchanges among non-state actors based across national borders", as Steven Vertovec (2009, 3) has explained. In this chapter, however, transnationalism is understood in a broad sense: in addition to movements across national borders, I am interested in exchange and movements across cultural and linguistic borders, which do not necessarily run congruently with national ones (see Pollari et al. 2015).

First, transnationalism plays an important role in Blasim's life, since he has crossed many borders: geographical, cultural and linguistic. He was born in Iraq, where he studied at the Academy of Cinematic Arts.[1] In 1998, he left Baghdad for Sulaymaniya (Iraqi Kurdistan), where he made the feature-length drama *Wounded Camera*, which tells about the forced migration of millions of people when Saddam Hussein's army entered Kurdistan after the uprising in 1991.[2] As the film contained direct criticism of the authorities and their treatment of the Kurdish population, Blasim had no choice but to leave the country. In 1999, he went into exile and in the following years travelled through Iran, Turkey, Bulgaria and Hungary, in 2004 finally settling in Finland, where he presently lives.

Second, the language that he writes in, Arabic, is a transnational language in itself, and his readers are scattered not only in the Arabic-speaking countries but around the world along the Arab diaspora.[3] As a transnational phenomenon, Arabic literature follows certain routes: according to an old Arab saying that illustrates the circle of literature in the Arab-speaking world, "Cairo writes, Beirut publishes and Baghdad reads." Recently, this circle of literary production has found new diasporic variations, since nowadays "an Arabic book of poetry could be written in Tampere [Finland], published in Milano and translated into several languages, awarded with the PEN prize in London, and censored in Jordan and most of the Gulf States", as Ahmed Al-Nawas (2017) writes in his report on the conditions of Arabic literature in the Nordic region; the reference to Blasim's career is evident. All of these changes have been accelerated by the digitalization of the international literary space; in the Arab diaspora, the internet is an important medium for writers. While living in Finland, Blasim has co-founded the website IraqStory.com, where he has published several of his texts in Arabic.

Third, Blasim's texts have been translated – and as such they have traversed both national and linguistic borders – into more than twenty languages, including English, Spanish, Turkish, German, French and all of the Scandinavian languages.[4] Because of the translations, Blasim continuously travels around the world, participating in various literary events and seminars. Nonetheless, these transnational encounters, although they are the result of successful border crossings, may create new linguistic barriers. In these international literary events, the language of social communication, as well as the presentations, is often English, a language in which Blasim's fluency does not match his mastery of Arabic and which therefore may limit the scope of what he would like to express. In the international literary space, English language skills can be considered valuable linguistic capital; poor knowledge limits access to the field.

In addition to IraqStory.com, Blasim has been active elsewhere on the internet, publishing essays, poems and other texts in several languages on his homepage,[5] as well as on Facebook. In one of the poems published on the internet, "A Refugee in the Paradise that is Europe",[6] Blasim criticizes the way refugees are used by Western journalists and politicians as well as academics. The poem, addressed to a refugee, reminds the reader of the power relations prevailing not only in the harsh realities of the world, but also in "international literary research":

> You escape death.
> They hit you on the border.
> They insult you in the racist newspapers.
> They analyse your child's dead body on television.
> They get together and discuss your past and your future.
> In their pictures they draw you drowning.
> They put you in their museums and applaud.
> They decide to stop hitting you and set up a military unit to confront you.
> Academics get new grant money to research your body and your soul.

Politicians drink red wine after an emergency meeting to
   discuss your fate.
They consult history in search of an answer for your daughter,
   who's freezing in the forest cold.
(Blasim 2017, trans. Jonathan Wright)

The Discovery of an Author

From the point of view of his readers in European languages, Blasim's story as an internationally renowned author began in 2009 with the first translation of a collection of his stories into English, *The Madman of Freedom Square*. However, Blasim had published his texts in their original Arabic prior to the English translation on the internet, as well as in a few literary magazines. The key actor in discovering Blasim in Europe was a UK-based "not-for-profit publishing initiative dedicated to promoting new writing, with an emphasis on the short story", as Comma Press describes itself on its homepage. "It is committed", the publisher continues, "to a spirit of risk-taking and challenging publishing, free of the commercial pressures on mainstream houses" (Comma Press n.d.). This absence of explicit commercial interests in the publishing policy of Comma Press draws attention to the ideological motifs behind the decision to assign Blasim. However, there are many other ways to measure the literary capital a writer may possess than commercial success: for example, media visibility, literary criticism, awards and attention given in literary research and reference books. In fact, commercial success can be interpreted as an opposite of literary capital. To declare one's pursuits as "free from commercial pressures" makes room for the accumulation of symbolic capital, as theorized by Pierre Bourdieu (1993, 75): "Symbolic capital is to be understood as economic or political capital that is disavowed, misrecognized and thereby recognized."

Ra Page, the founder and Editorial Manager of Comma Press, explains the discovery of Blasim by telling that the publisher had been particularly interested in the short story in the Middle East. There had been talk about "the great Arab novel" as well as the role of poetry in Arabic literature, but according to Page, in Europe very little was known about the short story in the area. The interest in the short story as a form of literature can be explained by the fact that it can "translate well" but is also a culturally portable, "intrinsically international" and "very political form". Page (2014) asserts, "It gives voice to [...] 'submerged population groups', people on the margins."[7] Correspondingly, Comma Press formulates its policy in order to "explore the power of the short story to transcend cultural and disciplinary boundaries, and to enable greater understanding across these boundaries" (Comma Press n.d.).

In consequence, Comma Press commissioned the Lebanese poet and journalist Joumana Haddad[8] to put together an anthology of stories from ten different Middle Eastern cities. For most of the cities, she selected well-established authors, but she thought that for Baghdad the book needed something different, a new writer. Haddad knew about Blasim because he had submitted poems to the newspaper which Haddad worked for in Beirut. So she invited Blasim to submit a piece for the book, which was to be called *Madinah: City Stories from the Middle East* (2008).[9] Blasim's short story in the book, "The Reality and the Record", attracted the publisher's interest and he was commissioned to write a whole book for Comma Press. The process was truly transnational:

> Hence we get the most circuitous route to a new author ever – an Iraqi refugee, based in Finland, found by a poet in Lebanon, translated by a former journalist based in Cairo, and commissioned by a tiny little press in Manchester!
>
> (Page 2014)

According to Page, Blasim's book initially "got very little attention" and "struggled to get the smallest reviews", but the publishing house kept promoting him over the following years. As Comma Press held the international rights to his work (except in Arabic and Finnish), Page was acting as Blasim's agent, selling the rights of his texts not only to other language areas but also to the US market:

> Eventually I managed to persuade John Siciliano at Penguin in New York to buy half of the first book and half of the second – this took about three years of horse trading which included me offering it to others in the States. Once Penguin had signed and with the second book (*Iraqi Christ*) out in the UK things finally started to move.
>
> (Page 2016)

In 2014, Penguin Books (US) published a selection of Blasim's short stories – chosen from the two collections published in the UK – with the title *Corpse Exhibition and Other Stories of Iraq*.[10]

Blasim has also received literary recognition in the form of awards. Literary prizes are "the most apparent of the mechanisms of consecration", Casanova (2004, 146–147) writes, as "they represent a sort of confirmation for the benefit of the general public". *The Madman of Freedom Square*[11] won an English PEN Writers in Translation Award and was nominated for the Independent Foreign Fiction Prize (IFFP), but the actual breakthrough for him in England was the winning of the IFFP with his second book in English, *The Iraqi Christ*, in 2014. Comma Press has continued to publish Blasim's work in English. In 2016, it published a collection of science fiction stories called *Iraq + 100*, edited by Blasim and including a short story by him.[12] Blasim's first theatre play, *Digital Hats Game*, premiered in Tampere in 2016 (see Litvin & Sellman 2016).

A heavily edited Arabic version of Blasim's debut collection was finally published in 2012 by the Arab Institute for Research and Publishing (Beirut). Al-Nawas (2017, 18) explains: "All direct critical comments against holy figures, and direct reference to the sex organs and to sexual activities were toned down by the editor." Furthermore, Al-Nawas (2017, 6) notes: "Such censorship is widely practiced by publishers to overcome different sets of criteria to introduce their books in the different Arabic speaking countries." However, despite the heavy censorship the book was soon confiscated and banned in Jordan and Kuwait. In 2014, the first uncensored collection of his stories came out in Arabic by the Al Mutawassit publishing house, stationed in Milan, Italy. In addition, it published a collection of Blasim's poetry, *The Shia's Poisoned Child*, in 2016.[13] After receiving death threats from several conservative and political parties, Al Mutawassit decided to redraw the poetry collection from Lebanon, Iraq and other Arabic book fairs (Al-Nawas 2017, 19).

All in all, Blasim's place in the Arabic literary space, as well as in the national literary field of Iraq, is complicated. In his introduction to *Iraq + 100*, Blasim depicts his "unease" about editing the anthology as an outsider who lives and works "out in the cold": "I am a writer whose work found its place in the wider, non-Arab world while I remained in the margins of the Iraqi literary scene – a scene I have always chosen to keep my distance from." He goes on to describe the Iraqi literature scene as "populated by 'official' writers who belong to the Writers' Union and other cultural institutions" and depending "on personal and cliquey relationships and on the corruption of the press and in the Ministry of Culture" (Blasim 2016, ix).

How, then, did the publishers in other language areas initially find out about Blasim? When I made an enquiry to the representatives of Blasim's publishers in Bulgaria, Finland, Norway and Sweden about how they had come across Blasim in the first place, they all told me that they had heard about the English translation. Asbjørn Øverås from Aschehoug, Norway, read about Blasim in an English paper and contacted him through Comma Press (Øverås 2016). Daniel Sandström from Albert Bonniers Förlag, Sweden, noticed that *The Iraqi Christ* had been nominated for the IFFP (but at the time did not know that Blasim was living in Finland). He also established contact through Comma Press (Sandström 2016). Neva Micheva from Bulgaria, who is a translator and as such also does some book scouting, was told by one of her colleagues about "a very interesting Iraqi book", and she ordered *The Madman of Freedom Square* from Amazon.com (Micheva 2016). The Finnish publisher's representative, Satu Harlahti, remembers reading about Blasim in a Finnish newspaper. She recalls that she had been astonished by the sheer fact that contemporary prose in Arabic had been translated into English, and not just any text but short stories, a genre that is not considered economically promising. In the case of Blasim's first book translated to Finnish, the publisher made the deal with Comma Press whereas the deal about the second book was made directly with Blasim who was living in Helsinki at the time (Harlahti 2017).

To sum up, all of the publishers I spoke with had heard about Blasim after his short stories had already been translated into English, and in all their negotiations concerning new translations, they dealt with Comma Press or with the author personally. It is clear that in the international career of Blasim, the English translation acted as a bridge between the original Arabic and translations in other languages than English – even though all those translations have been made directly from Arabic. In other words, it seems that the best way for contemporary Arabic literature to become a visible part in the international literary space in Europe is through English translation.

Born Translated

Rebecca L. Walkowitz writes about literature that she calls "born translated". By that she refers to books for which "[t]ranslation is not secondary or incidental [but] a condition of their production" (Walkowitz 2015, 4). While Walkowitz does not mention Blasim, in a sense he could be an illustrative example of a phenomenon that is likely to become more common in the international literary space. According to Walkowitz, writers such as J. M. Coetzee and Jamaica Kincaid incorporate certain forms, structures, themes and visual devices of translation in their writing to tell the story. In other words, the translation is present in the act of the original writing, thus challenging the dichotomy between the original and the translation. Although Blasim himself, when writing, does not recognize the pressure, for example, of contextualizing the particular cultural conditions his stories are set in for potential readers of other languages than Arabic – I once asked him about it and he replied "I just tell stories" – his texts come into existence and start their circulation as "born translated".

Blasim's first collection of short stories *The Madman of Freedom Square* was born translated in the sense that it was originally printed in book form as a translation. On the other hand, Blasim's work could also be depicted as "born digital", because he has published and still publishes a large part of his texts in Arabic on the internet, and this was also prior to the publication of the first English translation. All in all, the transnational as well as *translational* publishing history of Blasim's texts raises the question of their genesis, thus challenging the prevalent notion of the hierarchy of original text and translation, in which the former is seen not only as more authentic but also more significant than the latter.[14]

Blasim's career as a widely translated author has both conventional and unconventional features. It is interesting to speculate on what makes his work relevant in the eyes of international audiences. On the one hand, the topics and themes of his work can be viewed as appealing for readers in a variety of places and languages. In his report on the conditions of Arabic-Nordic literature, Al-Nawas (2017, 11–12) writes about the rising interest in Arabic exile and migrant literature in Europe, which can be explained by the growing number of migrant writers in that region as well as by public interest in the current wars in the Middle East and the migration caused by it. Many of Blasim's stories deal with the war in Iraq and the diaspora of Iraqi people caused by it; indeed, for years this has been an object of keen interest all over the world. Therefore, it can be claimed that there are large international audiences potentially interested in the themes covered in Blasim's work.

On the other hand, the interest among European readers in Blasim's stories is not only based on their topics, but also the literary quality of his work. Reading reviews of his books in English-language newspapers, for example, it soon becomes clear that the style of his writing – often compared to that of Franz Kafka, Nikolai Gogol, Jorge Luis Borges, Roberto Bolaño, Gabriel García Márquez, Carlos Fuentes, etc. – is considered to suit the taste of European readers. For example, in a critique of *The Iraqi Christ* published in *The Guardian*, Robin Yassin-Kassab (2013) writes that the collection is "Bolaño-esque in its visceral exuberance, and also Borgesian in its gnomic complexity".

To give some insight into the topics and style of Blasim's texts, I will briefly recapitulate and comment on a short story called "The Truck to Berlin" from *The Madman of Freedom Square*. The story is about the harsh realities – or rather horrors – of the "transnationality" presently taking place on the borders between Asia and Europe. As such, the story can be interpreted as an allegory of the contemporary global migration.

An extract from the beginning of the story illuminates Blasim's aesthetics, which often contain a level of metanarration that plays with the thin line between fantasy and reality:

> For sure most readers would see the story as merely a fabrication by the author or maybe as a modest allegory for horror. But I see no need to swear an oath in order for you to believe in the strangeness of this world. What I need to do is write this story, like a shit stain on a nightshirt, or perhaps a stain in the form of a wild flower.
> (Blasim 2009, 69)

The story is about a group of thirty-five young Iraqis who make a deal with a Turkish smuggler to take them from Istanbul to Berlin in the back of a truck. They are told that they will be travelling by night, while in daytime they will cautiously be let out of the truck. On the third day of the trip, the truck suddenly stops, makes a U-turn and retraces its path at high speed. After some time the truck comes to a halt, the engine is turned off and "an eerie and mysterious silence reigned inside the truck to Berlin, a satanic silence that would bring forth a miracle and a story hard to believe" (Blasim 2009, 73).

As the travellers have no way of communicating with the outside world, they have no idea of what has happened or what is going to happen next. Slowly their anxiety increases; after many long hours in the darkness, with their air running out, the thirty-five men start to quarrel and fight until they are too tired even for that. Eventually, after three days inside the pitch-black truck, complete chaos breaks out. There is a horrible scream, which sounds like "an unknown force which transformed the uproar and chaos of the truck into a cruel layer of ice", "a scream that emerged from caves whose secrets have never been unravelled" (Blasim 2009, 74). Something truly horrible is taking place inside the truck: "It seemed that the cruelty of man, the cruelty of animals and legendary monsters had condensed and together had started to play a hellish tune" (Blasim 2009, 74).

After a few days, the truck is found on the edge of a small border town in Serbia. The narrator says that it is not important to know what happened to the people smugglers, "for all these stories are similar" (Blasim 2009, 75). There may have been a dispute between mafia organizations, or maybe the police were after them; the ambiguity underlines the generalizability of the story. When a Serbian policeman opens the rear door of the abandoned truck, he finds the bodies of thirty-four dead Iraqi men torn apart by "claws and beaks of eagles, the teeth of crocodiles and other unknown instruments", while "the truck was full of shit and piss and blood, livers ripped apart, eyes gouged out, intestines just as though hungry wolves had been there" (Blasim 2009, 75). And just when the door is opened, a man jumps out of the truck and disappears into the forest. When the policeman afterwards tells his wife about the scene, he swears that "as soon as the man reached the forest he started to run on all fours, then turned into a grey wolf, before he vanished" (Blasim 2009, 75).

While it is clear that "The Truck to Berlin" is able to tell something profound about the inhuman conditions and the lack of self-determination many people are facing when embarking on their voyage from war and poverty in the Middle East to the high expectations of brighter prospects in Europe, the short story utilizes devices of fiction: nuances of language, levels of narration, allegory, symbolism and fantasy. In other words, the inclusion of a werewolf and other fantastic features requires specific contextual and intertextual knowledge from the reader. The symbolism is disturbing but revealing: the werewolf that escaped from the truck to Berlin keeps on howling on the Serbian border, as well as around other borders blocking the refugees' route to Europe.

To sum up, Blasim's success in the international literary space can be explained by the potential interest of readers in the topics and themes of the stories as well as in the quality and aesthetics of his craft. While Blasim's breakthrough as a translated author may be easy to pin down, it also contains unusual features, as he first self-published online in Arabic and his texts were collected in book form only upon English translation. In the international book market, it is rather extraordinary that he was "found" by a publisher and not by a literary agent. It is also unusual that he did not use the services of an established agent even after that. In addition, the fact that he shares some of his original writings for free on the internet can be regarded, at least within the book-publishing business, as a detrimental practice.

Casanova uses the notion of literariness, namely, "the literary credit that attaches to a language independently of its strictly linguistic capital", in reference to the form of consecration that works of fiction receive when they are translated into a major literary language. From the point of view of a major target language like English, "the importation of literary texts written in 'small' languages or ones belonging to neglected literatures serves as a means of annexation, of diverting peripheral works and adding them to the stock of central resources" (Casanova 2004, 135). It should be noted, however, that in the case of many languages the distinction between major and minor literary languages is not at all as clear as Casanova seems to suggest; the dichotomy serves here as a critical observation about the hierarchies of languages in the international literary space.

As an example of this kind of consecration, Casanova mentions the success of writers like Danilo Kiš, who writes in his native Serbo-Croatian but who entered the international literary space only through translation into French and recognition by French critics. In the same way, Casanova (2004, 135) writes, "The universal recognition of Rabindranath Tagore – symbolized by his Nobel Prize – dated from the Bengali poet's translation of his own work into English." Likewise, the translation of Blasim's texts into English provides them with the consecration needed to fully enter the international literary space (See also Walkowitz 2015, 11).

The world of translations is not just asymmetrical but also profoundly hierarchical. The number of translations from major literatures into minor literatures is considerably greater than vice versa. For example, only 4.5 per cent of the fiction works published in the British Isles are translations (Davies 2013). Walkowitz (2015, 20) explains: "Anglophone novels are more likely than novels in other languages to appear in translation: more works are translated out of English than out of any other language" (See also Bassnett 1993, 143). To be translated from a minor into a major language can increase the value of a text, and for a representative of minor literature, it is more significant than for a representative of major literature. Paradoxically, despite being a large language spoken in a vast region and having a rich literary tradition, in the European view Arabic literature belongs to the group of "minor literatures". For example, the IFFP awarded to *Iraqi Christ* was the first one ever given to a book translated from Arabic. Therefore, the English translation of Blasim's short stories invests them with the cultural prestige of Anglophone literature, thus increasing their attraction as potentially translatable texts from the point of view of other languages. Even though all of the translations of Blasim's texts have been made from the original Arabic, the English translation opened the way for awareness and circulation of his texts worldwide.

Author in a Strange Land

If translation into "major literary languages" like English ensures a certain status in the international literary space, what kind of position is acquired by translation into minor languages and the more or less corresponding national literary spaces? In this section I will discuss the precarious position of Blasim in the literary field of Finland, the country where he presently resides.

In Finland, Blasim is considered, perhaps first and foremost, a "stranger" in a Simmelian sense of the term. The German sociologist Georg Simmel ([1908] 1950, 402) wrote in the beginning of the 20th century that the figure of the stranger is always the product of a negotiation between the familiar and the alien. The stranger may be a member of a group in a spatial sense, but not in a social sense. In other words, a stranger is among "us" but not one of "us" (Löytty 2017). Accordingly, Camilla Haavisto (2011) has characterized the position of immigrant artists in Finnish as "conditionally one of us".

In Finland, as well as in the Nordic countries in general, one of the terms most commonly used and discussed by both critics and scholars with reference to transnational writers such as Blasim has been "immigrant author" or "authors with immigrant background" (e.g. Behschnitt & Nilsson 2013; Nissilä 2016). However, the problems implied by the concept are widely known, as a singular heading such as "immigrant literature" may limit "the representational scope of this literature" and may well result in homogenizing, essentializing and even racializing the ethnic minorities in question (Nilsson 2010; Löytty 2015; Nissilä 2016).

The concept of the stranger portrays the ambivalence of Blasim's position in the Finnish literary field. On the one hand, he has enjoyed many of the privileges provided for professional writers in Finland by the state and cultural institutions. He has won literary prizes and received grants from several foundations in Finland. He received the esteemed Finland Prize in 2015, awarded by the Ministry of Education and Culture, an award which is given "in recognition of a significant career in arts, an exceptional artistic achievement, or a promising breakthrough" (Ministry of Education and Culture 2015). His prospects to visit book fairs and festivals all around the world became notably easier when he was granted Finnish citizenship in July 2016, but even before that, he had become a representative of Finland. This was clearly shown at an event in London in spring 2015, European Literature Night; as one of the financers of the event, the Finnish Institute in London, stated on its webpage, Blasim represented Finland (The Finnish Institute in London 2015).

Shortly after their publication in English, both of Blasim's collections of short stories were translated into Finnish by Sampsa Peltonen. There have been a variety of articles about him and critiques of his books in Finnish media (see Löytty 2017), and the success of his books, particularly in the English-speaking world, has been widely noted. Literary scholars have recognized him as a member of the Finnish literary field; he is mentioned in the latest literary history of contemporary literature in Finland, *Suomen nykykirjallisuus II* (Hallila et al. 2013; Contemporary Finnish literature II), as an example of writers with an immigrant background living and working in the country.

Blasim actively takes part in the discussion about literature and politics in Finland. In May 2015, he was invited to Helsinki Lit, a literary festival specializing in translated literature, to read from his book while another author recited the Finnish translation, but instead he gave a powerful impromptu talk – or rather an oration – in which he criticized the way writers of immigrant background are treated in the country. He posed a question about the voice of immigrant authors: is it heard or is somebody else using it? This speech – delivered in English with occasional code-switching to Finnish – was broadcast live on television, and it created further discussion in media (Helsinki Lit 2015).

Despite his visible and audible presence in Finland, however, Blasim's place in the Finnish literary field is still ambiguous. The process of integration can be observed in the articles about him in Finnish media (see Löytty 2017), by whom he had been covered even before his first collection of short stories was translated into Finnish. In perhaps the first of these articles, he is discussed under the heading of "New Finnish Literature" (a concept that did not really catch on) and he is depicted working with his laptop in one of the trendy cafés of Helsinki. The caption of the article emphasizes his transnationality as a writer: "An Iraqi author is writing in Arabic in a bar in Helsinki for a British publisher" (Juntunen 2009). Some version of the narrative of his journey to Finland is told in almost all of the articles about him.

In 2010, when the first collection of his short stories was published in English but not yet in Finnish, *Helsingin Sanomat*, the biggest and perhaps the most influential newspaper in Finland, ran a lengthy article in which Blasim's story is told in detail but the focus is on the breakthrough of his texts in both the English and Arabic book markets. It is mentioned only briefly that a Finnish publisher was considering translating his first collection of short stories. In the article, the writer urges the Finnish readers not to be scared of his texts, since his short stories are much easier to understand than Salman Rushdie's books, which "touch the changeable interface of the East and West"; by contrast, Blasim is said to write "in a cool and laconic way without unnecessary intricacies or heavy cultural decorations" (Petäjä 2010). According to the view presented in the article, Finnish readers are more comfortable with texts that do not possess "unnecessary intricacies" (Petäjä 2010); perhaps the "heavy cultural decorations" refer to the Orientalist tradition implied by the origin of both Rushdie and Blasim.[15]

All in all, in many critiques, Blasim's literary style is presented to Finnish readers with references to both Eastern and Western literary cultures. An illustrative example is provided by *Kiiltomato* (6.3.2013), an online literary magazine: "If Gogol or Kafka were to write *One Thousand and One Nights* set in contemporary Baghdad, the outcome would resemble Hassan Blasim's collection of short stories *The Madman of Freedom Square (Majnun sahat al-hurriyya)*" (Salomaa 2013).[16]

In a critique of his first book in Finnish, Blasim is positioned as part of the Finnish literary field. The critic says that although "the topics of Blasim's short stories are far from Finnish average prose and short stories [...] it is great that the guild of Finnish authors have got an Iraqi-born author as a supplement" (Pääkkönen 2012).[17] According to the critique, Finnish literature is simply enriched and strengthened by Blasim, and it seems that writers like him do not cause pressure to refine the perceptions of Finnish literature.[18]

Although there is abundant evidence for the diverse ways in which Blasim is affiliated with the Finnish literary field, on the other hand, due to his writing language being Arabic, he cannot be a member of either of the national writers' associations, since one of them is for writers who compose their literary works originally in Finnish and the other one for writers who write in Swedish (see Korhonen & Paqvalén 2016, 19–20). In this sense, even though according to his passport Blasim is a Finn, due to their original language his texts cannot become "Finnish literature". The exclusive membership policy of the national writers' associations in Finland is just one but a nonetheless revealing manifestation of the unquestioned significance of Finnish and Swedish, the "national languages" of Finland, as they are officially called, in the national literary field. Although the linguistic landscape of Finland is changing in the wake of the present immigration, for example, the idea of "Finnish literature" being written in other than the "national languages" is still rather unthinkable.

Recently, there has been a discussion on the positions of literatures written in the majority and minority languages in Finland, as well as in the Nordic countries in general. Outi Korhonen, the coordinator of the project "Multilingualism and diversity as a resource in the cultural field – employment and integration through literature in the Nordic Countries", writes about the situation caused by the decision of the Finnish Writers' Union to rule out the possibility of writers using "non-dominant languages" (i.e. not Finnish or Swedish) to become members. She refers to a rationalization given by the Union stating that a "great part of their applicable funds comes from testament donations that have been defined with a specific language criterion and [...] if non-Finnish language writers were able to join, this would create inequality inside the organization". Korhonen's conclusion extends to the potentially even more multilingual future of the Finnish literary field: "Now the inequality remains between the ones who can be included and the ones who are completely outside. But what happens when the world changes?" (Korhonen 2017).

In order to analyse the significance of language in the integration of an immigrant writer into the Finnish literary scene, it is useful to compare Blasim to a representative of another art form, such as media art. Adel Abidin, like Blasim, was born in Baghdad and lives in Finland. Camilla Haavisto (2011) has studied the representations of Abidin in Finnish media, especially in relation to his status as an immigrant artist. According to her, when Abidin arrived in Finland at the beginning of the 21st century, the artistic value of his production was soon recognized, and since then he has had expositions both in Finland and abroad and received several nominations and awards. Abidin was elected as one of the representatives for Finland at the Venice Biennale, a highly regarded international art exhibition, where he participated in a work named "Abidin Travels" (see Abidin n.d.), which consisted of installations and video films that featured an imaginary travel agency organizing tourist trips to war-torn Baghdad. The dark humour of the grotesque travel agency is certainly not alien to the themes and artistic devices that Blasim utilizes in his short stories.

The ways how and degrees to which Abidin's background is mentioned and emphasized in media varies. Haavisto (2011, 117) noted that, of the thirty-three articles in which Abidin's name is mentioned, his background comes up more often than it is left unmentioned: "In 25 articles he is 'Iraqi', 'Finnish-Iraqi' or 'Finnish artist born in Baghdad/Iraq'. In eight articles he is simply 'artist', 'Adel Abidin', or 'Finnish artist'." Haavisto (2011, 117) concludes that over "the course of time his background is paid less attention to". Even in the cases when Abidin is mentioned like any other Finnish artist (e.g. in a listing of artists), he does not represent "typically Finnish": "He is, for example, asked to comment on how he feels about the Finnish winters, a question that a Finnish-born artist would hardly get" (Haavisto 2011, 118).[19]

The representations of Blasim and Abidin in Finnish media clearly have similarities. In both cases, it can be estimated that the more the artist has received international recognition, the more his work is counted as belonging to the Finnish art scene. However, there are also differences. For a visual artist like Abidin, although there are often linguistic elements in his work, it is relatively easy to get integrated into the art scene of Finland, whereas in the literary field, as in the case of Blasim, the language of a writer forms a much stronger barrier. And when it comes to the attitudes towards the internationalization of each form of art, one may also speculate about the differences between visual arts and literature. Perhaps one can consider media art, for example, as more international "by nature" than literature, which attains that level only through its consecration by translation.

Although the title as well as the status of "Finnish author" may be of very little use for Blasim, from the point of view of Finnish literature his presence in the country and involvement in the activities of the national literary field may have consequences for the perceptions of literature as something organized – or not – along national lines. The recognition of these kinds of consequences should be welcomed, as there is in this ever-changing world a growing need to understand literature as something that lives through the polyphony of different languages rather than their segregation from one another and categorization into neat linguistic and national containers.

The Translational Turn?

Even if Blasim is considered a stranger in Finland due to his background as well as his writing language, his books are available in Finnish. However, despite the fact that translations have provided "a primary shaping force" within literary history (Bassnett 1993, 142–143) and have had such an essential influence on the development of national literatures, as Susan Bassnet (2011, 72) writes, "translations tend to be seen as immigrants, not quite worthy of the status accorded to texts produced within a given literary tradition".

The recent changes in the international literary field caused by accelerating migration and digitalization have obviously influenced not only how literature as a form of art is perceived but also how literature is theorized. The significance of translations is being revalued. In their article on the multicultural literatures of Northern Europe in the era of globalization, Wolfgang Behschnitt and Magnus Nilsson (2013) refer to Bassnett's programmatic view of the future development of literary studies – presented already in 1993 – as something moving "[f]rom Comparative Literature to Translation Studies". In this view, rather than being a mere linguistic transfer, translation is conceived of as a cultural transformation shaped by intercultural hierarchies and power relations, as formulated by, for example, post-colonial criticism. Bassnett (1993, 158) challenges the idea of translation as a one-way process in which the translator complies with the authority of the original and the target text is perceived as secondary and subordinate. She questions the originality of the source text, for example, by referring to Jacques Derrida, who has written that the original text is not an original because it is an elaboration of an idea, of a meaning – a translation in itself. Thus, translation "enables a text to continue its life in another context, and the translated text becomes an original by virtue of its continued existence in that new context" (Bassnett 1993, 151).

In the context of the international literary space, the idea of translation as a one-way process can be further problematized. Instead of moving from one place to another in a more or less orderly fashion, translated texts can take different routes and circulate simultaneously in many directions. Translation, from this point of view, is a process that enables the international reception of literary texts. Hence, "world literature consists not so much of original compositions as of translations", as translation theorist Lawrence Venuti (2013, 193) highlights. Or, in the words of David Damrosch (2003, 5), "world literature is not an infinite, ungraspable canon of works but rather a mode of circulation and of reading".

In addition to its global nature, translation is fundamentally a localizing practice, as Venuti (2013, 193) points out:

> Every step in the translation process, starting with the selection of a source text, including the development of a discursive strategy to translate it, and continuing with its circulation in a different language and culture, is mediated by values, beliefs, and representations in the receiving situation.

In this view, translation is not so much about reproducing the source text, but transforming it "by inscribing an interpretation that reflects what is intelligible and interesting to receptors" (Venuti 2013, 193).

As a concept, translation may refer to a wide range of transformations. Not only are the texts taken from one cultural and linguistic context and transferred to another but also – in the same process – revised, modified, edited and rewritten. In addition, the place of publication can change: when translated, the texts can be published in different editions, anthologies or multimodal forums in general. In other words, they transcend media boundaries. For example, one of Blasim's short stories was adapted into a theatre play in the UK.[20] Blasim's translated short stories have been published in miscellaneous collections, anthologies, newspapers and magazines, as well as in different forums on the internet. The contents of his books in different languages are hardly ever identical, since Blasim has given permission for publishers to compile collections of his short stories according to their own preferences. Even though the names of these respective publications may be equivalent to the titles in English, *The Madman of Freedom Square* and *The Iraqi Christ*, it is possible for them to contain a different set of his short stories.

To understand the accelerating circulation of Hassan Blasim's texts around the globe, it is important to note that despite the number of Arabic speakers in the world, and despite the fact that all of the translations have been made from the original Arabic, it was the English translation and the publicity caused by the literary prize given to the translation in the UK that opened the door, so to speak, for his texts to be translated into other languages. The significance of English in the international literary space cannot be overstated. Even the translation from Arabic into Finnish, one of the "national languages" of the country where he presently lives, needed a detour via English in order to come into being. In this way, Blasim's case also demonstrates the influence of the international book market in a small country such as Finland and a small literary language such as Finnish.

Translation transcends borders between languages in the essentially multilingual international literary space, and by doing so it constantly affects the relationship between those languages and organizes their relations into new constellations; for example, Blasim's success will most likely draw more attention to contemporary literature written in the Middle East in general. Although literatures written in different languages are often considered, due to the intertwined histories of literature and modern nationalism (e.g. Bassnett 2011, 71–72), to lie in more or less separate containers, continuous movement in the form of translations across national as well as linguistic borders proves otherwise. In the words of Bassnett (2011, 69): "Reading literary history through the lens of translation has enabled us to see more clearly that the development of any literary system involves complex processes of import and export." However, these crossings over national and linguistic borders can also paradoxically affirm the separateness of different languages (Sakai 2009).

Blasim's case exposes the fact that languages within the international literary space are not equal as some possess more literary capital than others. The circulation of his works demonstrates how translations from minor to major languages – even though the concepts "minor" and "major" are both relational and mutable – may have profound effects on the literary value that a particular work of fiction is considered to have. English translations helped make Blasim's work noticed and valued on a global scale. However, by expanding the readership of translated texts and thus affirming their presence in the world literature of today, translations have a strong potential to dismantle the hierarchies between languages. After Blasim's success, perhaps there will be more room for contemporary Arabic literature in the international literary space.

Notes

1 As a student, Blasim made two short films, *Gardenia* (screenplay & director) and *White Clay* (screenplay), which won the Academy's Festival Award for Best Work in consecutive years.
2 As a director, he used the pseudonym Ouazad Osman because he feared for the safety of his family.
3 Arabic is also the universal language of Islam.

4 By 2017, the languages that Blasim's books have been translated into include Bulgarian, Catalan, Croatian, Danish, Dutch, English, Finnish, French, German, Icelandic, Italian, Japanese, Norwegian, Persian, Polish, Serbian, Spanish, Swedish, Turkish, etc.
5 Https://hassanblasim.net/
6 The poem is published in Finnish and English on his homepage; the Swedish translation was published also in *Dagens Nyheter*, the biggest newspaper in Sweden. There is also a video, made by the Finnish Broadcasting Corporation, of a popular Finnish singer, Maija Vilkkumaa, reading the poem in Finnish, while Blasim is seen in the background.
7 Although this blog has been completed, the webpage fails to mention Ra Page as its writer. The publisher Daedalus Books has promised to credit the rightful author with the text.
8 Joumana Haddad is a Lebanese author, journalist and women's rights activist. She has been selected by *Arabian Business Magazine* as one of the world's 100 most powerful Arab women for four years in a row for her cultural and social activism.
9 Madinah is "city" in Arabic.
10 Ra Page was not the only person negotiating the deal with Penguin. Concurrently, Ahmed Al-Nawas, Blasim's friend from Finland, was also discussing Blasim with potential literary agents in New York.
11 Including the short story "The Reality and the Record", published in *Madinah*.
12 It was chosen as one of *The Guardian's* best Science Fiction and Fantasy Books of the Year 2016 (Roberts 2016). The book was also published in Arabic in 2017.
13 Blasim says that the poems will not be translated to any other languages.
14 It seems that the author himself has a somewhat liberal view on the originality of his texts. As I was comparing the English and Finnish translations of one of his short stories, I noticed that there were whole paragraphs missing in one of them, and when I contacted Blasim and asked him about the differences in the translations, he explained that he "keeps on changing the texts".
15 "Länsimaisen lukijan on paljon helpompi lähestyä Hassan Blasimin novellikokoelmaa The Madman of Freedom Square kuin monia Salman Rushdien idän ja lännen häilyvälle rajapinnalle osuvia kirjoja. Hän kirjoittaa viileän lakonisesti vailla turhia koukeroita tai raskasta kulttuurista kuorrutusta" (Petäjä 2010).
16 "Jos Gogol tai Kafka kirjoittaisi *Tuhannen ja yhden yön tarinoita* nyky-Bagdadista, tulos voisi muistuttaa Hassan Blasimin novellikokoelmaa *Vapaudenaukion mielipuoli (Majnun sahat al-hurriyya)*."
17 "Blasimin novellit ovat aihepiiriltään kaukana suomalaisesta keskivertoproosasta ja novelleista. Siksi on hienoa, että suomalainen kirjailijakunta on saanut täydennykseksi irakilaissyntyisen kirjailijan."
18 One special feature about Blasim's image in Finland is his connection to the city of Tampere and especially to Pispala, the old residential area associated with working-class literature, where he used to live. After Blasim had been awarded the International Foreign Fiction Prize, the Tampere-based newspaper *Aamulehti* had a headline asking, "Does a future Nobelist live in Pispala?" The writer compares Blasim to "Finnish writers" whose texts are evaluated by considering their chances to win the Finlandia Literary Prize, whereas Blasim competes in a completely different league, such as winning the Nobel Literary Prize (See Löytty 2017).
19 Haavisto refers to the concept of the "ethnic mirror" used by Karina Horsti (2005, 291), which describes "a journalism which turns a story of

an immigrant into a story of Finnishness. The core idea with the mirror-metaphor is that the majority gets a possibility to mirror itself in the eyes of newcomers" (Haavisto 2011, 118).
20 *The Nightmare of Carlos Fuentes*, written by Rashid Razaq, premiered at the Arcola Theatre in London on 23 June 2014.

Bibliography

Unpublished References

Harlahti, Satu (2017) Telephone call with the writer February 3, 2017.
Micheva, Neva (2016) E-mail to the writer November 4, 2016.
Page, Ra (2016) E-mail to the writer September 1, 2016.
Sandström, Daniel (2016) E-mail to the writer September 14, 2016.
Øverås, Asbjørn (2016) E-mail to the writer September 1, 2016.

Published References

Abidin, Adel (n.d.) *Abidin Travels*. Accessed October 23, 2017, www.adelabidin.com/works/abidin-travels-2.
Al-Nawas, Ahmed (2017) *A View of the Conditions of Arabic Literature in the Nordic Region. Multilingualism and Diversity as a Resource in the Cultural Field*. Helsinki: Culture for All Service. Accessed August 28, 2017, www.cultureforall.info/doc/research_and_reports/A_View_of_the_Conditions_of_Arabic_Literature_in_the_Nordic_Region.pdf.
Bassnett, Susan (1993) *Comparative Literature. A Critical Introduction*. Oxford & Cambridge: Blackwell.
Bassnett, Susan (2011) From Cultural Turn to Translational Turn: A Transnational Journey. In Cecilia Alvstad, Stefan Helgesson & David Watson (eds): *Literature, Geography, Translation: Studies in World Writing*. Newcastle upon Tyne: Cambridge Scholars Publishing, 67–80.
Behschnitt, Wolfgang & Nilsson, Magnus (2013) "Multicultural Literatures" in a Comparatice Perspective. In Wolfgang Behschnitt, Sarah De Mul & Liesbeth Minnaard (eds): *Literature, Language, and Multiculturalism in Scandinavia and Low Countries*. Amsterdam & New York: Rodopi, 1–15.
Blasim, Hassan (2009) *The Madman of Freedom Square*. Translated by Jonathan Wright. Manchester: Comma Press.
Blasim, Hassan (2016) Foreword. Translated by Jonathan Wright. In Hassan Blasim (ed.): *Iraq + 100: Stories from a Century after the Invasion*. Manchester: Comma Press, v–x.
Blasim, Hassan (2017) A Refugee in the Paradise that is Europe. Accessed August 28, 2017, https://arablit.org/2017/01/31/hassan-blasim-a-refugee-in-the-paradise-that-is-europe-2/.
Bourdieu, Pierre (1993) *The Field of Cultural Production*. Edited and introduced by Randal Johnson. Cambridge & New York: Polity Press & Columbia University Press.
Casanova, Pascale (2004) *The World Republic of Letters*. Trans. M. B. DeBevoise. Cambridge, MA & London: Harvard University Press.
Comma Press (n.d.) *Comma Press*. Accessed August 28, 2017, http://commapress.co.uk.

Damrosch, David (2003) *What is World Literature?* Princeton, NJ: Princeton University Press.

Davies, Nia (2013) Three percent? New Research from Literature across Frontiers. *Literature Across Borders.* Accessed August 28, 2017, www.lit-acrossfrontiers.org/three-percent-new-research-from-literature-across-frontiers/.

The Finnish Institute in London (2015) No title. Accessed August 28, 2017, www.fininst.uk/en/articles/1451-european-literature-night-vii-brings-thecontinents-top-writers-to-london.

Haavisto, Camilla (2001) *Conditionally One of 'Us'. A Study on Print Media, Minorities and Positioning Practices.* Helsinki: University of Helsinki. Accessed August 28, 2017, https://helda.helsinki.fi/bitstream/handle/10138/26235/conditio.pdf?sequence=1-.

Hallila, Mika; Hosiaisluoma, Yrjö; Karkulehto, Sanna; Kirstinä, Leena & Ojajärvi, Jussi (eds) (2013) *Suomen nykykirjallisuus 2. Kirjallinen elämä ja yhteiskunta.* Helsinki: Suomalaisen Kirjallisuuden Seura.

Helsinki Lit (2015) Hassan Blasim. Accessed August 28, 2017, http://areena.yle.fi/1-2823609.

Horsti, Karina (2005) *Vierauden rajat: monikulttuurisuus ja turvapaikanhakijat journalismissa.* Tampere: Tampereen yliopisto.

Juntunen, Marko (2009) Irakilainen satiiri syntyy Kallion kuppilassa. *Maailman Kuvalehti* 10(2009), 14–17.

Korhonen, Outi (2017) Things We Don't Know about Our Language Diversity – Revisiting Non-dominant Language Writers' Possibilities in the Nordic Countries. *Multilingual Month.* Accessed August 28, 2017, https://multilingualmonth.org/2017/02/17/things-we-dont-know-about-our-language-diversity/.

Korhonen, Outi & Paqvalén, Rita (2016) *Wandering Words. Comparisons of the Position of Non-dominant Language Writers in Nordic Organizations.* Helsinki: Kulttuuria kaikille & Ministry of Education and Culture. Accessed August 28, 2017, www.kulttuuriakaikille.fi/doc/monikulttuurisuus_kansio/Wandering_Words.pdf.

Litvin, Margaret & Sellman, Johanna (2016) *Digital Hats, Analog Ambitions: Staging Hassan Blasim.* Arabic Literature (in English). Accessed August 28, 2017, https://arablit.org/2016/04/04/digital-hats-analog-ambitionsstaging-hassan-blasim/.

Löytty, Olli (2015) Immigrant Literature in Finland. The Uses of a Literary Category. In Ann-Sofie Lönngren, Heidi Grönstrand, Dag Heede & Anne Heith (eds): *Rethinking National Literatures and the Literary Canon in Scandinavia.* Newcastle upon Tyne: Cambridge Scholars Publishing, 52–75.

Löytty, Olli (2017) Welcome to Finnish Literature! Hassan Blasim and the Politics of Belonging. In Katrien De Graeve, Riikka Rossi & Katariina Mäkinen (eds): *Citizenships Under Construction: Affects, Politics and Practices.* COLLeGIUM 23. Helsinki: University of Helsinki, 67–82. Accessed December 18, 2017, https://helda.helsinki.fi/bitstream/handle/10138/228630/CollegiumVol23%205-Loytty.pdf?sequence=1.

Ministry of Education and Culture (2015) *Finland Prizes Awarded to Seven Artists.* Accessed October 23, 2017, http://minedu.fi/en/article/-/asset_publisher/opetus-ja-kulttuuriministeri-sanni-grahn-laasonen-jakoi-seitseman-suomipalkintoa.

Nilsson, Magnus (2010) Swedish "Immigrant Literature" and the Construction of Ethnicity. *Tijdschrift voor Skandinavistiek* 31(1), 199–218.

Nissilä, Hanna-Leena (2016) *"Sanassa maahanmuuttaja on vähän kitkerä jälkimaku". Kirjallisen elämän ylirajaistuminen 2000-luvun alun Suomessa.* Oulu: Oulu University.
Pääkkönen, Sirpa (2012) Sodan kurjistama maa. *Helsingin Sanomat* October 14, 2012.
Page, Ra (2014) *Guest Blog from Comma on the Iraqi Christ.* Accessed August 28, 2017, http://blog.dedalusbooks.com/2014/08/19/guest-blog-from-comma-on-the-iraqi-christ/.
Petäjä, Jukka (2010) Suomessa asuva irakilaiskirjailija tavoittelee englantilaista kirjapalkintoa. "Ihmisoikeudet kuuluvat kaikille". *Helsingin Sanomat* March 27, 2010.
Pollari, Mikko; Nissilä, Hanna-Leena; Melkas, Kukku; Löytty, Olli; Kauranen, Ralf & Grönstrand, Heidi (2015) National, transnational and entangled literatures. Methodological Considerations Focusing on the Case of Finland. In Ann-Sofie Lönngren, Heidi Grönstrand, Dag Heede & Anne Heith (eds): *Rethinking National Literatures and the Literary Canon in Scandinavia.* Newcastle upon Tyne: Cambridge Scholars Publishing, 2–29.
Roberts, Adam (2016) The Best SF and Fantasy Books of 2016. *The Guardian* November 30, 2016. Accessed October 23, 2017, www.theguardian.com/books/2016/nov/30/best-sf-and-fantasy-books-2016-adam-roberts.
Sakai, Naoki (2009) How Do We Count a Language? Translation and Discontinuity. *Translation Studies* 2(1), 71–88.
Salomaa, Tapio (2013) Irakin Kafka. *Kiiltomato* 6.3.2013. Accessed August 28, 2017, www.kiiltomato.net/hassan-blasim-vapaudenaukion-mielipuoli/.
Simmel, Georg (1950) The Stranger. In Kurt H. Wolff (ed.): *The Sociology of Georg Simmel.* Translated by Kurt H. Wolff. New York: Free Press, 402–408.
Venuti, Lawrence (2013) *Translation Changes Everything. Theory and Practice.* London & New York: Routledge.
Vertovec, Steven (2009) *Transnationalism.* London & New York: Routledge.
Walkowitz, Rebecca L. (2015) *Born Translated. The Contemporary Novel in an Age of World Literature.* New York: Columbia University Press.
Yassin-Kassab, Robin (2013) The Iraqi Christ by Hassan Blasim – Review. *The Guardian* March 20, 2013. Accessed August 28, 2017, www.theguardian.com/books/2013/mar/20/iraqi-christ-hassan-blasim-review.

3 Broken Lineages, Impossible Affiliations

The Russian Baltic Subject in Andrei Ivanov's "Zola" and *Peotäis põrmu*[1]

Eneken Laanes

In one of the first texts by the transnational Russian Estonian author Andrei Ivanov, the story "Zola" (2008, Ash), published in the New York-based Russian émigré journal *Novyi Zhurnal*, the protagonist offers a self-description that is characteristic of many persons in Ivanov's subsequent novels and, to a certain extent, of Ivanov himself as an author – a non-belonger, a man in-between. In the Russian original of the text, these descriptions are given in English because, as the protagonist explains, they stem from an international discourse of cosmopolitanism that was popular in the 1990s and is associated in the story with the name of Salman Rushdie. The narrator explains that a non-belonger is "someone who has not joined any collectivity, who does not belong to a certain place, who is a foreigner" (Ivanov 2011a, 319).[2] A man in-between is a person who "does not belong to any of the two sets, is literally between this and that" (Ivanov 2011a, 316). In this and Ivanov's other early novels, the non-belonging is linked to questions of non-citizenship and exile in mainly two contexts: his story "Zola" and the novel *Peotäis põrmu* (2011; A handful of dust) deal with stateless Russian Estonians in post-Soviet Estonia, and the novel *Puteshestvie Hanumana na Lolland* (2009; Hanuman's Travels) represents the life of the asylum seekers and paperless persons in Scandinavia in the 1990s.

In all of Ivanov's early novels and stories, the protagonists do not belong because they are stateless, migrant or exilic; they also actively refuse any political and cultural affiliation and consciously decide to be in-between as non-belongers. Some critics have linked this choice to Ivanov's extreme individualism, which he has expressed in many of his interviews, but in the following I will read this refusal to belong as a project of social, political and cultural critique of linguistic, cultural and national borders. In his seminal article on translation as a practice of bordering, Naoki Sakai argues that instead of borders we should study bordering, namely, the ways how borders are inscribed and distinctions are made (Sakai 2009, 71). He explores the processes of linguistic and national bordering that enforce each other mutually and create order and coherence within delimited linguistic, social or cultural spaces. Ivanov's project of non-belonging, both in terms of his institutional position in the linguistically defined Estonian literary field as well in terms of central themes of his fiction, is precisely such an exploration and critique of bordering, which at the same time is a process of ordering. In the first part of the chapter, I will discuss Ivanov's institutional position in the Estonian literary field and the crisis of (b)ordering that Ivanov's transnational work has created in it. In the second part, I will explore Ivanov's radical critique of (b)ordering, which grew out of his reflection on human existence at the borders of political and cultural identities. I will draw on Edward Said's ideas on exile and show how Ivanov harks back to T. S. Eliot and Salman Rushdie to carve out his own position, which is a critique both of cultural and national (b)ordering as well as certain versions of cosmopolitanism that try to defy these borders.

Crisis of (B)ordering: Ivanov's Position in the Estonian Literary Field

Andrei Ivanov (b. 1971) entered the Estonian literary field in 2010 with the translation of two of his stories: "Moi datskii diadiushka" (2007; My Danish uncle) and "Zola" (2008), which was originally published in Russian in *Novyi Zhurnal*. He was born in Tallinn in a Russian family, graduated from Tallinn Pedagogical University, and around the turn of the millennium spent several years as a paperless person in Denmark and other Scandinavian countries. He had been writing for a long time without publishing opportunities, but when he finally did manage to publish, he entered many literary fields at once. Along with "Zola" in the New York journal, 2009 also saw the Tallinn Russian press Avenarius publish his first novel *Puteshestvie Hanumana na Lolland*, which was subsequently nominated for the Russian Booker Prize in 2010. The New York publication and the nomination for the prize in Russia led to Ivanov's first translations into Estonian.

Even if Ivanov has been successful in establishing himself as a talented and prize-winning author in many literary fields that transcend national borders, his publication history shows that he and his fiction have been difficult to order. Despite successfully juggling multiple networks, the mismatch of linguistic, cultural and national borders revealed in the attempts to categorize his fiction has proved to be a stumbling block for his wider international success, and it has also highlighted the difficulties of fully transcending these borders.

I will briefly discuss Ivanov's publication history in order to highlight the quandaries of a transnational author in the specific cultural context of post-Soviet Estonia.[3] Most of Ivanov's novels have originally been published by Russian presses in Tallinn and then translated into Estonian. Some of the novels have then been republished in Moscow.

More recently, a few have been originally published in Moscow. However, there are also several texts published only in Estonian, having been translated from Russian manuscripts. The first of these, *Peotäis põrmu*, has provoked the most serious crisis of (b)ordering in the Estonian literary field, a crisis that has fundamentally redefined the linguistically determined understanding of Estonian literature and culture.[4]

The 2011 novel *Peotäis põrmu* was an immediate success among the Estonian reading public because it was the first novel to deal with the life of the Russian community in the country and to touch upon the Bronze Soldier conflict, which involved the relocation of the Soviet war monument from the centre of Tallinn to a military cemetery on the outskirts of the city in 2007, and resulted in riots by members of the Russian community. However, to the surprise of many, the novel was not nominated for any of the categories of the Annual Prize of Cultural Endowment of Estonia in 2012, the most important state literary prize. In their justification for the decision, prompted by the reactions of many journalists and cultural critics, the prize jury explained that the novel did not qualify for either of the two available categories – the prize for fiction or the prize for authors writing in Russian[5] – the former because it was not an original but a translation, and the second because it was not published in Russian (Lotman 2012). The ensuing public debate made apparent the way in which the (linguistic) categories that order literary fields make some productions impossible to order, if not invisible. Ivanov's novel, which was perceived as one of the best literary texts of the year, fell between the cracks of the prize categories, which were partly representative of the ways in which the whole literary field was (b)ordered (Laanes 2012).

The roots of the hard linguistic borders of the definition of Estonian literature and culture lie in the 19th-century nation-building process when the Estonian nation was defined according to the monolingual paradigm (Yildiz 2012), in terms of people speaking Estonian as opposed to German. Consequently, the history of Estonian literature was written on the basis of linguistic criteria, leaving much of the literary production in German out of the literary canon (Undusk 1999, 251, 2006, 464). Differently than in Finland, for instance, the beginning of Estonian literature has until recently been placed in the middle of the 19th century, excluding all literature that was written in German by people of both Estonian and Baltic German descent. The linguistic borders drawn in the 19th century continued to separate the different literary fields of Estonian and Baltic German literature at the end of the 19th century and the beginning of the 20th century and the Soviet Estonian and local Russian one in the second half of the 20th century in this potentially multilingual Baltic cultural space. The rigidity of linguistic borders that Undusk has characterized as "a fixation on language" (Undusk 1999, 251) has also been inherited by the post-Soviet Estonian cultural self-understanding.

As shown by the state's literary prize category for "authors writing in Russian", the phenomenon of Russian-language literature in Estonia has been widely recognized in post-Soviet Estonia, but I would still argue that, before Ivanov, there was no concept of Russian Estonian literature. This has its historical reasons. On the one hand, in the Soviet period there had always been a community of eminent Russian writers in Estonia whose members (e.g. Samoylov, Dovlatov) had a varied relationship to Estonia (Kotjuh 2012, 2013). After the collapse of the Soviet Union, some of the writers of that community continued to write in Russian and self-identified as Russian writers living in Estonia. Some of them, such as the writer and journalist Elena Skulskaya, have clearly been part of the Estonian cultural public sphere, but until very recently their texts have not been considered as part of Estonian literature.

On the other hand, for the few authors with mixed Russian Estonian background but writing in Estonian, their entrance into the Estonian literary field has been facilitated by the language criterion, and they have been unproblematically considered to be Estonian writers. Such is the case of Andrei Hvostov, a journalist and historian. Although he has sometimes been labelled a Russian by unsympathetic critics, his work has always been part of Estonian literature, not Russian Estonian literature. The crisis that Ivanov's entrance into the Estonian literary field provoked has related generational and thematic reasons.

Ivanov is a second-generation Russian Estonian who does not have any strong political or social ties to Russia. He argues for his cultural affiliation to Russia in terms of his attachment to the literary tradition, but in his novels his characters are often othered by the contemporary cultural community in Russia and debarred as somebody "from Estonia". Furthermore, Ivanov was the first to address in his fiction the existence of a Russian community in Estonia after the collapse of the Soviet Union, a truly local issue that not only interests local Russians but also, and most importantly, Estonians. When his first two texts appeared in Estonian, there was enormous relief and interest within the left-wing Estonian community, who had been waiting for some kind of insider account of the Russian Estonian community's life, compared to the outsider perspectives of the Estonian media.[6]

Since the 2012 debate, much has changed. Ivanov's fiction and personality caused a crisis in the (b)ordering of literature in the Estonian cultural field, initiating a process which has shifted and broadened the boundaries to a considerable extent. Ivanov has definitely established himself as one of the most interesting authors in contemporary Estonian literature. Despite continuing to write in Russian, for the last couple years, he has been included in the list of authors promoted internationally by the Estonian Literature Centre, the state-sponsored literary agency. It seems that the linguistic borders in the definition of Estonian literature have started to soften. However, there should be no illusion about the persistence of difficulties that the mismatch between the linguistic, cultural and national borders presents for transnational authors. The reach of the state literary agency, whose network of translators is mainly composed of those translating from Estonian, is obviously limited. As somebody from abroad writing about matters indifferent to Russia, the channels of literary travel and translation that run from Russian literary centres are equally difficult to reach. So far, Ivanov's work has been translated only into English, German, French, and Finnish in addition to Estonian (see Ivanov 2012, 2015, 2016, 2018a and 2018b).

In the following, I would like to show how the crisis of (b)ordering, but also the persistence of hard borders and the difficulties of defying them at the risk of becoming invisible revealed in Ivanov's publication history and reception, is also dealt with in Ivanov's texts on thematic and metaphorical levels. I will concentrate on two early texts by Ivanov, which deal with his existence as a Russian Estonian in post-Soviet Estonia: the story "Zola" and the novel *Peotäis põrmu*. "Zola" tells of the disintegration of the Soviet Union from the perspective of a young man from Estonia, who emigrates to Denmark and recalls his childhood in Tallinn while working as a fire stoker in an old castle squatted by a hippie commune. *Peotäis põrmu* is a story of a Russian Estonian who, after seven years in Scandinavia, is back in Tallinn leading an alienated and depressed existence in the second half of the 2000s. Against the background of the individualistic story, there unfolds the conflict around the Bronze Soldier. I will show how Ivanov tries in both texts to carve out a position that does not belong to any of the spaces and communities established by existing linguistic, cultural and national borders in post-Soviet Estonia.

Non-belonger: A Russian Estonian Subject in "Zola"

The story "Zola" opens with powerful metaphors of bordering and the breaking of borders. These are developed in the description of the birthplace of the protagonist on the edge of a swamp and dumping ground on the outskirts of Tallinn, in Pääsküla. He lives on the very last street of the suburb, whose houses are like dice rolling towards the swamp, constantly threatening to fall into it. They are decomposing, the steps leading to the houses crumbling. The fences around the houses are made of boards which have not been planned and are still covered with bark, creating for the child the impression of a fence that organically grows out of the ground. The fence is bent by bushes that press into it, making it look pregnant and finally breaking it. The houses are inhabited by mad and mutilated people, provoking fantasies of dismemberment in the child. The place is bordered from the rest of the world by a constant hum of passing cars, driving garbage to the dumping ground, and the crows and seagulls inhabiting the place.

The people of the neighbourhood are in a constant struggle with the swamp, which threatens to swallow the street. It often floods the ground, preventing use of the street and walking paths, and forcing people to take detours. The swamp is upheaving the earth. There is no balance, neither in houses nor in people:

> Everything – the doorjambs, the ceilings, the walls, the depth of wells, the height of the fence posts reaching the sky, the tilt of the ground and the position of the stars – was in a constant movement. The angles became more and more obtuse, the door opened and closed less and less properly, the window sills did not hold flowers anymore, the wells became deeper and the roofs lower, and even the sky rested on the shoulders of the old people sitting next to the fence and whispered something to them.
>
> (Ivanov 2008)

This exuberant, almost hysterical description of the oddity of the place brings the style of the story to the verge of magical realism. The protagonist confesses that the loss of his home to the swamp became for him a metaphor for the disintegration of the Soviet Union:

> In 1991 the outermost house, long without its inhabitants, crumbled and everything got messy and lost its sense. For me, and only for me, the corner of the Tallinn suburb with its future that was slipping away, with its cry, its garbage, its nose-picking, its dumping ground and trash, had long since turned into the metaphor of the historical spectacle ineptly staged at the beginning of the 1990s.
>
> (Ivanov 2008)

The protagonist perceives the disintegration of the Soviet Union as alienation from his hometown. As the political borders are re-drawn, the boundaries of the state he was born into shrink and he is left outside of them, to inhabit his home without the political and cultural meaning with which he had been brought up to give to the place. His exile at home is an exile in which the place he continues to inhabit is alienated from him, due to the change of cultural meaning given to it. He says:

> The city started to lose it familiarity, new faces, a new order appeared. It alienated itself from us, pushed us away. [...] The city ceased to belong to us. The best proof of the alienation from my hometown became the alien passport [...] From that day everything seemed to have slipped its chain, and the world raced along the streets like a mad dog, biting everyone and spreading the madness.
>
> (Ivanov 2008)

After the restoration of the independent Republic of Estonia, the protagonist, as well as Ivanov himself, opted for the so-called grey passport, the alien's passport for non-citizens.[7] The protagonist explains that he was unwilling to identify with his historical homeland, the former empire, and to take Russian citizenship, but he was also too proud to take the Estonian citizenship exam, because in that case he would have subscribed to the border drawn between himself and those who were born next to him in the hospital of Tallinn but happened to be of Estonian origin. In the retrospect of Danish exile, he reflects on his decision with full irony:

> I tried to poeticize my choice: "a man in-between", "no homeland, no flag", it is how it was said at the time. [...] That was the time when the idea of a Russian Balt was born in my mind. A person who is proud of what he lacks. Of what he does not even want to possess. Of what he has chosen not to possess. Who has chosen that he is not. Who is proud of the fact that in this new wondrous world he is nobody. [...] I decided to become this new Russian Balt who is willing to give up everything. I decided to become a person who, instead of "all", chooses "nothing". To become a person who does not want, cannot, does not bend, cannot be moulded – and is proud of it. I was proud of my status as a foreigner. I was against. I was a negative Nein. In my fight for the right to carry this disease I clutched to the word "non-belonger".
>
> (Ivanov 2008)

In the situation of redrawing of the borders, the protagonist opts to choose neither of the two sides. He is not inside any delineated whole or community; he is outside all of them. This is obviously an unbearable position and one that, as we saw in the case of his fiction, makes one invisible. After the protagonist's lover aborts their child behind his back, opts for Russian citizenship and leaves for Russia, the protagonist leaves Estonia, only to continue his paperless existence in the Danish hippie commune. The title metaphor of the story, *zola* ("ash"), refers to the actual ash he is shovelling out of the oven of the castle he is made to heat in the hippie commune. But the protagonist can also be said to be shovelling ash out of the oven by remembering and retelling the story of his Soviet childhood when in Danish exile.

The Post-Soviet Wasteland: *Peotäis põrmu*

Another of Ivanov's novels, *Peotäis põrmu*, features a similar Russian Baltic subject who, after seven years in Scandinavia, is working for a Scandinavian telemarketing company in Tallinn and tries in vain to establish his existence in the Russian Estonian community of the city.

As the title of the novel indicates, this time Ivanov sees the bleakness of the life of the Russian Baltic subject, in more universal T. S. Eliotian terms, as the demise of European civilization, displacement and broken communication. The post-Soviet wasteland is unliveable for the Russian Baltic subject not only because of its specific post-imperial uprootedness of the cuckoo whose mother has laid her eggs in the wrong nest (Ivanov 2011b, 23) but also because of neo-liberal capitalism, which has corrupted politics and rules the world. In *Peotäis põrmu*, Ivanov introduces a counterpart of the cultural crisis of the aftermath of the First World War expressed in Eliot's *Wasteland*. The protagonist laments:

> This country [Estonia] is in essence a similar subsidiary as our company. The whole country. A subsidiary. An offshoot. A cyst. A small territory for laundering money, partying at the company parties, buying real estate. [...] If only one could live without having anything to do with all that. But they have divided up the whole world. There is nowhere to run, companies, subsidiaries, bureaucrats [...] Where to run? Where to dive? Which worm in the corner of which bowel to turn oneself into?
>
> (Ivanov 2011b, 201)

Next to Eliot, Ivanov has another point of reference in this novel, Dostoyevsky's *Notes from Underground*. In the course of the novel, Ivanov's protagonist is slowly turned into the Underground Man, an utterly resentful misanthrope who hates everybody. He lives among a quirky set of Russian Estonians who, despite their bizarreness, are described with a degree of sympathy. At the end of the day, however, he is unable to find his home among them or identify with the community:

> It's easier to be a Muslim than a Russian Estonian! You have to do so much! Have to believe so many things! And give up so many things!
> If you're Russian you have to go to the Russian Drama Theatre.
> You have to admire Russian culture.
> You have to celebrate the New Year at the right time. Eleven o'clock! Together with Russia! Are you a Russian or not, damn it?!
> You have to follow what is happening in Russia, watch the Olympics and count the medals won.
> You have to read Pelevin, Prokhanov, Prilepin and another one from behind the baseboard...
> In football tournaments you should cheer for Russia and against Estonia. You must scream "Ros-si-ya-a-a!"[8] through a megaphone.
> You must lay flowers on the monument to the fallen.
> [...]
> You have to curse Estonian laws.
> You must drink and throw up with the others!

You must never fail to note that Russians are oppressed. You are obliged to notice it. If you do not, then you are no longer a Russian, since Russians are oppressed, and if you no longer feel that you are oppressed, you have gradually ceased to be a Russian.

(Ivanov 2011b, 153)

The (negative) epiphanies of *Peotäis põrmu* rehearse the drama of those of "Zola": the protagonists of both texts are unable to belong. Some affiliations are refused to them, while others they refuse themselves, choosing instead an existence outside any community. This kind of non-belonging seems not to be a problem for Ivanov himself as a writer. Considering the rich intertextuality of his novels, he is a typical modernist author who could not care less about national affiliation, having found his home in "the world republic of letters" (Casanova 2004). However, as Ivanov also shows the unbearable sadness of life without a community, one might ask what the point is of the thought experiment staged in these texts. Based on some of Ivanov's own remarks, many of his critics have read the credo of non-belonging as an expression of his extreme individualism. Yet I would argue that the experiment serves as a political critique. With the help of this miserable individualist subject, Ivanov considers human existence outside political and cultural communities.

Metaphors of Broken Lineage and Edward Said's Secular Criticism

Both of Ivanov's texts focussing on the bleak existence of an individual on the borders of various political and cultural identities close with similar central metaphors. In "Zola", in parallel to the political drama of the disintegration of the Soviet Union and the protagonist's process of becoming exilic, runs the drama of abortion and the protagonist's separation from his lover. In *Peotäis põrmu*, the protagonist and his wife are expecting a child, but the child is stillborn on the night of the Bronze Soldier conflict. In his interviews, Ivanov has warned that these private tragedies should not be read as metaphors for political events (Ivanov 2010, 125). However, their metaphorical potential – and, as such, their link to the condition of exile – is helpfully illuminated by Edward Said's reflections.

Said's thoughts about exile are tightly linked to the development of one of his central concepts, secular criticism, in the introduction to his book *The World, the Text and the Critics* (1983) and in the essay "Reflections on Exile" (1984). Without losing sight of the unredeemable horror of mass migration and physical homelessness, which has become the reality today for so many more people than was the case in the 1980s, Said is trying to retrieve a positive potential of exile. Said's approach

Broken Lineages, Impossible Affiliations 57

to exile is especially useful, because in thinking about the crisis of (b)ordering, he draws on modernist writers (in particular, T. S. Eliot) and the presence of "childless couples, orphaned children, aborted childbirths and unregenerately celibate men and women" (Said 1983, 17) in their work. Thus, the same motifs used by Ivanov are read by Said as metaphors for the crisis of natural filiation. In the following, I would like to discuss the notions of secular criticism, exile and the crisis of natural filiation in greater detail.[9]

For Said, exile is primarily a separation and alienation from home that is both a political and a cultural entity. To be at home in a place is to be part of a political formation, of a state, but even more to be part of a cultural community that nurtures the person and offers reassurance and comfort. In order to do that, culture has to designate the boundary that establishes what is extrinsic and intrinsic to the culture. Hence, culture is able to "authorize, to dominate, to legitimate, demote, interdict, and validate: in short, the power of culture to be an agent of, and perhaps the main agency for, powerful differentiation within its domain and beyond it too" (Said 1983, 9). Those who subscribe to these differentiations feel at home within the boundaries of this culture, while those who do not are left outside, homeless (Said 1983, 11). Therefore, culture is also

> a system of exclusions legislated from above but enacted throughout its polity, by which such things as anarchy, disorder, irrationality, inferiority, bad taste, and immorality are identified, then deposited outside the culture and kept there by the power of the State and its institutions.
>
> (Said 1983, 11)

Hence, culture often has to do with an aggressive sense of nation, home, community and belonging (Said 1983, 12).

It is clear from Said's definition of culture that exile, a separation from home, be it forced or voluntary, is an opportunity to look critically at aspects of belonging and being at home:

> The exiles know that in a secular and contingent world, homes are always provisional. Borders and barriers, which enclose us within the safety of family territory, can also become prisons, and are often defended beyond reason or necessity. Exiles cross borders, break barriers of thought and experience.
>
> (Said 2000, 147)

The condition of exile for Said becomes a privileged position through which to exercise a critical stance towards the community one is exiled from. Said develops his understanding of the positive potential of exile by discussing the birth of Erich Auerbach's monumental book *Mimesis*

(1946), written in his Istanbul exile from Nazi Germany. Said takes a cue from Auerbach's remark that he was only able to actually write the book due to the unavailability of all the necessary materials in Istanbul related to the European literature he was writing about. Said infers that the Istanbul exile gave Auerbach the critical distance from his culture necessary to write such a monumental work.

However, secular criticism, the distance from one's home and culture, can also take the form of inner exile. Said attributes to intellectuals the role of always being able to look at and resist the exclusions that every culture performs while defining itself. This would be a voice "out of place, but very much of that place" (Said 1983, 15). Said continues:

> individual consciousness is not naturally and easily a mere child of the culture, but a historical and social actor in it. And because of that perspective, which introduces circumstances and distinctions where there had only been conformity and belonging, there is distance, or what we might also call criticism.
>
> (Said 1983, 15)

So, if exile is primarily the opposite of nationalism for Said (2000, 140), then the "secular" in secular criticism is not so much opposed to religions, but to the religious in every definition of nation or culture, and to nationalism as a belief system (Robbins 1994, 26). To exercise secular criticism towards one's culture means to look at it from the outside, trying to see and to take into account what it excludes.

Said elaborates on the critical consciousness in terms of filiation and affiliation. To be filiated is to be born naturally from somebody, to be native in a place; to be affiliated means to become part of a place or community with which you do not have any natural bond. Said develops this opposition by looking at the whole generation of modernist writers and thinkers whose writing presents the crisis of natural filiation. More precisely, he looks at T. S. Eliot, an American expatriate in Britain whose early poetry is full of metaphors of the impossibility of natural filiation, aborted children and childless couples. For Said, Eliot actively searched for a way out of that crisis, for a way to conceive human relationships differently. Eliot's alternative, according to Said, is affiliation. Said argues that since *Ash Wednesday* (1930), Eliot finds this new community, whose existence is not guaranteed by biology but by a compensatory horizontal affiliation, in the Catholic Church – and for the rest of his life aspires to be more royalist and classicist than the English themselves.

However, there is a third part to the pattern, in which filiation is replaced by affiliation in exile. Said argues that affiliative communities tend to try to mimic filiative ones "to reinstate vestiges of the kind of authority associated in the past with filiative order" (Said 1983, 19). He is looking in particular at how cultural communities in exile often become closed and exclusionary and fetishize their condition of exile (Said 2000, 146). For Said, then, secular criticism also involves scrutiny of the ways in which affiliation reproduces filiation (Said 1983, 24).

Said's concepts of secular criticism, filiation and affiliation provide a vocabulary to elucidate what is at stake in Ivanov's protagonist's project of rejecting all ties to any cultural community through his refusal to be (b)ordered in any way. He is exiled by the disintegration of the Soviet Union, the only place he knows as his home. He refuses to affiliate with the new political and cultural community that lays claim to the place – the Estonian state – because of the exclusionary filiative nature of that community,[10] but he is also resistant to being part of the community of the people who are excluded just like him – the Russian minority – because of the ways in which the affiliative community tries to reproduce filiation. Ivanov's protagonist does not wish to be part of any community as long as it aims to secure a safe life for its members by excluding those who do not measure up to the criteria of belonging.

Said, Rushdie and the Question of Cosmopolitanism

To represent in fiction a position that rejects both filiative and affiliative ties is extremely illuminating. Yet, as Ivanov shows and Said is well aware of, the secular critical position in its radical version is an unbearably solitary one and thus practically unliveable in real life. Said is aware of the dangers of celebrating exile for its positive potential of critical secularism, which is pertinent also in Ivanov's case, considering the plight of his protagonists. Said argues that even if the exilic condition seems to be the prevalent motif of 20th-century extraterritorial literature, considering the scale of contemporary mass migration, to see this literature as "beneficially humanistic is to banalize its [the exile's] mutilations, the loss it inflicts on those who suffer them, the muteness with which it responds to any attempt to understand it as 'good for us'" (Said 2000, 138).

Despite this lucid awareness, some of Said's readers have criticized his notion of secular criticism because of its flavour of elite cosmopolitanism. Only intellectuals in European and North American metropolises can afford the secular critical position. Millions of poor and disenfranchised migrants have to deal with much more pressing issues of survival. However, Aamir Mufti has shown that Said's understanding of exile that enables the critical secular position is indeed firmly linked to minority existence and sometimes statelessness:

> Said's insistence on the critical imperative of the secular can appear elitist and hence paradoxical only if we fail to recognize this minority and exilic thrust in his work, if we forget the haunting figure of Auerbach in Turkish exile that he repeatedly evokes. It is in this

sense that we must read Said when he himself speaks of exile not as "privilege" but as permanent critique of "the mass institutions that dominate modern life." Saidian secular criticism points insistently to the dilemmas and the terrors, but also, above all, to the ethical possibilities, of minority existence in modernity.

(Mufti 1998, 107)

Ivanov's fiction highlights the distance between elitist cosmopolitanism and the minority position of his protagonists through its references to Salman Rushdie as a cultural icon of cosmopolitanism haunting all of Ivanov's early texts.

Rushdie is foremost present in Ivanov's fiction in terms of his style. All of his early novels – but in particular *Puteshestvie Hanumana na Lolland*, which deals with the absurd and tragic life of two paperless persons, Indian-born Hanuman and Russian Estonian Eugene, a truly Cervantine couple of Don Quixote and Sancho Panza in a Danish asylum camp – resemble Rushdie's exuberant and over-the-top prose. James Wood has called this style "hysterical realism", the description of which fits Ivanov's in many aspects but one. Wood argues that this style is characterized by "bonhomous, punning, travelling serenity of spirit" and that it is "incompatible with tragedy or anguish" (Wood 2004, 180). In Ivanov, however, the style is used to represent a completely desolate and unbearable existence of paperless people. So, even if Ivanov has affiliations with Rushdie in terms of style, he also marks his difference from him.

In the beginning of the 1990s, Rushdie was notably in the centre of the debate about cosmopolitanism in literary studies. Scholars like Timothy Brennan and others have criticized the elitist cosmopolitanism of Rushdie's novels and their indiscriminate celebration of hybridity (Ahmad 1992, 157–158; Brennan 1997, 306). Despite the affinity between Ivanov's and Rushdie's styles, and Ivanov's obvious appreciation of him, it is precisely with the help of Rushdie that Ivanov tries to draw attention to the unavailability of the cosmopolitan position for those who have been marginalized by the communitarian logic. The protagonist of "Zola" confesses:

> I clung to the word "non-belonger". I read Rushdie the way some punks read Bakunin. It seemed to me, I wanted to believe that this word somehow brought me closer to another word – cosmopolitan. To that luxury attainable only to holders of a British passport. Not to those who had a "grey passport" – there was only one step down from them: a wanted criminal.
>
> (Ivanov 2011a, 100)

In this passage, Ivanov's protagonist maps the distance between the non-belonger and the elitist cosmopolitan represented here by Rushdie, showing that both Ivanov and Said explore the processes of linguistic and political (b)ordering and criticize nationalism not in the name of cosmopolitanism, but in the name of those who are minoritized by national cultures.

Despite the unbearable loneliness brought about by isolation and uprootedness, the secular critical position has a utopian potential for Ivanov. The protagonist of "Zola" repeatedly compares the recounting of his wretched life in Danish exile to the shovelling of the useless ash out of the oven. However, towards the end of the story, it is said that he collects the ash in order to use it for the fertilization of a willow garden and for the purification of the groundwater, for some "utopian project of the improvement of the ecological environment and aura" (Ivanov 2011a, 102). If we look beyond the ecological metaphors in this passage, Ivanov's shovelling of ash in these texts serves a better politics to come for the people on the borders of political and cultural identities. In his article about a group of Russian Latvian poets and media artists called Orbita, Kevin M. F. Platt (2015, 309) has argued for their fragile lyrical cosmopolitanism, which "attempts to assemble a new and shareable world out of the shards of old ones", as the Baltic version of critical cosmopolitanism. Even if Ivanov's critique of both national cultures and elite cosmopolitanism is much more radical than that of the Orbita group, what he shares with them in these rare utopian moments is their awareness of the need to share the world beyond the communitarian logic.

Notes

1 The research for this chapter has been supported by the Estonian Research Council grant No IUT28-1 "Entangled Literatures".
2 If not stated otherwise, all translations in this chapter are mine.
3 My discussion of the institutional position of Ivanov and his work, as well as the crisis of (b)ordering it has provoked, is largely limited to the Estonian perspective. For a Russian Baltic and Russian perspective, see (Laukkonen 2012).
4 The novel was originally published in translation out of necessity rather than choice. The rights of the novel were bought together with Ivanov's earlier Booker-nominated novel, *Hanuman*, by the Moscow publisher AST in 2009, but it was not published until 2014, when it came out in the same volume with and under the book title of *Harbinskie motylki* (2014; Harbin moths). For a more extensive discussion of the debate around *Peotäis põrmu*, see (Monticelli & Laanes 2018).
5 The category for "authors writing in Russian" was added to the Annual Prize of the Cultural Endowment of Estonia in 2001.
6 In 2010, "Moi datskii diadiushka" and "Zola" were publicly discussed in one of the most popular Estonian literary forums of the time, the literary blog of the publishing house Varrak.
7 The alien's passport was chosen by people who did not want to take Russian citizenship, but were unable to be naturalized as Estonian citizens, generally because of the Estonian language requirement. In the 1990s, the alien passport was a serious impediment for travel. Since Estonia's

inclusion in the EU and the recognition of the alien passport, the alien passport was even preferred by many Russian Estonians because it enabled travel without a visa both in the EU and to Russia. As of 2019, there are still 76,000 stateless persons living in Estonia. Andrei Ivanov became an Estonian citizen in 2018.
8 My translation of the passage follows the original of the novel, which itself is an Estonian translation of the novel from a Russian manuscript. Hence, the code-switching here should be attributed to the Estonian translator.
9 My reading of Said is greatly inspired by Aamir R. Mufti's (1998) article "Auerbach in Istanbul: Edward Said, Secular Criticism, and the Question of Minority Culture".
10 Estonian citizenship is based on the *jus sanguinis* ("right of blood") principle.

Bibliography

Ahmad, Aijaz (1992) *In Theory*. London: Verso.
Brennan, Timothy (1997) *At Home in the World: Cosmopolitanism Now*. Cambridge, MA: Harvard University Press.
Casanova, Pascale (2004) *The World Republic of Letters*. Cambridge, MA: Harvard University Press.
Ivanov, Andrei (2008) "Zola". *Novyi Zhurnal* 253. Accessed August 10, 2017, http://magazines.russ.ru/nj/2008/253/iv1.html.
Ivanov, Andrei (2009) *Puteshestvie Hanumana na Lolland*. Tallinn: Avenarius.
Ivanov, Andrei (2010) Kes on Andrei Ivanov. Intervjuu kirjanikuga. In Andrei Ivanov (ed.): *Minu Taani onuke. Tuhk*. Tallinn: Loomingu Raamatukogu 7/8, 123–125.
Ivanov, Andrei (2011a) "Zola". In Andrei Ivanov: *Kopengaga*. Tallinn: KPD, 174–353.
Ivanov, Andrei (2011b) *Peotäis põrmu*. Translated by Ilona Martson. Tallinn: Varrak.
Ivanov, Andrei (2012) *Hanumans Reise nach Lolland*. Translated by Friederike Meltendorf. München: Kunstmann.
Ivanov, Andrei (2015) Jackdaw on a Snowdrift. In *Words Without Borders*. Special issue Writing from the Edge: Estonian Literature, October. Accessed August 10, 2016, www.wordswithoutborders.org/article/jackdaw-on-a-snowdrift.
Ivanov, Andrei (2016) *Le Voyage de Hanumân*. Translated by Hélène Henry. Paris: Le Tripode.
Ivanov, Andrei (2018a) *Hanuman's Travels*. Translated by Matthew Hyde. Glasgow: Vagabond Voices.
Ivanov, Andrei (2018b) *Kourallinen tomua*. Translated by Jukka Mallinen. Rajamäki: Aviador.
Kotjuh, Igor (2012) Eesti venekeelne kirjandus: kas osa eesti või vene kirjandusest? *Keel ja Kirjandus* 2, 134–139.
Kotjuh, Igor (2013) Eesti venekeelse kirjanduse nullindate põlvkond. *Methis* 11: 64–82.
Laanes, Eneken (2012) Andrei Ivanov ja rahvusülene (eestivene) kirjandus. *Sirp* March 8.
Laukkonen, Taisija (2012) Baltic-Russian Literature: Writing from Nowhere? *Baltic Worlds* 2, 24–26.

Broken Lineages, Impossible Affiliations 63

Lotman, Rebekka (2012) Milleks õhutada vaenu tühja koha pealt? *Sirp* March 2.

Monticelli, Daniele & Laanes, Eneken (2018) Battling around the Exception: A Stateless "Russian" Writer and His Translation in Today's Estonia. In Brian James Baer & Susanna Witt (eds): *Translation in Russian Contexts: Culture, Politics, Identity.* New York: Routledge, 321–335.

Mufti, Aamir R. (1998) Auerbach in Istanbul: Edward Said, Secular Criticism, and the Question of Minority Culture. *Critical Inquiry* 25(1), 95–125.

Platt, Kevin M. F. (2015) Lyrical Cosmopolitanism in a Postsocialist Borderland. *Common Knowledge* 21(2), 305–326.

Robbins, Bruce (1994) Secularism, Elitism, Progress, and Other Transgressions: On Edward Said's 'Voyage In'. *Social Text* 40, 25–37.

Said, Edward (1983) Introduction: Secular Criticism. In Edward Said (ed.): *The World, the Text and the Critic.* Cambridge, MA: Harvard University Press, 1–30.

Said, Edward (2000) Reflections on Exile. In Edward Said (ed.): *Reflections on Exile and Other Essays.* Cambridge, MA: Harvard University Press, 137–149.

Sakai, Naoki (2009) How to Count a Language? Translation and Discontinuity. *Translation Studies* 2(1), 71–88.

Undusk, Jaan (1999) Eesti kirjanduse ajast, ruumist ja ülesandest XX sajandil. *Looming* 2, 249–255.

Undusk, Jaan (2006) Peamiselt Victor Hehnist, aga veidi ka Faehlmannist. III baltisaksa kirjakultuuri sümpoosioni ainetel. *Keel ja Kirjandus* 6, 463–476.

Wood, James (2004) Hysterical Realism. In James Wood (ed.): *The Irresponsible Self: On Laughter and the Novel.* London: Macmillan, 178–193.

Yildiz, Yasemin (2012) *Beyond the Mother Tongue: The Postmonolingual Condition.* New York: Fordham University Press.

4 De-bordering Comics Culture
Multilingual Publishing in the Finnish Field of Comics

Ralf Kauranen

Multilingualism is an obvious trait when considering Nordic comics as a transnational, international and regional construct. It is constituted by the different languages used in the region as comics are published in Danish, Finnish, Icelandic, Norwegian and Swedish as well as in other less used languages. However, multilingualism is of relevance in another context as well, when Nordic comics are promoted to and read by readers outside the area. In this context, the linguistic variation in the region is of secondary interest as the audiences targeted belong to other language groups than those dominant in the Nordic countries. In these instances, English usually becomes the common Nordic language (See Cortsen & Kauranen 2016). This chapter focusses on attempts within the Finnish comics field to encompass readership in multiple languages and on the various practices of publishing comics multilingually. Finnish-English is the most usual language combination in such endeavours, but it is not the only one. One example of multilingual publishing within the Nordic context in the dominant Nordic languages is the interregional comics competition arranged in the northern Finnish towns of Kemi (1981–2012) and Oulu (2014–).[1] In 1981, Kemi became the home town of an annual comics festival, in connection to which a comics competition was arranged. At first the competition was national, but in 1999 its scope was broadened to cover the entire Nordic region. Since the second year of the competition, the prize-winning comics were published in an annual comics album. The first albums were entirely written in Finnish, but with the competition inviting contributions from Denmark, Iceland, Norway and Sweden, in addition to Finland, the publications became multilingual.

For example, the collection of comics from the competition in 1999 (Porkola 1999) contained comics in Danish, Finnish, Icelandic and Swedish, as well as a few pieces lacking any words. The book's multilingualism reflects (to some degree) the linguistic variety of the region and at the same time attests to the close ties between transnationalism and multilingualism in comics culture. The transcendence of national borders in comics production, appreciation and consumption presupposes that multiple languages come into play and interact in some way. This is

De-bordering Comics Culture 65

true of this particular case, but also for the promotion of Nordic comics in, for instance, English or French.

Whereas the Kemi album of 1999 presented the different Nordic languages in parallel, with each comic in its own language, the subsequent album collections have included translations, thus deepening the linguistic interrelations. In the 2002 album (Porkola 2002), for example, the comics published are in Danish, Finnish, Norwegian and Swedish, while the Finnish-language comics are supplemented with a Swedish translation and the comics in Scandinavian languages are translated into Finnish. Translations of longer comics stories are found at the end of the book, whereas the translations of texts in comic strips are located below each strip in the form of subtitles.

The publications from the Kemi comics competition highlight multiple aspects of the theme of this chapter. On a general level, they indicate the close ties between transnationalism and multilingualism in comics culture. This is the framework within which multilingualism is approached here. More specifically, the albums exemplify the means of presenting a comic multilingually in one publication, that is, both in an original language and, through translation, in one or more additional target languages. Furthermore, they illustrate the language variation in these multilingual publications as well as highlight the issue of how word-image relations in comics may potentially change with the addition of a second language.

My analysis of comics and multilingualism in this chapter is based on a presupposition that multilingualism is a consequence and central aspect of the increasing transnationalism of comics culture (see Beaty 2007, 111–137; Denson et al. 2013; Meneses 2013; Brienza 2016). Transnationalism and multilingualism in comics take many forms, as local fields are formed by increased travel of and cross-border communication between comics artists, readers and texts. My interest is not in language contact or multilingualism as a general trait of the comics field, nor in the multilingualism of individual comics artists or comics texts as works of art including, for example, code-switching. Instead, my focus is on multilingualism as a publishing practice in which comics are presented in multiple languages, in an original language and in translation.

One might ask whether these works are "born translated", to cite Rebecca L. Walkowitz's (2015, 4) concept used to describe contemporary world literature. According to her, "Translation is not secondary or incidental to these works. It is a condition of their production." The multilingual comics that are scrutinized here obviously are "born translated" to the extent that they are published multilingually and meant to be read by readers equipped with different language competencies. Still, in many cases languages are not equal in these publications and, in terms of presentation of the different languages, translation actually seems to be secondary. These works aspire in their multilingualism to the category of "world comics", to be part of the international space (Casanova 2004) of comics works, but at the same time they maintain hierarchies and borders in that world. Below I will present a typology of the practices of multilingual comics publishing and discuss them in terms of bordering, that is, how different types of multilingual publishing recast borders in comics culture on different levels, from the institutional to the textual.

Comics as Transnational Cultural Production

Multilingual publishing practices in the Finnish field of comics are motivated by the transnationalism of comics culture. In his analysis of trends in 1990s European comics culture, *Unpopular Culture: Transforming the European Comic Book in the 1990s* (2007), comics scholar Bart Beaty proposes that increasing transnationalism or internationalism is a significant trait in the culture of the period. He finds that comics artists, publishers, critics and readers meet and connect across national borders, thus creating an artistic community in which the global and local converge. The aesthetic disposition shared by comics artists forms the basis for a more – in the vocabulary of the anthropologist Ulf Hannerz (1996) used by Beaty – horizontal form of community than one based on national belonging.

Beaty (2007, 130–132) also pays attention to the field of Finnish comics production in this context. He states that, on the one hand, Finnish comics artists are an integrated group lacking clear-cut separate artistic cliques in the national context. On the other hand, Finnish artists demonstrate a transnational outlook and willingness to reach out to colleagues and readers beyond the borders of Finland. One means of transcending national borders and de-bordering comics culture is multilingual publishing.

As Beaty (2007, 131) notes, "Finnish publishers have made an important, and interesting, concession to globalizing market forces":

> these publishers have increasingly made their material – even among the smallest presses and at the fanzine level – available to readers by the inclusion of English translations packaged within the anthology. *Napa*, for example, began by presenting comics in Finnish, but included a pull-out insert containing the complete translation of the issue in English so that the dialogue could be read by English-language readers by turning from the printed book to the translation guide. When this method proved less than ideal, *Napa* began, with the fourth issue (2000), to include the English text on the printed page in small type, not unlike subtitles in film. This same technique has been adopted by the anthology *Laikku*.
>
> (Beaty 2007, 131)[2]

Beaty mentions two ways of including translations in a publication: the pull-out insert and so-called subtitles. The development described by Beaty of moving from inserts to subtitles is indicative of the general trend in Finnish comics publishing, with subtitles nowadays being the most popular form of translation. In her master's thesis, Saana Kaurala (2016) estimates that seventy comics albums with subtitled translations were published in Finland in 2000–2012. In addition to these albums, a number of comic books, magazines and fanzines have presented comics with translations in subtitles, one internationally recognized forum being the (until recently) tabloid-size comics magazine *Kuti*.[3] There is no reason to believe that the practice diminished after 2012. Contrary to Beaty's suggestion, it is actually small publishers who have adopted the custom (Kaurala 2016, 19), not the larger ones, who probably have less of a need to reach out to readers among non-Finnish speakers.

A Typology of Multilingual Publishing Practices

Whether comics subtitling is a Finnish innovation or has a prehistory elsewhere is another question. What is clear is that the practice is in use nowadays in several countries and linguistic communities in addition to Finland.[4] However, while the use of subtitles is a central practice in Finnish multilingual publishing, it is not the only one. The main types of multilingual publications – the ways in which a publication can present a comic multilingually in at least two languages – are, according to my proposed typology: supplementing, integration and doubling. The first type, supplementing, refers to publications in which one or more secondary language(s) are included but left out of the comic's pages proper. The practice of subtitling, as well as the pull-out insert mentioned by Beaty, provides one kind of supplement. By integration, I refer to the practice of including multiple languages within the frame of the comics page itself. Doubling – a very uncommon practice, to my knowledge – refers to the same comics page being printed in two (or more) versions, presenting the very same comic in different languages in one publication.

Multilingual comics not only differ in terms of presentation, but also with regard to the languages used. The most common case, as mentioned above, is a comic whose original language is Finnish and whose translation is in English. While the albums of the Kemi comics competition show that other language combinations do exist, altogether it seems clear that from the point of view of Finnish comics publishers, English is the lingua franca of comics culture. The presumption seems to be that English is the best language to reach readers unable to read Finnish. This interpretation is supported by the fact that comics in Finland in the 21st century are increasingly published in English, that is, in English only.[5] Whereas this practice is a monolingual one on the level of individual publications, on the level of the field in its entirety it means increasing multilingualism. In addition to the two traditional languages of comics publishing in Finland (Finnish and Swedish), more and more comics are now appearing in English.

Both the choice of publication languages and the chosen means of presenting comics multilingually have a bearing on the process of reading a comic. The reader's knowledge of the languages in a publication is an obvious prerequisite, but the multilingual presentation of a comic is essentially connected to one central aspect of how comics communicate and narrate. The word-image relation, considered crucial in analyses of the multimodal "language of comics", is constructed anew when a comic is presented multilingually. An added translation necessitates a different reading process and combination of the images and words of a comic than the reading of a monolingual comic with its conventional forms of integration. In the following sections, I will describe the different types of multilingual publishing practices through a number of examples, after which I will conclude with a discussion of the bordering processes involved in such practices.

Doubling and Supplementing

I am aware of only one case where what I call *doubling* is the chosen practice of multilingual publishing. It is an interesting example, as it breaks with the usual linguistic tendencies in Finnish comics publishing. Instead of being a publication in the Finnish and English languages, it contains Finnish and Swedish. Instead of being a publication aimed at a transnational or global audience through use of the English language, it addresses a local readership. The practice of doubling is used by Anita Lehtinen in her four self-published album collections of the comic strip *Hangö Lejon / Hangon Leijonat* (The Hanko lions; Lehtinen 2009, 2010, 2011, 2017). In this case, doubling means that each strip is printed twice with a Swedish and Finnish language version on each spread (see Figure 4.1).[6] Finnish is the source language and Swedish the target language in the translation process. The comic strip, which has a local character, is tied to the town of Hanko on the southern coast of Finland. The town is bilingual (in 2014, approximately 54 per cent was Finnish-speaking and 43 per cent was Swedish-speaking), and by means of the linguistic doubling practice the comics albums address both language groups in this local context. However, while the publications are bilingual, the comics themselves are monolingual. The reading process in Finnish and Swedish is the same when it comes to the issue of word-image relations. Neither of the languages has a secondary status with regard to the comics' images. That said, in the third book, the visuals of the comics in the two different languages are at times a bit different: in the Finnish version some additional grey tones colour the strips.

De-bordering Comics Culture   69

Figure 4.1 Anita Lehtinen, spread from *Hitaasti kävelevä turisti. Hangon Leijonat albumi 3. / En turist som rör sig långsamt. Hangö Lejon album 3* (2011), pp. 20–21. © Anita Lehtinen, Swedish translation © Björn Österman.

By *supplement*, I describe a practice that adds a second language (or more) to an original monolingual comic without the additional language(s) interfering or having a presence in the original comic's pages. In other words, the publication's multilingualism is brought about by means of some kind of addendum where the translation is included. This is done in various ways. In addition to the previously mentioned subtitles, supplements consist of different appendices. Furthermore, there is variation in the implementation of both appendices and subtitling, and hence the secondary language is posited in differing relationships with the original comic's pages and, consequently, its pictorial contents. In other words, there are different means and levels of integrating the supplementary text and language with the comics text in its entirety, that is, with the visual elements and the storyworld.

In the Finnish context today, subtitling is more common than different types of appendices, but they continue to be used as well. For instance, Matti Hagelberg's Finnish-language comic book *Läskimooses* (Fatso 2012–) is sold abroad with separate leaflets with English translations. To name another current example, Miissa Rantanen's small album *Kirjeitä / Letters* (2017) includes a small booklet with the Finnish text translated into English. While the addendum to *Läskimooses* is a sheet of printed text, Rantanen's translation leaflet has a handmade feel to it. The character of the addendum is reflected in how the comics are presented: *Läskimooses* only has a Finnish title, whereas Rantanen's book is titled bilingually.

As was mentioned by Beaty, the anthology *Napa* (published in 1997–2006), to which the innovation of subtitling was attributed, started by including the English translations of the Finnish text elements on a separate pull-out insert. Even before *Napa*, the small-press anthology *Gomix* offered English translations. The photocopied translation pull-out of the fifth issue, published in March 1994, is interesting (*Gomix* 1994). It is an A6 booklet, although the comic book itself is size A5, with the same amount of pages (40) as the original publication. In the translation booklet, the translated texts are in approximately the same position as the original text on corresponding pages (see Figure 4.2 with a page from

70 Ralf Kauranen

Figure 4.2 To the left a page from Petri Tolppanen, "Kissat" (*Gomix 5*, 1994, np.), and to the right the corresponding page from the translation leaflet. © Petri Tolppanen, English translation © Hans Nissen.

Gomix on the left and a page with translation on the right). Sometimes the original panel grid is copied on the translation booklet, but at other times it is not. This means of presenting a translation is taken a step further in Marko Turunen's *Rakkautta viimeisellä silmäyksellä* (2000; Love at last sight). The leaflet, about one-third smaller than the original book, consists of a photocopied version of the Finnish album with the original text covered by English translation. Here the supplement almost becomes a publication of its own, perhaps of a lower quality, but with the translation connected to the visuals of the comic. Of course, if a reader wishes to delve into the colouring of Turunen's book, the reading of the black and white translation appendix needs to be combined with a reading of the Finnish-language original.

In addition to separate pull-outs, translation appendices also appear in the pages of the publications themselves. The Kemi albums mentioned in the beginning apply this practice to the comics short stories in the books, such that the translations are posited in separate pages at the end of the book and typeset in a font that is distinct from the lettering used in the comics themselves. Contrary to this, Amanda Vähämäki's little book *Mestari / Maestro* (2011) presents a creative variant of the translation in an appendix. The comic is a 24-page story with one panel

De-bordering Comics Culture 71

on each page. The verbal content is limited: all the dialogue adds up to two dozen words. In addition to this, verbal elements are included in the comic's diegesis: on signs, a cafeteria window and a college shirt in the storyworld. One onomatopoetic sound effect is also spelled out.

The dialogue, which in the comic is in Finnish, is presented in English translation on the inside back cover of the book (see Figure 4.3). The diegetic texts on the signs, cafeteria window and college shirt are not translated, nor is the sound effect. The creative element in Vähämäki's solution to presenting the translation consists in it being framed by a ketchup bottle. Similarly, the bibliographic information is presented on the label of a mustard bottle. Neither ketchup nor mustard plays a role in the story, but they both hint at the main scene in which the story unfolds: a canteen or bar. In that way, although the translation is presented in a supplement, it is tied visually to the pictures of the comic and the storyworld being depicted. Furthermore, a connection is also made by the translated text being handwritten in the same style as the Finnish text in the comic. Still, to follow the dialogue a non-Finnish reader needs to "jump" between the comics pages themselves and the back cover. Readers with different linguistic competencies are dependent on differentiated reading processes with multiple implications, such as eye movement across the pages and spreads of the book as well as the physical turning of pages.

Figure 4.3 Amanda Vähämäki, *Mestari / Maestro* (2011), inside back cover. © Amanda Vähämäki.

Translations in Subtitles

Subtitling, notably the most popular way of supplementing comics with translations, refers to the placing of the translation in the bottom margin of a comics page or below a comic strip.[7] With regard to choice of languages, in Finnish comics publishing this means that the texts in the comic itself are in Finnish whereas the translations are in English.[8] Next I will discuss the practice of subtitling by means of three examples that are not completely representative for the practice, but can highlight its history and general characteristics, as well as variations. The first case is the comics anthology *Olmi Kolmonen*, the third issue of *Olmi* (1995; Olm), the other two being albums by individual artists. These are Wolf Kankare's debut, *Miska Pähkinä* (2013; Miska Nut), and Aapo Rapi's first album, *Pullapoika / Doughboy* (2005). All three are published by small presses, Arktinen Banaani (which since the publication of *Olmi* has grown to be somewhat larger than a small press), Suuri Kurpitsa and Napa Books, respectively. In this way, the subtitling is representative: small comics publishers such as the aforementioned, as well as Asema, Daada and Huuda Huuda, have been the most avid multilingual publishers.

The anthology *Olmi* and its third (and last) issue are worth mentioning for several reasons. It was published in 1995 and thus precedes *Napa* by a few years as a Finnish-language publication with English subtitles. It also includes a wide array of different ways of presenting subtitles. Furthermore, the novelty of subtitles is announced in capital letters on the cover and the spine of the book: "NOW WITH ENGLISH SUBTITLES". The foreword (written by editor Christer Nuutinen) states – in Finnish – that the translations are there to make it easier to introduce the book to foreign readers. The 64-page collection includes contributions by fourteen artists, mostly short stories but also a few comic strips. Again, just like the Kemi albums, the subtitles of the comic strips are placed under each strip, whereas the subtitles of the short stories are usually placed in the bottom margin of the page. In three stories, however, the subtitling is placed under each panel between the rows of panels.

The example in Figure 4.4 is the first page of Christer Nuutinen and Robert Ottosson's (1995) story "Slajka". It shows that the translations in the bottom margin are handwritten, just like the texts on the comic page. While a visual connection is thus maintained, the translation, however, does not differentiate between elements in the text which are characterized on the comics page by means of differently shaped speech balloons. The "electric" or artificial voice of the little flying robot, made visible and audible through rectangular balloons with lightning-shaped tails, does not appear in the translation. Yet the translation does indicate through numbering in which panel a textual element is to be found. In this case, the text in the target language does not repeat the title of the

De-bordering Comics Culture 73

Figure 4.4 Christer Nuutinen and Robert Ottosson, first page of "Slajka" (*Olmi kolmonen*, 1995, p. 10). © Christer Nuutinen and Robert Ottosson.

comic or the textual element naming the rocket or space station where the dialogue in the following panels takes place. Furthermore, the paratextual elements naming the writer and artist are left untranslated.

Wolf Kankare's *Miska Pähkinä* is a story about a young Finnish person named Miska, who is spending some time as an exchange student in Edinburgh. The central theme of the comic is gender identity and the struggle of being able to choose and live according to one's preferences in that regard. Due to the story's setting in Scotland, Miska

74   Ralf Kauranen

engages in a considerable amount of dialogue in English. Accordingly, the comic is bilingual to a great extent. The narrative captions that reflect Miska's thoughts are in Finnish, whereas the dialogue is in either Finnish or English, depending on whom Miska is speaking with. This has consequences for how the translation is presented in the subtitles: the English-language dialogue is translated into Finnish and the Finnish dialogue and captions are translated into English (Figure 4.5). The bilingual character of the comic also diminishes the hierarchy between source language and target language, putting different readers with different linguistic competencies in similar positions. The spread in Figure 4.5 illustrates both languages being used in the comic and the subtitled translation.

The translations on the left-hand page all present the English-language dialogue in Finnish. The exchanges in the discussion, marked in the comic with speech balloons, are numbered in the translation. Dialogue in the translation is presented with double quotation marks, indicating the text being direct speech. On the right-hand side, the text in the caption box is presented without quotation marks. It is also notable that the translation does not acknowledge the final turn in the dialogue: "Helmi". The personal name (which also means "pearl" in Finnish) is not translated or repeated in the subtitles. There are also other texts left untranslated in the comic. Some diegetic texts – that is, texts that exist in the storyworld and are visible to the characters of the comic,

Figure 4.5 Wolf Kankare, spread from *Miska Pähkinä* (2013), pp. 30–31. © Wolf Kankare.

such as signs (e.g. "Departures" at the airport, p. 19) or texts on computer screens (e.g. the letter of approval from the school in Edinburgh, p. 9) – are not translated. Others are translated: for example, a personal reflection written by Miska on the computer (p. 43). In this case, the text on the computer screen continues in the narrative caption in the following panel. Here the first-person narration usually kept in the captions crosses the border to the diegetic textual world and a translation is thus motivated.

In *Olmi* and *Miska Pähkinä*, the textual elements in the translation are numbered according to the order in which they appear on the comics page. The subtitling practice of indicating and separating different textual elements varies on a broader scale. Instead of numbering, elements are at times separated with slashes (/) (see, e.g. Reetta Niemensivu's *Aavepianisti ja muita kertomuksia / The Ghost Pianist and Other Stories* (2011)). For example, in Mika Lietzén's album *1986* (2014), panels on a comics page are indicated in the subtitled translation by encircled numbers, and elements within a panel are separated with a vertical bar (|). These different marking practices have the purpose of translating the visual topology or spatial organization of the verbal elements on the comics page (on the spatial aspect of comics, and especially the distribution of speech balloons, see Groensteen 2007, 67–85). As a key feature of text in comics is its position on the page, in the panel and within elements that have the purpose of framing verbal content, such as the speech balloon (and its variations, including the thought bubble) and the caption box, translations in the bottom margin of the page need to use different means to indicate these in order for a reader to be able to decipher the word-image relationships in the original comics page.

Aapo Rapi's *Pullapoika / Doughboy* is the story of a capitalist factory magnate's son, a young man concerned with the struggles of the working class, who ends up in a circus troupe. The setting for the story, which thematizes politics and entertainment, is reminiscent of early 20th-century Finland, but the mood is quite extraordinary and non-realistic. The Finnish-language comic's texts are translated into English. The translations in the bottom margins are written in the same, perhaps a bit sloppy-looking handwriting as the text on the comic's pages (see Figure 4.6). The page numbering in the bottom margins is also handwritten – or even, one could say, drawn differently – on each page. In addition, the bottom margins contain doodles, which, although they do not appear to be connected to the storyworld, narrow the gap between the imagery and panels of the comic and the bottom margin. The connection between translation and images is more organic than, for instance, in *Miska Pähkinä*. The drawn and handwritten character of the bottom margin is also bound to attract the attention of a reader otherwise sticking to the Finnish text.

Figure 4.6 Aapo Rapi, page from *Pullapoika / Doughboy* (2005), p. 9. © Aapo Rapi.

The sound effects in the comics pages are not translated, which, on the other hand, may draw the attention of the non-Finnish reader to the text in the images of the comic's pages. The translations are not connected to the panels of the page through numbering, for instance. The textual elements are instead separated with a short dash, demanding some work from the reader of the translations in connecting the translated text to the comic's page and its text elements, flow of dialogue and characters.

Integration as a Multilingual Publishing Practice

Among the previous examples of the addition of a translation to a comic, Vähämäki's *Mestari / Maestro* and Rapi's *Pullapoika / Doughboy* show how translated text can be tied to the visuals of the translated comic through different means: in *Mestari / Maestro* by the framing of the translated text and in *Pullapoika / Doughboy* by the creative use of the

De-bordering Comics Culture 77

bottom margins, in both by handwriting style. The visual aspects of the texts in translation integrate the spatially separate texts with the storyworld and imagery of the translated comic. This interconnection can be taken even further through a more or less complete synthesis of multiple languages within the frame of the comics page and its panels. I will discuss this phenomenon through three examples from the Finnish – or actually, as the examples will show, the Finnish-transnational – field of comics.

Invisible Forces / Näkymättömiä voimia (2011) is Juliacks's bilingual – English and Finnish – comics album, which forms part of a multidisciplinary art and transmedial project by the same name (see Juliacks n.d.). The poetic and non-realistic comic follows the American girl Rody Plane, who at the age of sixteen leaves her mother and the US to live with her father in Finland. This transnational journey is viewed through the imaginative and emotional inner life of the girl encountering events and forces in the surrounding world.

Invisible Forces / Näkymättömiä voimia is a translated work from English to Finnish. That Finnish is the "second" language also shows in occasional misspellings and missing diaereses, and the naming of a translator also obviously attests to this. Similarly to the subtitled comics discussed before, the translation (usually) is positioned in the margins, but here it is not only the bottom margin. An even more significant difference is that the margins containing translated text are also used for the presentation of a rich visual world (see Figure 4.7). The spread in

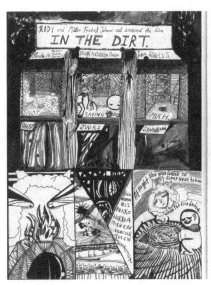

Figure 4.7 Juliacks, spread from *Invisible Forces / Näkymättömiä voimia* (2011), pp. 40–41. © Juliacks.

Figure 4.7 depicts a unique page on the left and a typical page on the right vis-à-vis the spatialization of the two languages. The non-typical page on the left-hand side shows how the hierarchy between languages can be played down. Both English and Finnish appear continuously on the page. While the captions at the top of the page and in the middle rows of images are arranged in such a way that the English narration is above the Finnish translation, the bottom row of the page turns the order on its head: the Finnish narration in the middle precedes the English original. In this case, one can no longer meaningfully divide the different language versions into an original English-language page and a secondary, target-language page. For the two languages to share the space of the page like this, the original (if there ever existed one) had to be radically altered. Furthermore, the Finnish-language narration unquestionably covers some of the page and therefore replaces something else (be it blank space or imagery).

In contrast, the centre of the typical page (on the right in the figure) contains a caption box ("SHE DREAMED") and four subsequent panels with the English narration continuing in the second to fourth panels. These are framed on all sides by blocks containing the Finnish translation. In this particular page, the centre and frame are stylistically different, with the line drawings and grey colouring being drawn with pencil in the centre panels, while ink dominates in the Finnish-language frame. Still, the images continue from centre panels to the outside frame, as in the case of the snake-like figure whose body stretches from the bottom left corner outside the centre "page" to the second and fourth panels. When the figure continues from the fourth to the third panel, it also crosses the right-hand frame of these. While the green and white patterns in the first panel continue outside the border in black and white, the colouring overall is consistent, with greens being the only other colours beside black-grey-white in both the centre piece and framing imagery. Almost all of the pages in *Invisible Forces / Näkymättömiä voimia* repeat this form of presentation with an "original" English-language page being surrounded by a Finnish-language frame. Although the parts are visibly separate, they are organically tied together with stylistic elements, such as line drawings, visual patterns, colouring and handwriting. This adds up to a bilingual comic with bilingual comics pages, where both languages in use are posited in the visual world of the comic – obviously not identically, but more equally than, for example, in the case of *sub*titles.

Sanna Ala-Ojala's second comics album, *Ättä ääriolosuhteissa / Mama to the Max* (published by Suuri Kurpitsa in 2013), shares anecdotes of family life with small children. There are some single-image cartoons, but most of the stories are two to three pages long. The two languages in Ala-Ojala's book, Finnish and English, the latter provided by the translator Terhi Kuusisto, seem to be equally interconnected with the images. There is an extraordinary balance between the languages.

De-bordering Comics Culture 79

Yet, despite the balanced presentation there are also evident differences between the ways in which the words of the two languages are visualized and tied to the images.

Each segment of the album has a title. The Finnish title is given on top of the English one: the writing in Finnish is in cursive writing in black and larger than the English title, which is printed in a light brown and written in block letters. Most pages in the book consist of one strip of irregular panels (see Figure 4.8). The Finnish text (captions, dialogue, sound effects) is positioned above the panels and the English below in the same colours as the title. The colours of the different languages and the positioning of Finnish above the panels and English below perhaps indicate a linguistic hierarchy, but the order need not be deemed in that way. Of course, the positioning of texts in respective language calls for different reading patterns, and it is not irrelevant if the texts are above or below the images. The reader's gaze is bound to wander differently, depending on the preferred language. In a few strips, the Finnish language is part of the imagery, that is, the text is positioned within the image and panel. In these cases, the English text found below the strip assumes the status of subtitle, and the language hierarchy between a translation's original language and target language is activated. Despite the exceptional bilingual character of Ala-Ojala's book, it is still a translated work, a fact indicated already in the imprint, which names the person who has translated the work from Finnish to English.

Figure 4.8 Sanna Ala-Ojala, page from *Ättä ääriolosuhteissa / Mama to the Max* (2013), p. 17. © Sanna Ala-Ojala, English translation © Terhi Kuusisto.

The final example of integration of translation in a comic broadens the view of the ways in which multilingualism is realized, as well as the scope of languages used in the transnationally connected Finnish field of comics. The comics collective Sanmagumo, formed in 2013, works in Finnish and Japanese; although it has its base in Finland, activities also take place in Japan. As the group states on its web page, it has "the goal of bringing together Finnish and Japanese culture" or "culture exchange through comics" (Sanmagumo n.d.). In this framework, bilingualism is a central strategy. Most publications have been published both in Finnish and Japanese. In addition, a couple publications are bilingual to the core.

The book *Suomusume* (Maro & Nieal 2016) is a curious collection of comics, artwork and an article relating stories and information about Finnish wartime history. At the same time, the album is a collection of fan art dedicated to the Japanese anime and manga series *Girls und Panzer*, whose central topic involves teams of high school girls who are active in the martial art of fighting with tanks. Among the groups is the Jatkosota High School ("jatkosota" being the Finnish word for the Continuation War, the war fought between Finland and the Soviet Union in 1941–1944), whose members are also depicted on the bilingual cover of *Suomusume*. The book is the result of intricate transnational cultural flows and connections: a Finnish book printed in Japan, in Finnish and Japanese, featuring art by Finnish and Japanese artists, depicting – albeit with artistic liberty – Finnish Second World War history while being dedicated to a Japanese animation and comics storyworld, which also features a Finnish team. No wonder that the book is bilingual – with minor components of English in some of the illustrations.

Figure 4.9 shows the first page of Sky and Cosmos's 8-page "Sota pesäpallon ytimessä" (War at the heart of *pesäpallo*), depicting the Finnish baseball game and the developer of the sport, Lauri "Tahko" Pihkala. The title, captions, speech balloons and dialogue presented without a balloon, as well as sound effects, are all in both Finnish and Japanese. What is significantly different from all the previous examples is that both captions and the speech balloons include both languages in the same space in the panel and on the page. Although this is unique in the contemporary Finnish field of comics, the method has a history. For example, in the early 1970s, a West German publisher launched a comic book series called *Eurocomics*.[9] The five issues that were published included comics adaptations of classic literary works, such as Goethe's *Götz von Berlichingen* and Dumas's *The Three Musketeers*. Reflecting the idea of European unity, the first issue was bilingual in English and German; the subsequent issues were trilingual, with French added to the other two languages.

Similarly to *Suomusume*, titles, caption texts and dialogue in speech balloons in *Eurocomics* are printed in multiple languages in the same space. Even diegetic text included in the imagery depicting the storyworld, such as a letter, is in multiple languages. The different languages

De-bordering Comics Culture 81

Figure 4.9 Sky and Cosmos, first page of "Sota pesäpallon ytimessä" (*Suomusume*, 2016), p. 50. © Sky and Cosmos, Jenna Suominen.

are separated from each other with a "colour code system" (see, e.g. *Eurocomics* 1973, inside front cover), which simply means that the texts in different languages are printed in different colours. This helps the reader focus on a particular language. In *Suomusume*, texts are in black on a white background, irrespective of language. On the other hand, differentiating Finnish from Japanese while reading is hardly a challenge due to their dissimilar orthography. An occasional Finnish word in Roman letters being sprinkled into the Japanese phrases does not change this.

In the fourth and fifth panels in Figure 4.9, Finnish and Japanese are separated: Finnish is kept within the balloons, whereas the corresponding Japanese is included in the images, reminiscent of sound effects. In these cases, the phrases in different languages acquire different relations to the imagery, based on comics cultural regional conventions. While the Finnish utterances are tied to the characters through the balloons – namely, through their positioning and the direction of their tails – the Japanese sounds are placed close to the mouths of the characters to indicate the source. In the final panel, the sound effect emanating from the character's glasses is presented in both Finnish and Japanese within the image, near to the source of the sound. According to Thierry Groensteen, the speech balloon "designates an opposition between the 'textual zone' and 'image zone'" in a panel. Whereas the image through different means "creates the illusion of three-dimensionality, [t]he text, on the other hand, frees itself from this mimetic transcendence" (Groensteen 2007, 69). From this perspective, the Finnish texts' position within and the Japanese texts' position without a speech balloon has some bearing. The Japanese texts not framed by a balloon are "closer" to the image-world of the comic than the Finnish texts separated from it. Perhaps in this case Japanese is more "audible" when the utterances reach out from the two-dimensional surface of writing to the three-dimensional visual world. Furthermore, the Finnish sounds are, thanks to the balloon, more word-like, while the Japanese words are, due to the lack of frame and their relation to the conventional presentation of sound effects, more sound-like.

Multilingual Comics Publishing and Processes of Bordering

There are two axes along which my presentation of different means of publishing and presenting a comic multi- or bilingually has revolved. One concerns the ways in which multiple languages are combined and presented in combination, that is, my proposed typology consisting of doubling, supplementing (including subtitles) and integration. The other axis is concerned with the linguistic variety of the Finnish multilingual comics publications. Both aspects are of interest when considering the transnationalism and multilingualism of the Finnish field of comics and the different processes of bordering implied by these phenomena.

While multilingual publications are most often aimed at a broad, global or international audience of non-Finnish readers, those readers are still assumed to be knowledgeable in certain languages. English dominates as the second language of multilingual publications, hence underlining the status of this language as a global lingua franca of comics culture. It is the means through which to transcend the national and linguistic borders confining Finnish comics. Obviously the use of English is all but neutral: it maintains the borders between English-speaking and non-English-speaking readerships, and it consolidates the position of English in the world of comics, perhaps at the expense of other, more peripheral languages. Still – and this is perhaps obvious, but needs to be said – a bilingual publication provides space for linguistic variation. Although the status of English is manifest, the publications usually also provide a privileged position to the "minor" language of Finnish.

The exceptions to the rule of the Finnish-English language combination show that the transnational comics culture has other dimensions than the one revolving around the presumed global accessibility provided by the English language. Transnationalism and multilingualism are maintained in spheres that vary in size. The use of Scandinavian languages, as in the albums produced in connection to the Nordic comics competition, attests that the regional Nordic dimension is of relevance to the Finnish comics scene and that such a network of transnational connections in fact exists. The combination of Finnish and Japanese, despite its uniqueness, makes apparent the fact that Japan's manga culture constitutes one of the centres (along with American and French comics cultures; see Beaty 2007, 111) in comics on a global level. It is also a sign of the importance of manga to some parts of the Finnish field of comics. Moreover, it interestingly adds to the multilingual character of a national comics culture, thereby diluting even further the traditional assumption of a connection between nation and language.

Multilingual translation and publishing practices constitute bridges between national and linguistic comics cultures and, as such, function as processes of de-bordering affecting comics culture. They also significantly change the crucial connection between images and words in the multimodal means of communication that is comics and, consequently, they affect the practice of reading comics. The different means of adding a secondary or even tertiary language[10] to a comic constitute new variants of the spatialization of words in a comic, thus creating alternative reading paths which are dependent on the language competencies and preferences of the reader.

One aspect of comics' multimodality is that their verbal elements are always also visual (this is true of writing in general, of course). They have visually determined positions on comics pages, in panels and in sequences of speech balloons and caption boxes. Words are connected to images of characters speaking or other sources of sound. In addition to this spatial dimension, words in comics also acquire meaning due to their appearance. Different typefaces, colours, stylistic renderings and forms of handwriting carry weight in the interpretation of words in comics. In both regards (the spatial dimension and the appearance of text), comics differ from most text-based works of prose, where the location and look of text are not considered crucial for the construction of meaning. In multilingual publications, the visual aspects of text vary for the different languages. Both position and often the look of writing are distinct.

Whereas multilingualism bridges linguistically separate comics cultures and is crucially connected to the transnationalism of the comics field, the revised relations between words and images in multilingual publications constitute a break in routinized reading practices. Reading a non-traditional translation – for example, in subtitles or in a pull-out leaflet – requires flexibility and a willingness by the reader to approach comics reading patterns anew. This requirement is probably somewhat of a hindrance to the diffusion of these comics and hence to the transnational dynamic itself. Readers can be assumed to prefer traditional translations in which one language has replaced another. It is likely the case, however, that multilingual comics most easily reach comics aficionados and people actively involved in the industry, that is, other artists, publishers and critics. These cultural gatekeepers are in a key position in the social process of constructing and furthering a transnational comics culture of world comics.

Notes

1 In 2013, the competition was arranged in connection to the Helsinki Comics Festival.
2 The first issue of the *Napa* (Finnish for "navel, centre, pole") anthology was published in 1997 and the final, sixth issue in 2006. *Laikku* ("spot" in English) was a series of anthologies from the small comics publisher Asema; the first issue was published in 2001.
3 The Finnish word *kuti* means "bullet", but it is also a term of endearment when tickling someone, as in *kutikuti* (from *kutittaa*, "to tickle").
4 Comics with translations in subtitles have been published at least in Croatia (the *Komikaze* anthology), Germany (the *Orang* anthology and Till D. Thomas's comic book *Zirp*), Italy (the *Canicola* anthology), Portugal (e.g. Janus's *Pénis Assassino* (2010) and the *Destruição* anthology (Farrajota 2010)), Slovenia (the *Stripburger* anthology: e.g. the *Madburger* issue) and Spain (e.g. publications from the publisher Apa Apa Cómics: Chema Peral's *Esperando a Jean Michel* (2013) and Alexis Nolla's *El Polo Sur* (2014)).
5 English-language original publications include, for example, Mari Ahokoivu's *Batuman* books (2010, 2012, 2016), Laura Pihl and Pau Norontaus's *False* (2011), Maura Manninen's *Trespasses 1: Initiation* (2013), Anayte Delahay and Matti Delahay's *Feral Gentry. Chapter One: Hermit Lord* (2014), Teemu Seuranen's *Stories of Pena the Unholy Black & White Devil* (2015) and Apila Pepita's *MOSSDASH* (2016), as well as several publications by Kaisa and Christoffer Leka (e.g. *I Am Not These Feet* (2003) and *Tour d'Europe* (2010)).
6 There are some exceptions to this. In the first book, subtitles actually dominate as the form of translation.
7 The only exception to the use of bottom margins that I have encountered is Monika Szydłowska's (2015) English- and Polish-language collection of one-panel cartoons *Do You Miss Your Country*, in which the translations are found in the outside margins of the book's pages.
8 One oddity in the field is the album republication of Tove Jansson's first Moomin comic in Swedish, "Mumintrollet och jordens undergång" (2007; *Moomintroll and the End of the World*, 2008). Here the original Swedish comic strips are accompanied by Swedish subtitles. This is explained by the fact that the penmanship and cursive handwriting in Jansson's original strips have been considered hard for readers to decipher.
9 I am grateful to comics artist and historian Ralf Palandt for making me aware of this series.
10 The 38th issue (2015) of the Helsinki-based comics tabloid magazine *Kuti* is dedicated completely to Alejandro Jodorowsky's comic "Fabulas Panicas", which was originally published in the late 1960s and early 1970s. The comics in *Kuti* are published in their original Spanish language with Finnish and English translations in the bottom margins.

References

Ahokoivu, Mari (2010) *Batuman No. 1*. Lahti: Daada.
Ahokoivu, Mari (2012) *Batuman No. 2*. Lahti: Daada.
Ahokoivu, Mari (2016) *Batuman No. 3*. Lahti: Daada.
Ala-Ojala, Sanna (2013) *Ättä ääriolosuhteissa. / Mama to the Max*. English translation by Terhi Kuusisto. Tampere: Suuri Kurpitsa.

Apila Pepita (2016) *MOSSDASH*. Helsinki: Lilies of the Streets.
Beaty, Bart (2007) *Unpopular Culture. Transforming the European Comic Book in the 1990s*. Toronto, CA: University of Toronto Press.
Brienza, Casey (2016) *Manga in America: Transnational Book Publishing and the Domestication of Japanese Comics*. London: Bloomsbury.
Canicola (2005) *Canicola 1*. Bologna: Canicola.
Casanova, Pascale (2004) *The World Republic of Letters*. Translated by M. B. DeBevoise. Cambridge, MA: Harvard University Press.
Cortsen, Rikke Platz & Kauranen, Ralf (2016) New Nordic Comics – A Question of Promotion? *Journal of Aesthetics & Culture* 8. Accessed December 21, 2017. Doi: org/10.3402/jac.v8.30253.
Delahay, Anayte & Delahay, Matti (2014) *Feral Gentry. Chapter One: Hermit Lord*. Helsinki: Anayte Delahay & Matti Delahay.
Denson, Shane & Meyer, Christina & Stein, Daniel (Eds) (2013) *Transnational Perspectives on Graphic Narratives: Comics at the Crossroads*. London: Bloomsbury.
Eurocomics (1973) *Goetz von Berlichingen. Der Ritter mit der eisernen Faust. / The Knight with the Iron Fist. / Le Chevalier au Poing de Fer*. Eurocomics Ausgabe 1. Trier: Verlag Druck und Vertrieb Paulinus-Druckerei.
Farrajota, Marcos (Ed.) (2010) *Destruiçao! Bandas desenhadas sobre como foi horrivel viver entre 2001 e 2010*. Lisbon: Chili Com Carne.
Gomix (1994) *Gomix 5*. Kuopio: Hans Nissen.
Groensteen, Thierry (2007) *The System of Comics*. Translated by Bart Beaty and Nick Nguyen. Jackson: University Press of Mississippi.
Hagelberg, Matti (2012–) *Läskimooses 1–44* [to date]. Lahti: Kreegah Bundolo.
Hannerz, Ulf (1996) *Transnational Connections: Culture, People, Places*. London: Routledge.
Jansson, Tove (2007) *Jorden går under! Tove Janssons första muminserie i Ny Tid 1947–48*. Helsinki: Tigertext Ab/Ny Tid.
Jansson, Tove (2008) *Moomintroll and the End of the World: Tove Jansson's First Moomin Comic Strip with Essays on Her Life and Work*. Edited by Anna Rotkirch & Trygve Söderling. Translated by Peter Marten. Helsinki: Tigertext/Ny Tid.
Janus (2010) *Pénis Assassino*. Lisbon: Mmmnnnrrrg.
Juliacks (2011) *Invisible Forces. / Näkymättömiä voimia*. Translations into Finnish by Katri Inkeri. Inner Tube Productions.
Juliacks (n.d.) Juliacks. Accessed July 18, 2019. Juliacks.com.
Kankare, Wolf (2013) *Miska Pähkinä*. Tampere: Suuri Kurpitsa.
Kaurala, Saana (2016) *Alaviitekäännös Suomessa 2000–2012 julkaistuissa sarjakuvakirjoissa*. Unpublished Master's thesis in German Translation, University of Helsinki.
Komikaze (2008) *Komikaze. Stripoteka Komikaze broj 7*. Zagreb: Komikaze.
Lehtinen, Anita (2009) *Hangon Leijonat. / Hangö lejon*. Swedish translation by Björn Österman. Hanko: Anita Lehtinen.
Lehtinen, Anita (2010) *Hangon Leijonat lomalla. / Hangö lejon på semester*. Swedish translation by Björn Österman. Hanko: Anita Lehtinen.
Lehtinen, Anita (2011) *Hitaasti kävelevä turisti. Hangon Leijonat albumi 3. / En turist som rör sig långsamt. Hangö Lejon album 3*. Swedish translation by Björn Österman. Hanko: Anita Lehtinen.

Lehtinen, Anita (2017) *Aurora & Conrad*. Translated by Björn Österman. Hanko: Anita Lehtinen.
Leka, Kaisa (2003) *I Am Not These Feet*. Helsinki: Absolute Truth Press.
Leka, Kaisa & Leka, Christoffer (2010) *Tour d'Europe*. Porvoo: Absolute Truth Press.
Lietzén, Mika (2014) *1986*. Oulu: Asema.
Madburger (2002) *Madburger: Comics Questioning Sanity*. Ljubljana: Strip Core, Forum.
Manninen, Maura (2013) *Trespasses 1: Initiation*. Helsinki: Pratfall Comics.
Maro & Nieal (Eds) (2016) すお娘 / *Suomusume*. Sarjakuvaryhmä Sanmagumo.
Meneses, Juan (2013) Reconsidering International Comics: Foreignness, Locality, and the Third Space. *Journal of Graphic Novels and Comics*. DOI: 10.1080/21504857.2013.842179.
Niemensivu, Reetta (2011) *Aavepianisti ja muita kertomuksia / The Ghost Pianist and Other Stories*. Tampere: Suuri Kurpitsa.
Nolla, Alexis (2014) *El Polo Sur*. Barcelona: Apa Apa Cómics.
Nuutinen, Christer & Ottosson, Robert (1995) Slajka. *Olmi kolmonen*: (Olmi three), 10–13.
Orang (Winter 2006) *Orang 6*. Berlin: Reprodukt.
Peral, Chema (2013) *Esperando a Jean Michel*. Barcelona: Apa Apa Cómics.
Pihl, Laura & Norontaus, Pau (2011) *False*. Turku: Pau Norontaus & Laura Pihl.
Porkola, Heikki (ed.) (1999) *Lifti ja muita sarjakuvia Kemin pohjoismaisesta sarjakuvakilpailusta 1999. / Lift och andra serier från den nordiska serietävlingen i Kemi 1999*. Kemi: Kemin sarjakuvakeskus / The Arctic Comics Center.
Porkola, Heikki (ed.) (2002) *Viimeinen kivi ja muita sarjakuvia Kemin pohjoismaisesta sarjakuvakilpailusta 2002. / Den sista stenen och andra serier från den nordiska serietävlingen i Kemi 2002*. Kemi: Kemin sarjakuvakeskus / The Arctic Comics Center.
Rantanen, Miissa (2017) *Kirjeitä. / Letters*. Helsinki: Miissa Rantanen.
Rapi, Aapo (2005) *Pullapoika. / Doughboy*. Helsinki: Napa Books.
Sanmagumo (n.d.) In English. Accessed December 21, 2017, http://sanmagumo.info/english/.
Seuranen, Teemu (2015) *Stories of Pena the Unholy Black & White Devil*. Vantaa: PTU Kustannus.
Sky & Cosmos (2016) Sota pesäpallon ytimessä. In Maro & Nieal (eds): すお娘 / *Suomusume*. Sarjakuvaryhmä Sanmagumo, 50–57.
Szydłowska, Monika (2015) *Do You Miss Your Country?* London: Centrala.
Thomas, Till D. (2010) *Zirp#4*. Berlin: Till D. Thomas.
Tolppanen, Petri (1994) Kissat. *Gomix 5*.
Turunen, Marko (2000) *Rakkautta viimeisellä silmäyksellä*. English translation by Liia Rissanen in separate booklet. Lahti: Ubu (Kreegah! Bundolo!).
Vähämäki, Amanda (2011) *Mestari. / Maestro*. Helsinki: Kutikuti.
Walkowitz, Rebecca L. (2015) *Born Translated: The Contemporary Novel in an Age of World Literature*. New York: Columbia University Press.

5 The Multilingual Landscape of Sámi Literature

Linguistic and Cultural Border Crossing in the Work of Sigbjørn Skåden

Kaisa Ahvenjärvi

Multilingualism is an essential feature of Sámi literature, culture and society. The Sámi area is located in the northern parts of Sweden, Finland, Norway and Russia, and many Sámi people are multilingual, typically in one of the Sámi languages and in Swedish, Norwegian or Finnish. Today there are nine living Sámi languages, some of which are mutually understandable but still defined as separate languages. With approximately 20,000 speakers, North Sámi is the most widely spoken of the Sámi languages. The total Sámi population is estimated to be approximately 75,000. More than 60 per cent of the Sámi live outside the Sámi homeland, which brings new challenges for the provision of education and services in the Sámi languages (Sámediggi – Saamelaiskäräjät 2017a, 2017b).

In the Nordic countries, the definition of a Sámi is mainly based on the Sámi language. According to the definition in Finnish legislation, a Sámi is a person who considers him or herself a Sámi, provided that this person has learnt Sámi as his or her first language or has at least one parent or grandparent whose first language is Sámi. The definitions of Sáminess are similar in Norway and Sweden. Language can be regarded as one of the most important factors that produce the sense of unity in the Sámi community. Knowledge of a Sámi language is a proof of being a Sámi[1] (Valkonen 2009, 245, 247).

Under the pressure of the dominant languages, many Sámi have lost their original mother tongue. Less than half of the Sámi people today speak Sámi as their mother tongue. Language still has a significant role in the drawing of ethnic boundaries, and since the 1960s, a variety of measures have been taken to preserve the Sámi languages (on the language revitalization process, see, e.g. Pasanen 2015). Six of the nine Sámi languages have a written language and a published corpus of literature: North Sámi, Lule Sámi, South Sámi, Inari Sámi, Skolt Sámi and Kildin Sámi. These languages, some of which have only a few hundred or a few thousand speakers, are used in many cultural spheres, such as media, children's literature and popular music.

A large part of Sámi literature is published in Sámi. There are Sámi publishing houses like DAT and Davvi Girji, which publish literature solely in Sámi languages. However, throughout its history Sámi literature has also been published in Nordic majority languages. This chapter discusses the different levels of multilingualism in Sámi literature. The focus is on the multilingualism of Sámi authors and their multilingual oeuvres and texts. The significance of the multilingual readership is also touched upon, as well as the importance of the literary institutions that influence the writing and publishing of Sámi literature. The chapter elaborates on two long poems by the Sámi poet Sigbjørn Skåden, who has applied multilingual elements in his work more than any other Sámi author.

Sámi literature is not only multilingual; it can also be defined as transnational (see, e.g. Parente-Čapková & Launis 2015, 5). According to Nissilä (2016, 31), transnational literature crosses ethnic, national, cultural and linguistic borders, and it is often linked to the bi- or multilingualism of the author. The oeuvre of Nils-Aslak Valkeapää (1943–2001), the most well-known Sámi author, demonstrates the different layers of transnationality: Valkeapää represents local (Sámi), national (Finnish or Norwegian) and regional (Nordic), as well as global (indigenous), cultures (Pollari et al. 2015, 12).

Writing and publishing literature in an indigenous language are exceptional in the global field of indigenous literatures. The majority of Maori, Aboriginal and Native American literature, for example, is published in English. Sámi and Greenlandic literatures are the only indigenous literatures mainly published in the indigenous languages – despite the fact that Greenlandic and Sámi are small languages with very limited readership and a short tradition of literary culture (Gaski 2000, 57). Writing in Sámi languages has not been a self-evident choice for the pioneers of Sámi literature. Many Sámi authors have had to learn to write their mother tongue as adults, because they did not have a chance to study it at school (Hirvonen 2011, 219).

Indigenous writers and researchers discuss globally if the definition of indigenous literature should be based on the writing language, the content of the book or the ethnic background of the writer (Gaski 2000, 27, 38, 43). As Sámi literature is published in several languages, the most important criterion in its definition is the Sáminess of the author, regardless of his or her writing language. Sámi language is, however, considered a very significant feature of Sámi literature (Paltto 2010, 50; Hirvonen 2011; Parente-Čapková 2015, 13; Heith 2016, 45).

The potential readership for books written in Sámi is relatively small; it is estimated that there are approximately 30,000–35,000 Sámi speakers altogether. The market is so small that publishing a book in a Sámi language is almost completely dependent on financial support from the Nordic governments[2] (Gaski 2011, 25). Sámi literature can reach larger amounts of readers only through translations. Because there are only a few professional translators from Sámi, there is a widespread practice of self-translation, in which an author translates his or her own text.[3] Self-translation is regarded as a border-crossing activity that reorganizes the relationships between languages and national literary canons, challenging the monolingual assumptions of the literary institution and of modern nation states (Grönstrand 2014, 116, 118).

Different Levels of Multilingualism in Sámi Literature

Vuokko Hirvonen (2011, 214) uses the term "multilingual landscape" in discussing the presence of several languages in Sámi literature as well as the ways Sámi literature describes multilingual environments and often unequal power relationships between different languages. Multilingual literature reflects the multilingual reality of Sámi society and the co-existence of different languages in everyday life. In this chapter, I will discuss the diverse levels on which languages co-exist in Sámi literary landscapes. Multilingualism can be a feature of texts, authors and readers, as well as the Sámi literary field as a whole.

In literature, multilingualism can be both a textual and a thematic phenomenon. Texts themselves may consist of words and expressions in more than one language, and the multilingualism of characters and settings can be thematically essential. In the work of the older generation of Sámi authors born in the 1940s and 1950s, experiences of the shame and inferiority connected with Sámi language are often described (Hirvonen 2011, 215–217). In contemporary Sámi literature published in majority languages, the lost "mother tongue" has been a recurrent theme. It comes up, for example, in the Norwegian-language collection of poetry *Et øyeblikk noen tusen år* (2009; A blink of an eye a couple thousand years) by Hege Siri (b. 1973). Siri's poems describe the speaker's attempt to get back the Sámi language she has lost. The collection shows that even though the language is both officially and symbolically one of the most important criteria in the definition of Sáminess, not knowing it is not an obstacle to identifying oneself as a Sámi (Ahvenjärvi 2015, 125).

The question of the lost language is also a central theme in Ann-Helén Laestadius's (b. 1971) Swedish-language young adult book *Sms från Soppero* (2007; SMS from Soppero). The protagonist, thirteen-year-old Agnes, lives between two cultures and surroundings: urban life in Solna, a town close to Stockholm, and her Sámi mother's home village Soppero in Northern Sweden. Agnes's mother has not spoken Sámi to her daughter. Agnes feels that without knowing the language, she is not a "real" Sámi. She finds that her Sámi identity is questioned by both Sámi and Swedish societies, as she is categorized by others as a "half Sámi" and even a "fake Sámi" (Jonsson 2012, 217, 226). To reach a fuller degree of Sáminess, Agnes starts to secretly learn Sámi language.

In *Sms från Soppero*, Sámi language is present, for example, in text messages that Agnes receives from a Sámi boy. Carla Jonsson, who has analysed the functions of multilingualism and code-switching (i.e. the use of both Swedish and Sámi in the novel), argues that multilingual literary texts offer a space where the reflection, construction and reconstruction of hybrid identities and experiences of "in-between-ness" can take place. Jonsson states that linguistic code-switching in Laestadius's novel has empowering functions, as the use of minority language legitimizes the often silenced voices of the minority (Jonsson 2012, 224–227; see also Rantala 2013).

Code-switching is a recurrent feature in the work of several poets who publish in Norwegian. Irene Larsen, Marion Palmer and the aforementioned Hege Siri, for example, embed fragments of Sámi language in their poems. This kind of multilingual strategy is common in indigenous literatures worldwide. Authors bring out their connections with the indigenous tradition by using indigenous words in their English texts (see, e.g. Allen 2002, 154). These untranslated indigenous words are directed at bilingual readers, which underline the internal differences of the readership and the specific nature of the indigenous cultures (Allen 2012, 160).

Hirvonen (2011, 210) has suggested that, by using Sámi words, Sámi writers who publish in majority languages want to express their Sámi background and their emotional ties with Sámi language. Even an incomplete knowledge of a language can generate a sense of belonging to a linguistic community. It can also be seen as a political gesture, a reminder of the existence of the minority language in the shadow of the majority languages. By using code-switching, authors resist monolingual norms that still prevail in the literary field. Code-switching turns the power relations of majority and minority languages upside down; the reader who does not understand the Sámi words becomes "the Other" (Jonsson 2012, 223).

Multilingualism has also become common in Sámi music culture. Sámi rapper Amoc practises a playful language mixing that combines local Inari Sámi language for lyrics, Finnish and English for interaction with the audience, and musical elements of the global genre of rap. Amoc reinvents an identity that draws on traditional Sámi culture but is also multilingual and hybrid (Pietikäinen & Kelly-Holmes 2012, 200). Another example from the field of music is Sofia Jannok's album *Orda – This Is my Land* (2016), which includes songs in English, Swedish and Sámi. The use of English exposes the album to an international audience, including other indigenous peoples, whereas the political message of the songs in Swedish is primarily directed at the Swedish society which has colonized the Sámi land. In the printed lyrics, English translations of the songs are provided, but only Sámi-speaking listeners are able to understand the nuances of the Sámi words.

One of the viewpoints on literary multilingualism is the question of readers' access to literature written in Sámi languages. In order to reach diverse readerships, collections of Sámi poetry are sometimes published with Sámi and Scandinavian or Finnish versions of the poems side by side.[4] This kind of "parallel bilingualism" is suitable for poetry, because it is typographically easy to place two versions of a poem in one spread. Sámi has also been juxtaposed with larger world languages: the trilingual publication *Roađđi – Rosa Boreal – Boreal Rose* (2016) contains poems by Inger-Mari Aikio and Niillas Holmberg in Sámi, Spanish and English. This kind of multilingual books open up Sámi literature to the international audience outside the Nordic countries.

Multilingual publishing is characteristic of Sámi children's literature. Children's books are often published simultaneously in different Sámi languages, most often in North, South and Lule Sámi. Sometimes the three languages are side by side in the same volume. This publishing strategy makes visible the multilingualism of the Sámi-speaking community. Linguistic revitalization projects have questioned the dominance of North Sámi and encouraged the use of small Sámi languages. Also Sámi media promotes multilingual practices in order to strengthen diverse linguistic identities and mutual understanding.

Basque author Iban Zaldua has discussed the linguistic and ideological choices that a minority language writer has to make in the present day when literature no longer needs to be a mere instrument of defending the minority culture or saving the minority language. First of all, the writer has to decide whether she wants to publish in a majority language with a larger amount of potential readers or in a minority language. A minority language writer also has to decide whether to draw attention to her "native exoticism" or to introduce herself as a "universal" writer (Zaldua 2009, 90–91, 108–109). Choosing the status of an "ethnowriter" is connected not only to the writing language but also to the themes the author discusses in her work.

Those Sámi authors who know both Sámi and majority languages can bring out the possibilities and positive effects of multilingualism (Hirvonen 2011, 210). A good example of a multilingual Sámi author is the poet Niillas Holmberg (b. 1990), who is active in several linguistic and literary fields. During the last few years, he has published three collections: one in Finnish (*Jos itseni pelastan itseltäni*, 2015; If I save myself from myself), one in English (*The Way Back*, 2016) and one in North Sámi (*Oaidnaleapmai, čáhcesiellu*, 2016; See you, watersoul). A multilingual publishing strategy has also been adopted by Sigbjørn Skåden (b. 1976). Skåden has written two collections of poetry, *Skuovvadeddjiid gonagas* (2004; The king of the shoemakers) and *Prekariáhta lávlla* (2009; The song of the precariat), and a blog novel, *Ihpil: Láhppon mánáid bestejeaddji* (2008; Ihpil: the saviour of the lost children), in North Sámi, as well as a novel, *Våke over dem som sover* (2014;

Wake up those who sleep), in Norwegian. Furthermore, Skåden has self-translated his first collection into Norwegian as *Skomakernes konge* (2007). The last section of this chapter concentrates on a detailed analysis of the multilingual features in Skåden's poetry.

Language-mixing in the Poems of Sigbjørn Skåden

Skåden's work does not meet the traditional conceptions of nature-oriented Sámi poetry. This is ironically commented on in Maren Uthaug's comic: Skåden is accused of being the only Sámi writer to neither compose about nature nor use rhymes with the words "sun", "bear" or "eagle" (Uthaug 2012, 74). Skåden can be characterized as a Sámi postmodernist, whose poems are characterized by fragmental form, unpoetic language, mixtures of different styles and humour generated from surprising combinations (on the postmodern features in literature, see Kantola 2001).

In his poems, Skåden often crosses linguistic borders and mixes fragments of different languages. A long poem "Mu Muhammad Ali" (My Muhammad Ali) in *Prekariáhta lávlla*, for example, is written in North Sámi but includes English phrases in italics: "*Moore in four*" and "*you out, sucker!*" (Skåden 2009, 30, 32). Another poem in the same collection includes phrases in Swedish and Meänkieli, Tornedalian Finnish, which is spoken in Northern Sweden. Sámi, Tornedalian Finnish and Swedish expressions follow each other: "*Mon boađán, mie tulen / min älskade*" (Skåden 2009, 46). These examples of code-switching can be seen not only as an expression of the poet's multilingual identity and his position in different cultural traditions, but also as a linguistic political gesture. The fragments of majority languages scattered in the text are secondary to Sámi, which usually is overshadowed by bigger languages.

Skåden's first collection *Skuovvadeddjiid gonagas* is an example of multilingual literature par excellence. It is written in Skåden's own Sámi dialect (Skånland dialect), which differs from standard North Sámi to such an extent that Skåden has included a short dialect–standard language glossary at the end of the collection. In the poems, there are fragments of several languages: Norwegian, French, German, Latin, Spanish and Sanskrit. Repetition is a central poetic technique used in the collection, and this also applies to the use of different languages. For example, the French phrase "c'est moi, mes enfants"[5] is repeated several times in the poems.

The collection is not only multilingual, but thoroughly multicultural. It combines elements from, for example, Sámi, Hindu and Christian traditions. The fourteen parts of the collection constitute a story with a main character called Jusup. Jusup identifies with the figures of the Wandering Jew and Christ. The Wandering Jew is a mythical immortal man in a medieval Christian legend. The name of Skåden's collection *Skuovvadeddjiid gonagas* refers to another name for this figure, the Shoemaker of Jerusalem. The legend concerns a Jew who insulted Jesus on the way to the Crucifixion and was then cursed to walk the earth until the Second Coming. There are countless versions of the story, both in European oral traditions and in literature and art, ever since the 1600s. With his collection, Skåden joins this tradition:

> Est-il rien sur la terre
> qui soit plus surprenant
> que la grande misère
> du pauvre Juif-Errant![6]
> I bear the name of all the holy books,
> the king of the shoemakers,
> have you seen me?
> I walk in the marketplaces
> and the paths of your village,
> along the riverbends of your nightmare:
> Laqedem,
> Buttadeo,
> Ahasverus,
> Kartafilus,
> I make shoes for everyone
> so that my small world wouldn't stop turning around;
> without shoes I wouldn't be Jusup,
> lively hands sew the ribbons of the edges of the mind,
> walking hunchbacked through the history in the bright clothes
>   of a king,
> have you seen me?
> shoes make
> miraculous noises
> when I drift the Earth:
> da datta dayadhvam
> shantih shantih shantih!
> de dette diebbelii[7]
> Satan Satan Satan![8]
>
> (Skåden 2004, 19; my translation)

The poem is a mixture of diverse cultural and linguistic materials and allusions. It begins with four verses in French, a citation from a French children's song about the destiny of the Wandering Jew. The different names used for the Wandering Jew – "Laqedem, / Buttadeo, / Ahasverus, / Kartafilus" – appear in the middle of Skåden's poem. Names from different cultural traditions can be seen as a form of multilingualism.

At the end of the poem there are two Sanskrit verses, "da datta dayadhvam, / shantih, shantih, shantih", which mean "be charitable, be compassionate, / peace, peace, peace". Here Skåden makes a "double allusion": The verses are a mantra from a holy Sanskrit text, one of the Upanishads, which also concludes T. S. Eliot's *The Waste Land* (1922), a central work of European modernist poetry. In Skåden's poem, the mantra is followed by Sámi words that phonetically resemble the Sanskrit verses: "de dette diebbelii / sáhtán sáhtán sáhtán", which literally translates "then yet that way, / Satan, Satan, Satan". Skåden's language play can be seen as a parody of the holy Sanskrit text. In the poem, the holy Hindu virtues transform into Sámi nonsense, and "shantih" ("peace" or "bliss") turns into "sáhtán", the Sámi word for Satan. The word "sáhtán" is, however, very ambiguous: it could also be translated as "I can", "I escort" or "I give a ride". This ambiguity puts the final verse "on the move" and reinforces the images of walking and wandering repeated in the poem.

Skåden's connection to T. S. Eliot is more profound than just a single citation. Skåden's use of mythology resembles that of Eliot. *The Waste Land* repeatedly alludes to the legend of the Fisher King, and similarly *Skuovvadeddjiid gonagas* refers to the Christian legend of the Wandering Jew. Eliot's *The Waste Land* has obviously given inspiration to Skåden's work. Multilingualism, intertextuality, disjointed structure and the mixture of styles, modes and cultural traditions in *The Waste Land* were revolutionary literary features in the European poetry of the 1920s. The same features in Skåden's *Skuovvadeddjiid gonagas* and *Prekariáhta lávlla* reshape and rewrite Sámi poetry in the 2000s.

Skåden's "stylistic multilingualism" includes integration of exalted, classical style with banal, everyday expressions. In the following poem "Backstage, Sámi Grand Prix", the rhythm and structure are adopted from Shakespeare's play *Henry V*, which is written in iambic pentameter, the most common meter in English poetry and verse drama.[9] Skåden's poem is situated in a contemporary scene, the annual "yoik"[10] and song competition, the Sámi Grand Prix, which is organized during Easter in Kautokeino, Northern Norway. Nowadays, the Sámi Grand Prix show resembles the Eurovision Song Contest.[11]

BACKSTAGE, SÁMI GRAND PRIX

Enter our hero. The audience is heard in the background.

OUR HERO
O dear God, strengthen my heart,
And grant me extraordinary powers today,
When I see the time of the times getting closer,
And I hear the familiar pull in my body:
The call of the black blood of my ancestors.
[...]

AUDIENCE
O, more!

OUR HERO
Ohmygod, my blood is boiling!
O shit, now I don't remember the lyrics!
What to do? Breathe, young boy,
Let the air in, don't throw up,
And remember that now your time has come,
Remember now the hours alone in your room,
Remember now the sound of the old Casio,
As today humankind will see
All of me on a big stage.
[...]
Now listen, the damned, the gnomes, and all,
And Gods, too, turn your ears towards me,
When my tune tells that I have reached
Adulthood go lo lo go lo la!

AUDIENCE
Wow, listen to that!

OUR HERO
God, **please**, if I will now throw up,
O don't let the juices fall on my dress,
As you remember, I have been confirmed at the church,
And last Christmas I also visited you,
And in the funeral of my godmother Ánne.
If everything goes fine tonight,
I promise to visit you every now and then,
I will even come though no-one has died
And eat your biscuits with clasped hands.
[...]
Enter Sámi Grand Prix Host

HOST
Now come!

OUR HERO
Is it the host?
I know thy errand, I will go with thee.
The day, my friends, and all things stay for me. *Exeunt*[12]
 (Skåden 2009, 35–37; bold text by me)

The central figure of the poem, ironically entitled as "our hero", is a competitor who is nervously awaiting his turn backstage. The inner monologue of this hero is written in a Shakespearean style, which creates a humoristic tone for the whole poem. The context of the poem – a popular contemporary song contest – and its exalted style are in a parodic relationship with each other. The first line by "our hero" is full of old-fashioned expressions, but as the poem proceeds the classical style starts to break down: "the call of the black blood of the ancestors" gives way to memories of an old Casio keyboard. In the middle of the poem "yoik syllables" suddenly appear in the text: "go lo lo go lo la". This is an example of code-switching: iambic pentameter shifts to an aspect of Sámi musical tradition. The third line of "our hero" is a list of ridiculous proofs of religiousness and promises that the speaker gives to God. Earlier he has prayed for strength of heart, but now he only hopes that vomit will not spoil his clothes. The contradiction between the style and the content of the poem continually grows until the end.

The largest part of Skåden's poem is written in North Sámi, but there are a few colloquial expressions in English, which I have highlighted in bold text in the English translation. The code-switching from classical style to the spoken language creates a humorous effect. "Ohmygod", "O shit" and "please" are English words and expressions that are commonly used as a part of everyday speech in many languages. The citation from Shakespeare at the end of the poem is also humorous. The nervous speaker, who does not remember the words of the song he is going to perform, suddenly speaks with the voice of a Shakespearean character in *Henry V*. This stylistic shift can be seen as a counterpart to a technique which T. S. Eliot uses in *The Waste Land* (1922). In the second part of Eliot's long poem, a vulgar scene in a pub ends up with a citation from Shakespeare's *Hamlet*.[13] Skåden has adopted the same technique of bringing a classical allusion into a contemporary setting.

The poem that follows "Backstage, Sámi Grand Prix" represents a stylistic shift from traditional English meter to trivial pop lyrics. The poem "My Grand Prix Song"[14] is the piece "our hero" performs at the competition. It is a parody of a naïve love song: "I took your hand, / you took my soul, / and our hearts were beating // I held youuuuu, / I held youuuu / Be mi-i-ne, be mi-i-ne"[15] (Skåden 2009, 38). The spelling simulates the pronunciation of the words when they are sung. This can be seen as yet another form of code-switching or multimodality in Skåden's poems.

Political Multilingualism

This chapter has discussed the different levels of multilingualism in Sámi literature and shown how they meet in the work of Sigbjørn Skåden. Skåden has a multilingual oeuvre in which he uses and mixes different languages, linguistic registers and multicultural allusions. He uses citations from European classical writers such as T. S. Eliot and William Shakespeare, but he also refers to Sámi poetry. In *Skuovvadeddjiid gonagas*, for example, there is a direct allusion to Rauni Magga Lukkari's collection *Mu gonagasa gollebiktasat – Min konges gylne klær* (1991; The golden clothes of my king): the speaker refers to a king dressed in his finest golden clothes (Skåden 2004, 57).

Using elements from the Western literary canon and critically rewriting specific works is a postcolonial literary strategy (Marx 2004, 83, 89). This kind of postcolonial stance is present in some of Skåden's poems. *Prekariáhta lávlla* contains a pastiche of a poem by the classical Norwegian writer Henrik Ibsen (Skåden 2009, 12–15). Here Skåden mocks the national pathos connected to Norwegian Independence Day. The ironic attitude is underlined with a metalyrical comment: "The writer wants to thank Henrik [Ibsen] and Terje [the character in Ibsen's poem] who have lent such an excellent structure with which one can ridicule the habits of history" (Skåden 2009, 15).[16] The poem can be described as an ironic, postcolonial rewriting of a Norwegian classic. Skåden's way of using Ibsen's poem as "raw material" for his own writing challenges the traditionally hierarchical relationship between minority and majority literatures.

Direct ethno-political comments are scarce in Skåden's work. Instead of writing in a critical opposition to Western tradition, he often uses this tradition very playfully. He does not draw or re-draw borders between literary canons but positions himself in the continuum of European literature as an equal. Skåden has the capacity to do this because he knows his classics: he has a Western academic education and a Master's degree in literature. Also, the implied reader of Skåden's poem is an educated person who is adept in several languages and recognizes the frequent intertextual allusions in Skåden's text. Sámi literature has never been written in a void, but Skåden's way of mixing diverse cultural and linguistic materials has broken borders in the field of Sámi poetry. By removing the invisible yet still existent border between Sámi literature and majority literatures, Skåden shows that Sámi poetry has a place in the Western canon.

Notes

1. Obviously, language skills alone do not suffice: a non-Sámi person does not become Sámi if she or he acquires knowledge of a Sámi language.
2. A special feature of Nordic art and culture policy is governmental financial support for individual artists. Authors can apply for grants for writing a book, and there are also institutional grants for translating literature from Nordic majority languages into Sámi and vice versa.
3. Inger-Mari Aikio (b. 1961), for example, has translated two of her collections from North Sámi into Finnish: *Máilmmis dása* (2001; in Finnish *Maailmalta tähän*, 2006) and *Suonat* (2008; in Finnish *Suonet*, 2009). These collections have also been translated into English, the first as "From the World and Home" as a part of the anthology *Female Voices of the North II* (2006) and the second as *This Beloved Homeland* (2009).
4. Examples of bilingual collections are, for example, *Ruohta muzetbeallji ruohta – Løp svartøre løp* (2011; Run blackear run) by Rawdna Carita Eira

(Sámi/Norwegian), the Sámi/Swedish anthology *Viidát. Divttat Sámis – Vidd. Dikter från Sápmi* (2006; The expanse: Poems from Sápmi) and *Beaivváš čuohká gaba – Aurinko juo kermaa* (2014; The sun drinks cream) by Inger-Mari Aikio (Sámi/Finnish).

5 "It's me, my children".

6 The French beginning of the poem translates roughly as follows "Is there anything on the Earth / that would be more surprising / than the great misery / of the poor Wandering Jew!" My translation.

7 This line has been left untranslated in order to convey the phonetic content of the Sámi words.

8 "Est-il rien sur la terre / qui soit plus surprenant / que la grande misère / du pauvre Juif-Errant! / Juohke bássi girjji namma lean mon, / skuovvadeddjiid gonagas, / leak gus mu oaidnán? / Mon jodán du márkana selju, / du giláža bálgáid, / du deattáma roaŋkejogaid: / Laqedem, / Buttadeo, / Ahasverus, / Kartafilus, / skuovaid reiden mon juohkehaččii / aman máilmmážan jorráma bisánit; / skuovaid gehtte in lihčo mon Jusup, / virkos giedak gorrok mielarabdda deattáldagaid, / goavrume historjjá čada gonagasa šerres biktasiigo, / leak gus mu oaidnán? / skuovak jitnek / impasiid / go eatnama jodásan: / da datta dayadhvam / shantih shantih shantih! / de dette diebbelii / sáhtán sáhtán sáhtán!"

Skåden has himself translated the poem into Norwegian:

> Est-il rien sur la terre / qui soit plus surprenant / que la grande misère / du pauvre Juif-Errant! / Alle hellige skrifters navn bærer jeg, /skomakernes konge, / har du sett meg? / Min streifen krysser ditt travle kirketorg, / din grends stier, / ditt mareritts elvebuktninger: / Laqedem, / Buttadeo, / Ahasverus, / Kartafilus, / jeg skor dere alle, / for å dreie min lille verden; / uten sko var jeg ikke Jusup, / virksomme hender syr sinnsrandens pyntebånd, / krumbøyd vandrende gjennom historien i en konges skinnende klær, / har du sett meg? / skoenes skritt skaper / underlyder / i min drift gjennom verden: / da datta dayadhvam / shantih shantih shantih! / de dette deiligste / satan satan satan!

(Skåden 2007, 19)

9 The meter used in the original Sámi version is not reflected in my translation of the poem into English.

10 The yoik is traditional Sámi music, being unaccompanied singing. North Sámi yoiks mainly consist of non-semantic syllables like the ones in Skåden's poem.

11 The Eurovision Song Contest is an annual international TV song competition held among the member countries of the European Broadcasting Union.

12 *Enter min sáŋgár. Geahččit gullojit.* / MIN SÁŊGÁR / O Jipmil, ráhkis, nanusmahte váimmun, / Ja lodne munnje odne amas fámuid, / Go oainnán áiggiid áiggi lahkoneame, / Ja gorudis dál gullo oahpes geassu: / Mu máttarmáttuid čáhppes vára gohčču. [...] GEAHČČIT / O eambbo! / MIN SÁŊGÁR / Ohmygod, mus duoldá várra / O shit, dál in šat muitte čállon sániid! / Maid dahká olmmoš? Vuoiŋŋa, unna lunttaš, / Dál luoitte áimmu sisa, ale vuovsse, / Ja muitte dál de lea du áigi boahtán, / Hal muitte diimmuid aktonassan lanjas, / Hal muitte boares Casioa jienaid, / Go odne galgá oaidnit olmmošsohka / Mu ollisvuođa máilmmi stuorra lávddis. [...] / Dál guldalehket neavrrit, ulddat, visot, / Ja Jipmilat vel lodne munnje bealji, / Go šuokŋan muitala mu ođasvuiton / Go rávisvuođa go lo lo go lo la! / GEAHČČIT / Wow dette! / MIN SÁŊGÁR / Jipmil, please, jus dál de vuovssán, / O ale divtte gáktái goaikut liema, / Go muittát, rihpaid válden firkolanjas, / Ja mannan juovllaid ledjen vel du luhtte, / Ja Ánne-ristamuota hávdádeamis. / Jus

odne eahkedis buoragit manna, / De lohpidan dus fitnat duollet dálle, / De vaikko boađán olbmojápmingehtte / Ja ristagieđaiguin boran du čeavssaid. [...]*Enter Sámi Grand Prix Koferansiera* / KONFERANSIERA / Na boađ'ál! / MIN SÁŊGÁR / Konferansiera go? / I know thy errand, I will go with thee. / The day, my friends, and all things stay for me. *Exeunt.*

13 Eliot's citation from *Hamlet* consists of the last words of Ophelia: "Good night, ladies, good night, sweet ladies, good / night, good night" (Eliot [1922] 1998, 61).

14 "Mu Grand Prix-lávlla".

15 "[D]u gieđa válden mon, / mu sielu váldet don, / ja váimmut lakkastedje. / Dollen duuuuu, / dollen duuu-u-uu! / Šaddos muuuuu, / šaddos muuu-u-uu!"

16 "Čálli hálida giitit Henrik ja Terje go leaba sutnje lodnen nu earenoamáš buori hámádaga man bokte bilkidit sáhttá historjjá vugiid".

Bibliography

Ahvenjärvi, Kaisa (2015) Reindeer Revisited: Traditional Sámi Features in Contemporary Sámi Poetry. In Ann-Sofie Lönngren, Heidi Grönstrand, Dag Heede & Anne Heith (eds): *Rethinking National Literatures and the Literary Canon in Scandinavia*. Cambridge: Cambridge Scholars Publishing, 104–129.

Allen, Chadwick (2002) *Blood Narrative: Indigenous Identity in American Indian and Maori Literary and Activist Texts.* Durham & London: Duke University Press.

Allen, Chadwick (2012) *Trans-Indigenous: Methodologies for Global Native Literary Studies.* Minneapolis: University of Minnesota Press.

Eliot, T. S. ([1922] 1998) *The Waste Land and Other Poems.* Edited by Frank Kermode. New York: Penguin Books.

Gaski, Harald (2000) *Njealját máilmmi Čiegáin. Álgoálbmotgirjjálašvuohta.* Kárášjohka: Davvi Girji.

Gaski, Harald (2011) Song, Poetry, and Images in Writing: Sami Literature. In Karen Langgård & Kirsten Thisted (eds): *From Oral Tradition to Rap: Literatures of the Polar North.* Nuuk: Ilisimatusarkif/Forlaget Atuagkat, 15–38.

Grönstrand, Heidi (2014) Self-translating: Linking Languages, Literary Traditions and Cultural Spheres. In Leena Kaunonen (ed.): *Cosmopolitanism and Transnationalism: Visions, Ethics and Practices.* Helsinki: Helsinki Collegium for Advanced Studies, 116–137. Accessed December 21, 2017, https://helda.helsinki.fi/bitstream/handle/10138/45246/06_GRONSTRAND_1305.pdf?sequence=1.

Heith, Anne (2016) Postcolonial, Transnational, Literary Fields: Sámi and Tornedalian Counter-Histories. *Joutsen/Svanen* 2016, 44–57.

Hirvonen, Vuokko (2011) "Te opetitte minut kirjoittamaan – kiitoksia!" Valta- ja vähemmistökielen kohtaamisia saamelaisten naiskirjailijoiden tuotannossa. In Heidi Grönstrand & Kristina Malmio (eds): *Både och, sekä että. Om flerspråkighet – Monikielisyydestä.* Helsinki: Schildts, 201–222.

Jonsson, Carla (2012) Making Silenced Voices Heard: Code-switching in Multilingual Literary Texts. In Mark Sebba, Shahrzad Mahootian & Carla Jonsson (eds): *Language Mixing and Code-Switching in Writing: Approaches to Mixed-Language Written Discourse.* New York: Routledge, 212–231.

Kantola, Janna (2001) *Runous plus. Tutkielmia modernismin jälkeisestä runoudesta*. Helsinki: Palmenia-kustannus.
Marx, John (2004) Postcolonial Literature and the Western Literary Canon. In Nail Lazarus (ed.): *The Cambridge Companion to Postcolonial Literary Studies*. Cambridge: Cambridge University Press, 83–96.
Nissilä, Hanna-Leena (2016) *"Sanassa maahanmuuttaja on vähän kitkerä jälkimaku". Kirjallisen elämän ylirajaistuminen 2000-luvun alun Suomessa.* Oulu: Oulun yliopisto.
Paltto, Kirsti (2010) Publishing Sámi Literature – from Christian Translations to Sámi Publishing Houses. *Studies in American Indian Literature* 22(2), 42–58.
Parente-Čapková, Viola (2015) Kirjallisuudentutkimuksen asema saamentutkimuksessa ennen ja nyt – Keskustelua Veli-Pekka Lehtolan kanssa. *Avain* 3(2015), 13–18.
Parente-Čapková, Viola & Launis, Kati (2015) Saamelaiskirjallisuuden ylirajainen historia ja nykypäivä. *Avain* 3(2015), 3–12.
Pasanen, Annika (2015) *Kuávsui já peeivičuovâ. 'Sarastus ja päivänvalo': Inarinsaamen kielen revitalisaatio*. Uralica Helsingiensia 9. Helsinki: Helsingin yliopisto & Suomalais-ugrilainen seura.
Pietikäinen, Sari & Kelly-Holmes, Helen (2012) The Dangers of Normativity – The Case of Minority Language Media. In Jan Blommaert, Sirpa Leppänen, Päivi Pahta & Tiina Räisänen (eds): *Dangerous Multilingualism: Northern Perspectives on Order, Purity and Normality*. Basingstoke: Palgrave MacMillan, 194–204.
Pollari, Mikko; Nissilä, Hanna-Leena; Melkas, Kukku; Löytty, Olli; Kauranen, Ralf & Grönstrand, Heidi (2015) National, Transnational and Entangled Literatures: Methodological Considerations Focusing on the Case of Finland. In Ann-Sofie Lönngren, Heidi Grönstrand, Dag Heede & Anne Heith (eds): *Rethinking National Literatures and the Literary Canon in Scandinavia*. Cambridge: Cambridge Scholars Publishing, 2–29.
Rantala, Katja (2013) *Att leva i ett mellanrum. Kulturell identitet i Populärmusik från Vittula, Ett öga rött och Sms från Soppero*. Unpublished master's thesis. Åbo: Åbo Akademi.
Sámediggi – Saamelaiskäräjät (2017a) *Saamelaiset Suomessa*. Accessed August 29, 2017, www.samediggi.fi/index.php?option=com_content&task=blogcategory& id=105&Itemid=167.
Sámediggi – Saamelaiskäräjät (2017b) *Saamen kielet*. Accessed August 29, 2017, www.samediggi.fi/index.php?option=com_content&task=blogcategory& id=253&Itemid=405.
Skåden, Sigbjørn (2004) *Skuovvadeddjiid gonagas*. Evenskjer: Skániid girjie.
Skåden, Sigbjørn (2007) *Skomakernes konge*. Evenskjer: Skániid girjie.
Skåden, Sigbjørn (2009) *Prekariáhta lávlla*. Evenskjer: Skániid girjie.
Uthaug, Maren (2012) *Dan botta go vuordit beaivváža*. Kárášjohka: ČálliidLágádus.
Valkonen, Sanna (2009) *Poliittinen saamelaisuus*. Tampere: Vastapaino.
Zaldua, Iban (2009) Eight Crucial Decisions (A Basque Writer is Obliged to Face). In Mari Jose Olaziregi (ed.): *Writers in Between Languages: Minority Literatures in the Global Scene*. Reno: University of Nevada, 89–112.

6 Kjartan Fløgstad's *Pampa Unión*

A Travel on the Border of Languages in Latin America

Anne Karine Kleveland

With more than fifty published books since the late 1960s, Kjartan Fløgstad is one of the most prolific and renowned Norwegian authors. Although his work is written in Norwegian, multilingualism has been part of his literary language from the start. His first books of poetry, *Valfart* (1968; Pilgrimage) and *Seremoniar* (1969; Ceremonies), as well as his first collection of prose, *Den hemmelege jubel* (1970; The secret cheer), contain words and phrases from several European languages in addition to Norwegian. In his first book of prose we also find that the author is preoccupied with languages and translation on a meta-level, and these topics steadily become more important throughout Fløgstad's oeuvre.

Travel constitutes another *leitmotif* of Fløgstad's. *Valfart* can be read as a travel narrative through different historic epochs and European intellectual history. Already in some of the texts from *Seremoniar* and *Den hemmelege jubel*, the author orients himself towards the Latin American continent. In fact, travel to this part of the world is central in his later work, such as in the case of *Pampa Unión. Latinamerikanske reiser* (1994; Pampa Unión: Latin American travels), which is the book that this chapter focusses on.

Although *Pampa Unión* contains a great variety of texts and might be classified as a scrapbook, it is also a travel book. This is suggested in the subtitle and also on the dust cover: "*Pampa Unión* is a love song about and dedicated to Latin America. Like the continent itself, this travel book is full of contrasts" (Fløgstad 1994; my translation). The thirty-eight short texts that compose the volume describe the first-person narrator's encounter with Latin American societies and cultures, people and languages. Through these texts the narrator touches upon a number of different topics, varying from intellectual questions to popular culture and Andean myths.

As is common in travel literature, *Pampa Unión* claims to be written on the go, in this case during the narrator's visit to South America in the mid-1990s. The narrator is a writer, and to some extent he can be said to mirror the real-world author, Kjartan Fløgstad. Significantly, the two share a Northern European background and similar physical appearance, as well as anti-imperialist and anti-capitalist ideas. In order to stress how the narrator of *Pampa Unión* has a double function as traveller and writer, I will call him the "traveller-narrator", an expression taken from Michael Cronin (2000).

Multilingualism is an essential part of the travel in *Pampa Unión*. The Norwegian "matrix language" – understood here as the main language of the text – is continually interrupted by words or phrases from other languages, mainly ones with European origin (e.g. Spanish, English, French, German, Portuguese and Latin), but also words from native languages of South America, such as Aymaran, Mapudungün and Quechuan.[1] In addition, the pages of *Pampa Unión* raise questions about the written representation of language, group languages, regional jargon and how the power relations of the post-colonial societies are reflected in language. In fact, although the pages of *Pampa Unión* show a physical displacement, or wandering, through different cities, regions and countries, the linguistic and meta-literary aspects of the travel are just as important. In this chapter, I shall study how the traveller-narrator of *Pampa Unión* seeks to understand – and even become one with – the languages and people that he meets, and how he, through his pen, communicates his insights and shortcomings to the reader. I will analyse text fragments where he confronts the challenges of handling different kinds of linguistic borders drawn by the languages and language communities of the South American continent, and I will show how he also points to the borders between the literary world and the material world. However, before analysing the text fragments, I shall briefly address the concept of "otherness", a central aspect of travel literature.

Travel Literature and "The Other"

Historically, travel literature has been closely linked to European colonialism. As Mary Louise Pratt (1992) shows in *Imperial Eyes*, this literature contributed to producing an idea of "the rest of the world" for European readership during the 18th and 19th centuries. When studying European fiction that deals with the colonial context, Abdul R. JanMohamed (1985, 63) affirms that "[t]he dominant model of power- and interest-relations in all colonial societies is the Manichean opposition between the putative superiority of the European and the supposed inferiority of the native". This model has provided what he – with a glance to Fredric Jameson's work – calls the "the Manichean allegory". JanMohamed defines it as "a field of diverse yet interchangeable oppositions between white and black, good and evil, superiority and inferiority, civilization and savagery, intelligence and emotion, rationality and sensuality, self and Other, subject and object" (JanMohamed 1985, 63).[2] This way of thinking, he claims, constitutes a central feature of the literary texts preoccupied with the colonial period. So, when travel literature has drawn borders between "us" and "them" or "self" and "Other", it has indeed contributed to expressing and maintaining the imperialist way of imaging the world.

Studying modern travel literature from the 1930s and onwards, Arne Melberg describes these texts as follows:

> This travel literature can aim to tell the truth about reality and to engage in politics, but it still has a problematic relationship to truth and reality: it shows that truth must be produced by literary means, and that politics and aesthetics do not always pull evenly. On the other hand, it develops a number of possible strategies for managing the relationship between the traveller and the foreign country, or the "otherness" that he or she meets.
> (Melberg 2005, 31–32; my translation)

Regarding the traveller's encounter with otherness, Melberg (2005, 32) states that the meeting between the traveller and the foreign "Other" constitutes the essence of travel literature. Thus, even in travel literature from the 20th century, it seems to be difficult to avoid dualism altogether. After all, these texts are essentially a glance into another culture – a meeting with other people, their habits and languages. However, this does not mean that modern European travel literature must reproduce the Eurocentrism of the past or contribute to a Manichaean image of the world. In *Pampa Unión*, the travel takes place in previously colonized territory, and the discourse is influenced by post-colonial thought. As in any travelogue, otherness is central also in Fløgstad's book. Still, as we shall soon see, when Fløgstad's traveller-narrator makes use of the concept of the Other it is with a twist.

Losing Letters and Starting the Literary Travel

The linguistic dimension of travel becomes clear in the first text of the volume, the prose poem "Maskinen" (The machine). This poem depicts the act of writing *per se* and questions around how written words portray reality:

> **The machine**
> is connected to the mains
> standing solidly on my desk
> It writes ae for æ, oe for ø, and aa for å.
> The lines in the writing are veins of the pure ore of history
> running through the grey rock of the past. Through the machine
> the words take root deep down in reality.
> With every touch the keys extract

letters with their roots intact
leaving open wounds and drifts
transformed by the writing to black omens
on paper, where eyes sow seeds
in freshly written words, or see
the pain in freshly torn wounds.[3]

(Fløgstad 1994, [9]; translated by
Annjo Klungervik Greenall)

Here the machine is a reference to a typewriter that cannot reproduce the Norwegian language correctly, as it does not have the three last letters of the Norwegian alphabet: "æ", "ø" and "å". ("It writes ae for æ, oe for ø, and aa for å.") This suggests that the author is in a foreign place, using someone else's typewriter, a typewriter that is designed for another language than his own. We could say that the machine embodies a physical border between languages. Thus, from the very beginning of the book, the reader understands that the traveller-narrator is forced to express himself differently than he usually does in his maternal language. He manages to overcome the linguistic obstacle of the missing letters by adapting his writing to an international keyboard. Accordingly, we could say that the traveller-narrator accepts that his own language has to change in his approach to the other culture. It is a physical change, as his letters have to adapt to the foreign. This can be interpreted as a first attempt to dissolve the dichotomy of "self" and "other" typical of the travel book, and reinvent the self as a hybrid being. From the first text, the traveller-narrator's intentions to adapt to the surrounding society are obvious.

Paradoxically, the words of "Maskinen" do contain the letters ("æ", "ø" and "å") not found on the aforementioned typewriter, so the poem we are reading does not come directly out of that machine. Clearly there is a gap between the reality *described* in the poem and the poem that meets the eye. In this way, the reader is reminded of the border between the literary world (*diegesis*) and the real world. Interestingly, the existence of a gap between the literary representation and the real world is not communicated through the traveller-narrator's reflections on the topic, but by the use of language itself. It is up to the reader to spot the incoherence, to see that the letters are not really missing. Therefore, from the very beginning of the book, language itself is given a defining role in the traveller-narrator's encounter with the Latin American people and society.

The division between fiction and reality is a highly relevant topic in travel literature. As explained above, Melberg underscores the problematic relationship between truth and reality typical of this literary mode. In fact, travel literature has been considered one of the ideological apparatuses of the empire during the colonial period (Pratt 1992). "Maskinen" brings forth the meta-dimension of picturing a reality through words. This is found, for instance, in the following verses:

> The lines in the writing are veins of the pure ore of history
> running through the grey rock of the past. Through the machine
> the words take root deep down in reality.
> With every touch the keys extract
> letters with their roots intact
> leaving open wounds and drifts
> transformed by the writing to black omens
> on paper...

These poetic images, where the words transform into an almost tangible root system, are a forceful way of connecting the literary world to the material world. In fact, the writing digs deep into the ground and becomes one with the most solid substances of all: metal ore and grey rock. It touches upon one of the cornerstones of the colonial history of South America, namely, the mining industry. The words "open wounds" and, in the last verse of the poem, "freshly torn wounds", in combination with "grey rock" and "black omens", suggest how the mining history of this region is one of ruthless exploitation of manpower and natural resources.[4]

As one can expect from the opening poem, the mining industry is a recurrent topic in the pages of Fløgstad's travel book. In fact, one of the main topics is the negative economic effects of colonialism and neo-colonialism, especially the effects visible in the Chilean and Bolivian mining industry. The title *Pampa Unión* is also the name of a city constructed to house the miners in the Antofagasta region of Chile. Being a well-functioning society in the golden years of the industry, between 1910 and 1930, it was gradually abandoned during the 1950s and 1960s. Today – as when the travel book was written – it is a ghost city.

All in all, Fløgstad's poem shows its willingness to depict reality with words, even though this is not unproblematic, and declares that the words will have to adapt to a foreign culture. As such, language defines the travel. With this pronouncement, the literary journey begins.

Inverting Otherness and Alienating the Matrix Language

Throughout the pages of *Pampa Unión*, the traveller-narrator observes and comments upon the traces of colonialism and neo-colonialism in Latin American society. We find it in "Malmbyen" (Ore city), a nickname for the Norwegian city of Narvik, which is well known as a port for the great volume of iron ore coming from Kiruna in Sweden. In this text, the traveller-narrator recalls how he lived in that city for a year before moving to the small mining community of Bjørnevatn, where ore was the main product. He is thinking about his experience with Norwegian miners' settlements as he visits the slum areas of another city dependent on the mining industry, Lota, which used to be the centre of coal mining in Chile but faced economic recession and the definitive closure of the mines in the late 1990s. Here we find a parallel with the ore mines of Bjørnevatn, which were closed down during the same period of time. Without saying it directly, Fløgstad's text suggests that the traveller-narrator's experience in Norway makes it easier for him to understand how the Chilean mining community is facing economic downturn. In fact, he visits Lota only a few years before the major mining company closes its doors for good, and thus he is able to observe how the city is severely impacted by the economic situation.

To some extent, the discourse preserves the distinction between the European traveller, on one hand, and the previously colonized individuals of Latin America, on the other. But the hierarchical mould of colonialism is questioned when Fløgstad's traveller-narrator calls *himself* "the Other":

> More or rather less consciously some of us seek a role and a place in life where we are easily visible and recognizable as the Foreigner. As the Other. It must be motivated deep inside us. Here we are a head taller. Here we stand out. And we can live with it. I think we even enjoy it. We enjoy being something in between provocation and temptation. Yes, we enjoy the inversed racism that ensures us a privileged treatment. [...] We are wandering and unattainable advertising columns of wealth. We can feel how the stares of everyone we pass desire us. [...] While we are the Other that exposes his own body, we know that the others want to escape their bodies, and stab us with a knife, cut deep into the Foreigner, drain us of the fortune and wealth we embody, and then place themselves in our pink, slightly sunburnt bodies, [...] in order to see wealth from the inside, with the blue gaze of wealth itself.[5]
>
> (Fløgstad 1994, 48–49; my translation)

Arguably, the traveller-narrator is a representation of the colonial heritage. He has the physical appearance, lifestyle and living standards of the First World, and he receives the privileged treatment that Europeans have enjoyed since the colonial period. When he deliberately inverts the situation, redefining the idea of who is the Other, this can be read as an anti-imperialist statement, a rejection of the asymmetric power relations of the past.

In the second paragraph of the quote, the traveller-narrator not only *says* that he is the Other, he metaphorically gives up his body to an imaginary exploitation. It is as if his flesh embodies the mines of the

Travel on the Border of Languages 107

continent or, even stronger, as if his body is the abused soil of South America. When the traveller-narrator lets his own body suffer the colonial exploitation, the anti-imperialist protest becomes more striking. Interestingly, this imagery recalls the work of the Chilean poet Pablo Neruda, who is well known for using poetic images where man and nature merge. This is found in his most political work, *Canto General* (1950), where Neruda dedicates several poems to miners and the mining industry. In fact, Fløgstad's traveller-narrator comments upon some of these elsewhere in the book, explaining how he considers "Hambre en el sur" ("Hunger in the South"), a poem written in Lota, to be especially successful. In the first verses of the poem we find the fusion of coal and man: "I see the sob in Lota's coal / and the humiliated Chilean's wrinkled shadow / Picking the innards' bitter vein, dying" (Neruda 2000, 207).[6] The metaphors used by the traveller-narrator and the approximation to Pablo Neruda's poetry remind us how this is a literary travel, even when the topic is highly material.

While, in "Malmbyen", the traveller-narrator's voice redefines the Other in poetic terms, in the text "Barnet til hesten" (The horse's child), we find a redefinition of otherness in the use of language itself. Here the traveller-narrator visits a coal mine in the Chilean city of Coronel. In an attempt to understand the hard life of the workers, he enters the deepest galleries of the mine. The title of the text reflects a situation where the traveller-narrator does not remember "potro", the Spanish word for "foal", and rephrases what he wants to say. The local miners find the rephrasing amusing and mock the traveller-narrator:

> I say the horse's child, and the people that accompany me in the elevator laugh. Am I referring to the horse's son or daughter? Strictly speaking horses do not have children, and the foals – los potros – didn't really become blind.[7]
>
> (Fløgstad 1994, 16)

The linguistic shortcomings of the traveller-narrator create a comic situation. In *Across the Lines*, Michael Cronin shows how modern literary travel accounts often exploit the comical potential of mistranslations: "The translation mistakes, the misunderstandings, the rough approximations provide the dialogue for the mock-sentimental drama of intercultural encounter", he states (Cronin 2000, 45). This comic *Verfremdung* of translation, he explains, can be self-directed (e.g. directed towards the traveller-narrator) or other-directed. Regarding the first mode, Cronin holds that:

> the traveller-narrator is a picaresque hero or heroine whose cultural knowledge and linguistic assuredness are undermined or relativized by interlingual travelling. The sovereign ego is humbled by the

intractable detail of foreign language and the traveller is no longer at the centre of his/her own language world but on the margins of another.

(Cronin 2000, 45–46)

This description is also fitting for Fløgstad's traveller-narrator. His non-native dominion of Spanish forces him to use a rephrasing that deviates from standard Spanish. In this way, he places himself in what Cronin calls the *margins* of the language he encounters, and we can say that he linguistically takes on the role of the Other.

Research on code-switching commonly treats the language or languages that deviate from the matrix as foreign elements. Here I understand "code-switching" in a broad sense, following the researcher Carla Jonsson, who defines it as "the use of two or more codes (e.g. languages, varieties, dialects, styles) in writing" (Jonsson 2012, 212). If we were to apply this logic to the text "Barnet til hesten", the words "los potros" would be the foreign element. But in the plot the foreign words are "barnet til hesten" ("the horse's child"), and the traveller-narrator is the foreigner. Thus, Fløgstad has changed the most common rule of the multilingual game. The matrix language has become the alien language, and the Spanish language is not only revealed as the spoken language of the plot, but also as the linguistic centre. That is, the Spanish language – used very scarcely in the text – has become the language that has the power to define right and wrong, foreign and native, and to draw the line of otherness.

From a reader-oriented perspective, this change offers the Norwegian reader the possibility to free herself from the common idea that the code-switched element (here "los potros") is a foreign element in the text. If she is able to identify with the traveller-narrator, she might even experience that *she* is in fact the Other, even though the matrix language of the text is her mother tongue. This being the case, the use of multilingualism has managed to evoke in the reader a feeling of being on the margins of another language that is similar to the one experienced by the traveller-narrator of *Pampa Unión*.

Fløgstad's use of multilingualism questions how linguistic reality is reproduced in literature. Meir Sternberg addresses this topic through the concept of "translational mimesis". This concept describes how literary texts imitate the multilingual reality that surrounds us in different ways (Sternberg 1981, 221–239). Michael Cronin emphasizes the same process in his approach to modern travel accounts:

> The reality that is happening in a foreign language is being conveyed to the reader in the language of the narrative; in other words, it is being continuously translated into that language but foreign words remain as witting or unwitting reminders of how fraught the process

of translation is in the first place. Lexical exoticism is a palpable written trace of the foreign for the reader, a legible indication that, although the account has been written in English, French, Irish, Italian or Russian, the country is elsewhere, the language and mores different.

(Cronin 2000, 40–41)

In the extract from Fløgstad's text, it is obvious that the traveller-narrator says "barnet til hesten" ("the horse's child") in *Spanish*, although it is reproduced in Norwegian (In Spanish, it would be "el hijo/ niño del caballo"). But only "los potros" is actually expressed in Spanish.[8] If the reader notices this paradox, she might find that the homogenizing convention which for a long time has allowed us to consider monolingual texts as the norm is somewhat deceiving or misleading. I follow Sternberg (1981, 225–227) in understanding the "homogenizing convention" as texts where the literary world appears monolingual because everything is written in the matrix language, although it is obvious that the plot takes place in a multilingual universe. To a great extent, this convention conceals how different languages coexist in a text that on the surface might appear monolingual. If the reader is made aware of the translational processes that go on in the text (e.g. the *translational mimesis*), she will be more prone to appreciate the literary craftsmanship of the author. Perhaps she will even be more apt to appreciate the literary text as a piece of art where different linguistic realities come together.

The Perpetual Movement in and Out of Languages

Although the traveller-narrator of *Pampa Unión* plays on his own otherness in the encounter with the Latin Americans, I find that the texts of the volume testify how he is constantly trying to overcome this condition. The dominion of the languages of the continent is seen as the key to integration; throughout the book, the traveller-narrator attempts to merge with Latin American society by acquiring detailed knowledge about local words and idioms. Accordingly, we find several sociolinguistic remarks, for example, detailed descriptions of how the Spanish word *mina* has several denotations, and how the people of specific Chilean cities use these. Still, the traveller-narrator is aware of the fact that there is more to learn, and he pursues a deeper comprehension of the local culture (for instance, when he is trying to learn the in-group language of the Chilean coal miners). The following example, taken from the text "Løyndemålet" (Secret language), displays some of the difficulties he encounters:

What does the silent secret language of the miners in Lota and Coronel tell us? [...] In subterranean mines the ore is always extracted in secret and darkness. Normally no intruders can see what is going on. How can they be expected to react when a long huinca and gringo comes down into the darkness and wants to learn their secrets? One thing is clear: they will not speak the secret language from the deepest galleries.[9]

(Fløgstad 1994, 113)

Once again the traveller-narrator shows awareness of his otherness. But while the lack of the precise vocabulary ("potro") previously did not prevent a successful communication between the traveller-narrator and the locals, here he is not granted access to the language he seeks. Why is this so? Why do the local miners erect a border that limits his integration? The pages of *Pampa Unión* do not provide any definitive answers to these questions. Still, the choice of words in "Løyndemålet" suggests a reason for the exclusion: the term "huinca", from Mapudungün, is used by the Mapuche community for a person who is not Mapuche. The Spanish "gringo" denotes someone who is not originally from Latin America, and it is often used, more specifically, about someone from the US. Thus, both terms underscore the foreignness of the traveller-narrator. And, notably, both point towards the mining history of the region, in which miners were first cruelly exploited by the Spanish Empire during the colonial era and, from the 19th century, by the North American industry. The traveller-narrator's ethnicity and Northern European appearance might be too much of a reminder of the usurpations of the past. After all, who would share their secrets with their oppressors? In *Pampa Unión*, language is seen as the key to understanding society, but the colonial wound may still be an obstacle for the traveller-narrator in his quest for an in-depth understanding of the Latin American people and cultures, even if he tries to change the traditional patterns by taking on the role of the Other.

Yet these lines from "Løyndemålet" contain an interesting paradox: semantically they show that the traveller-narrator finds himself unable to learn a particular group language. This is communicated in the Norwegian matrix language. But the words "huinca" and "gringo", which break up the matrix, prove that the traveller-narrator indeed understands and uses terminology which places him on the inside of other group languages. Although he cannot access the local miners' secret language, he understands why he is excluded. This reveals how he is at once on the inside and outside of different levels of the local languages. Accordingly, his travel is a perpetual movement between the different layers of the linguistic reality – what Bakhtin calls *heteroglossia* – a perpetual struggle to overcome otherness. As we recall, Bakhtin uses this term to denote the regional and social variations that exist in any language at any given time (Bakhtin 1996, 272–273).

Bordering Travel Literature, Attempting to Dissolve Dichotomies of the Past

The pages of *Pampa Unión* explore how different kinds of borders co-exist in travel literature. From the very beginning, the meta-literary idea of picturing a reality is a central topic: the alleged missing letters of the typewriter that are still there in the poem "Maskinen" show that the depicted reality and the outside world are not the same. The way the matrix language is revealed as the foreign language in "Barnet til hesten" shows how the depicted linguistic reality and the letters or languages that compose the text might not be the same. These are crucial ideas in a literary mode that, albeit its historical role of picturing "the rest of the world" to the European readership, has always been a fictional representation and never a faithful reproduction of a journey.

As opposed to Eurocentric travel literature that contributed to the colonial power discourse by creating Manichean dichotomies of "us" and "them", and "self" and "other", neither the identity nor the values of the travelling "self" are fixed in *Pampa Unión*. Instead we find an attempt to transcend the mental borders of the past. Both through his thoughts and reflections, and in the way language is used in the text, the traveller-narrator presents himself as an individual willing to dissolve the dichotomy of "self "and "other" in order to reinvent himself as a hybrid being. From the outset, he gives up a part of his own identity as he accepts slight changes in his written language. In addition, he metaphorically gives up his body, letting it suffer the exploitation of the South American bedrock. Admitting that his own language is not at the linguistic centre of the travel, he finds himself on the margins of the languages of South America. From this position, he pursues a fuller comprehension of the continent by learning the secret language of the miners but finds himself unable to access this group language. Still, his use of selected words from the continent reveals how he has access to other group languages and jargons. Conclusively, his travel can be read as a perpetual movement between different languages and between different linguistic realities.

Notes

1 I have borrowed the term "matrix language" from Carol Myers-Scotton (2001), who, however, makes a more specific use of the concept.
2 Bill Ashcroft, Gareth Griffiths and Helen Tiffin ([1989] 2005, 169) refer to the same concept as "Manichean aesthetics", citing Fredric Jameson's work.
3 **Maskinen**

> er kopla til lysnettet
> og står støtt på skrivebordet.
> Den skriv ae for æ, oe for ø, og aa for å.
> Linjene i skrifta er årer av historias reine malm
> gjennom fortidas gråberg. Gjennom maskinen

har orda røter djupt ned i det verkelege.
For kvart anslag riv tastane
bokstavar opp med rota
og let det stå att åpne sår og gruvegangar
som skrifta skaper om til svarte teikn
på papiret, der augo sår
i nyskrivne ord, eller ser
smerten i nyopprivne sår.

4 In the Norwegian original, "svarte teikn" is not quite as alarming as the "black omens" of the English translation.
5 "Meir og helst mindre medvite søker nokre av oss ei rolle og ein plass i livet der vi er lett synlege og gjenkjennelege som Den Framande. Som Den Andre. Det må vera ein gir djupt inne i oss. Her er vi eit hovud høgare. Her stikk vi oss ut. Og vi meistrar det. Et trur vi nyt det også. Vi nyt å vera ei blanding av provokasjon og freisting. Ja, vi nyt den omvende rasismen som gjer at vi blir altfor godt behandla. [...] Vi er omvandrande og uoppnåelege reklamesøyler for rikdom. Vi kjenner at blikket til alle vi passerer, begjærer oss. [...] Slik vi er den Andre som framhevar sin eigen kropp, veit vi at dei andre ønsker å rømma frå sin eigen kropp, og stikke kniven i oss, skjera djupt inn i den Framande, tømma oss for gods og gull og all den rikdommen vi lekamleggjer, for så sjølve å ta plass inne i våre rosa, lett solbrende kroppar, [...] for slik å kunna sjå rikdommen frå innsida, med rikdommens eige blå blikk."
6 Fløgstad (1994, 149) has translated this poem from Spanish into Norwegian and quotes his own translation in *Pampa Unión*: "Eg ser klagen i kolet frå Lota / og den krøkte skuggen av ein vanvyrd chilenar / ser eg bryta den bitre malmen djupt under jorda, døy."
7 "Eg seier barnet til hesten, og dei som står rundt meg i heisen flirer. Er det sonen eller dottera til hesten eg meiner? Strengt tatt får vel ikkje hestar barn, og føla – los potros – blei vel ikkje akkurat blinde."
8 Sternberg (1981, 225–227) calls this technique the "selective reproduction" of code-switched elements, meaning that chosen speech fragments uttered by (fictive) speakers point towards the heterolingual communication that takes place in the text.
9 "Kva fortel det tause løyndemålet til gruvearbeidarane i Lota og Coronel? [...] I underjordiske gruver går utvinninga av malmen alltid føre seg i løynd og mørker. Ingen uvedkommande ser vanlegvis kva dei driv på med. Korleis skal dei få reagera når ein lang huinca og gringo kjem ned i mørkret og vil læra å kjenna løyndommane deira? Ein ting er sikkert: dei vil ikkje tala løyndemålet frå dei djupaste gruvegangene."

Bibliography

Ashcroft, Bill; Griffiths, Gareth & Tiffin, Helen ([1989] 2005) *The Empire Writes Back: Theory and Practice in Post-colonial Literatures*. London & New York: Routledge.

Bakhtin, Michail M. (1996) Discourse in the Novel. In Michael Holquist (ed.): *The Dialogic imagination: Four Essays by M. M. Bakhtin*. Austin: University of Texas Press, 259–422.

Cronin, Michael (2000) *Across the Lines: Travel, Language, Translation*. Cork: Cork University Press.

Fløgstad, Kjartan (1968) *Valfart*. Oslo: Samlaget.

Fløgstad, Kjartan (1969) *Seremoniar*. Oslo: Samlaget.
Fløgstad, Kjartan (1970) *Den hemmelege jubel*. Oslo: Samlaget.
Fløgstad, Kjartan (1994) *Pampa Unión*. Oslo: Gyldendal.
JanMohamed, Abdul R (1985) The Economy of Manichean Allegory: The Function of Racial Difference in Colonialist Literature. *Critical Inquiry* 12(1), 59–87.
Jonsson, Carla (2012) Making Silenced Voices Heard. Code-switching in Multilingual Literary Texts in Sweden. In Mark Sebba, Shahrzad Mahootian & Carla Jonsson (eds): *Language Mixing and Code-Switching in Writing: Approaches to Mixed-Language Written Discourse*. New York & London: Routledge, 212–232.
Melberg, Arne (2005) *Resa och skriva. En guide till den moderna reselitteraturen*. Göteborg: Daidalos.
Myers-Scotton, Carol (2001) The Matrix Language Frame Model: Developments and Responses. In Rodolfo Jakobson (ed.): *Codeswitching Worldwide*. Berlin & New York: Mouton de Gruyter, 23–58.
Neruda, Pablo (2000) *Canto General*. Translated by Jack Schmitt. Berkeley, Los Angeles & London: University of California Press.
Neruda, Pablo (2011) *Canto General*. Madrid: Cátedra.
Pratt, Mary Louise (1992) *Imperial Eyes: Travel Writing and Transculturation*. London: Routledge.
Sternberg, Meir (1981) Polylingualism as Reality and Translation as Mimesis. *Poetics Today* 2(4), 221–239.

7 Humour and Shifting Language Borders in Umayya Abu-Hanna's Autofictional Novel *Sinut*

Heidi Grönstrand

Cross-cultural autobiographies, which stem from personal recollections of experiences of moving across two (or several) languages and cultures or living in them simultaneously, have an important role in bringing into discussion issues of cultural change and the ways in which language questions are intertwined with them (e.g. Seyhan 2001; Karpinsky 2012; Leonard 2013; Doloughan 2016). Also in Finland, autobiographical writing has been an important genre in which these themes have appeared in recent years (Rantonen 2010, 168–170; Nissilä & Rantonen 2013, 64; Hyvärinen & Mäki 2014). One example is Umayya Abu-Hanna's *Sinut* (2007; You),[1] which tells the story of the author's arrival from Palestine to Finland in the beginning of the 1980s.

Umayya Abu-Hanna is known in Finland as a writer but also as a journalist and politician, being a former member of the Helsinki City Council (Green Party) who has actively been engaged in public discussions on intolerance and racism. She has published several non-fiction works, but her debut was the autobiography *Nurinkurin* (2003; Upside down, inside out), in which she portrayed her childhood in Haifa. Abu-Hanna entered the literary field as a Finnish-language writer. In particular, *Sinut* (the sequel to *Nurinkurin*) depicts how language is interwoven in the process of integration and becoming a recognized citizen who has full legal rights and is treated with appreciation and respect by the community. Since 2010, Abu-Hanna has lived in Amsterdam in the Netherlands.

Language Learning

Umayya Abu-Hanna's relations to the Finnish language constitute an important theme in *Sinut*. The protagonist's attempts to learn Finnish are depicted in detail. In the beginning, Finnish is for her a language consisting of a continuous flow of incomprehensible sound in which it is impossible to differentiate anything familiar. Much attention is given to the difficulties in finding the right words and grasping the correct pronunciation. For example, Abu-Hanna has difficulties in following the pronunciation of Finnish vowels, which, in turn, leads to different meanings and misunderstandings. By focussing on language questions, *Sinut* follows many current autobiographical works on immigration, which foreground the desire for mastery of the dominant language of the new country and the struggle to acquire it as one's own medium (see, e.g. Seyhan 2001, 88; Kellman 2009, 21; Wanner 2015).

The main language of *Sinut* is Finnish, but it also includes English – even containing long passages – and Arabic appears in a few single words and expressions. These languages become important in the portrayal of the protagonist's life, in which many languages are present at the same time. Yet it is worth noting that in contrast to such Swedish novelists as Alejandro Leiva Wenger, Jonas Hassen Khemiri and Marjaneh Bakhtiari, who are known for their literary strategies of employing youth slang spoken in immigrant suburbs in their writing and have given it literary status, Abu-Hanna does not actively mix languages or create a slang of her own.

But linguistic playfulness, creativity and variety, which define the above-mentioned authors' literary language (e.g. Behschnitt 2013),[2] are important features of *Sinut* as well. The multilingual traits of Abu-Hanna's literary language in *Sinut*, especially the playful and humoristic elements, become a form of bordering. This marks linguistic belonging and exclusion in new ways and challenges the dominant power relations between languages in society and in the literary field in Finland. At the time when *Sinut* came out, there was not much room for literature in other languages than Finnish or Swedish. Ranya El Ramly's *Auringon asema* (2002; Position of the sun) is often counted as a forerunner of "immigrant literature" in Finland (Löytty 2015, 67; Nissilä 2016). The novel is in Finnish, however, although multilingualism is present as a theme (Grönstrand 2019).

In the following, my approach is inspired by discussions on multiethnic youth slang in contemporary literature, especially in Sweden (see, e.g. Behschnitt 2013; Behschnitt & Nilsson 2013), as well as by Doris Sommer's idea of language games and humour as a tool for resisting monolingualism and the notion of a "one-to-one identity" between a language and a people (Sommer 2004, xv). Sommer is most of all interested in language games that operate between languages. They stem from "poaching and borrowing, and crossing lines", as Sommer puts it (2004, 34). In her view, interruptions, delays, code-switching and syncopated communication are rhetorical features of bicultural language games (Sommer 2004, 176), but what is crucial is the effect of surprise. According to Sommer (2004, 37): "code switching prefers the surprise element of an estranged (literally foreign) expression to the predictability of one legitimate language; it values artistry over stable identity, and it invites an acknowledgement of aesthetic agency over a politics of cultural recognition." When writing about surprise effect, Sommer draws on the Russian formalist Victor Shklovsky, for whom defamiliarization was an important key concept. Language is made strange by a surprise effect; this is accomplished by roughening conventional material in unconventional ways (Sommer 2004, 29). Sommer gives value to language that is arbitrary and slippery, and interestingly, the surprise effect can also be caused by a mistake (Sommer 2004, xii).

"I Have One Cursor at the Right, one at the Left" – A Model of Living in More Than One Language

It is possible to read Abu-Hanna's *Sinut* as a kind of development story characterized by assimilationist rhetoric. The novel puts emphasis on social mobility and success, a movement from the margins to the centre (see, e.g. Pearce 2010, 152–153; Karpinsky 2012, 31, 138). Already the foreword alludes to a narrative that has resulted in a situation in which wholeness and balance have been achieved. The author interprets the title of the book and provides the reader with guidelines on how to approach the work at hand:

> To become familiar with oneself requires that one steps outside of oneself, to be another to oneself. In the Finnish language the state of balance is expressed beautifully.
> This book tells about life in Finland from the beginning of the 1980s and encompasses about one-third of the history of Finland's independence. It depicts life from one migrant's perspective and it is meant to be read as such. Forgive me its excesses and remember that I am only a human being, although I am a Finn.
> The book is a compilation of life, diary entries, correspondence, lectures and columns. Read it as you wish.[3]
>
> (Abu-Hanna 2007, 9; my translation)

In many regards, the foreword introduces *Sinut* as a traditional autobiography. The references to diary entries and correspondence lead one to think that the story is based on material that indicates truth and authenticity (e.g. Smith 2000, 6–9, 12–13). The individual "migration story", which is at the heart of the story, is also put in historical perspective. The mentioned fact that the story encompasses almost thirty years of the period of Finland's independence places the story in a broader social context, reminding that migration is an integral part of Finnish history. But despite these features, conventional genre conventions are questioned as well. The documentary material is not presented as any kind of evidence of truth or authenticity. Instead, the reader is given the advice to read the book "as you wish". *Sinut* stretches the borders between autobiography and fiction; thus, it can be regarded as autofiction.

The narrator-protagonist Umayya Abu-Hanna comments upon the rigid conventions of autobiographical writing in the story as well. In a short scene in which she portrays her visit to an Academy of Life Writing course where ordinary people are taught how to write their life story, she expresses her doubts about being able to follow the requirements of the genre. She finds it impossible to condense her life into a compact story which touches readers emotionally but does not contain elements which could be considered dubious or might question the values of the community. Abu-Hanna feels that she is forced to censor herself, and she decides to leave the Academy before presenting her own life story. By bringing into discussion the genre conventions of autobiographical writing, *Sinut* not only defies expectations that have been applied to the autobiographical genre in general, but also to the specific category of "immigrant literature". As many scholars have pointed out, "immigrant literature" has been viewed almost exclusively as an expression of ethnic experience and identity (Nilsson 2013, 41; Löytty 2015, 71–73). Whether or not the author has presented his or her work as autobiography, critics have tended to interpret it in an autobiographical frame (Leonard 2013, 153).

How does Abu-Hanna then narrate her story in *Sinut*? The life story begins with events that highlight her experiences of how it was to move to Finland, to a small town with a community that was not used to foreigners in the early 1980s. However, the linear and chronological narrative autobiographic style is soon discontinued and a depiction of isolated events starts to alternate with, for example, the narrator's essayistic reflections on the problems that foreigners meet with in Finland or on religions from a global perspective.

The structure of *Sinut* is episodic. For example, longer jokes and anecdotes are incorporated in the main storyline. This episodic structure is further strengthened by the use of documentary material, such as published interviews with Abu-Hanna or emails and faxes she has written or received. This kind of fragmentary structure, in which chronology and a straightforward narrative of adaption and growth are abandoned, points to a postmodern rather than a traditional autobiography (see, e.g. Kosonen 2000, 14–20). Occasionally the book's layout also contributes to increase the fragmentary impression, as a page might contain only one single sentence, such as "They do not dance in Finland"[4] or "and it makes the Arab totally sad of illness"[5] (Abu-Hanna 2007, 30–31). These sentences are surrounded by a large empty space; thus, the layout further underlines the loneliness expressed by the sentences.

Stories in which the inability to communicate in the dominant language of the surrounding society leads the protagonist to isolation and crisis are common in literature dealing with immigrant experiences, especially when looking at the phenomenon from a historical perspective. In Eva Hoffman's well-known autobiography *Lost in Translation: A Life in a New Language* (1989), which focusses on language and particularly on immigrants' language as an important means for self-construction and self-exploration, young Ewa's arrival in Canada is portrayed as a traumatic experience. As Eva C. Karpinsky (2012, 137) puts it: "The world around her is covered with 'the verbal blur', and she fears that she is losing her identity." The fear is also connected to pain and grief over a lost or receding mother tongue (e.g. Seyhan 2001, 70; Karpinsky 2012, 135–137; Doloughan 2016, 31–33). In Swedish-Finnish literature, especially of the 1970s and 1980s, depictions of Finnish immigrants' difficulties learning Swedish and communicating in the new language are characteristic features (see, e.g. Vallenius 1998, 123–127). Eija Hetekivi-Olsson's *Ingenbarnsland* has also been regarded as one of the contemporary Swedish-Finnish novels to deal with the social and collective traumas connected to social discrimination (Melkas 2018). The traumas caused by assimilation policies, language loss and the marginalization of one's own identity are recurrent themes in Tornedalian[6] and Sámi literature as well (Hirvonen [1999] 2008; Heith 2009).

In *Sinut*, there are glimpses of how the protagonist-narrator is forced to adopt a new identity in her new home country. The most obvious example is her new name, Maija Hänninen: Maija is a Finnish form of Umayya and Hänninen is the last name of her Finnish husband. In the beginning of the story, Umayya underlines that she would not have been able to move to Finland without getting married. Furthermore, in 1981, women were not allowed by law to keep their own family names, even though Arab women traditionally do that. When the narrator sets her old and new home countries against each other, it becomes clear that she experiences this Finnish habit and piece of legislation as a more or less violent and traumatic act. The feeling of outsiderness and foreignness is further strengthened as the first-person narration suddenly changes into the third person and the past tense into the present tense: "Umayya, i.e. nowadays Maija H., lives with her husband at Teräs street in Naantali"[7] (Abu-Hanna 2007, 11).

Also, the joy Abu-Hanna expresses when her mother comes to visit her and she has a possibility to speak Arabic for the first time since moving to Finland can be seen as testifying to feelings of loneliness and longing for a possibility to speak her mother tongue:

> I can speak my mother tongue right in the morning! We sit on benches at the kitchen cottage table and open the Za'atar (a mixture of sesame seeds and oregano) jars that mum brought. I have baked plait bread, whose recipe I found in *Kotiliesi*. Mouths full of food, close to each other we speak and laugh.[8]
>
> (Abu-Hanna 2007, 17)

The atmosphere in this scene is very warm and, interestingly, it is created by a combination of Arabic and Finnish elements. It highlights the significance of the mother tongue, but does not question Abu-Hanna's interest in learning to know Finnish culture. The food which the mother and daughter are eating while speaking consists of both "Za'atar", a Middle Eastern spice blend, and Finnish bread. Abu-Hanna has baked the bread herself, according to a recipe in a well-known Finnish magazine which specializes in cooking and other household matters. The whole context in which Arabic is spoken seems to be of importance: in addition to the verbal communication, physical closeness and laughter contribute to the cosy atmosphere. Years later, when Umayya's brother visits Finland, the same kind of feeling is present between them: "Everything feels so familiar. The sun and the mother tongue"[9] (Abu-Hanna 2007, 197).

Throughout the story, Abu-Hanna refuses to choose between Arabic and Finnish. Even after having lived many years in Finland, she still states: "I cry and notice that I have sighed in Arabic. And the language comforts"[10] (Abu-Hanna 2007, 139). While she admits that the letters of Arabic and Hebrew are not self-evident to her any more, this is not a problem. Instead she expresses enjoyment about the script and "dives" into it, as she puts it: "I enjoy the twisting script for a moment, and then I dive in. There are new names, new terms, new slang and inventions, but soon I forget the language and become emotionally and intellectually involved"[11] (Abu-Hanna 2007, 93). When Abu-Hanna's knowledge of Finnish increases, the value of Arabic does not decrease. The expression "I have one cursor on the right, one on the left"[12] (Abu-Hanna 2007, 95), which she uses to illustrate her efforts to write in Finnish with her parents' computer, which produces text from right to left, aptly illuminates her position in two cultures and languages. She has two homes, one in Haifa and one in Helsinki.

Although the story emphasizes the significance of the two languages in the protagonist's life, Arabic appears relatively sparsely in the text. The Arabic words occur only occasionally. In the quote above, for example, there is only one single word in Arabic, "Za'atar", written in Roman script and provided with an explanation in Finnish. The same practice applies to most Arabic words and expressions in *Sinut*. In addition to the above-mentioned "Za'atar", there are such words and expressions as "La'shukran" ("No, thank you"), "Kibd" ("liver") and "Shu" in a question that mixes Arabic and Finnish "Shu tapahtuu?" ("What happens?") and "habibi" ("friend"). The few Arabic words and phrases are not highlighted in the text (e.g. by italicization). In the question "Kidneys habiibi, onko mulla sellaiset?" ("Kidneys habibi, do I have those?") (Abu-Hanna 2007, 166), which is a mixture of English, Arabic and Finnish, the word "habibi" is not necessarily understood as an Arabic word for "friend", as it is adapted to the Finnish orthography. It is written with two "i" letters, which makes it look even less foreign than it would look in Arabic writing. This impression is further heightened by the placement of the word right after a more familiar English word. The fact that there is no translation may also make it difficult to identify the word as "a foreign word" in the first place.

"Kidneys habibi, do I have those?" is a question that Umayya asks in a phone conversation when ill and at the hospital. She contacts her brother in order to get some good advice, but is unable to remember what the right word for kidneys might be in Arabic. Umayya explains that her brother answers her in Arabic, but uses English vocabulary when he mentions medical terms or body parts. What she does not mention is the language she uses herself. Is it English, in order for the doctors and nurses, who might be present, to understand the conversation? Or is it Arabic, which apparently is the siblings' mutual language?

The minimal use of Arabic can be regarded as an adjustment to the prevalent language hierarchy, which favours languages other than Arabic. Yet it can also be seen as an important means by which *Sinut* portrays an immigrant life in which questions of ethnicity, origin and mother tongue are not foregrounded, and in which writing in Finnish, for the most part, becomes an act of empowerment and a sign of assimilation. As the example of "habibi" shows, the language use in *Sinut* is unpredictable. However, while Arabic is disguised or nearly absent and used only in a private context with family and friends, this does not apply to English. It is associated with the public sphere and considered as a language of wide, international dimensions. English is the language that really makes Abu-Hanna's life story multilingual, and it challenges the hegemony of Finnish as a self-evident language of Finnish literature.

Collisions with Language Borders – And Humour as an Attempt to Overcome Them

Most notably, English is visible through extensive jokes or anecdotes in *Sinut*. Tales such as "Arab hell" or "Basketball rules in Palestine", which are written in English, bring an international story repertoire into Abu-Hanna's work while also pointing to the global dimensions of racism. The story "Scene which took place on a British Airways flight between Johannesburg and London" (Abu-Hanna 2007, 112), which tells about an air hostess who gives a moral lesson to a woman because of her racist behaviour, circulates on the internet. In *Sinut*, it is located in the chapter that discusses how prejudices concerning race and religion are dealt with in popular culture and media at large, and how racism is part of the narrator's own life in Finland as well. Abu-Hanna recalls applying for a job as a reporter on cultural issues at the national broadcasting company in Finland. At the interview she is asked why she is interested in working as a reporter on culture and what kinds of programmes she would do. After her answers, the employer advises her to apply for a job at the programme called *Basaari*

(Bazaar), a show focussing on immigrant issues. Abu-Hanna's comment to this suggestion, by which she is excluded from the Finnish-speaking community, is laconic and charged with irony: "Fortunately I was reminded: 'You have forgotten your place, go into the box'"[13] (Abu-Hanna 2007, 116).

After living in Finland for twenty years, learning Finnish and pursuing academic studies, Abu-Hanna's language skills are still questioned. For example, she is not accepted as a reporter for TV programmes on topical issues, as she speaks Finnish with an accent. *Sinut* not only illuminates the problematic linguistic power relations from a migrant perspective, but also actively gives English an equal status as a literary language along with Finnish: English is never translated, neither in the form of extensive jokes nor sequences of English in dialogue.

For young Abu-Hanna, who has just arrived in Finland and does not yet know Finnish, English becomes an important language. It is the language that she uses for communication with the surrounding community, which, however, is represented in a rather monolingual light. While Abu-Hanna communicates in English, the neighbours and relatives, among others, speak Finnish. Their difficulties in meeting the newcomer are depicted in various scenes right at the beginning of *Sinut*. The narrator-protagonist's eagerness to get to know her new home country is often met with silence or racist comments.

The opening scene of *Sinut* reveals the strong relationship between whiteness and the Finnish language, setting the stage for the themes of racism that run through the story. The protagonist and narrator Abu-Hanna, whose name at that time is Maija Hänninen, is waiting to see the doctor. When he calls her, she arises from the chair, and by so doing she surprises the doctor:

> "Not your turn. You wait", the doctor says nervously [in English]. I return and sit down on the waiting room's children's chair, the kind which is used in this country for adults. "Maija Hänninen!" the same white coat shouts. I push my head down and purse my lips. I gather strength and walk again to the doctor. The doctor's face is angry now. "You wait. Not your turn. We have turn here." [in English] "I am Maija Hänninen." [in English][14]
> (Abu-Hanna 2007, 11)

The doctor's abrupt comment in English, "Not your turn. You wait", reveals not only that he assumes Abu-Hanna to be a non-Finnish-speaking person, but also that he does not expect a woman with a very Finnish name like Maija Hänninen to look like Umayya Abu-Hanna. He is confused, and he gets angry. The impression of the rude behaviour is further strengthened when his speech is represented in a way that does not include any kind of phrase of politeness.

The stiff language use of the doctor resembles that of a person who might talk to somebody who does not know the language. The language is simplified in order to aid the communication, but this kind of simplification can also be regarded as an insulting gesture. However, the conventional – or expected – power positions are destabilized as the doctor is the one whose language is represented as insufficient, not the newcomer. The representation, which foregrounds grammatical incorrectness and impoliteness, whittles away the authority of the doctor. He is the one who becomes emotionally involved in the situation, while Abu-Hanna stays calm. The overall impression of the scene is comic, and it is further strengthened when the doctor tries to maintain order by commanding the patient without any reason. The opening scene draws a sharp border between the Finnish doctor and the patient, who is linked with non-Finnishness, but from the protagonist-narrator's point of view, at least when recounting the event from a distance of many years, it does not seem to be a traumatic experience. Instead of a trauma narrative, the collisions with the language border are recalled in a humorous light. Humour is used to demonstrate the language border, but also to question it. The scene reveals an implicit expectation of whiteness connected to the Finnish language and challenges the idea that knowledge of Finnish language is required in order to become a true member of the community. Here Doris Sommer's idea about valuing failed communication and ignorance is put into practice. Play and laughter that bubbles out of mistakes are used to challenge linguistic power relations (Sommer 2004, xiv).

New Dimensions of Mother Tongue

For Sommer, creativity is the norm for language games and, as mentioned above, mistakes are also an important part:

> Mistakes can brighten speech with a rise of laughter [...] or give the pleasure of a found poem. Always, they mark communication with a cut or a tear that comes close to producing an aesthetic effect. The risk and thrill of speaking or writing anything can sting, every time language fails us.
>
> (Sommer 2004, xii)

When the protagonist Umayya Abu-Hanna is learning Finnish, she does not express any kind of embarrassment over her mistakes. For her, "haudutettu tee" ("steeped tea") is "haudattu tee" ("buried tea"), and instead of saying "kakku" ("cake") she says "kukka" ("flower"). Although her mistake of saying "pillu" ("cunt") when she means "pulla" ("bun") causes an awkward silence among her new relatives, the protagonist-narrator herself deals with the mistakes compassionately and with humour. What is strange and new for Abu-Hanna is presented as strange and new for the reader as well. Finnish language spoken by a newcomer, "broken Finnish", is introduced as a literary language and assigned a positive value.

The newcomer's language is present from the beginning alongside both standard Finnish and English. When in the beginning the narrator tells the story of how in Finland she has been turned into a new person, Maija Hänninen, she concludes the passage by saying: "So I am 'mamad Hänninen, I presume'"[15] (Abu-Hanna 2007, 10). The short sentence includes standard Finnish "joten olen" ("so I am"), incorrect Finnish "mamad" ("ruova" being the mispronounced and misspelt version of "rouva", the Finnish word for Madam), and English "I presume". Compared to the previous examples, such as "haudutettu" ("steeped") / "haudattu" ("buried"), the incorrect version of Madam does not imply a different meaning, as it is nonsensical. Although strange and grammatically incorrect, it is, however, understandable. Abu-Hanna explains how it took a year before she understood that she pronounces the word in a wrong way, and when portraying her first months in Finland the false spelling is repeated in the text. In this respect, Abu-Hanna's speech is not adapted into standard language. Moreover, the conclusion "So I am 'mamad Hänninen, I presume'" is, of course, an allusion to the explorer Henry Morton Stanley's famous words upon finding Dr Livingstone in Tanzania. Abu-Hanna thus positions herself as an explorer who is located in an unknown territory and making acquaintances with its inhabitants, the Finns.

Unpredictability and creativity in speaking Finnish are present when Abu-Hanna's mother once surprises her daughter by speaking it on the phone. She has learnt Finnish from a record, a Christmas gift from her daughter, which includes the famous Finnish Christmas song "Sika" (Swine) by the rock singer and songwriter Juice Leskinen:

"Listen!" Mother coughs and gets ready to speak Finnish. She lowers her voice and sucks her lips and mimics Juice: "Pig, nanana nananaa, pig."
"Merry Christmas Mum!"
"Bay, goddamn, elevator."
"Okay, okay mum, you speak brilliant Finnish. Hugs and kisses."[16]

(Abu-Hanna 2007, 82)

The mother seems to enjoy speaking Finnish. The way the language sounds, and how the language is realized, is foregrounded instead of grammar and the understanding of the meaning of the words. Most likely the mother does not understand a single word of the Finnish she is producing, but there does not seem to be a need for translation. The conversation between the mother and daughter echoes with laughter and connection: for a moment, Finnish is, literally, Umayya Abu-Hanna's mother tongue. Finnish becomes tied to affective and corporeal intimacy, natural kinship, which is closely linked with the concept of mother tongue. For Yasemin Yildiz, "mother tongue" is more than a metaphor, because it constitutes a condensed narrative about origin and identity through "mother", the first part of the term in "mother tongue" (Yildiz 2012, 10). At the same time that the conversation is brimming with closeness and enthusiasm, it is also loaded with irony. Umayya's line "Okay, okay Mum, you speak brilliant Finnish" is meant to be a fun, supportive comment for her mother, but it also points to a discourse where a person says one thing and means something else, while also invoking elements of hierarchy and judgement (see, e.g. Hutcheon [1994] 1995, 2, 17). It recalls the normative aspect embedded in language questions and the fact that language is not only a private matter; it is not one's own, as Jacques Derrida (1998) writes.

Yildiz places the concept of mother tongue at the heart of the monolingual paradigm, namely, practices by which "individuals and social formations are imagined to possess one 'true' language only, their mother tongue, and through this possession to be organically linked to an exclusive, demarcated ethnicity" (Yildiz 2012, 2). She emphasizes the role of disciplines and institutions in the linguistic socialization, which links the individual to the national collective in a way that stresses a static mode of belonging. Although "mother" in the concept of mother tongue stands for a unique, irreplaceable, unchangeable biological origin, this connotation is an outcome of different kinds of social practices, with historical roots especially in 19th-century nationalism (Yildiz 2012, 2, 9–10).

In the conversation between Umayya and her mother, the mother breaks down the expectation of sticking with Arabic, the actual "mother tongue". She dismantles the connection between language, birth and national belonging, and she gives Finnish the emotional function that is often attached to the concept of mother tongue. The ironic tone of the scene, however, indicates that the question of linguistic belonging is more complex than how it is performed in the dialogue. The emotional aspects of language and linguistic belonging are tightly linked with social dimensions, and this perspective is dealt with further in *Sinut*, when the narrator-protagonist writes about her brother's visit to Finland.

Artistic joy or the joy of becoming acquainted with a new language characterizes Umayya's brother's way of speaking Finnish when he visits Finland. Like his mother, he enjoys speaking the language of his sister's new homeland and invents his own way of communication. For example, he repeats single words and makes precise observations about the pronunciation. By speaking English and adding the letter "i" to the nouns his language resembles Finnish: "film" is "filmi", "bank" "pankki", "post" "posti", "kiosk" "kioski, "bus" "bussi", "restaurant" "restaurantti" and "food" "fuuti" (Abu-Hanna 2007, 196). Adding an "i" to the end of an English or Swedish word is a relatively common way of word formation in Finnish, but, in the cases of "restaurantti" and "fuuti", the result is not a proper Finnish word. These unorthodox forms serve as a reminder of the creative potential of language and of the fact that standard forms of a language are a result of conventions and common agreements, not "natural" laws.

Umayya comments on her brother's language use are laconic: "Sister has to make guesses every day, when mister 'speaks Finnish'"[17] (Abu-Hanna 2007, 196). The word "mister", referring to Umayya's brother, creates a feeling of distance and hierarchy between the two, even if the tone is certainly also warm and playful. It is as if Umayya would have difficulties understanding the kind of Finnish her brother speaks and that she would consider his language use as not only improper, but arrogant, haughty and excluding. Her attitude resembles that of the Finns she met when she herself was a newcomer. There seems to be not much space left for language play. Ironically, her attitude can be interpreted as a sign of her becoming, finally, a true Finnish citizen. She clearly signals that she knows the border drawn between normative and non-normative language and how to react to this kind of language use.

The depiction of Umayya's brother's language learning entails humoristic dimensions. The brother is presented as a cheerful fellow who is more interested in discovering "the rules" of the language on his own than through grammar books or language teachers. In the end, the narrator's attitude towards innovative language experiments is two-sided. While Umayya makes it clear that she knows her brother's language is improper, she does not correct it. Instead, she adopts some of his favourite words. When the brother has left, in her longing she parrots the phrase "hullu hissi" ("crazy elevator") (Abu-Hanna 2007, 197). Here, as in the conversation between Umayya and her mother, the humoristic use of Finnish strengthens the bonds between the family members, and it underlines the cultural connection that exists between language and family ties, especially through the concept of mother tongue. At the same time, it is evident that the emotional relations that Umayya and her family have with the Finnish language do not pave the way for inclusion in Finnish society, as their common language lacks social legitimacy. The humour marks a sharp border between the private and public worlds, but also signals a demand for a change of attitudes towards interpretations of questions about language and belonging.

Conclusions

Umayya Abu-Hanna's autobiographical work *Sinut* is a migrant story that discusses the importance of mastering the language of the new home country. The main language of *Sinut* is Finnish, but there is a tendency to contest its central position as a literary language. Especially in the beginning of the story, when the narrative centres on Umayya's first experiences in Finland, English is explicitly present in the dialogue. For a newcomer, English is an important language for communication, but also later in the story, when a global repertoire of jokes and stories are woven into Abu-Hanna's life story, English is used. The English elements are never translated into Finnish, reflecting an effort to make English equal with Finnish as a literary language.

Elaboration and play with the concept of mother tongue are also a means of questioning the conventional relationship between the nation and its languages. Arabic, the mother tongue of the protagonist-narrator in *Sinut*, has importance for her, but it is not foregrounded or explicitly present in the narrative. Instead of Arabic, Finnish is highlighted. It is connected to Abu-Hanna's work and everyday life in Finland, and also to close family relations, and thus it is given a status usually reserved for the mother tongue. From the protagonist's point of view, the Finnish that her mother and brother use fulfils both kinship requirements and the emotional ties often connected with the mother tongue, but from a larger perspective, their language does not meet the standards that are set for normative language use and for the mother tongue.

The story foregrounds the narrator-protagonist's efforts to meet the required language standards in Finnish, but the border between her language use and the norm remains clear. Yet the protagonist's collisions with the language border are addressed through humour, and humour thus becomes an important means by which the language norms of the nation-state are questioned. By giving space to the newcomer's language, which is characterized by mispronunciation and misunderstanding, *Sinut* destabilizes a clear-cut border and hierarchy between standard Finnish and non-standard Finnish. It uses humour as a means to convey, on the one hand, the protagonist-migrant's critical attitude towards nation-states and their stiff language norms, and, on the other hand, her need to define her position in the community on her own terms. *Sinut* combines autobiographical writing with a playful and humoristic style. While widening the language repertoire of Finnish literature, it shows that the protagonist and writer Umayya Abu-Hanna has the ability to simultaneously meet the language norms and enter the literary field as a Finnish-language writer.

Notes

1 *Sinut* is the accusative form of the pronoun *sinä* ("you"), and it also is a noun which refers to a kind of state of mind: you are not only familiar with something, but you feel comfortable as well.
2 Among the above-mentioned authors could also be included Eija Hetekivi-Olsson, a Swedish author who debuted with the novel *Ingenbarnsland* (2012; No land for children), a story of a second-generation Finnish immigrant named Miira. *Ingenbarnsland* was received with enthusiasm and nominated for the Swedish August Prize (see Melkas 2018). Hetekivi-Olsson

connects the migrant theme to a new type of language with its own kind of vocabulary and grammatical rules. Especially in *Miira* (2016), the sequel to *Ingenbarnsland*, the protagonist refuses to adopt a position on the margins of society, a position she feels she is forced into because of her family background and language skills, and her language use echoes the same attitude.

3 "Sinuiksi itsensä kanssa päästään asettumalla itsensä ulkopuolelle, olemalla itselleen toinen. Suomen kielellä tasapainon tilan on kauniisti ilmaistu.

Tämä kirja kertoo elämästä Suomessa 1980-luvun alusta lähtien ja kattaa Suomen itsenäisyyden historiasta noin kolmanneksen. Se on yhden siirtolaisen kautta käsiteltyä elämää ja tarkoitettu luettavaksi juuri sellaisena. Antakaa anteeksi ylilyönnit ja muistakaa, että minäkin olen vain ihminen, vaikka olenkin suomalainen.

Kirja on kooste elämästä, päiväkirjamerkinnöistä, kirjeenvaihdosta, luennoista ja kolumneista. Lue sitä kuten haluat."

4 "Suomessa ei tanssita."
5 "ja se tekee arabin aivan surullisen kipeäksi."
6 Tornedalians are a small minority in Northern Sweden, living in the border area of Sweden and Finland.
7 "Umayya, eli nykyään Maija H., asuu miehensä kanssa Teräskadulla Naantalissa."
8 "Voin puhua äidinkieltäni heti aamusta! Istumme keittiön pirttipöydän penkeillä ja avaamme äidin tuomat Za'atar-purkit (seesaminsiementen ja oreganon sekoitusta). Olen leiponut palmikkoleivän jonka reseptin löysin *Kotiliedestä*. Suu täynnä ruokaa puhumme lähekkäin ja nauramme."
9 "Kaikki tuntuu niin tutulta. Aurinko ja äidinkieli."
10 "Itken ja huomaan huokaisseeni arabiaksi. Ja kieli lohduttaa."
11 "Nautin koukeroista hetken, sitten sukellan. On uusia nimiä, uusia termejä, uutta slangia ja keksintöjä, mutta pian unohdan kielen ja olen tunne- ja älytasolla mukana."
12 "Minulla on kursori oikealla ja toinen vasemmalla."
13 "Onneksi muistutettiin: 'Olet unohtanut paikkasi, mene lokeroon.'"
14 "'Not your turn. You wait', lääkäri sanoo hermostuneena. Palaan takaisin ja istun odotushuoneen lastentuoliin jota tässä maassa käytetään aikuisille. 'Maija Hänninen!' huutaa sama valkoinen takki. Painan pään alas ja mutristan huuleni. Kerään voimia ja kävelen taas lääkärin eteen. Lääkärin ilme on nyt vihainen. 'You wait. Not your turn. We have turn here.' 'I am Maija Hänninen.'"
15 "Joten olen 'ruova Hänninen I presume.'"
16 "'Kuuntele!' Äiti yskii ja valmistautuu puhumaan suomea. Hän madaltaa äänensä ja suipistaa huulensa ja matkii Juicea: 'Sika, nanana nananaa, sika.'

'Hyvää joulua äiti.'
'Lahti, jumalautanen, hissi.'
'Joo joo äiti, puhut loistavaa suomea. Pus hali.'"

17 "Sisko joutuu joka päivä arvailemaan, kun herra 'puhuu suomea.'"

Bibliography

Abu-Hanna, Umayya (2007) *Sinut*. Helsinki: WSOY.
Behschnitt, Wolfgang (2013) The Rhythm of Hip Hop: Multi-Ethnic Slang in Swedish Literature after 2000. In Wolfgang Behschnitt, Sarah De Mul & Liesbeth Minnaard (eds): *Literature, Language, and Multiculturalism in Scandinavia and the Low Countries*. Amsterdam & New York: Rodopi, 175–195.

Behschnitt, Wolfgang & Nilsson, Magnus (2013) "Multicultural Literatures" in a Comparative Perspective. In Wolfgang Behschnitt, Sarah De Mul & Liesbeth Minnaard (eds): *Literature, Language, and Multiculturalism in Scandinavia and the Low Countries*. Amsterdam & New York: Rodopi, 1–15.
Derrida, Jacques (1998) *Monolingualism of the Other, Or, The Prosthesis of Origin*. Translated by Patrick Mensah. Stanford: Stanford University Press.
Doloughan, Fiona J. (2016) *English as a Literature in Translation*. New York, London, Oxford, New Delhi & Sydney: Bloomsbury.
Grönstrand, Heidi (2019) "Joo joo äiti. Puhut loistavaa suomea". Maahanmuutto, kieli ja valta 2000-luvun suomalaisissa romaaneissa. In Elina Arminen & Markku Lehtimäki (eds): *Muistikirja ja matkalaukku. 2000-luvun suomalaisen romaanin muotoja ja merkityksiä*. Helsinki: Suomalaisen Kirjallisuuden Seura. (Forthcoming.)
Heith, Anne (2009) Voicing Otherness in Postcolonial Sweden: Bengt Pohjanen's Deconstruction of Hegemonic Ideas of Cultural Identity. In Vesa Haapala, Hannamari Helander, Anna Hollsten, Pirjo Lyytikäinen & Rita Paqvalén (eds): *The Angel of History: Literature, History and Culture*. Helsinki: University of Helsinki, 140–147.
Hirvonen, Vuokko ([1999] 2008) *Voices from Sápmi: Sámi Women's Path to Authorship*. Translated by Kaija Anttonen. Kautokeino: DAT.
Hutcheon, Linda ([1994] 1995) *Irony's Edge: The Theory and Politics of Irony*. London: Taylor and Francis. Available from: ProQuest Ebook Central. Accessed November 8, 2017.
Hyvärinen, Anna-Riitta & Mäki, Tuija (2014) *Elämäkertoja ja elämäkerrallisia teoksia*. Helsinki: Avain.
Karpinsky, Eva C. (2012) *Borrowed Tongues: Life Writing, Migration and Translation*. Waterloo, ON: Wilfrid Laurier University Press.
Kellman, Steven (2009) Translingual Memoirs of the New American Immigration. *Scritture Migranti* 3, 19–32.
Kosonen, Päivi (2000) *Elämät sanoissa. Eletty ja kerrottu epäjatkuvuus Sarrauten, Durasin, Robbe-Grillet'n ja Perecin omaelämäkerrallissa teksteissä*. Helsinki: Tutkijaliitto.
Leonard, Peter (2013) Bi- and Multicultural Aspects in the Literary Writing of Translingual Authors in Sweden. In Wolfgang Behschnitt, Sarah De Mul & Liesbeth Minnaard (eds): *Literature, Language, and Multiculturalism in Scandinavia and the Low Countries*. Amsterdam & New York: Rodopi, 149–174.
Löytty, Olli (2015) Immigrant Literature in Finland: The Uses of a Literary Category. In Ann-Sofie Lönngren, Heidi Grönstrand, Dag Heede & Anne Heith (eds): *Rethinking National Literatures and the Literary Canon in Scandinavia*. Newcastle upon Tyne: Cambridge Scholars Publishing, 52–75.
Melkas, Kukku (2018) Literature and Children in-between – The Entangled History of Finland and Sweden in Susanna Alakoski's *Svinalängorna*, Klaus Härö's *Mother of Mine* and *Ingenbarnsland*. In Satu Gröndahl & Eila Rantonen (eds): *Migrants and Literature in Finland and Sweden*. Helsinki: Finnish Literary Society, 83–96.
Melkas, Kukku & Löytty, Olli (2016) Sekoittuneita ääniä. Johanna Holmströmin *Asfaltänglar* ja lomittuvat lukemiskontekstit. In Heidi Grönstrand, Ralf Kauranen, Olli Löytty, Kukku Melkas, Hanna-Leena Nissilä & Mikko

Pollari (eds): *Kansallisen katveesta. Suomen kirjallisuuden ylirajaisuudesta.* Helsinki: Suomalaisen Kirjallisuuden Seura, 118–138.

Nilsson, Magnus (2013) Literature in Multicultural and Multilingual Sweden: The Birth and Death of the Immigrant Writer. In Wolfgang Behschnitt, Sarah De Mul & Liesbeth Minnaard (eds): *Literature, Language, and Multiculturalism in Scandinavia and the Low Countries.* Amsterdam & New York: Rodopi, 41–61.

Nissilä, Hanna-Leena (2016) *"Sanassa maahanmuuttaja on vähän kitkerä jälkimaku". Kirjallisen elämän ylirajaistuminen 2000-luvun alun Suomessa.* Oulu: Oulun yliopisto.

Nissilä, Hanna-Leena & Rantonen, Eila (2013) Kansainvälistyvä kirjailijakunta. In Mika Hallila, Yrjö Hosiaisluoma, Sanna Karkulehto, Leena Kirstinä & Jussi Ojajärvi (eds): *Suomen nykykirjallisuus 2. Kirjallinen elämä ja yhteiskunta.* Helsinki: Suomalaisen Kirjallisuuden Seura, 55–71.

Pearce, Lynne (2010) Beyond Redemption? Mobilizing Affect in Feminist Reading. In Marianne Liljeström & Susanna Paasonen (eds): *Working with Affect in Feminist Readings: Disturbing Differences.* London & New York: Routledge, 151–164.

Rantonen, Eila (2010) Maahanmuuttajat ja kirjallisuus Suomessa ja Ruotsissa. In Eila Rantonen (ed.): *Vähemmistöt ja monikulttuurisuus kirjallisuudessa.* Tampere: Tampere University Press, 163–191.

Seyhan, Azade (2001) *Writing Outside the Nation.* Princeton & Oxford: Princeton University Press.

Smith, Sidonie & Watson, Julia (2000) *Reading Autobiography: A Guide for Interpreting Life Narratives.* Minneapolis & London: University of Minnesota Press.

Sommer, Doris (2004) *Bilingual Aesthetics: A New Sentimental Education.* Durham & London: Duke University.

Vallenius, Erkki (1998) *Kansankodin kuokkavieraat. II maailmansodan jälkeen Ruotsiin muuttaneet suomalaiset kaunokirjallisuuden kuvaamina.* Helsinki: Suomalaisen Kirjallisuuden Seura.

Wanner, Adrian (2015) Writing the Translingual Life: Recent Memoirs and Auto-Fiction by Russian-American and Russian–German Novelists. *L2Journal* 7, 141–151. Accessed August 2, 2017, http://escholarship.org/uc/item/85t9d1xh.

Yildiz, Yasemin (2012) *Beyond the Mother Tongue: The Postmonolingual Condition.* New York: Fordham University Press.

8 An Author's View
To Be a Bridge between Cultures

Zinaida Lindén

In the contemporary literature of Finland, I am often called an immigrant writer. Such characters are still rare in Finland, though the number is increasing.

Since my literary debut in 1996 I have written seven books, three novels and four collections of short stories. I write in two languages: Swedish (one of the two official languages of Finland) and Russian (my mother tongue). I regard both versions, the Swedish and the Russian, as my original texts. I publish my novels and short stories in both languages, and others have translated my work into additional languages: Finnish, Danish, Croatian, English and German.

My first book, a collection of short stories, *Överstinnan och syntetisatorn* (The colonel's wife and the synthesizer), appeared in Swedish in Helsinki in 1996. My second book, *Scheherazades sanna historier* (The true stories of Scheherazade), appeared in Swedish in 2000. In 2003, it was also published in Russian in Moscow as *Подлинные истории Шахразады* (Podlinnye istorii Shahrazady). So far, five of my seven books have also appeared in Russian.

My basic identity is connected to my home city, Leningrad/Saint Petersburg. On my father's side I can count many generations of the city's natives, dating back to the 1860s. My mother's side has lived there since the 1930s.

There were some features of multilingualism in my upbringing. Since early childhood I have been exposed to foreign languages and cultures. I was not brought up bilingual, but my mother (who had been taught English by a native speaker) used to read English books to me, mainly nursery rhymes and fairy tales. This resulted in my learning to read both in Russian and in English when I was five.

I am well acquainted with Russian classic literature, but in our home, as well as in many other homes in Leningrad, we regarded even foreign classics as our own. Ever since I can remember I have been an ardent reader. I have no formal education in creative writing. The books and authors I have read throughout my life have been my teachers. I still like to reread some old favourites. I go back to them as other people return to their homes.

English was taught at my school. At that time, children could study only one foreign language in Soviet schools. When I was sixteen I also studied some French, privately. I was strongly motivated and learned how to speak French in half a year. Sadly enough, I have never had an opportunity to proceed with my French studies, but I remember some basic grammar, and I can still recite some poems by Alfred de Musset. At the age of twelve, I also learned from my Polish relatives how to speak Polish.

As a child I loved languages. I still do.

*

In 1981, I entered the Philological Faculty of Leningrad University. My major was Swedish and Swedish literature. I also studied English and Danish. The subject of my diploma thesis was Selma Lagerlöf's Ring trilogy (1925–1928; *The Löwensköld Ring, Charlotte Löwensköld, Anna Svärd*).

During my university years, I travelled widely around the former Soviet Union, working as a tourist guide, translator and interpreter. I led many journeys with Scandinavian and English-speaking tourist groups to Central Asia, the Caucasus and other places.

At that time, most Soviet students had no opportunity to study abroad. I was no exception. My knowledge of Swedish is a product of my university studies and extensive reading, as well as my vast experiences as a guide and interpreter. When it comes to expression, Swedish became a language of my feelings during my journeys with tourists around the former Soviet Union. As a university student, I used to read a lot of Swedish literature, magazines and newspapers, but it was through interaction with people that I acquired knowledge of Swedish on a deeper emotional level. I was young and perceptive, and some of those journeys were quite dramatic. I made friends and fell in love.

In 1987–1990, I worked at the Film Department of Leningrad State Institute of Theatre, Music and Cinematography, nowadays the Russian State Institute of Performing Arts. The subject of my research were films by Ingmar Bergman and Andrei Tarkovsky. My film studies influenced me profoundly as a person and as a prosaist.

*

In the beginning of the 1990s, I married a young Swedish-speaking physicist from Finland and moved to the Helsinki region. We moved to Turku in 1995, because of my husband's work. In 1999–2000, we lived in Japan, in Yokohama and Tokyo. Since then we have visited Japan frequently. For me, the Kanto area (which includes Yokohama and Tokyo) feels like one of my homes.

I wrote my first short story in the winter of 1993/1994, shortly after giving birth to my first child. My first two books were never translated into Finnish, but they got positive reviews in the Finnish press, and my persona aroused some interest in the media.

In the 1990s, I also translated some prose and poetry by several Finnish authors who write in Swedish into Russian: Monika Fagerholm, Kjell Westö, Claes Andersson, and Martin Enckell.

Before I had my second child I had been teaching Russian literature and translation at Åbo Akademi, the Swedish language university in Turku. Later, I would deliver lectures on the cultural history of Saint Petersburg, on Russian urban folklore and on contemporary Russian cinema.

As a translator I have mostly focussed on historic literature. I have translated two books by Professor Henrik Meinander of Helsinki University from Swedish into Russian: *Finlands historia/ История Финляндии* (A history of Finland) and *Finland 1944/ Финляндия 1944 год* (Finland 1944). I would like to believe that these books are important for the bilateral contacts and mutual understanding between Finland and Russia. Books on history give me balance and tools in my daily interaction with the complicated issues of the relationships of our countries. Such books also provide inspiration for me as a publicist.

In 2017, my colleague Eleonora Joffe and I published the anthology *Голос женщины* (The woman's voice) in Saint Petersburg, comprised of our translations into Russian of a number of female poets of Finland. Joffe translated from Finnish and I translated from Swedish. We wrote the introduction together.

Besides fiction, I have been writing newspaper columns, reviews and essays in the Swedish language press of Finland for many years. Since 2001, I have worked as a columnist at *Hufvudstadsbladet*, the main Swedish language newspaper in Finland, and also as a film critic at *Åbo Underrättelser* and *Ny Tid*. I have also published numerous essays in magazines such as *Nya Argus* and *Finsk Tidskrift*. Recently I wrote some reviews of my Russian colleagues' books (e.g. in *Nezavisimaya Gazeta*).

*

Since my years as a student, I have dreamed of becoming a living bridge between cultures and nations. When I was nineteen, I followed this urge by beginning to work as a tour guide and interpreter. Today I am a member of two writers' unions: the Society of Swedish Authors in Finland and the Saint Petersburg Writers' Union. The Finnish-speaking majority in Finland considers me not only a representative of the Russian minority but also a representative of the Swedish-speaking population.

*

Metaphorically speaking, there are many floating bridges around us in our everyday life. A foreign language is such a floating bridge. In my case, many circumstances were complicated. I moved to Finland at the age of twenty-seven, possessing very good knowledge of Swedish, but in my situation it was difficult to get a job. I had a great deal of experience and competence, but in Finland I was hardly able to use my translator's skills, partly because I could not compete with the numerous translators who were perfect in Finnish and Russian, partly due to the absence of necessary contacts. I understood that I would not be able to compete in the translators' market. Nonetheless, I tried hard to get some work. I took four Finnish language courses at the University of Helsinki. I got through the "pieni kielikoe", the basic Finnish language test, but I was realistic about my situation: since I did not speak Finnish at home (my husband is Swedish-speaking), and I could not even get a job at McDonald's, there was no way for me to develop my Finnish to a more advanced level.

A year after moving to Finland, I passed the official state translator's exam in Swedish and Russian. Today I am an authorized translator in Finland with this combination of languages. Sometimes I get some assignments, like translating official documents from Swedish into Russian or interpreting for a court in one of the regions where Swedish predominates.

Finnish is not one of my working languages, but I like it and I would love to know it better. I have a large Finnish vocabulary, but my Finnish grammar is not sufficient. Sometimes I have to use English in my everyday life. I have never lived in any of the regions in Finland where you can get by with Swedish.

On a professional level, my unusual language situation can cause some problems. Almost all the other Swedish-speaking authors of Finland speak fluent Finnish, since they have studied it from their early childhood. Five of my books have been translated into Finnish, and I proofread all of these and commented on them before they were published. Since my knowledge of Finnish is rather passive, I am not able to deliver writer's lectures in Finnish. But when I meet my Finnish-speaking readers, I always have a good connection with them. I cannot read advanced fiction in Finnish, but Finnish rock and pop songs are of huge importance to me. They are a source of inspiration, and sometimes they define the rhythm of my prose.

*

My sense of otherness has much to do with some identity issues. I did not learn Swedish, my second working language, in my new country of residence. I brought it with me from my home country. I have a strong bond to Saint Petersburg and I spend a great deal of time there. In addition, the Swedish writers of Finland usually have a strong national identity.

It is often connected with their environment and characterized by their life circumstances: closeness to the Baltic Sea, the beauty of the local nature, the somewhat contradictory relationship between Finns and Swedes, and the variety of Swedish dialects of Finland. For me, writing in Swedish is not a question of national identity, it is just one way to tell a story – a story that can use any environment as a starting point. Telling a story is more important for me than telling it in a specific language.

Nevertheless, I also have a strong bond to Swedish. After many years I still love and admire it. Figuratively speaking, I have been married to the Swedish language since the age of seventeen, when I began my university studies. Swedish has become a part of me, almost physically. The protagonist/narrator in my novel *I väntan på en jordbävning* (Waiting for an earthquake), Ivan Demidov, an internationally acclaimed Soviet weightlifter, is in some ways a metaphor of my career as a writer. Demidov can hardly remember what his life was like before he developed his muscles. I can hardly remember myself not knowing Swedish. "I am no superstar", Demidov says, "I am but driftwood floating on the current."

*

How do I write in two languages, Swedish and Russian? It is a sensitive subject. Usually I avoid it. Maybe because I am afraid of disappointing my readers. Maybe because I do not wish to define myself as a representative of any national literature. I really believe that the essence of my writing is the narrative – and building bridges between people.

When asked about my method, I feel like Stefan Högl from my epistolary novel *Takakirves – Tokyo* (in the Russian version *По обе стороны*). He is a mathematician and an illusionist. At the end, when Högl is about to get married and he is supposed to let his friends meet his somewhat secretive mother, he feels as if all his tricks are going to be revealed.

Most often, when I am writing a first draft, I use both Russian and Swedish (but seldom in the same phrase), and sometimes even fragments of English, Finnish, Polish, Japanese, and so on (if I have to quote some songs or poems). Then I usually make two versions of my text. In some cases I have written the whole first draft in Russian or only in Swedish, depending on the subject, but more often I combine these languages. I thus operate both as an author and as a translator. My method is tricky, time-consuming and rather difficult to explain. It has its pros and cons.

*

Concerning the advantages: I am not a translator of someone else's work, I do not have to stick slavishly to the "original". I can always make amendments in the "original", and I can transform both versions in a way that suits my purposes.

An obvious advantage is my ability to address my readers directly in Swedish and in Russian during book fairs, public readings, author talks, discussions, interviews and other events. In addition, Norwegians and Danes are able to read my books in Swedish, since their languages are similar to it (my latest book, *Valenciana*, has also been translated into Danish). There are many Russian-speaking people in the US, Israel and the Baltic countries, which gives me an opportunity to widen my audience, for example, through libraries.

There are also some difficulties. One of my main problems is that the cultural references of my readers are not the same. My Scandinavian readers have different life experiences than my Russian readers. Many facts of history, culture and everyday life that are obvious to most Russian readers are not necessarily known to a foreign audience. And vice versa. Specific allusions (i.e. bonds of culture between people of the same origin or similar experiences) sometimes say nothing to a foreign audience. An example is my frequent reference to a pair of my favourite Russian authors, including quotes from Ilya Ilf and Yevgeniy Petrov, whose satiric books enjoy great popularity among Russian speakers.

In my novel *För manga länder sedan* (Many countries ago), there is a mention of the Badayev warehouses. Anyone born and raised in my home city knows what I mean. Most Russians do not need any explanation: the Badayev warehouses are found in many books and in songs (e.g. in a song by Vladimir Vysotsky). In other countries, the Badayev warehouses are known only to historians. Used to store food in pre-war Leningrad, at the beginning of the siege in 1941 they were bombed by the Germans and burned – one of the reasons of famine during the war.

In one of my short stories, a severe Finnish policeman asks the main character: "Varför ler du som ett Hangökex?" ("Why are you smiling like a Hanko cookie?") Most people in Finland know this round cookie with a smiling face printed on it, but the expression says nothing to a Russian reader.

Not even a well-educated Russian reader can imagine the specific language situation in Finland and how it exactly works (or does not work). Some details and allusions have to be sacrificed. I am used to it.

My third country is Japan, and since I often use Japan as a literary environment, some words and details can be a challenge for both my Russian and my Scandinavian readers.

The difficulty of translating idioms is obvious. Sometimes there is a good idiomatic expression in my Swedish version, but it is not always possible to find an equally good Russian idiom.

In the title story of my collection of short stories *Lindanserskan* (The tightrope walker), there is an episode where the female narrator remembers being molested as a child by a stranger while her unsuspecting grandparents are enjoying the summer day in the park. The man asked them if he could play badminton with the little girl, and they "gave him a free hand" (in Swedish "gav honom fria händer"). In Russian there is no similar idiom, so in the Russian edition I had to write that they "gave their consent".

Alliteration is important to me. In my novel *Takakirves – Tokyo* (in Russian: "По обе стороны"), there is an episode where I use the visual similarity of Foster (a surname) and *foster* (which means "embryo" in Swedish): "Jag är inte längre Jodie Foster. Jag är ett foster." ("I am no longer Jodie Foster. I am an embryo.") This detail is lost in my Russian version of the novel published by *Novyi Mir* magazine, as well as in the Finnish translation. Another example is my heroine's dilemma, if she should sit by her toddler's bed or continue working on her writing: "min dotter"/ "min dator" ("my daughter"/ "my computer"). In both cases it is impossible to recreate the alliteration.

In my short story "I bergakungens sal" (In the hall of the mountain king), the female main character feels attraction to a hotel owner who goes by the nickname of The Mountain King. Here I use some allusions to Edward Grieg's music and to Thomas Mann's novel *Magic Mountain* (in Swedish *Bergtagen*, literally "taken by the mountain"). "Bergtagen" is also an idiom in Swedish, meaning "spellbound". The heroine is "bergtagen av en sådan karl" ("spellbound by this sort of man"). In the Russian version, *berg* ("mountain") disappears.

There are many examples of the contrary. Some matters are obvious to Russian speakers, but not known to my foreign readers. For example, the name of the Finnish town Huittinen sounds indecent to Russian speakers; this detail has to be explained to foreigners, or else the comic effect is lacking.

Song lyrics are important to me. In "Esperal", a short story with two narrators, there are some embedded quotes from "Från Djursholm till Danvikstull" (From Djursholm to Danvikstull), a song by the Swedish singer Orup. In two of my short stories I use basically the same ending, a quote from a hit by the Russian singer Maxim Leonidov.

*

Another source of inspiration to me is cinema. One episode in which the narrator dreams about being Jodie Foster is derived from *The Silence of the Lambs* (dir. by Jonathan Demme, 1991). The language of the film is one of the most powerful languages on Earth. It is a real floating bridge – actually, a language more powerful and more international than literature. Literature needs good translators. It loses its strength if translators are poorly educated or careless. But a film can also work if the translation of its dialogue is poor, because of the specific language of images. Sometimes it is possible to get a strong impression of a film, even if you do not understand the language it is made in.

I remember a trip with a group of Swedish tourists to North Ossetia. One of my Swedish tourists, a man from Kumla, did not understand any language but Swedish. Once he told me that he and one of his fellow travellers had visited a local cinema. I was astonished when he told me, quite convincingly, the plot of the Soviet film he had seen there. I was able to recognize it: it was "Человек-невидимка" (1984, The Invisible Man) directed by Alexander Zakharov. I remember that Swedish man from Kumla warmly, because he made an effort to understand something totally unknown to him, to cross a border. Such things can give you an opportunity to use your imagination. This point, making an effort, has become scarce in our modern attitude, when we view ourselves as consumers and expect to be spoon-fed.

*

A question I often hear is: "Are you able to write only in Russian? Or only in Swedish?" The answer is yes. I have written columns, essays and film reviews only in Swedish. I am able to do the same in Russian. I have written some columns for a Russian-language paper in Tallinn.

Another aspect is a question of translation. I cannot imagine my works being translated from Swedish into Russian or vice versa by someone else. But it has happened a couple of times. In my eyes, the results were disastrous. Twice I had to stop the publication of such translations. Maybe my attitude is wrong, but if I see a Russian text with my name on it, it has to be my own Russian, my way of expressing myself. It is about integrity. It is the same with my Swedish. I am quite possessive when it comes to such matters.

I know other authors who are like me. Some of my Swedish-speaking colleagues in Finland tell me that their Finnish translators sometimes become angry with them, since the authors are never happy with their Finnish translations. They would like to change every phrase in the Finnish translation of their works. Many Swedish prosaists in Finland know Finnish at a very advanced level and are even able to write fiction in Finnish.

There are some differences in the perception of my books in Finland and in Russia. An example is my epistolary novel *Takakirves – Tokyo*. In Finland, it has mainly been read as a contribution to the discussion on identity, since many people in Finland (especially Swedish-speaking readers) are accustomed to that kind of debate. In Russia, my novel attracted attention as a depiction of customs and manners in Finland and in Japan; the details of everyday life in these two countries were the most interesting aspect for my Russian readers, while the identity debate was hardly noticed there.

Although some details are inevitably "lost in translation", something else is gained instead. As a bilingual writer, I represent Finland in Russia and many things Russian abroad. I have reinvented the word "we", and I use it in more than one sense. Win or lose, I have been fortunate to be able to walk through life on a tightwire, using my writing as a balancing pole. One of my collections of short stories is actually called *Lindanserskan* (The tightrope walker).

9 The Pilot's Son (Short Story)
Zinaida Lindén
Translated by Eric Dickens

Of all places on this Earth he liked hotels best.
Staying at a hotel was being on a visit, travelling through. Hotels were a no-man's-land, a terra nullius. And yet they were populated. Hotels were never deserted.
Staying at a hotel was a homecoming. Here he could set himself at zero, delete his history. It was like being born anew.
Once arrived at some hotel or other he felt rest and peace in his soul, as if someone had pulled a thorn out of it. He especially liked semicircular buildings such as Hotel Cosmos in Moscow. Russia was foreign to him, yet the Cosmos felt like an open embrace.
There are people who are struck with anxiety if they have to stay at a hotel. They feel isolated. They call it a soulless environment. With him it was otherwise. It was at hotels that he felt secure. Nothing bad could happen to him there. Even if there was a fire. He always made sure that he had checked the emergency exits.
Hotels were places you could dream yourself away to. When he was at his one-roomed flat in Kallio he often longed to be staying at some hotel or other. During one period things got so far that he would travel to a city simply to be able to stay at a hotel which the *Condé Nast Traveler* magazine had declared to be the best in that hotel chain.
When the Eyjafjallajökull volcano paralysed the airspace above Northern Europe, he stayed for five nights in Budapest. He loved his exile existence. During the day, he and the other cabin crew would volunteer as knowledge base for stranded travellers. In the evenings he would sit around in his hotel room wearing terry cloth slippers and watch news bulletins. On the hotel radio, the Charlatans whispered seductively:

> You're so pretty, we're so pretty
> Call me anywhere
> I don't have a care
> This is my world

He couldn't understand celebrities that made demands on hotels: that the fridge should have a glass door, that the furniture should be covered with colourful loose covers, that the staff should provide light that smelt newly baked or fill the lavatory with mineral water.

People would swear about the hotel breakfast, but he liked it. He even liked those strange works of art that would decorate hotel rooms. He has even bought one such painting and hung it in his one-roomed flat in Kallio. The flat was twenty-five and a half square metres in area. The bathroom was as cramped as that of an aircraft. The shower was located right above the toilet seat. The wash basin looked like a soap dish.

The rest of the cabin crew accepted him. He was a trustworthy colleague. Behind his back they would call him the Door-Locker. When the flight was over he didn't want to join the rest of them, but would make straight for his hotel room and turned the key in the lock. But no one knew that he would take photos of his room before he threw himself on the newly made bed. However, when he checked out, he didn't take any photos. He just cast a last glance over his shoulder and shut the door.

Between flights, the rest would often go to a nightclub. Some would drink a lot. They lived a quiet life back home and were in search of adventure when abroad. They knew exactly where to shop for this or that: men's shirts and golf clubs in Tokyo, Uggs in all the colours of the rainbow in Sydney, sausage and orange marmalade in Mallorca.

He didn't look for excitement. He simply loved hotels. As opposed to the rest, he didn't use the hotel gym. Now and again, he would take a swim in the hotel pool. That gave him a feeling of seclusion.

He didn't want to start life all over again. He simply wanted to free himself of the pressure to start living. He had never experienced anything tragic. He had never lost anyone close to him. Nor had he rescued anyone from a burning building. He had just been born different, with an intensive need for seclusion. That's what monks sometimes become. Presupposing that they believe in God. But he had been brought up in a secular family.

The boy turned out to be insufferable.

"Mummy says I shouldn't talk with anyone, except those in uniform", – was what he would babble as they were passing passport control. "So I thought of talking to you!"

"Of course you can do so. But we are twelve people on board. The one who is free at the time can come and talk to you."

"But I want to talk only with you!"

"And why is that?"

"Because I already know you."

All the lad knew was his name: Henrik Lappalainen. He asked for it immediately.

The boy's mother's large face, especially her pinkish, porous skin, made you think of pork luncheon meat, the ham in a can that Henrik had got as a child when there was no one at home. She spoke pidgin Finnish and hesitated after every word. The boy spoke Finnish without an accent, but in a slightly odd way, as if trying to imitate someone from an American blockbuster movie.

While Henrik was looking at his travel documents the boy made rude faces at his little sister. She had straight flaxen hair. Her skin was a little pink, just like her mother's. The little girl was wriggling about in her pram and covered her eyes with her hands. Her small face screwed up in irritation. In the end she managed to get hold of the blue plastic pocket with the letters UM printed on it, i.e., Unaccompanied Minor, that her big brother had around his neck. She tugged angrily at the plastic pocket. The tape was a strong one, but the woman became nervous and started shouting at the little girl.

Henrik looked at the woman's address in the boy's document. They lived in Lahti. In order to take her son to Helsinki Vantaa airport, she had been forced to drag along her little girl. Not in the car but on the bus. She clearly had no babysitter.

"Time to go, Aleksey", said Henrik and held out his hand to the boy.

"I'm not called Alexey!" the boy replied sulkily.

"You're not? But in your papers it says..."

The woman cut him short. She nodded and tried to explain something in her excruciating Finnish, but the boy was determined:

"I'm called Aleksi. But in America they call me Alex."

***

Somewhere above Trondheim or Bergen he asked:

"Can you move me to business class?"

"I'm afraid that isn't possible."

"But those two elephants moved."

Henrik gave a wry smile. It was not his job to preach sensitivity to the boy. Two extremely overweight passengers, a Finnish man and his American wife had entered the plane last of all. They found difficulties sitting down in their seats in economy class. They couldn't even fold down the tray in front of them.

"Aleksi, that was a special case. I can't upgrade you to business class."

This was an intercontinental flight, but there were a good deal of empty seats. Maybe this was on account of the downgrade of the flight company's reputation. In May they had really had bad luck. Within four days two incidents occurred on this same route. An A330 Airbus on its way to New York had landed at Halifax in Canada, because of engine trouble. Two days later a New York – Helsinki flight was cancelled after a hard landing at JFK where the undercarriage was damaged.

Neither incident involved him personally. During those days he was first in Saint Petersburg, then in London.

"Is this your first flight?" he asked the boy as they were flying over Scotland.

"Course not."

The boy gave him a superior look.

Was he perhaps one of those small children who were forever commuting between their two parents, from one continent to the other? When Henrik was little there were children of divorced parents who commuted between two homes – in the same town. Nowadays there were Unaccompanied Minors.

"Have you flown a lot on your own?"

"Not really. Only with mummy and Kari. We were on the Canaries."

"How nice. Was that a long time ago?"

"I don't remember. It was winter in Finland. I was little went to the kindergarten."

"Is Kari your mother's husband?"

The boy shook his head and gave a grimace.

"Not any more. She's got another one. He's not much... But Kari was nice. He took me to the Linnanmäki amusement park and trained karate with me. Do you know any lethal karate chops?"

"Maybe."

The boy giggled.

"If some wicked men try to hijack the plane, can you put them out of action?", he asked with uncertainty in his voice.

"Kari sent me a Christmas card", he continued, without waiting for an answer. "But Mummy doesn't want me to meet him."

"Did he move out a long time ago?"

"No so very long ago. He's in prison. Mum's got a new husband. And she's got Lilja, my little sister."

Henrik shuddered, as if he had peeped into a prison cell by accident.

"Listen, Henrik... Can I also get one of those?"

The boy was referring to a play packet that a small girl was puffing over, two seats away: a colouring pad with pictures from the latest animation film "Nico and his Flying Brothers". Two felt-tips were lying under the girl's seat, along with plastic cutlery and the remains of the on-flight meal.

"But that's just for small children", said Henrik sagely.

The boy looked crestfallen.

"So I won't get one?"

He pressed his thickish lips together. It was as if he were about to burst into tears.

"But of course you can", said Henrik hastily. "You'll get a set."

When he had finished the tax free round and returned to the boy, they were already flying over Greenland.

"Look what I've got for you!"

On the tray in front of the boy lay half a dozen collector's cards with pictures of football stars. Henrik sat down on the free seat next to him.

Few things interested him less than football. He knew Cristiano Ronaldo. Lionel Messi was less familiar to him. Luis Suárez was a completely unknown name.

The boy gave him a condescending look.

"I know all of them!" he said. "Pity I didn't get any pocket money this month otherwise I'd have bought more cards."

"Why didn't you get any pocket money?" wondered Henrik without meaning to ask.

"I didn't do anything wrong. They just said that I was on my way to see dad in any case. He'll buy me masses of football cards."

"Sure."

Aleksi scratched his head. He was clearly suffering from some sort of eczema. He had a short retroucé nose and large lively eyes.

"D'you know, Henrik. I want to tell you something. A secret!"

Henrik began to want to move away. He didn't like other people's secrets. He had enough of his own. Nor did he like unwelcome confidences.

"I took a forbidden object onto the plane!" whispered the boy audibly.

To impress Henrik with objects that had evaded airport security was not an easy thing to do. During his eight years as flight attendant he had seen all kinds of snakes and scorpions, bottles of hair spray, toy pistols that closely resembled real ones, all sorts of cigarette lighters, large screwdrivers and even a double-edged Samurai sword. Now and again, a female passenger would try to do her manicure on the plane. And he had lost count of all the small children that had attempted to cut pictures out of newspapers with large pairs of scissors.

"A forbidden object? What is it? Got it in your pocket?"

"In my rucksack."

The boy's face lit up with pride. He opened his rucksack and produced a transparent snow globe filled with liquid and glitter, and a tiny plane inside.

"I see..."

Henrik smiled.

"When I was small I used to collect them"; he said thoughtfully while shaking the snow globe. "I had about ten of them. Maybe a dozen... I have to disappoint you, Aleksi. It's quite alright to have one of those things in your hand-luggage. If it had been larger than a tennis ball, it would have been forbidden."

For the first time, the boy began to show some humility because of Henrik's skills.

"I got it from my dad", he said shyly. "I don't remember when he did. He sent it me through the post, Mummy says. My dad's a pilot."

"Is he really? How nice for you. The son of a pilot! As in that song. Sorry Aleksi, I've got to go. Do try to sleep a little. Or watch a video. All you have to do is press this button, and choose your channel."

"I know. I'll have time to see two films. Or even three! We've still got eight hours to go."

"No, no. Not quite that much..."

"Henrik... when we've landed, will it be night over there?"

"When we get there, the time will be roughly the same as when we left. The time difference eats up the time."
"Eats it up?"
The boy looked fearfully at Henrik, as if the Big Bad Wolf had just gobbled up Little Red Riding Hood.
"You mean it's as if this flight never existed?" And he continued, "As if me and you had never met?"
Henrik had to laugh.
"It's only a way of speaking", he explained. "It's because of the time zones."
He got up from his seat.
"I went and forgot", he said in an apologetic tone of voice. "Did you get your colouring book pack?"

* * *

The service round was over. He made himself comfortable in the rest room and dutifully shut his eyes, but could not fall asleep. He was thinking of Katri who had met a former classmate on board. The joyful cries of the ladies echoed in his head. He saw Katri open a little bottle of champagne and offer her classmate some. In actual fact, their enthusiasm soon ebbed. It was followed by strained smiles. They had nothing further to say to one another. But nevertheless... A classmate. Even he has former classmates somewhere out there in the world.

He suddenly remembered a task at school when they were in the third class: write something positive about one of your classmates. One girl wrote about him: "Lives a long way from school." This was clearly the most positive thing she could write about him. If he were to meet one of his classmates on board he would hardly offer them champagne.

How do Aleksi's schoolmates relate to him back in Lahti? He has a Russian mother. And his dad... His dad sent him a snow globe. And will buy him a mass of football cards.

Henrik couldn't help smiling. Aleksi no doubt resembles his father. He doesn't take so much after his mother. He's flying to the USA for the first time, on summer vacation. If he likes it, he'll move there for good, is what he says. His mother does, after all, have Lilja and her new man. Who isn't much fun. But her ex was good. Now he's in prison.

Henrik yawned. In a few hours he will, as usual, have tramped through the hotel corridors with his travel bag with the text: Crew. Numbered rooms will rush past him, shiny glass doors will open. Nice to see you. Welcome home.

And the eight-year-old Unaccompanied Minor will change planes at JFK and carry on to Seattle, with his colouring block and his snow globe. Not a short journey; it will take about four hours or so.

Henrik felt annoyance at his failed nap and otherwise – at himself. He put his feet down into his shoes, absent-mindedly buttoned up his uniform jacket and stretched. He took a handful of sweets that the cabin crew usually handed out before landing, pushed them into his pocket and began to walk down to aisle.

Just as he had imagined, the boy's seat was empty. There were only two passengers in the same row. In the next row sat a young red-haired man who was reading the score of some symphony or other. On the other side of the aisle sat two women in their forties. They were both wearing a nun's headscarf. One of them seemed to be of Slavic extraction. She had a luxuriant figure, broad shoulders and eyes as dark blue as a thundercloud. The other woman was bloodless and thin. She hid her little rather dark face behind a pair of tinted spectacles. Both nuns were silent and were fingering their rosaries.

After waiting a minute, Henrik started to look for the boy. He found him at a window not far from the toilets.

"What are you doing here?" Henrik asked gently.

"I'm just watching what's going on… Can't I have a look inside the cockpit? Just a quick one."

Henrik shook his head.

"No one, with the exception of cabin crew is allowed into the cockpit", he said in his official voice. "Those are the rules."

"When I was little, it used to be OK. I was actually allowed in to have a look", he added soothingly.

"I see. When was that?"

"In the 1990s. Before the 9/11 attacks."

Aleksi sighed glumly.

"I wasn't really interested", Henrik continued almost guiltily, "but my dad wanted to have an excuse to go in and have a look himself…"

"Weren't you interested? Didn't you want to be a pilot when you were little?"

"No."

"What did you want to become? A flight attendant?"

Henrik shrugged his shoulders. In those days, like now, he lacked any ambition in life. As a child he had been attracted by the idea of becoming an architect or dinosaur researcher if someone had asked him.

"Well, what did you want to become?" Aleksi repeated impatiently.

"A millionaire."

Henrik wanted to laugh away the question, but the boy took his answer seriously and nodded respectfully. He let himself be obediently taken back to his seat. On the way they bumped into Katri. She stared at her always so phlegmatic colleague in the role of an eager babysitter. Henrik tried to give a humorous smirk, but at the same time he felt himself blushing for some reason. Luckily, Katri didn't notice.

In Aleksi's seat the colouring pad with pictures from Nico and his Flying Brothers could be seen.

"Do you like this cartoon film?" asked Henrik.

"Yes, but the first one about Nico the Reindeer Calf was better! He goes out to look for his dad. His dad works for Father Christmas, as a flying reindeer."

Henrik took out a few sweets, but stopped short.

"Aleksi, why haven't you drunk your water? During a long flight you lose a lot of liquid."

In the net underneath Aleksi's tray an unopened can of drinking water could be seen.

"I drank some juice."

"That was a long time ago. Now you should drink some water."

Unaccompanied Minor pulled a face, but Henrik opened the can with a determined gesture. The boy drank up the water in three large gulps, as if the water were medicine.

Henrik brought out the sweets.

"Pozhaluista!" he said

Aleksi looked almost shocked.

"Can you speak Russian?"

Henrik gave a wry smile.

"Dobro pozhalovat'. Pristegnite remni. Kofe, chay, sok", he rattled off. "Vino krasnoye, beloye. Dosvidaniya. Like that. That's it."

Aleksi burst out laughing.

"But surely you speak Russian at home?" Henrik wondered.

"Only with mum. Her Finnish isn't so good."

The boy gave him a worried look.

"I'm not a Roosky!" he said suddenly. "When I grow up no one will find out that I know Russian."

"It's good to know many languages", said Henrik diplomatically. "Do you speak English with your father?"

"Not yet... He doesn't know Finnish, but my English isn't good enough. So it'll have to be Russian to start with."

"You mean that your father's Russian?"

Henrik immediately regretted his question, but the boy didn't seem to have been hurt by it.

"No, but he isn't a negro either", he explained, his face serious. "My dad's an American!"

Henrik sighed resignedly. It wasn't his job to lecture the kid about race questions.

"How come your dad knows Russian?"

"He studied in Leningrad, at a cadet school. He became a military helicopter pilot."

Henrik was astonished.

"Jesus. An American that was trained as a military pilot in the Soviet Union..."

"In those days he was still a Cuban. He became an American later."
"I see. That explains matters… So he was retrained to become a civilian in the USA?"
"No. In the States he became a businessman. He often travelled to Saint Petersburg. That's where he met my mum. I don't remember that. I wasn't born yet."

His dark little hand flew up to his curly hair. He scratched his scalp for a long time. Maybe he doesn't wash his hair often enough. Or too often? For some reason he couldn't imagine how the woman with the pink, porous skin, whips up lather and washes his hair. Despite her unassuming clothes and her sad greasy hair, she wore stylish false fingernails with silvery tips.

"Why did you move to Finland?"
"Mum married Kari. She had never been married to my dad. I simply got born."
"Were you born in Saint Petersburg?"
"Yes."
"A very pretty ci…"
Henrik didn't manage to end the word.
"In America there's also a city with the same name!" interrupted the boy. "When I go and live in America they'll think I came from that Saint Petersburg. I'm no Roosky. And no negro either. They shouldn't say so at school. I'm a Finn! And in the USA I'll become an American."

Henrik glanced at the clock.
"We can talk some more later, Aleksi."
His voice quailed. He pressed the boy's hand together and surprised himself by doing so.
"You're clever", he added for some reason. "You'll surely have a good time in America."

Once they had landed at JFK he had to deal with a handicapped traveller in a wheelchair. Or, rather, the passenger's luggage. It was Katri who took the boy to Passport Control. As they hurried past, she whispered to Henrik:
"Here comes Baby Jesus…"
But there was no sarcasm on her face.

Henrik knew that they had got out among the first passengers. Nevertheless he looked for Aleksi's curly head among the crowds. The boy was likely to be wearing a peaked cap, he finally thought.

Everything was as usual. They had a short debriefing in the crew bus on the way to the hotel, when they went through the flight. This time there had been no incidents.

Then he went to bed. To his surprise he felt a rocking motion. He didn't usually have problems with his balance. For the first time for ages he hardly noticed the interior of his hotel room. Nor did he take any pictures of it.

He fell asleep entirely satisfied. Today had been a really lucky day: none of the passengers had been disruptive, no one had fallen suddenly ill, everything had simply floated by and his colleagues had been pleasant.

A day had passed, nothing had darkened it, an almost happy day.

***

According to the preliminary passenger list this time, there were no Unaccompanied Minors. On the other hand, there were six families with small children.

One of these families, with two children, had been allocated seats spread out through the plane. Henrik and Katri were fully occupied dealing with them. In the end they were allowed to sit together.

Were these really entirely new passengers? It was as if Henrik had flown with them to some other destination, to some other city. Or had dealt with them somewhere down on the ground.

An exhilarated business lady was chatting with a fellow-passenger:

"By this point I know exactly to the second how much time I need at various airports, so that I don't have to sit and wait too long..."

"... and that's how you get lots of bonus points!" her husband agreed.

The same faces, the same small talk. Henrik almost knew whether they drank coffee or tea.

"Heathrow, Terminal Three", the man continued, "is the worst I know! There are small insects there that bite..."

The fasten your seatbelts sign had hardly been switched off before the American blonde from row 20 started doing stretching exercises outside the toilet. Everyone was staring at her but she carried on in her woollen stockings. Her pink skin reminded you of luncheon meat.

It was time for the lunch round. While they were busy getting the meals ready, Katri suddenly asked:

"Henrik, do you remember that Sánchez boy? The Unaccompanied Minor? You were looking after him."

"Alexei Sánchez?"

"Yes."

"Why d'you ask?"

"He was sent back to Helsinki."

Henrik nearly dropped a sandwich in plastic wrap on the floor.

"Oh dear. Did he have problems with Immigration?"

Katri shook her head grimly.

"No. Nothing wrong with his papers. You've looked at them yourself. He had everything: passport, health certificate. He changed planes and flew on to Seattle."

"So, what happened?"

"No one came to collect him on arrival."

Suddenly, Henrik felt a lump in his throat. He didn't need to hold back his tears. They didn't come. He felt sick instead. Thank goodness the urge to vomit wasn't so strong.
"Christ Almighty", he managed to utter in the end.
Katri nodded.
"Exactly" she said without looking up. "I really mean it. Christ Almighty."
For a few minutes longer preparation continued in silence. Henrik was swallowing saliva. The nausea eased little by little.
"It's the first time a thing like that has happened as long as I can remember", he said apathetically.
"Same here."
"He stayed the night in Seattle", Katri added. "It took some time... to get a grip on the situation."
"I understand. So he flew back with another airline, not with us."
It was as if Katri was reading his thoughts. She answered questions he had never asked – jerkily, unwillingly. She was shaking her head the whole time, almost imperceptively, and looking past him.
"I don't know any details, Henrik... I got to hear about it in the crew room this morning, quite by chance."
Here voice was strangely low, she sounded like a boy whose voice was breaking.
"There must have been some kind of misunderstanding", she continued. "Take it easy. Nothing bad happened to him. It was just that no one answered the phone over there. Then they followed the rules. He was sent back to his original point of departure. Everything's OK. He's safely home in Finland."
As she pushed past him on her way into the lounge she suddenly placed her hand on his shoulder. For some reason he didn't feel surprised. Perhaps he didn't have the time to feel surprised. It happened so quickly. He automatically pressed her hand onto his uniform shoulder. For a second they stood close together, like two footballers when one had been injured on the field.
For some reason, he was reminded of a school exercise from when he was in the fourth form. Write and wish anonymously something positive about one of your classmates. He too received an anonymous slip of paper. Judging by the handwriting it was the same girl who had written one year previously: "lives a long way from school".
If he thought about it, she even said hello to him sometimes. She had nails bitten down to the quick and bulging eyes with dark rings under them. She was as thin as a rake. And yet she had something in common with the robust, sporty Katri.
That girl had written: "I wish you didn't get beaten so much".
Thinking about it, it didn't matter what would happen to the Sánchez boy. Did he really exist? Wasn't that refugee swallowed up by the time difference? Just like so much in Henrik's life.

Even his own childhood had been swallowed up by all sorts of differences. After his parents had got divorced, time was measured for quite a while in birthday cards that his dad sent him. They stopped arriving once Henrik had come of age. He himself kept on sending cards now and again. Mostly from Moscow when he got the opportunity. Sending cards was one of his secret rituals. His mother had mentioned that his father liked Moscow.

"Are you coming along for a drink?"

The question took him by surprise.

It was raining at JFK. Katri nearly slipped when leaving the plane.

"Come on, life is beautiful!" she continued.

By that time Henrik had already switched on his psychological defence mechanisms.

"Will this be a debriefing about Alexei Sánchez?" he wondered a shade sarcastically.

"Maybe. Or about the boy Henrik Lappalainen."

Katri's eyes shone like two nightlights. Nil irony, nil ulterior motives. Henrik cleared his throat.

"All right", he said with a provocative grin. "We'll go for a drink, on one condition."

"What sort of condition?"

Now Katri looked dissatisfied. A small crease could be seen between her eyebrows.

Henrik giggled. He felt light at heart which, like a small balloon was bobbing up and down in his chest.

"On condition that I pay."

Part III
Multilingualism as Problematization of Language

Part III

10 Language Play and Politics in Contemporary Swedish Hip-Hop

Karin Nykvist

"All rappers are poets; whether they are good poets or bad poets is the only question" (Bradley 2009, 193). When Adam Bradley wrote his hip-hop study *Book of Rhymes: The Poetics of Hip Hop* in 2009, there seemed to be a need for that assertion, the question of genre apparently being an important one. Today the question of genre does not seem pressing. When done right, hip-hop lyrics can prove to be a powerful force, no matter what the genre label is, and hip-hop rhymes succeed in making a great impact through the inventive and conscious use of literary devices and distinctly poetic aesthetic strategies. Historically, some hip-hop rhymes have done just that: rappers such as Melle Mel from Grandmaster Flash and the Furious Five, KRS-One from Boogie Down Productions and Chuck D from Public Enemy have combined commercial and critical success with enormous ideological influence, combining poetical finesse with political conviction.

Over the past twenty years, hip-hop scholarship has studied the political impact of hip-hop from different perspectives. Understandably, this scholarship has mostly been geared towards US hip-hop (Rose 1994; Keyes 2002; Perry 2004; Ogbar 2007; Hess 2007; Bradley 2009; Rabaka 2011 and many others). Recently, scholarly interest has widened to include hip-hop as a global form of cultural expression as well, thus opening up questions of appropriation, multilingualism and hip-hop as a global cultural movement. In Scandinavia, however, the scholarship is still limited, mainly consisting of studies concerned with musicological, sociological or purely linguistic issues (see Sernhede 2002; Söderman 2007; Krogh & Stougaard Pedersen 2008; Sernhede & Söderman 2010; Berggren 2014; Lindholm 2016).

In this chapter I will turn to a field that is still waiting to be fully problematized, mapped and explored, namely Swedish rap poetics, and more specifically the part played by multilingualism therein. I will investigate how, in terms of language, Swedish rap aesthetics have become increasingly more overtly political in the last two decades: it is my conviction that the mixing of languages and the blurring of borders between them have become distinctly more radical over the years.

Many scholars and artists alike agree that hip-hop is not a product but an act, in the performative sense of the word, as a strong maker

154   Karin Nykvist

and marker of identity. According to Simon Frith, hip-hop performance is all about the production of identity: "The aesthetic question about this postmodern music, at least, concerns not meanings and their interpretation – identity translated into discursive forms which have to be decoded – but *mutual enactment*, identity produced *in* performance" (Frith 1996, 115). Music, Frith points out, is not a reflection of identity, but rather an important part of the process by means of which identity is created (Frith 1996, 115). Language and a language-conscious aesthetic marked by radical heteroglossia that make use of code-switching, blending and blurring play an important part in this production and performance of identity.

In the following pages, I will show how contemporary hip-hop lyrics often explore multilingualism and turn to multilingual aesthetics in order to destabilize and question ideas of national identity and to deconstruct the monolingual ideals that those ideas are founded on. My investigation is related to linguistic research but is literary in its foundation: I will be investigating multilingualism as a literary device in terms of design and effect. The use of multilingual aesthetics is at the core of hip-hop lyrics written outside of the US and not as visible in a US context, even if examples of multilingual rap can be found, for example, in the work of the partly Latino rap collective Cypress Hill (Ogbar 2007, 45ff.). In today's Sweden – as in many other countries and regions of the world – many successful hip-hop acts are using multilingual devices in order to chip away at what Yasemin Yildiz has called the monolingual paradigm. Her term is intended to describe the widespread idea that "individuals and social formations are imagined to possess one 'true' language only, their 'mother tongue', and through this possession to be organically linked to an exclusive, clearly demarcated ethnicity, culture, and nation" (Yildiz 2012, 2). In my study, I will show just how some of the more successful chipping is done.

I will be making three claims. The first one is that over the past twenty years or so, Scandinavian – most notably Swedish – hip-hop culture has become acutely and consciously more multilingual. In order to make this claim, I will briefly discuss the work by hip-hop artists from three decades: the ground-breaking Latin Kings in the nineties, the female rapper Feven, who had a short-lived but very successful career in the aughts, and the contemporary rapper Erik Lundin, who started releasing material in Swedish in 2015 and whose debut, *Suedi*, will be the main subject of my study. These three artists are carefully chosen because of their emblematic quality – they are characteristic and representative – but also because of the attention given to them in the public sphere, from critics as well as from fans, and their success in the charts. It may be added that, in addition to their lyrics, these three artists can be studied from a broader perspective. Interviews, public acts, CD inserts and other paratexts can all be interpreted as performative acts creating artistic personae that are aligned with the hip-hop lyrics. Reviews and other journalistic texts also become part of this creation by reacting to the actions of the artists in ways that further or alter their effects. All in all, the material I have chosen opens to a study of how the idea and ideology of what it means to be and to speak Swedish has been destabilized and redefined within Swedish hip-hop culture since the 1990s.

Second, I aim to show that in the process of chipping away at the monolingual paradigm, hip-hop lyrics in later years have turned radically more political, going from a sometimes extrinsic, organic, authenticity-performing multilingualism to a radical, consciously politically performing one. That this is so becomes even more apparent when one takes into account the context of the musical scene: media coverage, interviews and award acceptance speeches. My argument will borrow its terminology from the work of sociolinguists Elizabeth Gordon and Mark Williams (1998). Although they speak of code-switching instead of multilingualism and their interest rather lies within the realm of bilingualism, I find their terminology useful and instructive. They suggest that multilingual practice has three main functions: extrinsic, organic and political (Gordon & Williams 1998, 80). While extrinsic multilingualism adds an outlandish flavour to the text, and marks the otherness of the presence of the supposedly foreign content – such as the word "bonjour" in an American text about a trip to Paris – organic multilingualism is an integral part of the text that conveys authenticity, while still being easily understood by non-speakers of the languages used because of context and/or explanations within the text. Gordon and Williams use the term "political multilingualism" to designate a radical multilingual performance consciously aiming for political affect. The aim of this performance is not necessarily to be understood or to communicate; rather, language takes on a symbolic function where the language itself is the message. Here the question of effect is also worth looking into: the radically multilingual text is known to evoke strong feelings in the listener, who feels excluded or included, with or without reason. The value and nature of these feelings are difficult to analyse, but I am convinced that they are worthy of attention nevertheless. Scholars such as Doris Sommer, Julia Tidigs and Markus Huss have taken on the challenge and address the possible affective effects of multilingual texts on the reader (or listener) in some of their work (Sommer 2004; Tidigs & Huss 2017). Gordon and Williams make sure to point out that literature often takes part in "cultural negotiation" (Gordon & Williams 1998, 75) and that code-switching in speech or writing is part of the "larger struggles for power that are continually being conducted in and through language" (Gordon & Williams 1998, 79). Naturally, the same goes for multilingual speech or writing. Thus, the political substance of a text can lie within its very form – with or without content backing it up.

My third claim concerns the construction of national identity. I will show that the politically performing multilingualism of contemporary hip-hop lyrics disturbs and alters the notion not only of the Swedish language, but the idea and ideology of Swedishness itself as well. In fact, these two are difficult to separate. Language and nation are intrinsically connected in complex ways, as has been discussed by many scholars from different fields, famously by political scientist and anthropologist Benedict Anderson in the eighties (Anderson 2006, 67ff.) and more recently by, for example, the already mentioned Germanic scholar Yasemin Yildiz (2012, 7ff.). In order to show how the disturbances of the idea of nation and language are set in motion, I find the work of Mikhail Bakhtin and his writings on heteroglossia and the complex stratification of speech to be quite useful (Bakhtin 1982, 263–275). He suggests that there are centrifugal and centripetal forces at play in any utterance. This notion offers a fruitful way of exploring the politically and ideologically performative aspects of multilingual hip-hop lyrics. To Bakhtin, popular genres have historically been marked by more prominent heteroglossia, where sometimes "there was no language-center at all" – an idea that in itself is subtly politically subversive (Bakhtin 1982, 273). Whereas Bakhtin always situates the literary utterance within a context, the model of territorialization and deterritorialization put forth by Gilles Deleuze and Félix Guattari goes one step further through their idea of the complex nature of their interrelation, where the utterance and its context are interrelated in multifarious ways (Deleuze & Guattari 1988). I will therefore also make reference to this Deleuze and Guattari model, as I believe it can illuminate the complex way in which hip-hop lyrics, their performance and reception work in the world.

A Glocal Genre

In the introduction to her ground-breaking 1994 study *Black Noise: Rap Music and Black Culture in Contemporary America*, called "a landmark moment for hip-hip culture" (Woldu 2010, 9), Tricia Rose states that "hip-hop is a cultural form that attempts to negotiate the experiences of marginalization and brutally truncated opportunity and oppression within the cultural imperatives of African-American and Caribbean history, identity and community" (Rose 1994, 21). For the most part, she is right. Hip-hop does indeed attempt to negotiate experiences of marginalization and truncated opportunity – but that experience is not limited to African-American and Caribbean spheres. The question of identity and the creation of diasporic narratives are not limited to US culture, or even to the culture that Paul Gilroy (1993) has named the Black Atlantic. Instead, hip-hop has proven to be a genre that can express and negotiate experiences of marginalization locally, but on a global level. Diaspora, questions of identity formation, and the experience of truncated opportunity and oppression play an important part in the daily lives of many youths, most notably from marginalized and unprivileged groups of youths everywhere. The aesthetics of hip-hop has proven to travel well, as many scholars of late have pointed out. How the genre of hip-hop combines global and local poetics has been explored for some time now, most notably by scholars from fields of linguistics and sociology (see, e.g. Mitchell 2001; Alim et al. 2008; Terkourafi 2010; Aidi 2014). Many suggest that this combination of the cosmopolitan and vernacular is quite logical, especially when one considers that hip-hop has demonstrated itself to be a deterritorializing force from the start, with the perspective of the underprivileged and marginalized as its focus – a position that can be translated into many areas of the world. The act of combining global and local aesthetics sets deterritorializing as well as reterritorializing forces into play, and the locality of the lyricist becomes important. The act of "repping one's hood" has, however, been an important part of US hip-hop aesthetics from the start (Potter 1995, 146; Ogbar 2007, 44). Thus, the act of naming places and making allegiance to certain neighbourhoods can be read both as acts of marking authenticity and as markers of genre.

Swedish Hip-Hop Lyrics

Perhaps not very surprisingly, Swedish hip-hop has gone from mimicking its North American roots musically as well as lyric-wise to becoming a local genre, combining international hip-hop aesthetics with a vernacular voice. Apart from a few exceptions, early Swedish hip-hop relied heavily on inspiration from US performers in terms of both their music and lyrics. The first Swedish rap recording, which came out in 1980, was a light, fun and forgettable affair, surely not intended for posterity and bearing more than a little likeness with the contemporaneous The Sugarhill Gang's "Rapper's Delight" (Hedemyr 1980; Strage 2001, 69). However, hip-hop soon gained a huge following in Sweden, with many artists working within the genre and making it their own.

While I suggest that today's hip-hop practice is radically language-political, it is, however, also important to remember that the question of language has been at the forefront for more than twenty years in the Swedish production and reception of hip-hop. The first known rap recording in Swedish was a low-fi production made by MC Tim in 1989 (MC Tim 1989; Strage 2001, 81), while the first successful group to release rap records with Swedish lyrics was the Stockholm group Just D, who emerged in the early 1990s. The name of their second release, *Svenska ord* (Swedish words), gives testimony to the fact that the group was making a conscious language choice. Their playful strife to turn hip-hop into a Swedish genre also became apparent through their use of their recurrent choice of Swedish children's songs and Swedish evergreens for samplings. Albeit filled with slang, witty wordplay and alternative spellings, the lyrics of Just D were decidedly monolingual in their aesthetic, and the playfulness of the music was mirrored in the fun and trivial rhymes.

The first hip-hop CD that can be regarded as practising any postmonolingual language politics, as Yildiz would surely call it because of its conscious and foregrounded use of a non-standard version of Swedish marked by heteroglossia (Bakhtin 1982; Yildiz 2012), was released in Swedish in 1994 by the Latin Kings as *Välkommen till förorten*. This title literally translates as "welcome to the suburb", but in Swedish, "suburb" does not bear the middle-class connotations attached to the word in US English, resembling rather its French counterpart, *banlieue*, a term bringing to mind council housing, low income, petty crime, unemployment and other social problems. The debut received attention because of its use of a vernacular then known as "Rinkebyswedish" – the name derived from the multilingual, multi-ethnic Stockholm suburb of Rinkeby, where, incidentally, the Latin Kings did not originate. In a forcibly centripetal move, a professor of the Swedish language, Ulla-Britt Kotsinas, even went on to make a book with the lead singer Dogge Doggelito (Douglas Léon) on the slang of multilingual origin spoken in the Stockholm suburbs, namely *Förortsslang* (Suburban slang; Doggelito & Kotsinas 2004). The claim made by the Latin Kings was quite mimetic and suggested that the multilingualism of the lyrics organically reflected that of the crew's neighbourhood. Incidentally, rap has prompted the compilation of dictionaries in other places as well. In 1998, the Sorbonne professor Jean-Pierre Goudaillier published a dictionary on the plenitude of French slang, called *Comment tu tchatches !* (How you talk!), which, according to Mitchell, raised some controversy (2001, 14).

When one hears those Latin Kings lyrics today, the multilingualism which made such an impression in 1994 is not at all that striking. The impression is rather that of lyrics filled with Swedish slang and some Spanish to boot. I would suggest that one reason the multilingualism of the Latin Kings was given such attention at the time of their debut was that it was not geared towards US English. It made use of the languages present in the Swedish context at the time, such as Turkish and Spanish. And like Just D, who sampled many Swedish classic songs, the Latin Kings chose to include quite a few Swedish samplings in their music – for example, they used a children's song by Astrid Lindgren in the track "Snubben" (The dude) about racist violence – thus bringing multilingualism into the musical medium as well. A few years later, the outspokenly feminist rapper Feven, who was just as politically progressive, had a short but very successful career and received a Grammis, the Swedish equivalent of the Grammy, for the best hip-hop act of 2001. She mixed Swedish and easily understood urban US English, and yet she did not at all get the same attention for her brand of code-switching and multilingualism as the Latin Kings had. I am convinced that the main reason for this is the fact that her lyrics gave an impression of mimicry and appropriation of outlandish US vernacular, and therefore did not answer to the great rule of authenticity within the genre of hip-hop, nor to the public's urge to read hip-hop lyrics as testimonials. Proving that one is "real" is more important than anything. Even though the content of Feven's songs often was openly political within a Swedish context – for example, in "Bränn behån" (Burn your bra), the Swedish Social Democrat Mona Sahlin is hailed as the expected first female Swedish prime minister (this, however, did not come to pass) – her code-switching openly mimicked a North American aesthetic and was therefore not accorded the level of attention that the Latin Kings had received. Although delivered in Swedish, Feven's Grammis acceptance speech in January 2001 was peppered with words like "yo" and expressions such as "where my peoples at?", which added a definite extrinsic Bronx-sound to it, despite the fact that she herself has no personal ties to the US.

In spite of her mimicry, Feven was language-conscious and engaged in language politics in her paratexts, if not in her actual rhymes. On her debut album, she included a skit called "Språka på svenska" (Språka in Swedish) (Feven 2000). Språka was the name of a short TV show in common immigrants' languages, often containing news and public information, which was a constant in Swedish television broadcasts for almost twenty-five years, from April 1974 to December 1998. The name of the show was somewhat of a pun: "språka" can be translated as "talk" but it is also a play with the Swedish word for language: språk. The show was always presented along with the language of the episode in question: "Språka in Finnish", "Språka in Arabic", et cetera. A show called "Språka in Swedish" never aired, but in the name of her short skit, Feven turned the othering of the show on its head. The skit contains two young men speaking to each other in US English and a third person who joins the discussion in Swedish. After the latter asks one of the former if he is Mowgli – a move that leads the audience to guess that this is a racist white Swedish person, othering and stereotyping a black youth – he or she goes on to exclaim: "I know that you can speak Swedish, stop it, do you think you're from Queens or what?" Here the two young men answer in Swedish that they have no interest in talking to him or her (the gender of the voice is unclear). Even though Feven rapped in Swedish on her debut album, moves like this one show that she did not regard the Swedish soundscape as a monolingual space. In the opening of her "Bränn behån" video, Feven arrives at her job in the Stockholm subway, talking much in the same way as in her Grammis acceptance speech, provoking a confrontation with her older, white male boss who remonstrates: "Swedish! Speak in Swedish!" in a way that echoes the Swedish person in the "Språka in Swedish" skit (Feven 2000b). Although Feven was on the whole a politically progressive artist, her multilingual practice can be regarded as extrinsic and thus, more than anything else, underlining the monolingual paradigm: the foreignness of her English phrases is never seriously questioned; the centrifugal effect is there but rather subtly so. My guess is that the choices she made language-wise were perceived as genre-specific and therefore safe. Even though their aims and thematics were deterritorializing, their effects were reterritorializing. On the contrary, the multilingual practice of the Latin Kings had a deterritorializing, worrying effect when it was first introduced in the 1990s – making apparent the need for a reterritorializing dictionary.

Political Multilingualism

The focus on language in the reception of the Latin Kings suggests that language politics, as well as questions of identity and place, has been a part of Swedish hip-hop culture and reception from the start. Some twenty-odd years later, it is striking how subdued the multilingual content of the Latin Kings' debut is, especially compared to what is produced in the 2010s, but the attention given then shows that at the time it was received as radical and new. If one compares Feven's acceptance speech upon being awarded her Grammis with that of her 2016 counterpart Silvana Imam, the difference speaks volumes. Although Imam spoke for almost a full minute, she used only four Swedish words, "Jag är naturkraft" ("I'm natural force"), which was the title of her lauded album, and "Tack" ("Thank you"). The remainder of the speech was held entirely in Arabic and Lithuanian. The majority of viewers did not understand her speech, which made its multilingualism political, in the terminology of Gordon and Williams. The fact that Imam mainly chose Arabic and Lithuanian for an acceptance speech in the public setting of a Swedish awards ceremony effectively turned those two languages into Swedish languages – if only for a few seconds. Her bold choice was not missed by the press, with articles in newspapers (Haidl 2016; Thomsen 2016) and comments on television (Weiderud 2016) and in social media. Her act was definitely one of political multilingualism – language was at the core, albeit not necessarily literal communication, forefronting the sound of language and its potentiality to include and exclude, rather than the dispersing of semantic content. In an interview with Sveriges Radio, Imam stated that she wanted all Swedes to experience what it was like not to understand – and that the experience would teach them empathy (Kulturnytt 2016).

Silvana Imam is a frequent collaborator with fellow rapper Erik Lundin, and her act at the Swedish Grammis was indicative of the mindset of many of the contemporary hip-hop artists in Sweden. Lundin, whose full name is Ibrahima Erik Lundin Banda, used to record tracks in English under the name of Eboi, but when he started to produce music with Swedish lyrics in 2015 – to huge success, commercially as well as critically – he chose to use the name Erik Lundin. In doing so, he was clearly performing Swedishness and authenticity in a conscious play with the often unconscious practice of stereotyping that pervades popular culture, in addition to some parts of the political sphere, and which is centripetal in its effect (on stereotyping in the reception of hip-hop and American black culture overall, see Ogbar 2007, 17ff.). In an interview he commented on this choice, saying that Erik Lundin was not an act, it was his name, and that a person with his looks could have a name like that was a provocation to xenophobes as well as to some immigrants.

In Lundin's version of hip-hop music, however, heteroglossia is a fundamental part of the aesthetic and constitutes a strong deterritorializing, centrifugal force. It is formed from a multitude of modes, media and languages, which are brought together and apart through Lundin's use of rhyme and rhythm, collage, repetition, flows and ruptures, all of which are typical to the hip-hop genre but accentuated and brought to the forefront through – among other devices – unexpected choices, sonic play and metapoetic commentary. Languages from many continents, as well as from different social strata, are mixed over samplings from music from various regions and styles. These quite conscious choices push his aesthetics into a political realm, insisting on change and the blurring of borders while simultaneously performing this very blurring.

All in all, there is clearly quite a leap from the multilingual performances of Feven and the Latin Kings to those of Silvana Imam and Erik Lundin. There are, however, a few factors that are important in making the political stance of Swedish contemporary hip-hop lyrics as forceful as it is. One of these factors is the fact that the borders between rap lyrics and poetry are more blurred than ever. Adam Bradley's assertion that hip-hop artists are poets might not be as needed in Sweden as in the US; to many Scandinavians it is already a given. At the turn of the millennium, the genres of hip-hop and poetry met in two critically acclaimed literary debuts that preceded Bradley's claim. In Johannes Anyuru's poetry collection *Bara gudarna är nya* (2003; Only the gods are new), allusions to the hip-hop duo Mobb Deep are seamlessly mixed with allusions to Homer's *Iliad*. And Daniel Boyaciaglu, who had made a name for himself in the Poetry Slam circuit, chose the name *Istället för hip hop* (2003; Instead of hip-hop) for his first collection of poetry. I would argue that both of these paved the way for a more literary approach in the reading and writing of Swedish hip-hop lyrics, showing and performing the close kinship between spoken word, hip-hop and poetry. This affinity is furthered by acts by many Swedish rappers. Douglas Léon (Dogge Doggelito, the lead singer of the Latin Kings) has written two children's books (Doggelito 2011a, 2011b, 2012), and *The Latin Kings: Texter* (2004) is a publication of the lyrics of the group, including a foreword by the aforementioned poet Johannes Anyuru. Petter Alexis, the most successful rapper in Sweden, has also published his rap lyrics in a book where he additionally writes about dyslexia and the importance of reading (Alexis Askergren 2014). A quote by Jason Diakité, better known as the very successful rapper Timbuktu, adorns one of the buildings of Malmö University, and the rapper received great praise for his bestselling autobiography (Diakité 2016). The fact that Erik Lundin, along with a few fellow rap artists, was asked to contribute to the Swedish literary magazine *10TAL* in 2016 (Lundin et al. 2016) confirms the literary status that hip-hop lyrics are starting to enjoy in Sweden.

Lundin himself is preoccupied with the question of the status of his writing. In "Haffla", he raps, "Authors should be contacting me / Fuck it, brother, I should be an author."[1] His lyrics are also richly crafted, filled with euphonies such as alliterations, sonic repetitions, end-rhymes and in-rhymes, as well as rhetorical tropes such as chiasmi ("vännerna delar på abiat / abiat delar på vännerna" ("friends divide up the cocaine / cocaine divides up the friends")), epiphora and anaphora. Furthermore, he is no stranger to the use of metaphor – if it rhymes well.

Another factor that furthers the political force of hip-hop writing is the demand for authenticity that is at the core of the genre. Many scholars and artists alike have made this point, artists often by means of lyrics that claim to "keep it real" and demand others to do the same, and scholars in countless studies on hip-hop aesthetics. Hip-hop scholar Jeffrey Ogbar has even suggested that hip-hop is characterized by a "cult of authenticity" (Ogbar 2007, 8, 37ff.). Others offer similar views (Terkourafi 2010, 6ff.), with artists themselves returning to the importance of being real (Jay-Z 2010, 248). Here the question of language becomes important: is it used as a marker of authenticity, making mimetic claims of realness and truth, or is it used playfully, marking the constructedness and fleeting quality of politically charged ideas of identity and origin? I would suggest that the two can often be at play simultaneously. The acceptance speech by Silvana Imam and the lyrics of the Latin Kings can definitely be read as acts performing authenticity in line with established hip-hop aesthetics, but also as language-conscious games questioning the idea of Sweden as a monolingual nation.

Authenticity is not only about form, however, but also about content. In an interview given at the release of *Suedi*, Lundin stated that he regarded himself as a griot, someone who recounts and records history. "History must be told honestly, just like it happened", he says to his interviewer (Roney 2015, 25). In choosing hip-hop as his mode of expression and griot as his role, Lundin combines the West African concept of the oral history teller with the narrativity that plays and has played an important part for many US hip-hop artists, including Nas, Common and A Tribe Called Quest. It also shows that Lundin's self-understanding connects hip-hop to oral poetry, a stance he shares with many scholars and artists alike, which furthers the notion of hip-hop as a literary genre (Rose 1994, 64; Bradley 2009, 175ff.; Gates 2010; Jay-Z 2010).

The demand for authenticity is double-edged, however. Racialized authors and authors who are perceived as belonging to or originating from marginalized groups are often given the role of witnesses in the public sphere, while the narrative voices of their work are often mistaken as authentic rather than belonging to dramatis personae. Women, working-class authors and authors with foreign-sounding names have historically often been read as truthsayers and representatives of their respective groups – a tendency which in complex ways can be viewed as the flip side of stereotyping. This practice has led to a certain mode of reading: while the literariness and question of certain texts' literary value may be overlooked or played down, the truth-value of the texts are correspondingly played up. Sometimes the authors in question have accepted or even actively taken that role, and sometimes it has been forced upon them. A white middle-class public is – for all kinds of reasons, good and bad – hungry for stories told by the perceived other, a hunger that more often than not places the burden to bear witness, explain and analyse on the minority writers themselves. The reception in Sweden of the authorial debut of Jonas Hassen-Khemiri is a case in point: the protagonist of Hassen-Khemiri's novel *Ett öga rött* (2003; One eye red), which went on to become one of the most read and appreciated novels of the aughts, was viewed by quite a few reviewers as a self-portrait, even though the protagonist lacked almost all resemblance with the text's author; apart from their common North African heritage. The two did not share name, age, social class or circumstance. Seeing the text as an authentic testimony led even experienced critics to grossly misread the text and caused them to question the values and perceived anti-Semitism, sexism and violent ideology of the author (Strömberg 2003). The fact that the text was written in non-standard Swedish may have contributed to this misconception, since, as many scholars have shown, multilingualism is often taken as a signal of authenticity as well (Tidigs 2014, 83–88).

Of course it is not that simple: the concept of authenticity is a slippery one, with intentions and receptions sometimes corresponding, sometimes not. As Paul Gilroy (1993, 99) has pointed out, "representing authenticity always involves artifice". Traditionally in hop-hop lyrics, there is often an ambivalence – within the work of the artist or even within the same song – between what T. S. Eliot called the second and the third voice of the poet – that is, between the poet himself addressing his audience and the poet taking on the voice of a dramatic role (Bradley 2009, 162ff.). This adoption of different voices and the often quite seamless move between them create a tension which allows for biographical as well as more literary readings. In his lyrics, Lundin plays with this tension, sometimes assuming the identity of a clichéd hip-hop character (in songs such as "Araba" and "Abiat", he is the drug dealer, the small-time yet larger-than-life gangster), sometimes using a voice leaning more towards the political speaker. Such is the case in songs like "Haffla" where the voice of the rapper is partly the voice of the successful hip-hop artist who has made it and can spend tons of money to party in style – "the cheese is aged and the whisky has reached the age of majority"[2] – and partly the more authentic-sounding voice of the aspiring writer urging others to give witness as well, and to do it in the languages they know best.

Swedish Redefined

Through his expressed wish of acting as a griot, Erik Lundin showed that he intended to convey a message and tell a story with his *Suedi* album. Its title pointed to where his main message lay. The word "Suedi" is Arabic for Swede and has been used widely with negative connotations for decades, mostly in ethnically mixed and urban working-class areas, to designate a stereotypical, generic Swede. When using it to designate his act as Erik Lundin as well as himself – Lundin wore a black hoodie with the word on the front for most interviews, TV appearances and live performances following the release – Lundin brought all the connotations of the word into play and altered their performance. Lundin is Swedish – born and raised, with a Swedish passport – but his father hails from Gambia; thus, he is not your stereotypical Swede, and therefore not the prototypical Suedi. Lundin consciously used a stereotype and confronted it with another stereotype, the non-Suedi, thus blurring the nationalist borders of the notions of being Swedish and non-Swedish, both calling them out and deconstructing them, and in the end broadening the idea of what Swedishness is.

What is most remarkable about this act is the degree to which it highlighted the volatile nature of the question of nationality. In order to focus on this issue, Lundin made use of his Swedish passport, which he repeatedly included in the paratexts of the album. An old passport of his graces the cover of the album, and for an interview with the main Swedish daily *Dagens Nyheter*, Lundin chose to be photographed holding up a Swedish passport. The image was clearly echoing a very famous picture of the aforementioned Swedish hip-hop artist Jason Diakité, who in 2013 caused quite a stir by holding up his passport while giving a speech in Swedish parliament where he was awarded a prize; in this way, he reminded everyone of his citizenship and claimed allegiance to the country of his birth. The event was quite controversial and became the topic of heated debate, since not long before being awarded the prize Diakité had released an outspokenly political song where he seemingly instigated violence, suggesting that the leader of the xenophobe and racist party the Swedish Democrats – holding seats since 2010 in the very Swedish Parliament where he was awarded his prize – should be beaten up (Kartellen 2013). In spite of – or because of – the controversy, the image of Diakité holding his passport was spread widely, shown on television as well as in printed media and on the internet. In one of Lundin's later songs, "Välkommen hem" (2016; Welcome home), he would rap about Diakité's act,

Language Play and Politics 165

confirming its symbolic importance for him: "All hype, see my passport in the air like Timbuk's."[3]

Diakité's message in the Swedish Parliament was that he is no stranger, that he is not the other, and that the hatred he and other Swedes who look like him experience in real life and in social media is never xenophobia but should be called for what it is: racism. To simply state the fact that one is Swedish can sometimes prove to be a political performance. During his tour in the spring of 2017, Lundin would address his Swedish nationality in between songs, as well as the fact that it has repeatedly been questioned throughout his life (Lundin 2017).

On the cover photo of *Suedi*, the names Ibrahima and Banda are blacked out, an act that furthers the performative and political stance of the album. By blacking them out, Lundin performed a Suedi kind of Swedishness, putting forth an unambiguously Swedish name. But the black lines give the picture a palimpsest-like, deterritorializing quality, underlining the supposed otherness of the child in the photograph, pointing to his history of being othered, and marking the monolingual-sounding name as a construct and an act of forced reterritorialization. The non-Swedish sounding names are not wiped out, however – they are marked. And the complexity that comes with this layered identity, the album cover suggests, is also what *Suedi* is about. Thus, the signified of the signifier Suedi was not only broadened, it was also made more ambiguous, no longer simply negative, with its racial and monolingual connotations weakened. In this way, the political performance of the album can be said to begin even before the first song is played.

The EP album itself is 17 minutes long and consists of five songs. It was released electronically on 6 November 2015. The five songs on the album, in the order they appear, are: "Suedi", "Annie Lööf", "Haram", "Västerort" and "Haffla". Just from the titles of the songs, one gets an impression of the themes and the post-monolingual mode of the album: titles such as "Suedi" and "Haram" evoke thoughts on national, cultural and religious identity, while "Västerort" is a geographical destination, very much located in Swedish reality. Annie Lööf is a Swedish Liberal politician, and the word *haffla* is Swedish slang derived from the Arabic word *khafla*, which means "party" or "feast". Thus, the order of the songs makes an interesting weave of Arabic–Swedish–Arabic–Swedish–Arabic. Annie Lööf is a name that connotes Swedishness – much like the name Erik Lundin. One could believe that the song is about Swedish party politics, but it is actually a play of words about making money: Swedish 500-kronor notes are orange, in slang often being referred to as "reds" (*rödingar*), matching the colour of Lööf's hair, while the Swedish word *löv* ("leaf") is metaphorically – and sometimes in slang – used for cash. It is clear that Lundin plays with language on many levels here, not only through multilingual games, but through semantic language games and puns as well.

The fact that "Suedi" is the first song on the album is significant: it is a manifesto of post-monolingual and post-monoethnical life, of turning life in-between into a new way of being Swedish; in the form of a coming-of-age narrative, it tells the story of finding one's place in what Homi K. Bhabha (1994, 36–39) has termed the third space. The lyrics are a narrative – and in this way they are in line with a certain kind of central hip-hop tradition which, in turn, derives from the Black Atlantic vernacular tradition of oral storytelling and the practice of what often is called "signifying", a narrating style where language games, double entendres, polyglossia and intertextuality play a major role (Gates 1988, xxv–xxviii, 2010; Bradley 2009, 181). The song is a short but effective coming-of-age story of choosing the identity of being Suedi. It starts out with childhood: a non-problematic Swedish cultural environment and upbringing with Swedish food and Swedish children's television shows are contrasted against the racism experienced, and the much-hated expression "second-generation immigrant" is used. Here it should be noted that while in the US the expression "second generation" implies "second-generation American", in Swedish it denotes a "second-generation immigrant" – a seemingly subtle but very significant difference. The experience of being othered prompts a reaction, and here language serves as a tool. Rather than never fitting in, one can carve out one's own third space:

> He who does not fit in does everything to stand out, to endure / We corrupted our dialect / stole words from the family / What was the effect? / Ghetto slang, that gave respect / Grammar turned bad, R's sharper.[4]

A youth spent in a multicultural environment is then described in the song, and is on the whole given a very positive description. In a clumsy, literal translation, the lyrics go: "I was happiest in my hood, perhaps a bit fussy / but never boring, diversified, multilingual."[5] Lundin evokes positive memories, such as friendships and international food, and negative experiences, including petty crime and police harassment. The protagonist finally decides to leave Sweden for his non-Swedish family and discovers that with them he is perceived as a Swede. On returning, he finds that many of his old friends have moved on. Some have record deals, while some have even become policemen, started families, use snuff, own Volvos and houses, and have children who are born in Swedish hospitals – in other words, they have turned to a Suedi lifestyle.[6] At the end of the song, the protagonist says that he remembers the day he "found himself". He invites his parents to coffee (the word used is *fika*, a Swedish idiomatic expression for sharing coffee and more often than not, a cinnamon roll or the like, an act that plays a large part in Swedish national self-understanding), a behaviour that surprises his father. The song ends with him telling his parents that he might as well not be ashamed: he is Suedi.

Thus, the opening song of the album – and the song where the artist Eboi reinvents himself and presents himself as a rapper rapping in Swedish – is a narrative about finding and claiming a national identity. However, the Swedish that this Suedi artist uses is what I would call "weird Swedish" after the work of Evelyn Nien-ming Ch'ien, who in her book *Weird English* discusses how the non-standard, hybrid and marked English of writers such as Irvine Welsh, Junot Díaz, Vladimir Nabokov and Arundhati Roy is a "conscious appropriation of hybridity", an aesthetic choice that has ideological and political implications and that "deprives English of its dominance" (Ch'ien 2004, 5–11). The language that Lundin uses to write about multilingualism, racism and othering is in itself thoroughly multilingual, moving freely between and mixing Spanish, English, Arabic, Turkish, French and Polish – to name just the obvious ones – in an aesthetic that goes beyond simpler notions of code-switching and rebels against any ideas of language purity.

Lundin's "weird Swedish" constitutes an act of political multilingualism that destabilizes the traditional notion of nationhood, turning it into something else, new and more inclusive. In this lies the political message of the song. A few months after the release of *Suedi*, the song "Välkommen hem" (Welcome home) was released as a video on YouTube in time for the European football championship in 2016, featuring children, Lundin himself and various footballers in the European Championship gear of the Swedish team. This is the song discussed above where Lundin not only makes references to his Swedish passport and employs the iconic passport picture with Timbuktu, but also mentions his song "Suedi", which he calls his "victory speech" (*segertal*). The song "Välkommen hem" clearly has two sides: it is partly a cheer for the national team playing in the championship and also as much of a political statement as the song "Suedi". An occasion that is usually of national interest, the football championship, is used in order to question and rebuild the notion of national identity once more. "My identity is my own choice", Lundin states early on in the song.[7] The rest of the lyrics can be read as an explanation of the facets of this identity, which in itself is a poetical, multilingual description of the third space and a claim of Swedish nationality – "the flag, we used to diss it / now we hoist it" – as well as Swedish geography: "This is where I plan to stay, this is my home."[8] An important theme in the song is the non-white Swede and the Swede of non-Swedish heritage: Lundin refers to himself as "zinji", Arabic for "black", and all of the Swedish football players he hails are partly or entirely of non-Swedish origin: "To Olsen, Guidetti, to Zlatan my brother, Henke Larsson, Dahlin and Ravelli: / Welcome home!"[9] Here Lundin reminds every listener that these players – and, implicitly, everyone who is like them – are in fact Swedes and have the right to call Sweden their home. The title of the song can be understood not only as a greeting to the football team upon returning to Sweden, but also as a greeting to the

168 *Karin Nykvist*

countless people who are seeking a new place in the world to call home, or those who are struggling with the question of where their home is – much like the protagonist of the lyrics in the song "Suedi".

The practice of releasing songs in connection with big championships is decades old. Such tracks are often nationalist in the happy-go-lucky manner associated with sports. In his use of the genre, Lundin combines this tradition with the political agenda from *Suedi*. When performing the song in Copenhagen on 20 April 2017, Lundin in a tongue-in-cheek way introduced the song as "the new Swedish national anthem", making his political and aesthetic ambitions clear. The fact that his version of the national anthem problematizes the notion of what Swedishness entails – and, furthermore, includes a multitude of languages, such as Somali, Arabic, Spanish, English and Turkish – gives the song a political edge that is all but subtle. The radical multilingualism of the text is underlined by the practice of using many different languages within the same phrases, such as in the line "Visste nada om Dunya" ("Knew nothing about the world"), where Swedish, Spanish and Arabic are combined in a four-word sequence.

Suedi: A Weird Swedish Poetic

What language is Swedish? Or perhaps, what language is "Suedi"? In the aesthetic of Erik Lundin, the question is not easily answered, but his version of Swedish/Suedi – his "weird Swedish" – is clearly a much broader concept than the language described in Swedish dictionaries. The symbolic potential of the physical dictionary is not lost on Lundin: upon the release of *Suedi*, he told journalists that a glossary would be accompanying it. This glossary never materialized, but the intention gives testimony to the mindset of the artist: language is at the heart of the matter, and he recognized the centrifugal as well as the centripetal potential of his enterprise. In the songs themselves, language is highlighted not only thematically in the lyrics, but, as we have seen, also in the very form of the lyrics. Lundin mixes languages from different countries, and yet he goes further, mixing languages from different social spheres, turning his rhymes into radical examples of multi-layered heteroglossia. The song "Haram", which on the surface is a song about partying one's troubles away, also includes reflections on police harassment, drug dealing, and multicultural friendships and identities. Traditionally coarse language full of cursing and slang is mixed with high-brow Latin terms, such as "momentum", "tempus" and "consensus", showing the wide scope and far-reaching range of Lundin's vocabulary. Language-wise, the song moves from Swahili to Turkish, Latin, Portuguese, Greek, Spanish, Wolof and English. Furthermore, seemingly Swedish words are often semantically multilingual, since they are literal translations of non-Swedish idiomatic translations. The Spanish expletive "hijo de puta", for example, is translated into the Swedish "horungar" – a term that exists in the Swedish language but historically – apart from surprisingly enough being a typographical term – only has been used literally about children born out of wedlock. It is furthermore worth noting that US vernacular – supposedly the language of hip-hop – is quite absent here. The opening of the song is a play with contrasts:

Hakuna Matata
Hakuna Matata
Aina persona non grata
SD persona non grata

No English translation is needed, as these four lines contain no Swedish vocabulary. Instead, the Disney Swahili expression "hakuna matata" rhymes with "persona non grata", thus mixing popular culture and language traditionally not taught at university with the lingua franca of diplomacy, Latin, which is part of curricula all over the world. While "aina" is a word of Turkish origin used in Swedish slang for "police", and SD is short for the Sweden Democrats – the populist right-wing party mentioned in the text above, "aina" is also Finnish for "always", a denotation that could also be invoked here: Swedish Democrats are never welcome.

If one compares versified poetry with hip-hop rhymes, one fundamental difference stands out. In poetry, the beat of the verse is abstract, constructed from the rhyme and rhythm of the words of the poem. In hip-hop, the rhyme and rhythm of the words remain, but the beat of the music is also there. And while poetry is often read privately, hip-hop lyrics are always performed, adding the voice and delivery of the performer to the mix (Rose 1994; Bradley 2009). In Lundin's aesthetic, rhyme and rhythm are at the forefront, and they are both an important factor in the deterritorializing force of his multilingual lines. Lundin's way of rhyming words from different languages in a seamless flow brings out their similarities of sound and rhythm and thus blurs the borders between them, deepening the multilingual quality of the lyrics.

In many instances, Lundin combines words from many different languages and social spheres in very short sequences delivered in a flow so tight and fast that the words are often almost impossible to pick up from just hearing the songs. The fact that the lyrics published online by fans are full of errors is clear evidence of this fact. Lundin's delivery highlights rhythm and sound rather than semantic content. In some instances, the lyrics stretch towards a space where sound is prior to meaning and almost resists it, turning the lyrics into a play with sound and repetition. Ch'ien writes about the acoustic aspect of language and claims that "human beings have a relationship with language that is satisfying beyond its function of delivering meaning"; furthermore, she asserts, "Weird English highlights these aesthetic aspects of linguistic presence in human life" (Ch'ien 2004, 7). Lyrics come close to being music. In the song discussed above, the vowel sequence [a: / a:] is absolutely central to the lyrics, often in combination with the [u:] sound found in the expression "hakuna matata". This repetition creates rhythm while pointing towards the central hook: "min bror är haram" ("my brother is Haram") where the *u: / a: / a:* sounds cannot be missed, as they are repeated. The reduction of a multitude of languages to one repeated sound almost has a deconstructive quality to it, turning language into rhythmic noise. There is no point of origin here, as words from different countries, continents and social strata are mixed and combined, cutting through hierarchies as they go. This aesthetic reaches far beyond code-switching; rather, it questions the notion of language as a clearly demarcated monological system. As Tidigs and Huss (2017) have pointed out, language reduced to noise is not without meaning and not without effect. I would say that it might often prompt reflections upon the nature of language itself. In the case of Lundin, language is also used as a musical instrument through the making of patterns in sound, tone, rhythm and pitch. The aesthetic of the lyrics and its conversion of language into music and noise are also mirrored in the musical aesthetic of hip-hop used here. Samples and repetitive loops deconstruct and question the notion of originality. This is in line with a recurring discussion not only among hip-hop scholars, but also among scholars of modern poetry (Bradley 2009, 212; Perloff 2010, 123–145).

The centrifugal force that is at work here through the radical multilingualism of the lyrics can, however, also be understood as a centripetal force: through the use of sound repetition and rhythm, all of these words, expressions and music samplings are turned into one language, a wider and broader sense of Swedish – or Suedi. The cultural and linguistic context and origin of every word are heterogeneous, while in a broad sense they are part of Swedish discourse. In her acceptance speech at the Swedish Grammis, Silvana Imam turned Arabic and Lithuanian into Swedish languages – if only for a moment. I would argue that Lundin promotes the same idea in his lyrics through his use of many languages, but also through highlighting the many languages that are in fact spoken in Sweden and by pointing out that the Swedish soundscape in itself is post-monolingual, if one cares to listen. In the song "Haffla", he proposes that he and others should be writers:

Our travels are underestimated
[...]
So take it back, take it in Aramaic,
Take it in Arabic, take it in Hebrew
All the Suedis who are non-European
Here's to immortalizing the histories, *haffla!*[10]

Language Play and Politics 171

The point here is clear: Swedes of non-European origin should tell their stories, as they are still untold and unheard. Arabic, Hebrew and Aramaic are languages that are spoken in different variants in Sweden today in spite of being all but invisible in the public domain. However, outside of Sweden (and Europe), the histories of these languages and their literary histories are both glorious and important to the origins of literature, Occidental as well as Oriental. Thus, Lundin subtly suggests, implicit language hierarchies and the question of minority and majority are a matter of perspective. Since Suedis speak these languages, they effectively become Swedish languages. Simply put, Lundin and all other Swedes of other, often ignored origins have stories to tell and should be published as well as included in the realm of Swedish literature.

In the excerpt above from "Haffla", multilingual Swedishness is thematized, but languages are not really mixed – if one disregards the use of the words "Suedi" and "haffla". As we have seen, however, multilingual Swedish is the very foundation of Lundin's poetics, as it is an inherent part of its form. Lundin already has a political pathos that he shares with those who came before him: the Latin Kings and Feven were outspokenly political, as are many other Swedish and Scandinavian rappers. Through Lundin's repeated focus on language and his radical heteroglossia, his hip-hop lyrics become language politics as well.

Conclusion and Outlook: The Force of Post-monolingual Nordic Hip-Hop

In this chapter, I have explored how rap lyrics in Sweden have become increasingly more multilingual in the past twenty years, going from the extrinsic and organic multilingualism of the 1990s to the radical and political multilingualism of today. A short study like this one can never be exhaustive, and while Erik Lundin has been my main example – and his multilingualism is exceptional – he is far from alone in mixing languages and blurring language borders, thus negotiating questions of identity, nation and language. In the other Nordic countries, multilingualism and heteroglossia in hip-hop have – so far – taken on other, often subtler, forms. Greenland is an interesting example, where groups like Nuuk Posse perform in Inuit, Danish and English, making linguistic choices that in themselves highlight language hierarchies in Greenland – a territory that is still a part of the Danish kingdom – and thus practise language politics (Mitchell 2001, 12). In Finland, the highlighting and blurring of languages and identities in hip-hop has not yet become very common, although the scene is starting to change, with hop-hop taking an increasing part in the often quite heated political debate on Finnish ethnicity and identity (Westinen 2016).

In Denmark, hip-hop has historically been less language-political than in Sweden, one exception being the tremendously successful group

Outlandish, notwithstanding the fact that their language politics are not visible in all of their work. Internationally speaking, their biggest hit was a cover of "Aicha" (1996), a song by the Algerian raï singer Khaled, which itself is a mix of Arab raï, French chanson and European pop. Outlandish performed this song in English and a few words of French. Their 2006 song "Kom igen" (Come on) uses English, Danish, Spanish and Arabic to convey a message about selflessness and the empty lures of money, but the multilingualism is of a type that upholds the borders between languages, as it switches languages – and often performers – with each verse. The group uses this modus operandi in many other songs as well, employing a post-monolingual stance and aesthetic which, however, does not reach the radical multilingual performance of Erik Lundin's lyrics. In Norway, the genre widely known as "dialect rap" has been quite influential, with groups such as Tungtvann and more recently Yoguttene rapping in a quite heavy local dialect – often, but not always, aiming for comic effect. In Sweden, the fact that a few successful hip-hop acts use dialect (more often than not Southern Swedish vernacular, as in the work of Timbuktu) has not really been given any attention, perhaps since dialect is not attached to political connotations in Sweden as it is in Norway, where, due to the history of the Norwegian language, dialect is often a marker of both class and ideology (Bucken-Knapp 2003, 1–23).

Cultural studies scholar Toni Mitchell suggested already in 2001 that hip-hop had become "a tool for reworking local identity all over the world" (Mitchell 2001, 1–2). Clearly, this holds increasingly true in a Swedish context – and language plays a huge part in this reworking enterprise. Erik Lundin raps in Swedish, but his is not the Swedish of the standard dictionary. The choice of Swedish signals sameness, while the choice of deterritorializing "weird Swedish" signals otherness, thus setting both centrifugal and centripetal forces in motion. In analogy with Ch'ien's study on deterritorialized English, *Weird English*, where the existence of many Englishes is suggested, one both could and should talk about Swedish in the plural: there are many Swedishes. Unwittingly or not, contemporary Swedish rappers such as Erik Lundin highlight this very fact, and through their work they question what it means to be and to speak Swedish.

Notes

1 "Jag borde bli kontaktad av författare / Fuck it bre, jag borde bli författare."
2 "Osten har hunnit åldras och whiskyn har blivit myndig."
3 "Helt hype, kolla passet upp i luften som Timbuks."
4 "Den som inte passar in gör allt för att stå ut, för att stå ut / Vi förvrängde dialekten / snodde en massa ord från släkten / Vad blev effekten / Förortsslang, det gav respekten / Grammatiken den blev kassare, R:en vassare."
5 "Trivdes bäst i orten, kanske bråkigt / men aldrig tråkigt, mångfald, flerspråkigt."

6 "Nu går dom på snus / och har skaffat hus / Volvon står på grus / deras barn föds på svenska sjukhus."
7 "Min identitet är mitt eget val."
8 "Flaggan vi brukade dissa den / nu vi lyfter och viftar den." [...] "Är hemma nu det är här jag vill stanna."
9 "För Olsen, Guidetti, för Zlatan min bror, Henke Larsson, Dahlin, och Ravelli / Välkommen hem!"
10 "Våra resor är underskattade [...] Så ta det tillbaka, ta det på arameiska / Ta det på arabiska, ta det på hebreiska / Alla dom suedis som är utomeuropeiska / Skål för att historierna förevigas, haffla!"

Bibliography

Aidi, Hisham (2014) *Rebel Music: Race, Empire, and the New Muslim Youth Culture*. New York: Vintage.
Alexis Askergren, Petter (2013) *16 rader*. Stockholm: Brombergs.
Alim, H. Samy; Ibrahim, Awad & Pennycook, Alastair (eds) (2008) *Global Linguistic Flows: Hip Hop Cultures, Youth Identities, and the Politics of Language*. New York & London: Routledge.
Anderson, Benedict (2006) *Imagined Communities: Reflections on the Origin and Spread of Nationalism*. Revised edition. London & New York: Verso.
Anyuru, Johannes (2003) *Bara gudarna är nya*. Stockholm: Bonniers.
Bakhtin, Mikhail (1982) *The Dialogic Imagination: Four Essays by M. M. Bakhtin*. Edited By Michael Holquist. Translated by Caryl Emerson & Michael Holquist. Austin: University of Texas Press.
Berggren, Kalle (2014) *Reading Rap: Feminist Interventions in Men and Masculinity Research*. Uppsala: Acta Universitatis Upsaliensis.
Bhabha, Homi K (1994) *The Location of Culture*. London & New York: Routledge.
Boyacioglu, Daniel (2003) *Istället för hiphop*. Stockholm: Tiden.
Bradley, Adam (2009) *Book of Rhymes: The Poetics of Hip Hop*. Philadelphia, PA: Basic Civitas.
Bucken-Knapp, Gregg (2003) *Elites, Language and the Politics of Identity: The Norwegian Case in Comparative Perspective*. Albany: State University of New York Press.
Ch'ien, Evelyn Nien-Ming (2004) *Weird English*. Cambridge & London: Harvard University Press.
Deleuze, Gilles & Guattari, Félix (1988) *A Thousand Plateaus: Capitalism and Schizophrenia*. Translated by Brian Massumi. London: The Athlone Press.
Diakité, Jason (2016) *En droppe midnatt*. Stockholm: Bonniers.
Doggelito, Dogge & Kotsinas, Ulla-Britt (2004) *Förortsslang*. Stockholm: Norstedts Ordbok.
Doggelito, Dogge & Rivera, Yoria (2011a) *Izzy & gänget*. Stockholm: Bonnier Carlsen.
Doggelito, Dogge & Rivera, Yoria (2011b) *Izzy & gänget – lata dagar*. Stockholm: Bonnier Carlsen.
Doggelito, Dogge & Rivera, Yoria (2012) *Izzy & gänget – vänskapen växer*. Stockholm: Bonnier Carlsen.
Frith, Simon (1996) Music and Identity. In Stuart Hall & Paul du Gay (eds.): *Questions of Cultural Identity*. London: Sage, 108–127.

Gates, Henry Louis, Jr. (1988) *The Signifying Monkey: A Theory of Afro-American Literary Criticism.* New York & Oxford: Oxford University Press.
Gates, Henry Louis, Jr. (2010) Foreword. In Adam Bradley & Andrew DuBois (eds): *The Anthology of Rap.* New Haven & London: Yale University Press, xxii–xxvii.
Gilroy, Paul (1993) *The Black Atlantic: Modernity and Double Consciousness.* London & New York: Verso.
Gordon, Elisabeth & Williams, Mark (1998) Raids on the Articulate: Code-Switching, Style-Shifting and Post Colonial Writing. *The Journal of Commonwealth Literature* 33(2), 75–96.
Haidl, Kajsa (2016) De läckta vinnarna var de riktiga på Grammis. *Dagens Nyheter,* February 24, 2016. Accessed June 1, 2017, www.dn.se/kultur-noje/musik/de-lackta-vinnarna-blev-de-riktiga-pa-grammis/.
Hess, Mickey (2007) *Is Hip Hop Dead? The Past, Present, and Future of America's Most Wanted Music.* Westport & London: Praeger.
Jay-Z (2010) *Decoded.* New York: Spiegel & Grau.
Keyes, Cheryl L. (2002) *Rap Music and Street Consciousness.* Urbana & Chicago: University of Illinois Press.
Krogh, Mads & Stougaard Pedersen, Brigitte (eds) (2008) *Hiphop i Skandinavien.* Århus: Aarhus Universitetsforlag.
Latin Kings (2004) *The Latin Kings: Texter.* Uppsala: Ruin.
Lindholm, Susan (2016) *Remembering Chile: An Entangled History of Hip-hop in-between Sweden and Chile.* Malmö: Fakulteten för lärande och samhälle.
Lundin, Erik et al. (2016) Third culture kids. Samtidens skildrare. *10TAL* 23/24 2016.
Mitchell, Toni (ed.) (2001) *Global Noise: Rap and Hip-Hop Outside the USA.* Middletown: Wesleyan University.
Ogbar, Jeffrey O.G. (2007) *Hip-Hop Revolution: The Culture and Politics of Rap.* Lawrence: University Press of Kansas.
Perloff, Marjorie (2010) *Unoriginal Genius: Poetry by Other Means in the New Century.* Chicago & London: Chicago University Press.
Perry, Imani (2004) *Prophets of the Hood: Politics and Poetics in Hip Hop.* Durham & London: Duke University Press.
Potter, Russel A. (1995) *Spectacular Vernaculars: Hip Hop and the Politics of Postmodernism.* New York: State University of New York Press.
Rabaka, Reiland (2011) *Hip Hop's Inheritance: From the Harlem Renaissance to the Hip Hop Feminist Movement.* Plymouth: Lexington Books.
Roney, Marimba (2015) I en klass för sig. *Sonic* 82, June 2015, 24–26.
Rose, Tricia (1994) *Black Noise: Rap Music and Black Culture in Contemporary America.* Hanover: Wesleyan University Press.
Sernhede, Ove (2002) *Alienation is my nation: hiphop och unga mäns utanförskap i Det nya Sverige.* Stockholm: Ordfront.
Sernhede, Ove & Söderman, Johan (2010) *Planet Hiphop: Om hiphop som folkbildning och social mobilisering.* Malmö: Liber.
Söderman, Johan (2007) *Rap(p) i käften: Hiphopmusikers konstnärliga och pedagogiska strategier.* Malmö: Malmö Academy of Music.
Sommer, Doris (2004) *Bilingual Aesthetics: A New Sentimental Education.* Durham, NC: Duke University Press.
Strage, Fredrik (2001) *Mikrofonkåt.* Stockholm: Atlas.

Strömberg, Ragnar (2003) Räkna med bråk. *Aftonbladet* August 4, 2003. Accessed June 1, 2017, www.aftonbladet.se/kultur/article10384554.ab.
Terkourafi, Marina (ed.) (2010) *The Languages of Global Hip Hop*. London & New York: Continuum.
Thomsen, Dante (2016) Silvana Imams hårda kritik mot Grammis. *Expressen* February 24, 2016. Accessed on June 1, 2017, www.expressen.se/noje/silvana-imams-harda-kritik-mot-grammis/.
Tidigs, Julia (2014) *Att skriva sig över språkgränserna: Flerspråkighet i Jac. Ahrenbergs och Elmer Diktonius prosa*. Åbo: Åbo Akademis förlag.
Tidigs, Julia & Huss, Markus (2017) The Noise of Multilingualism. *Critical Multilingualism Studies* 5(1), 209–235.
Weiderud, Hanna (2016). Silvana Imam om tacktalet. *SVT Nyheter* February 24, 2016. Accessed June 1, 2017, www.svt.se/kultur/musik/silvana-imam-om-tacktalet.
Westinen, Elina (2016) Multiscalarity and Polycentricity in Rap Artists' Social Media Communication: Multisemiotic Negotiations of Otherness and Integration. In Jaspal Naveel Singh, Argyro Kantara & Dorottya Cserző (eds): *Downscaling Culture: Revisiting Intercultural Communication*. Newcastle: Cambridge Scholars Publishing, 280–310.
Woldu, Gail Hilson (2010) The Kaleidoscope of Writing on Hip-Hop Culture. *Notes* 67(1), 9–38.
Yildiz, Yasemin (2012) *Beyond the Mother Tongue. The Postmonolingual Condition*. New York: Fordham University Press.

Discography

Feven (2000) *Vägen ut*. Stockholm: Sony BMG Music Entertainment.
Hedemyr, René (1980) *Record Pool Rap*. Stockholm: White / Record Pool. Accessible at www.youtube.com/watch?v=PuVcx22sQzc.
Just D (1991) *Svenska ord*. Stockholm: Telegram Records.
Kartellen (2013) Svarta duvor & vissna liljor (feat. Timbuktu). In *Ånger & kamp, del 2*. Stockholm: Universal.
Latin Kings (1994) *Välkommen till förorten*. Stockholm: Warner Music Sweden.
Lundin, Erik (2015) *Suedi*. Stockholm: RMH Sweden.
Lundin, Erik (2016) *Välkommen hem*. Stockholm: RMH Sweden.
MC Tim (Timothy Wolde) (1989) *Jag Är Def*. Accessible at www.youtube.com/watch?v=Ca98hF1yHuI.

Videography

Feven (2000b) "Bränn BH'n". Stockholm: Sony BMG Music Entertainment. Accessible at www.youtube.com/watch?v=Q35QbnS-TNQ.

Other Sources

Kulturnytt (2016) "Silvana Imam om vad som sades i tacktalet och varför". Radio interview from February 24, 2016. Accessed December 17, 2017, http://sverigesradio.se/sida/artikel.aspx?programid=478&artikel=6375779.

11 "Conversations in misspelled English"
Partial Comprehension and Linguistic Borderlands in Tomas Tranströmer's *Östersjöar. En dikt (Baltics)*

Markus Huss

Scholarship on the relationship between literature and multilingualism, sometimes referred to as *literary multilingualism*, is growing rapidly, not least in the Nordic region.[1] Situated in the intersection between literary studies, sociolinguistics and translation studies, the field – although one might still hesitate to call it a unified field, considering the many different theoretical frameworks and foci – emerges as a particularly fruitful approach to addressing general cultural and political issues associated with processes of globalization in Northern Europe: the concept of *world literature* and how to understand the circulation of minor language literatures in a global context, the politics of translation and how to negotiate and critically scrutinize the resilience of nationalism and monolingualism in an increasingly transnational literary field. For the purposes of this chapter, however, I wish to address the *concept* of literary multilingualism and suggest that we need to critically reflect on the dangers of considering multilingual literature as a separate category from so-called "normal" or monolingual literature. Theoretically, I take my departure from translation studies scholar Naoki Sakai's understanding of *bordering* in the context of translation in order to illustrate the contingency and perpetual mobility of linguistic borders (Sakai 2009, 83). The fact that languages never cease to change and develop – and that the borders between languages as well as their labels (language? dialect? sociolect? Creole?) also change due to historical, political, economic and cultural power relations and processes – is, of course, not new. Still, the tendency to regard multilingualism in literature as a separate sphere of interest, outside the realm of so-called monolingual literature, is strong (e.g. see Tidigs & Huss 2017, 211–212).

Many literary works considered to be part of the monolingual literary canons of the Nordic countries do in fact exhibit features associated with multilingual literature, such as the mixing of linguistic registers. I argue for a re-examination of canonical works of Nordic literature from the perspective of literary multilingualism for two main reasons. First, canonical literary works' linguistic interconnections and entangled literary relationships with other languages and traditions usually associated with that particular national canon generally tend to be downplayed, which hinders a better historical understanding and aesthetic appreciation of them. Yasemin Yildiz's reading of Kafka has reminded us of the fact that "what looks like a monolingual text may, in fact, suggest the contours of a multilingual paradigm" (Yildiz 2012, 35). Second, canonical literary works and their histories of reception offer fascinating examples of how over the course of time they have been regarded as nationally and culturally representative. Simultaneously, however, they may – on a linguistic and literary level – work against such an understanding.

With these considerations in mind, I will analyse Tomas Tranströmer's long poem *Östersjöar. En dikt* (in Robert Fulton's translation, *Baltics*).[2] The poem offers straightforward instances of lexical multilingualism (e.g. words in English, Latin, French and Old East Norse (Sw. "fornöstnordiska"), which clearly depart from standard Swedish), but these will not be my sole concern. Rather than only pointing to these examples, I wish to demonstrate how the poem draws attention to the malleable border between sound and language, understanding and misunderstanding in a poetic meditation whose recurrent motif and prism consists of the *border* itself. Tranströmer's poem, in my view, thematizes partial fluency, misunderstanding and precarious communication in a transnational, multilingual setting, opening up a space for philosophical, existential and political reflection – a space that I claim to be of fertile ground also for a general, theoretical discussion on literary multilingualism and how the concept might be understood. Drawing on my analysis and previous research on the poem, I wish to discuss the possibility of defining literary multilingualism in a wider sense, involving a multimodal and reader-oriented approach to the phenomenon.

Partial Fluency as Aesthetic Asset?

Before turning to the analysis of *Östersjöar*, however, I briefly wish to discuss the topic of incomprehension, not only because it recurs as a motif throughout the poem, but also due to its role in literary multilingualism and the interaction between diverse groups of readers and the literary text. The question of whether or not a text is considered to consist of intelligible language/languages or incomprehensible gibberish – that is, only a random cluster of letters foreign to the reader – depends, of course, on the audience, and this can, in turn, give rise to various aesthetic effects on the part of the reader. In contrast to previous scholarship arguing that multilingual literature requires multilingual readers, I instead follow Doris Sommer's and Julia Tidigs's theoretical considerations (Sommer 2004, 30; Tidigs 2014, 102f.). Sommer and Tidigs highlight the relationship between partial fluency and aesthetic effects on the part of the reader of the multilingual literary text, exemplifying how his or her lack of linguistic knowledge may in some cases work as an asset, an invitation to consider the linguistic foreignness of a text as a sphere of experimentation and *deautomatization* of everyday language usage (Sommer refers here to Viktor Shklovsky's term). Furthermore, Rebecka Walkowitz identifies these features as significant for the contemporary novel "in an age of world literature": "Instead of identification, these texts offer readers partial fluency, approximation and virtual understanding" (Walkowitz 2015, 30).

I also wish to briefly recapitulate Monika Schmitz-Emans's argument in the article "Geschriebene Fremdkörper – Spielformen und Funktionen der Integration fremder Schriftzeichen in literarische Texte" (Alien scripts – forms and functions of the integration of foreign characters in literary texts), in which she follows the trope of the incomprehensible "foreign" text in literary examples from the Romantic era up to present times in German literature, but also from the sphere of German language philosophy, in this case focussing on Johann Georg Hamann (Schmitz-Emans 2004, 111–173). Schmitz-Emans illustrates how Hamann insists on the aesthetic qualities of different written languages in his own writings – their particular typographical shapes in terms of visual artefacts, but importantly also their acoustic qualities – qualities that have the power to arrest the reader's desire for instant translation and comprehension. In fact, Schmitz-Emans argues, it is exactly this desire for instant comprehension and the extraction of meaning into an abstract sphere of thought somehow considered to be beyond language that Hamann vehemently criticizes. According to Schmitz-Emans, Hamann's main point is that instead of striving towards translation and comprehension, we should pay attention to the sensual characteristics of language, in other words, its aesthetic qualities. This is in line with a multimodal approach to literary multilingualism, which I will try to demonstrate in my analysis of *Östersjöar*.

Tomas Tranströmer's *Östersjöar* and Previous Research

No contemporary Swedish poet has been so widely celebrated around the world – a phrase truly apt in this case – as Tomas Tranströmer. This was also the case long before he was awarded the Nobel Prize in Literature in 2011 "because, through his condensed, translucent images, he gives us fresh access to reality" (Swedish Academy 2011). His poetry comprises thirteen published collections, from *17 dikter* (1954; 17 poems) to *Den stora gåtan* (2004; The great enigma). According to an email from Monica Tranströmer on 9 October 2017, Tranströmer's work had been translated as of that date into sixty-nine languages, including the dialects of Bavarian and "jamska" spoken in the Swedish province of Jämtland.

Partial Comprehension & Linguistic Borderlands 179

Östersjöar. En dikt was published in 1974 and was, according to Kjell Espmark, the author's most extensive effort to develop a longer and "freer, rhythmic verse and a less strict, dense diction" (Espmark 1983, 225; my translation). The Virtual Baltic Sea Library, a web portal dedicated to publishing and translating "representative literary texts broadly connected with the Baltic Sea", which "seeks to provide multiple insights into the Baltic Sea region", has so far published eleven translations of *Östersjöar*: in Danish, English, Estonian, Finnish, German, Icelandic, Latvian, Lithuanian, Norwegian, Polish and Russian (Baltic Sea Library n.d.). The subject matter, already stated in the poem's title, naturally invites translations into the other languages of the Baltic Sea region, and the Baltic Sea Library's side-by-side compilation of translations offer a good opportunity to study differences between them. Even though this will not be the focus of my analysis, the various possibilities of translation exhibited in the different language versions cast new light on the Swedish original, sometimes offering fresh interpretations and strategies of reading.

The scholarship on Tomas Tranströmer is vast. I have deliberately chosen to limit my use of previous research to works dealing with *Östersjöar* in an elaborate manner (Espmark 1983; Bankier 1993; Ringgren 1997; Falk 2001; Rönnerstrand 2003; Madsen 2014). The poem is divided into six parts; as previous scholarship has demonstrated, these constitute a thematic whole, ultimately structured by the title's Baltic Sea as its spatial and temporal dimension. Magnus Ringgren follows numerous other interpreters in comparing the poem to a musical suite in six movements, a multimodal dimension of the poem, to which I will return below (Ringgren 1997, 9). Joanna Bankier regards the poem as Tranströmer's deliberate attempt to make "a form of inner time" by combining the "structural similarity between music and memory" (Bankier 1993, 130). In a Deleuzian reading of the poem, Claus K. Madsen has instead highlighted its structure in terms of intertwined fragments, which, according to him, express a longing for a lost, unifying narrative (Madsen 2014, 65). In my view, these descriptions do not necessarily contradict each other; rather, they testify to the rich interpretative possibilities that the poem offers. Thematically, *Östersjöar* revolves around miscomprehension and the problems of communication, which are also linked to the poem's historical scope: The I-narrator repeatedly reflects on and tries to interpret traces of the past in the geographical surroundings of the Stockholm archipelago, as well as through historical documents, such as a photograph and notes on vessels that his pilot grandfather made in his almanac (see quote below). Hence, the theme of communication and the problems associated with it are not only restricted to interpersonal communication between people who speak different languages, but also fundamentally to the problem of historical distance. In both of these cases, the *border* (or "frontier", as Robin Fulton has chosen to translate

180   *Markus Huss*

the Swedish *gräns*) comes across as a multifaceted and even paradoxical image for this communicative difficulty. In a short description of *Östersjöar* that was printed on the cover of the 1990 edition (see Ringgren 1997, 16), the border is also highlighted by Tranströmer himself as a "keyword" in the poem. Here Tranströmer describes it as inspired by his own childhood and the lives of his grandparents, along with two trips to Estonia and Latvia in 1970. The poem is furthermore described as "geographical, historical, political and introspective".[3]

Partial Comprehension and Metaphors of Writing and Reading in *Östersjöar*

In order to return to the link between my analysis of the poem and the more general theoretical discussion on the concept of literary multilingualism that I wish to pursue, I would like to suggest the need to widen the scope of research on literary multilingualism to also include those instances of language usually not counted in our analysis as language proper, such as sounds and noises (also discussed in Tidigs & Huss 2017). We need to focus on these seemingly peripheral phenomena, since they highlight the borders or limits of what we usually tend to regard as language and that which tends to be discarded as superfluous or uninteresting noise. As Douglas Kahn has noted, "noise" is usually understood as that which disturbs communication, such as "[i]mperfections in script, verbal pauses, and poor phrasing" (Kahn 1999, 25). As his work on the history of sound in modern art demonstrates, however, sounds and noises should not be defined as the opposite of meaning, as somehow transcending signification in contrast to an articulated language. They are, on the contrary, part of a social, cultural and political space imagined by humans. Following this view, instances of "noise" in multilingual literature *do* signify in many important ways and furthermore have the potential to help us rethink common theoretical assumptions in the field of literary multilingualism. Sounds and noises are also part of our phenomenological experience of language, the acoustic materiality of language surrounding us in our everyday lives. Literature has the ability to heighten our sensitivity to the acoustics of language itself, an ability to arrest the reader's desire for instant comprehension and instead open up a sphere of a strange but captivating foreign linguistic territory. Stephen Connor has described this sphere, or perhaps this acoustic dimension cohabited by sounds and languages, in the following way:

> If the two extremes of human existence are the animal or biological being of the body, and the power of thought and self-representation given by language, then the realms of sound, voice and music lie between body and language. They are no longer merely body, for they are the emanations of the body, the body put forth or doubled. But

neither are they yet language, in the sense of grammar, syntax, or semantics. Rather, they are the body of language, sometimes thought of as the inert mass of form out of which music will be shaped, or words selected, sometimes as an unchallenged impetus or power.

(Connor 2002, 4)

Tranströmer's poem returns, again and again, to this sphere between language and body; in fact, it could even be described as the centre of *Östersjöar*, around which its six parts revolve. Already in the first part of the poem, the theme of precarious communication in a foreign language is introduced, accompanied by reiterated questions posed by the narrator, which never receive an answer:

1

It was before the age of the radio masts.

Grandfather was a new-made pilot. In the almanac he wrote
 down the vessels he piloted –
names, destinations, drafts.
Examples from 1884:
Steamer Tiger Capt. Rowan 16 ft Hull Gefle Furusund
Brigg Ocean Capt. Andersen 8 ft Sandöfjord Hernösand
Furusund
Steamer St. Petersburg Capt. Libenberg 11 ft Stettin Libau
Sandhamn

He took them out to the Baltic, through the marvellous
 labyrinth of islands and waters.
And those who met on board and were carried by the same
 hull for a few hours, or days,
how much did they come to know one another?
Conversations in misspelled English, understanding and
 misunderstanding but very little conscious falsehood.
How much did they come to know one another?

When it was thick fog: half speed, half blind ahead. At one
 single stride the cape emerged from the invisible and was
 right on them.
Every other minute a bellowing signal. His eyes read straight
 into the invisible.
(Had he the labyrinth in his head?)
The minutes passed.
Shallows and skerries he memorized like psalm verses.
And that feeling of "we're just here" that must be kept, like
 carrying a brimful pail without spilling a drop.

A glance down in the engine room.
The compound machine long-lived as a human heart toiled
with great supple bouncing movements, acrobats of steel,
and the smells rose as if from a kitchen.[4]
(Tranströmer 2006, 127; trans. Robin Fulton)

The first line of the poem introduces the theme of long-distance communication through historical contrast. In Fulton's translation, one reads: "It was before the age of the radio masts." The reader is presented with abbreviations made by the I-narrator's grandfather for the various vessels trafficking the archipelago; this is a kind of miniature poem, which in itself demonstrates the transnational routes as well as the names of the captains and harbours of the Baltic Sea. In the age before radio masts, ships had to rely on the knowledge of pilots like the grandfather, who took them "through the marvellous labyrinth of islands and waters". The verbal conversations between the grandfather and the seamen of the foreign vessels are, if not as equally precarious as the ships passing through thick fog in the waters of the archipelago, depicted as cautious and preliminary:

And those who met on board and were carried by the same hull for a few hours, or days, how much did they come to know one another? Conversations in misspelled English, understanding and misunderstanding but very little conscious falsehood. How much did they come to know one another?

Here communication takes place in a "misspelled English", highlighting the written word, as opposed to "broken English", which could come across as a more natural phrase in this context. Espmark interprets it as a "playful shift from pronunciation to orthography" that "simultaneously captures the mutual language's bridging as well as the limits of the linguistic connection" (1983, 235). Rönnerstrand (2003, 145) argues that the phrase introduces three motifs that will recur in Tranströmer's later poetry, namely, "'the border between silence and the articulable', the aphasia motif and the thought that every act of language involves a kind of translation". These points are all correct, but they overlook how "misspelled English" evokes a recurring metaphor of writing and reading used to describe the grandfather's activity as a pilot (for Tranströmer's use of textual metaphors in landscape descriptions, see Falk 2001, 29). In the fourth stanza of this first part of the poem, the grandfather's "eyes read straight into the invisible", and the "[s]hallows and skerries he memorized like psalm verses". The pilot, in short, *reads* the landscape and the sea. The connection thus established between topography and memorized hymns lends the pilot's activity a literary – as well

Partial Comprehension & Linguistic Borderlands 183

as ritual – character. Interpreted in this context, the "[c]onversations in misspelled English, understanding and misunderstanding but very little conscious falsehood" lend the pilot the role of a reader and writer of the Baltic Sea, who despite the precariousness of the communicative situation and poor English skills all around succeeds in escorting the vessels to safety. Still, the iteration of the question "How much did they come to know one another?" underlines how the conversations that took place long ago will remain unheard and unwritten, unreachable for the I-narrator as well as for the readers of the poem. Together with the I-narrator, we are left to interpret the "misspelled conversations" of the past, thus experiencing a similar kind of partial fluency as the grandfather and the crews of the foreign vessels.

The fact that the "[s]hallows and skerries" are "memorized like psalm verses" requires further scrutiny, since it highlights the poem's recurring conflation of language, literature and a broader, acoustic sphere. In the act of memorizing the seascape "like psalm verses", the Baltic Sea is elevated to a hymnic language (psalms) connoted with the sphere of music. This motif reappears in the poem's fifth part, which includes a short narrative about a composer:

>Music comes to a man, he's a composer, he's played, makes a
>   career, becomes Conservatory Director.
>The climate changes, he's condemned by the authorities.
>His pupil K is set up as prosecutor.
>He's threatened, degraded, removed.
>After a few years the disgrace lessens, he's rehabilitated.
>Then, cerebral hemorrhage: paralysis on the right side
>   with aphasia, can grasp only short phrases, says the
>   wrong words.
>Beyond the reach of eulogy or execration.
>But the music's left, he keeps composing in his own style,
>for the rest of his days he becomes a medical sensation.
>
>He wrote music to texts he no longer understood –
>in the same way
>we express something through our lives
>in the humming chorus full of mistaken words.[5]
>
>(Tranströmer 2006, 135–136)

Aside from the peculiar biographical fact that Tranströmer himself suffered from a similar medical condition sixteen years after the publication of the poem, which in 1990 caused paralysis and aphasia (see Bergsten 2011, 350f.), this passage turns the lack of verbal understanding ("can grasp only short phrases, says the wrong words") into an asset, at least partly: he is now "[b]eyond the reach of eulogy or execration", a state that seems to enable him to continue composing "in his own style". Moreover, his linguistic predicament of writing "music to texts he no longer understood" is elevated to a general human condition, when Tranströmer introduces the comparison "in the same way we express something through our lives in the humming chorus full of mistaken words". Interestingly, Espmark has pointed to the fact that this passage echoes an earlier draft of the poem, including the following lines that are not to be found in the published version:

> The recruit sat in his rock shelter on the outskirts of the archipelago. And tapped on the telegraph / key its crypto: K D A N S B E N X D / passed through his hands, he did not understand it (as so much else that passes through our hands and we do not understand it) / J K L A N F R T X S.[6]

Just as in the published passage about the composer, this communication of encrypted messages unknown to the private who is handling the telegraph is elevated to a general condition through the phrase in parentheses: "(as so much else that passes through our hands and we do not understand it)". In the published passage about the composer, our lives are full of "mistaken words" and are ascribed meaning (they express "something through our lives"), but they also give rise to a collective "humming chorus", whereby the sphere of language and music again blend (I will return to the "humming" acoustic quality of incomprehensible language further on). In sum, the passages from the first and fifth sections of the poem thus demonstrate a precarious communicative situation where verbal language comes across as fragmented and provisional. However, this fragmented state of language also introduces a new mode of experience and aesthetic orientation (the pilot) as well as aesthetic creation (the composer): the acoustic sphere of sound and, ultimately, music. Thus, *Östersjöar* seems to conflate partial verbal and textual comprehension – and, in the case of the composer, even *incomprehension* – with creative, aesthetic possibilities. Furthermore, this recalls the emphasis on the creative potential of partial fluency in recent scholarship on literary multilingualism (discussed earlier in this chapter). *Östersjöar* seems to demonstrate this potential on a thematic level.

"Where everything becomes a frontier" – Listening to Language Borders in *Östersjöar*

Where the first part of the poem invokes the metaphor of reading and writing as a way to experience the Baltic Sea, the second section (almost twice as long as the first) highlights *listening* as the primary sense of experience. By listening to the sounds of the Baltic Sea, the I-narrator gains access to past lives, but also to a sphere where language and sound meet, and the borders between them momentarily seem to dissolve:

2

> The wind is in the pine forest. Sighing heavily and lightly.
> The Baltic is also sighing in the middle of the island, far within
>   the forest you are out on the open sea.
> The old woman hated the sighing in the trees. Her face
>   stiffened in melancholy when the wind picked up:
> "We must think about the men out in the boats."
> But she heard something else as well in the sighing, as I do, we are kin.
> (We are walking together. She's been dead for thirty years.)
> There's sighing, yes and no, understanding and misunderstanding.
> There's sighing, three sound children, one in a sanatorium and two dead.
> The great current that blows life into some flames and blows others out.
>   The conditions.
> Sighing: Save me, O God; for the waters are come in unto my soul.
> You go on, listening, and then reach a point where the frontiers open
> or rather
> where everything becomes a frontier. An open place sunk in darkness.
>   The people stream out from the faintly lit buildings. Murmuring.
>
> A new breath of wind and the place lies desolate and silent again.
> A new breath of wind, sighing about other shores.
> It's about war.
> It's about places where citizens are under control,
> where their thoughts are made with emergency exits,
> where a conversation between friends really becomes a test of
>   what friendship means.
> And when you are with people you don't know so well.
>   Control. A certain sincerity is in place
> if only you don't take your eyes off what's drifting on the
>   outskirts of the conversation: something dark, a dark stain.

>   Something that can drift in
>   and destroy everything. Don't take your eyes off it!
>   What can we compare it to? A mine?
>   No, that would be too concrete. And almost too peaceful – for
>   on our coast most of the stories about mines have a happy
>   ending, the terror short-lived.
>   As in this story from the lightship: "In the autumn of 1915 we
>   slept uneasily..." etc. A drift-mine was sighted
>   as it drifted slowly toward the lightship, then sank and
>   resurfaced, sometimes hidden by the
>   waters, sometimes glimpsed like a spy in a crowd.
>   The crew was in a sweat and shot at it with rifles. No use. At
>   last they put out a boat and made fast a long line to it and
>   slowly and carefully towed it to the experts.
>   Afterward they set up the dark shell of the mine in a sandy
>   plantation as an ornament
>   together with the shells of Strombus Gigas from the
>   West Indies.
>
>   And the sea wind is in the dry pines further away, hurrying over
>   the churchyard sand,
>   past the leaning stones, the pilots' names.
>   The dry sighing
>   of great doors opening and great doors closing.[7]
>   (Tranströmer 2006, 128–129)

The Baltic Sea initially marks its presence through sound: "The Baltic is also sighing in the middle of the island, far within the forest you are out on the open sea." Fulton has translated the Swedish word "susar" with "sighing", lending the sound a stronger verbal and anthropomorphic connotation ("susar" could also be translated as "whistling"). In both cases, the sound of the wind recalls memories when the old woman listens to it, but also simultaneously on the part of the I-narrator listening to the same sound thirty years later, as if sound itself might collapse the temporal distance between the two:

> But she heard something else as well in the sighing, as I do, we are kin. (We are walking together. She's been dead for thirty years.) There's sighing, yes and no, understanding and misunderstanding. There's sighing, three sound children, one in a sanatorium and two dead.

As Espmark and Rönnerstrand have pointed out, "understanding" and "misunderstanding" are repeated from the first part of the poem, albeit in a mirrored way, thereby establishing a connection to its theme of precarious communication (Espmark 1983, 239; Rönnerstrand 2003, 145).

The theme of the acoustic sphere as that of past lives is emphasized in the end of the first stanza, when the account of the old woman is followed by a section written in the present tense: "You go on, listening, and then reach a point where the frontiers open or rather where everything becomes a frontier. An open place sunk in darkness. The people stream out from the faintly lit buildings. Murmuring." Apart from the paradoxical image of opening frontiers paired with "everything" becoming a frontier, it is striking how this border crossing or border merging is experienced through listening. Here the dimension of sound is not constructed by discrete acoustic categories such as sounds of nature, in turn, evoking memories of the past, succeeded by a final "murmuring". Instead, the reader is presented with an auditory continuum ("You go on, listening") without any clear temporal distribution or division. In this borderlessness of sound where "everything becomes a frontier", a preliminary unity between past and present, but also between distance and closeness, is established in terms of a shared sound of a distant, indecipherable language: "Det sorlar." / "Murmuring." I draw on Espmark's interpretation of the people's murmuring as a "modulation of the constant sighing of the wind" and as "the audible sign for an all-embracing human community, a mutual understanding which prefigures a larger one in which voices from the countries around the open sea come together" (Espmark 1983, 239).

I would like to supplement Espmark's point, which underscores "mutual understanding", by highlighting how this vision of a future "all-embracing human community" is illustrated by a *lack* of verbal, literal understanding of what the people who "stream out from the faintly lit buildings" are saying, and how it instead rests upon a supralinguistic sphere of non-verbal sounds (in the sense that the "murmuring" cannot be assigned to any particular language). This state of commonality of sounds also resembles the "humming chorus" of "mistaken words" in the poem's fifth section, discussed earlier, as well as the first section's "[c]onversations in misspelled English". The sound of verbal interaction without any, or only partial, access to its semantic content thus seems to signify a preliminary state of transnational unity, or at least the possibility of such a future, precisely by sidestepping language itself and turning it into sounds which border on music.

This state of commonality is soon replaced, however, by a new, silent state announcing the themes of war and political repression in the historical context of the Cold War: "A new breath of wind and the place lies desolate and silent again. A new breath of wind, sighing about other shores. It's about war." In this second stanza, the theme of precarious communication from the poem's first part continues, but now the threat has shifted from shallows and skerries to language itself:

> It's about war. It's about places where citizens are under control, where their thoughts are made with emergency exits, where a

> conversation between friends really becomes a test of what friendship means. And when you are with people you don't know so well. Control. A certain sincerity is in place if only you don't take your eyes off what's drifting on the outskirts of the conversation: something dark, a dark stain.

As previous commentators have noted (see, e.g. Espmark 1983, 239), the passage most likely refers to the self-censorship and repressive control through mutual mistrust exercised in the Soviet Union under Stalin, as well as in the Nazi-occupied territories in the Baltic countries during the Second World War. It is, as Espmark (1983, 240) points out, a striking contrast to the unifying murmur from the passage before, but also comparable to the verbal interaction between the pilot and the foreign vessels, characterized by "understanding and misunderstanding but very little conscious falsehood".

The passage also alludes to an example of multilingualism within one language (see Schmitz-Emans 2004, 11–16), which is prevalent in totalitarian societies where an ideologically streamlined language is forced upon its citizens. Ulla Fix, a scholar of language and communication of the former German Democratic Republic, has described citizens' adoption to the officially sanctioned discourse in politically repressive societies as "code-switching", defined as

> the adoption of public language as a manifestation of belonging, in compliance with the respective system, partly critically reflective, partly non-reflective, uncritically executed. This often happened in the belief that you could not act differently, since you would otherwise expose yourself as linguistically disloyal and face sanctions.
> (Fix 2014, 75; my translation)

Interpreted in the light of Fix's definition, the poem's descriptions of thoughts "made with emergency exits" and "where a conversation between friends really becomes a test of what friendship means" testify to a kind of linguistic double consciousness, since speakers constantly have to keep in mind how their utterances might be interpreted by a hostile listener loyal to the political system (echoed in the passage "if only you don't take your eyes off what's drifting on the outskirts of the conversation: something dark, a dark stain.)" or by a kindly disposed political ally who is able to decipher layers of subversion in superficially conformist discourse (for examples of linguistic resistance in repressive societies, see Fix 2014, 75ff.). Conversely, citizens in repressive societies learn to listen for ambiguities and multiple meanings in seemingly straightforward communication, in order to navigate the pitfalls of unreflective discourse. On a broader level, then, the poem thus demonstrates how communication within a language officially considered to be one and

Partial Comprehension & Linguistic Borderlands 189

the same can entail at least two separate, highly ideologically charged registers, whereby a border or frontier running *through* language itself is highlighted.

Materiality of the Block Letter in *Östersjöar*

Aside from the theme of precarious communication, metaphors of reading and writing, and an emphasis on listening and the acoustic sphere of language, *Östersjöar* features instances of lexical multilingualism. In this concluding part of the analysis, I will focus on three names (one personal name and two names of species) that are central to the poem's themes and laden with meaning, not least due to the fact that they deviate from standard 20th-century Swedish. In addition, the narrator meditates on the materiality of the letters themselves as a way to reflect on the relationship between language, representation and historical distance. Importantly, they are the only words in the poem written in block letters (aside from "UFO" in part III; Tranströmer 1974, 20, and "TBC" in Part VI; Tranströmer 1974, 36), thereby underscoring the text's visual component: "HEGWALDR" (Tranströmer 1974, 19), "ALRUNA" (Tranströmer 1974, 22), "AURELIA" (Tranströmer 1974, 29). Even though Tranströmer does not insert another writing system than the Latin alphabet into the poem, the deviation from standard Swedish and capitalized letters evoke a defamiliarizing effect, common in the tradition of modernist, materialist poetry, as well as in contemporary multilingual poetry (see Perloff 2010; Tidigs & Huss, 2017, 221).

"HEGWALDR", the Old East Norse[8] name of a 12th-century mason whose works are still visible in medieval churches on the island of Gotland, occurs in the first section of *Östersjöar*'s third part:

3

In the half-dark corner of a Gotland church, in a glimmer of soft mildew
there's a sandstone font – 12th century – the mason's name
is still visible, shines out
like a row of teeth in a mass grave:
             HEGWALDR
             the name's left. And his pictures
here and on the sides of other pots, human swarms, figures
   stepping out of the stone.
There the eyes' kernels of good and evil are split.
Herod at table: the roasted cock flies up and crows "Christus
   natus est" – the waiter was executed –
close by, the child is born, under clusters of faces dignified and
   helpless as those of young apes.

And the fleeing steps of the pious
echoing over dragon-scaled sewer openings.
(The images stronger in memory than when seen direct,
strongest when in memory the font turns like a slow rumbling
merry-go-round.)[9]

(Tranströmer 2006, 130)

In his elucidating commentary, Espmark notes how Tranströmer seems in this passage to highlight the permanence of art despite the passage of time and the unavoidable death of the artist – "the name's left. And his pictures" (Espmark 1983, 243ff.). The name, in turn, is followed by descriptions of Hegwaldr's pictures bringing the biblical legends to life: "human swarms, figures stepping out of the stone" (for a discussion of biblical allusions in the passage, see Espmark 1983, 244). Here I only wish to pause on the striking simile of the name HEGWALDR as "a row of teeth in a mass grave", since it is particularly interesting from the perspective of multimodal, literary multilingualism. Aside from the individualizing move – the artist's name in Old East Norse is highlighted against the background of an anonymous mass, which is interpreted by Espmark as an image of the great unknown history (Espmark 1983, 243) – the reader is prompted to read "HEGWALDR" as a sequence of letters as well as a picture, "a row of teeth". According to Espmark, this passage alludes to a baptismal font in the church of Etelhem on Gotland, on which the name Hegwaldr was doubly inscribed, in Latin block letters as well as in runes (Espmark 1983, 306). Following Lars Ellerström's typology of intermedial relations – in particular, the three modes of what he terms "the semiotic modality": "convention (symbolic signs), resemblance (iconic signs) and contiguity (indexical signs)" (Elleström 2010, 22) – the narrator of *Östersjöar* thus reads "HEGWALDR" as an *iconic sign*, resembling teeth. Simultaneously, another iconic relationship is established in the passage between "HEGWALDR" and the script inscribed in the sandstone font, mentioned in the poem's narrative. In an article on literary multilingualism and contemporary multilingual poetry, Julia Tidigs and I have argued for the need to include a multimodal approach to literary multilingualism, since "multilingual poetry has a strong tendency to utilize and highlight the visual and material qualities of letters and sign systems" (Tidigs & Huss 2017, 221). The case of the 12th-century mason's name in *Östersjöar* demonstrates an affinity with this tradition and the need for readers of the poem to take this into consideration, precisely because the multilingual component (a name written in Old East Norse) coincides with a multimodal emphasis of the letters' visuality and materiality. The fact that the poem's narrator meditates on a name *literally* carved into sandstone underscores the materiality of the name itself. In sum, it is as if the linguistic defamiliarization and

Partial Comprehension & Linguistic Borderlands 191

capitalization mutually reinforce a visual reading of "HEGWALDR", turning the historically distant script into human remains.

The second name in block letters occurs in the final part of the same section. As was the case with the inscription of "HEGWALDR" in the sandstone font, the second name also turns out to be a quote:

> I don't know if we are at the beginning or coming to the end.
> The summing up can't be done, the summing up is impossible.
> The summing up is the mandrake –
> (See the encyclopedia of superstitions:
> MANDRAKE
> miracle-working plant
> which when torn out of the ground gave off such an appalling scream a man would drop dead. A dog had to do it.)[10]
> (Tranströmer 2006, 132)

Here the poem expresses the impossibility of "the summing up", combined with a temporal disorientation – "I don't know if we are at the beginning or coming to the end" – testifying to a general disbelief in the ability of language to represent the totality of life. Furthermore, this impossibility is equated with the "MANDRAKE", a plant whose root is hallucinogenic and, according to folklore, could bring good fortune and was therefore often made into amulets. When torn out of the ground, however, the plant would give "off such an appalling scream a man would drop dead", as the poem retells the legend. In order to avoid such deaths, animals would be assigned the task of removing the plant. In other words, Tranströmer chooses to draw on this piece of folklore in order to illustrate the impossibility – or at least the danger – of a "summing up", with an ominous scream possibly leading to death. In short, the quest for linguistic all-encompassing representation is turned into noise, whereby the poem again realizes an acoustic dimension closely connected to the problem of communication and representation. The Swedish original term for the plant also carries with it another significance, which the English translation lacks: "ALRUNA" includes the Swedish word for "rune", *runa*, which designates the proto-Swedish "runskrift" sign system or the "runic" of Old Norse before the introduction of the Latin alphabet in the North (etymologically, *runa* draws on the Gothic word for "secret"; see Svenska Akademien 1898). Thus, for the reader of Tranströmer's original version of the poem, the Swedish name of the mythological plant simultaneously evokes the ancient, "foreign" sign system of proto-Swedish, even though it is written in Latin script. This allusion, alien and indecipherable for most readers of contemporary Swedish, seems to heighten the sense of mystery and awe in this line of poetry. The capitalized letters prompt the reader to focus on the plant's evocative name, while the allusion to the sign system creates a virtual, bilingual effect. In comparison to Schmitz-Emans's studies on the trope of the incomprehensible in the German Romantic tradition mentioned in the article's introduction, the allusion to runic script in "ALRUNA" seems to enhance and deepen the mystery in a similar manner, rather than dispelling it: we are reading a script that we do not understand, and this seems to be the whole point.

The last name in block letters is to be found in the first section of the poem's fifth part, anticipating the narrative about the composer, who is diagnosed with aphasia:

5

July 30th. The strait has become eccentric – swarming
   with jellyfish today for the first time in years, they pump
   themselves forward calmly and patiently, they belong to the
   same line: *Aurelia*, they drift like flowers after a sea burial,
   if you take them out of the water their
entire form vanishes, as when an indescribable truth is
   lifted out of silence and formulated into an inert mass,
   but they are untranslatable, they must stay in their own
   element.[11]

(Tranströmer 2006, 135)

As in the case of the name Hegwaldr, Tranströmer uses similes in order to establish connections to specific materialities: the jellyfish of the genus *Aurelia* are compared to "flowers after a sea burial", whose form, in turn, vanishes if taken out of the water. Then, the simile connecting the jellyfish and the flower with the problem of representation is introduced, "as when an indescribable truth is lifted out of silence". Like the inscription of Hegwaldr being compared to "a row of teeth in a mass grave", the theme of death is present on this occasion as well. Here, however, the name "Aurelia" – because of its chain of associations leading to "an indescribable truth" – comes across as far more vulnerable, given the risk of its turning into an "inert mass" if removed from its "own element". The passage thus testifies to a similar dynamic as in the case of "Alruna", since they both signify something "untranslatable": "the summing up" and "an indescribable truth". In both cases, the narrator seems to conclude, we must halt and pause over the names themselves, not try to translate or comprehend them, for that matter.

The motif of an untranslatable text finds its mirror image in the poem's final and sixth part, where the narrator describes the roof of an old fishermen's hut: "Tegelpannorna med lavarnas skrivtecken på ett okänt språk är stenarna på skärgårdsfolkets ghettokyrkogård, stenarna uppresta och hoprasade. –" (Tranströmer 1974, 37) / "The tiles with their lichen-script in an unknown tongue are the stones in the ghetto cemetery of the archipelago folk, the stones raised and tumbled. –" (Tranströmer 2006, 139). Still, this "unknown tongue" written by nature itself comes to actually represent the past lives lived in the archipelago, a paradox which is perhaps able to capture an overarching tension in *Östersjöar* with the inability to reach across time towards lives long lost while at the same time demonstrating the power of poetic language to imagine precisely such temporal leaps and historical connections.

Conclusion

In my reading of *Östersjöar*, I have aimed to show how the poem uses instances of literary multilingualism to explore themes such as partial fluency, incomprehension and problems of communication. I have also explicated how the poem helps us to think through the concept of literary multilingualism by turning the focus to the acoustic and visual dimensions of language.

Östersjöar's overarching thematic focus on the *border* has proven to be particularly fruitful for a theoretical endeavour seeking to widen the scope of the term "literary multilingualism", not least against the backdrop of Naoki Sakai's discussion of translation as a *bordering process*. Indeed, the task of defining literary multilingualism is also an ongoing bordering process: seeking to delineate it in terms of its "other", creating a typology suited to describe and analyse the phenomenon, and so forth. In my reading of *Östersjöar*, I have directed my attention to aspects that are not usually regarded as language proper, such as sounds and noises. Precisely because these seem to fall outside the sphere of language while simultaneously being overdetermined with meaning in Tranströmer's poem (centring on the problem of interpersonal and historical communication), we need to pay closer attention to them. The acoustic sphere of literary multilingualism is an important part of a multidimensional understanding of the category, taking the literary text's material and sensorial dimensions seriously. Such an understanding is also dependent on a nuanced approach to the category of the reader. Just like literary texts, readers are situated in different cultural, political, historical and – not least – linguistic contexts, bringing different sets of skills into their readings. *Östersjöar* conflates the themes of precarious communication and partial fluency with new aesthetic possibilities, pulling the reader into a border area of known and unknown languages, verbal and non-verbal alike. This sphere is also where a discussion on literary multilingualism needs to take place.

194 *Markus Huss*

Notes

1 See introduction to this volume for examples of current research.
2 Quotes in this chapter from "Baltics" by Tomas Tranströmer, translated by Robin Fulton, are reprinted by permission of New Directions Publishing Corp. "Baltics" is included in the collection THE GREAT ENIGMA, copyright ©2006 by Tomas Tranströmer. Translation © 2006 by Robin Fulton. Reprinted by permission of New Directions Publishing Corp.
3 "Dikten är geografisk, historisk, politisk och introspektiv." (Tranströmer quoted in Ringgren 1997, 16.)
4 I

>   Det var före radiomasternas tid.
>   Morfar var nybliven lots. I almanackan skrev han upp de fartyg han lotsade –
>   namn, destinationer, djupgång.
>   Exempel från 1884:
>   Ångf Tiger Capt Rowan 16 fot Hull Gefle Furusund
>   Brigg Ocean Capt Andersen 8 fot Sandefjord Hernösand Furusund
>   Ångf St Pettersburg Capt Libenberg 11 fot Stettin Libau Sandhamn
>
>   Han tog ut dem till Östersjön, genom den underbara labyrinten av öar och vatten.
>   Och de som möttes ombord och bars av samma skrov några timmar eller dygn,
>   hur mycket lärde de känna varann?
>   Samtal på felstavad engelska, samförstånd och missförstånd men mycket lite av medveten lögn.
>   Hur mycket lärde de känna varann?
>
>   När det var tät tjocka: halv fart, knappt ledsyn. Ur det osynliga kom udden med ett enda kliv och var alldeles intill.
>   Brölande signal varannan minut. Ögonen läste rätt in i det osynliga.
>   (Hade han labyrinten i huvudet?)
>   Minuterna gick.
>   Grund och kobbar memorerade som psalmverser.
>   Och den där känslan av "just här är vi" som måste hållas kvar, som när man bär på ett bräddfullt kärl och ingenting får spillas.
>
>   En blick ner i maskinrummet.
>   Compoundmaskinen, långlivad som ett människohjärta, arbetade med stora mjukt studsande rörelser, akrobater av stål, och dofterna steg som från ett kök.
>   (Tranströmer 1974, 7–10)

5 Musiken kommer till en människa, han är tonsättare, spelas, gör karriär, blir chef för konservatoriet.
   Konjunkturen vänder, han fördöms av myndigheterna.
   Som huvudåklagare sätter man upp hans elev K***.
   Han hotas, degraderas, förpassas.
   Efter några år minskar onåden, han återupprättas.

Då kommer hjärnblödningen: högersidig förlamning med afasi, kan
bara uppfatta korta fraser, säger fel ord.
Kan alltså inte nås av upphöjelse eller fördömanden.
Men musiken finns kvar, han komponerar fortfarande i sin egen stil,
han blir en medicinsk sensation den tid han har kvar att leva.

Han skrev musik till texter han inte längre förstod –
på samma sätt
uttrycker vi något med våra liv
i den nynnande kören av felsägningar.
(Tranströmer 1974, 30)

6 "Rekryten satt i sitt bergrum i havsbandet. Och slog på telegraf nyckeln sitt krypto: K D A N S B E N X D passerade genom hans händer, han förstod det inte (liksom så mycket annat som passerar genom våra händer och vi inte förstår det) J K L A N F R T X S" (Tranströmer quoted in Espmark (1983, 227–228)).

7 II

Vinden går i tallskogen. Det susar tungt och lätt,
Östersjön susar också mitt inne på ön, långt inne i skogen är man ute
på öppna sjön.
Den gamla kvinnan hatade suset i träden. Hennes ansikte stelnade i
melankoli när det blåste upp:
"Man måste tänka på dem som är ute i båtarna".
Men hon hörde också något annat i suset, precis som jag, vi är släkt.
(Vi går tillsammans. Hon är död sen tretti år.)
Det susar ja och nej, missförstånd och samförstånd.
Det susar tre barn friska, ett på sanatorium och två döda.
Det stora draget som blåser liv i somliga lågor och blåser ut andra.
Villkoren.
Det susar: Fräls mig Herre, vattnen tränger mig inpå livet.
Man går länge och lyssnar och når då en punkt där gränserna öppnas
eller snarare
där allting blir gräns. En öppen plats försänkt i mörker. Människorna
strömmar ut från de svagt upplysta byggnaderna runt om.
Det sorlar.

Ett nytt vinddrag och platsen ligger åter öde och tyst.
Ett nytt vinddrag, det brusar om andra stränder.
Det handlar om kriget.
Det handlar om platser där medborgarna är under kontroll,
där tankarna byggs med reservutgångar,
där ett samtal bland vänner verkligen blir ett test på vad vänskap
betyder.
Och när man är tillsammans med dem som man inte känner så väl.
Kontroll. En viss uppriktighet är på sin plats
bara man inte släpper med blicken det där som driver i samtalets
utkant: någonting mörkt, en mörk fläck.
Någonting som kan driva in
och förstöra allt. Släpp det inte med blicken!
Vad ska man likna det vid? En mina?

196 Markus Huss

> Nej det vore för handfast. Och nästan för fredligt – för på vår kust har
> de flesta berättelser om minor ett lyckligt slut, skräcken begränsad
> i tiden.
> Som i den här historien från fyrskeppet: 'Hösten 1915 sov man oroligt
> ... ' etc. En drivmina siktades
> när den drev mot fyrskeppet sakta, den sänktes och hävdes, ibland
> skymd av sjöarna, ibland
> framskymtande som en spion i en folkmassa.
> Besättningen låg i ångest och sköt på den med gevär. Förgäves. Till sist
> satte man ut en båt
> och gjorde fast en lång lina vid minan och bogserade den varsamt och
> länge in till experterna.
> Efteråt ställde man upp minans mörka skal i en sandig plantering som
> prydnad
> tillsammans med skalen av Strombus gigas från Västindien.
>
> Och havsblåsten går i de torra tallarna längre bort, den har bråttom
> över kyrkogårdens sand,
> förbi stenarna som lutar, lotsarnas namn.
> Det torra suset
> av stora portar som öppnas och stora portar som stängs.
>
> (Tranströmer 1974, 11–15)

8 *Östersjöar*'s fifth section includes a quote from Erikskrönikan, a medieval Swedish chronicle written in Old Swedish, derived from the earlier linguistic variety of Old East Norse.

9 III

> I den gotländska kyrkans halvmörka hörn, i en dager av mild mögel
> står en dopfunt av sandsten – 1100-tal – stenhuggarens namn
> är kvar, framlysande
> som en tandrad i en massgrav:
>   HEGWALDR
>   namnet kvar. Och hans bilder
> här och på andra krukors väggar, människomyller, gestalter på väg ut
> ur stenen.
> Ögonens kärnor av ondska och godhet spränger där.
> Herodes vid bordet: den stekta tuppen flyger upp och gal "Christus
> natus est" – servitören avrättades –
> intill föds barnet, under klungor av ansikten värdiga och hjälplösa som
> apungars.
> Och de frommas flyende steg
> ekande över drakfjälliga avloppstrummors gap.
> (Bilderna starkare i minnet än när man ser dem direkt, starkast
> när funten snurrar i en långsam mullrande karusell i minnet.)
>
> (Tranströmer 1974, 17–19)

10 Jag vet inte om vi är i begynnelsen eller sista stadiet.
> Sammanfattningen kan inte göras, sammanfattningen är omöjlig.
> Sammanfattningen är alrunan –
> (se uppslagsboken för vidskepelser:
>   ALRUNA
>   undergörande växt

som gav ifrån sig ett så ohyggligt skrik när den slets upp ur jorden
att man föll död ner. Hunden fick göra det ...)
(Tranströmer 1974, 21–22)

11 "Aurelia" is not written in block letters in Fulton's translation. My analysis is based on the Swedish original:

V

30 juli. Fjärden har blivit excentrisk – idag vimlar maneterna för
första gången på åratal, de pumpar sig fram lugnt och skonsamt,
de hör till samma rederi: AURELIA, de driver som blommor efter
en havsbegravning, tar man upp dem ur vattnet försvinner all form
hos dem, som när en obeskrivlig sanning lyfts upp ur tystnaden och
formuleras till död gelé, ja de är oöversättliga, de måste stanna i sitt
element.
(Tranströmer 1974, 29)

Bibliography

Baltic Sea Library (n.d.) Accessed August 16, 2019, http://www.balticsealibrary.info/home/about-us.html.
Bankier, Joanna (1993) *The Sense of Time in the Poetry of Tomas Tranströmer.* Berkeley, CA: University of California.
Bergsten, Staffan (2011) *Tomas Tranströmer: ett diktarporträtt.* Stockholm: Albert Bonniers förlag.
Connor, Steven (2002) *Seeing Sound: The Displaying of Marsyas.* Accessed August 12, 2016, www.stevenconnor.com/marsyas/.
Elleström, Lars (2010) The Modalities of Media: A Model for Understanding Intermedial Relations. In Lars Elleström (ed.): *Media Borders, Multimodality and Intermediality.* Houndmills: Palgrave Macmillan, 11–48.
Espmark, Kjell (1983) *Resans formler: en studie i Tomas Tranströmers poesi.* Stockholm: Norstedt.
Falk, Erik (2001) Epifanins Plats. Om topografi och epifani i Tomas Tranströmers Östersjöar. *Tidskrift för litteraturvetenskap* 30(2), 21–32.
Fix, Ulla (2014) *Sprache, Sprachgebrauch und Diskurse in der DDR: Ausgewählte Aufsätze.* Berlin: Frank & Timme.
Kahn, Douglas (1999) *Noise, Water, Meat: A History of Sound in the Arts.* Cambridge, MA: MIT.
Madsen, Claus K. (2014) Indskrivning – en postmoderne læsning af Tomas Tranströmers Östersjöar. *Finsk tidskrift: kultur, ekonomi, politik* 7–8 (2014), 63–77.
Perloff, Marjorie (2010) *Unoriginal Genius: Poetry by Other Means in the New Century.* Chicago & London: The University of Chicago Press.
Ringgren, Magnus (1997) *Det är inte som det var att gå längs stranden: en guide till Tomas Tranströmers Östersjöar.* Stockholm: Bokbandet.
Rönnerstrand, Torsten (2003) *"Varje problem ropar på sitt eget språk": om Tomas Tranströmer och språkdebatten.* Karlstad: Karlstad University Press.
Sakai, Naoki (2009) How Do We Count a Language? Translation and Discontinuity. *Translation Studies* 2(1), 71–88.

Schmitz-Emans, Monika (2004) Literatur und Vielsprachigkeit. Aspekte, Themen, Voraussetzungen. In Monika Schmitz-Emans (ed.): *Literatur und Vielsprachigkeit*. Hermeia: Grenzüberschreitende Studien zur Literatur- und Kulturwissenschaft 7. Heidelberg: Synchron, 11–26.

Sommer, Doris (2004) *Bilingual Aesthetics: A New Sentimental Education*. Durham, NC: Duke University Press.

Svenska Akademien (1898) *Svenska Akademiens Ordbok*. Spalt A 1142 band 1. www.saob.se/artikel/?seek=alruna&pz=1.

The Swedish Academy (2011) *Press Release*. October 6, 2011. Accessed November 3, 2017, www.nobelprize.org/nobel_prizes/literature/laureates/2011/press.html.

Tidigs, Julia (2014) *Att skriva sig över språkgränserna. Flerspråkighet i Jac. Ahrenbergs och Elmer Diktonius prosa*. Åbo: Åbo Akademis förlag.

Tidigs, Julia & Huss, Markus (2017) The Noise of Multilingualism: Reader Diversity, Linguistic Borders and Literary Multimodality. *Critical Multilingual Studies* 5(1), 208–235.

Tranströmer, Tomas (1974) *Östersjöar: en dikt*. Stockholm: Bonnier.

Tranströmer, Tomas (2006) *The Great Enigma: New Collected Poems*. Translated by Robin Fulton. New York: New Directions.

Walkowitz, Rebecca L. (2015) *Born Translated: The Contemporary Novel in an Age of World Literature*. New York: Columbia University Press.

Yildiz, Yasemin (2012) *Beyond the Mother Tongue: The Postmonolingual Condition*. New York: Fordham University Press.

12 Transcending Borders through Multilingual Intertextuality in Ville Tietäväinen's Graphic Novel *Näkymättömät kädet*

Aura Nikkilä

In this chapter I analyse how through multilingualism, which manifests itself most visibly in the form of intertextual references, borders are both represented and crossed in the graphic novel *Näkymättömät kädet* (2011; Invisible hands)[1] by the Finnish comics artist Ville Tietäväinen. *Näkymättömät kädet* tells the story of Rashid, a poor Moroccan man, who crosses the Mediterranean to Spain in search of work and a better life for himself and his family. Tietäväinen's graphic novel deals with global inequality, irregular migration, questions of ethnicity and racism, religion, honour and insanity. Since its original publication in 2011, *Näkymättömät kädet* has been translated into Swedish; German; French; and, most recently, Arabic. This graphic novel of Finnish origin has succeeded in crossing borders in the form of translations, but the original work in itself is far from monolingual. Even though it was originally written in Finnish, the dialogue teems with Arabic words, and Spanish diegetic texts are recurrent in the storyworld. In addition to these, other languages also make occasional appearances.

The multilingualism of *Näkymättömät kädet* is not carried out exclusively by intertextual references, but they are perhaps the most visible multilingual aspect of the work. The intertextual references in the graphic novel are represented both in verbal and in visual forms, and they originate from history, literature and popular culture. According to Monika Schmitz-Emans (2011, 195), representation is based on a transfer process when words, images or panel structures in a comic are recognized to be borrowed from another context. Thus, intertextuality is perceived as a process in which texts travel from one context to another, carrying with them earlier meanings while also receiving new ones.

My argument is that borders and border-crossings are present in the graphic novel not just in its thematics, but also in the overall expression of the comic. The interplay of visual and verbal elements, a fundamental aspect of comics expression, makes comics intermedial or multimodal by nature. In *Näkymättömät kädet*, borders are verbalized and visualized throughout the work, and in my analysis I observe how the intertextual references that frequently make use of multilingualism transcend both cultural and national borders as well as the borders of different media. Furthermore, I look at other multilingual elements in Tietäväinen's graphic novel to see how these form part of the transnational thematics and expression of the comic.

Intermedial and Multilingual Combination of Words and Images

The ten-page prologue of *Näkymättömät kädet* opens with a page of an aerial view of parts of North Africa and the southernmost tip of Spain. The continents seem to reach towards each other across the Strait of Gibraltar, the point where the Atlantic and the Mediterranean meet. In the middle of the page is a sentence written on the surface of the dark sea: "In the name of God, the entirely merciful, the especially merciful!"[2] (Tietäväinen 2011, 5). A wide, almost entirely black panel opens the next page, where the prayer continues while the view approaches the sea (Figure 12.1). A boat cleaving the dark water is shown from above, and in the next panel we see the boat against a reflection cast by an enormous full moon. In the penultimate panel of the page, the boat is shown up close; we see the backs of the people aboard it and a strip of land looming on the horizon. A speech bubble emanating from one of the passengers contains just one word: "Europe". The last panel reveals Rashid's face from behind his friends, Wafiq and Nadim, who are partially cropped outside the frame. Rashid finishes his sentence: "...looks just like Africa from the sea"[3] (Tietäväinen 2011, 6).

This page from the beginning of the graphic novel illustrates how comics tell stories through images, by making use of different points of view and with versatile transitions from one panel to another, and through text, both in the form of dialogue placed inside speech bubbles and as captions, in this case in the form of the words of a prayer flowing without frames on the surface of the picture. The portrayal of this nocturnal crossing begins far above, from the air, and panel by panel the boat is shown closer and closer, all the way to a close-up that reveals the faces of the passengers. This scene invites the reader into the location of the story: we are on the Mediterranean Sea on a boat stacked full of people. Quite a lot is accomplished in just two pages, as the gradual zoom from the stratosphere to Rashid's face in five panels works as a transition from the general to the personal. The story begins on the border between Africa and Europe, a border depicted in the form of the Mediterranean Sea. Rashid's words highlight the artificiality of this border: seen from the sea, the continents look the same.

The very first page includes an indication of the graphic novel's multilingualism. Even though the reader sees the words of the prayer in Finnish, in the storyworld this Islamic prayer is in fact recited aloud in Arabic. The storyline eventually comes back to the boat, and by now the

Multilingual Intertextuality 201

Figure 12.1 Ville Tietäväinen, *Näkymättömät kädet*, p. 6. © Ville Tietäväinen.

reader has become acquainted with Rashid and his friends, and knows that they are Muslims who speak Arabic. This kind of portrayal of one language through another is certainly nothing extraordinary, since this is how most translations of literary works operate. What is of interest in the case of *Näkymättömät kädet* is that it is a Finnish graphic novel, originally directed towards a Finnish-speaking audience, in which Finnish represents other languages – Arabic, Spanish, Catalan – but also itself. In addition to this dual nature of the preliminary language of the graphic novel, it also contains recurrent use of other languages as themselves: mostly Spanish, but also Arabic, English, Catalan, German, French and, last but not least, Bambara. In what follows, I will trace these language changes, or code-switches, and analyse how and why they occur.

Language is a topic that in comic studies is discussed primarily in connection to the translation of comics, but there is also an evident linguistic tendency, especially among the theorists stemming from semiotic approaches, which defines comics as a code that incorporates two media (see Rippl & Etter 2015, 194). For example, Thierry Groensteen (2007, 3) regards comics as a language in itself, consisting of visual and verbal signs, the latter being subordinate to the former. It is also possible to think of images and words as modes, which is the case when comics are seen as multimodal (Stein 2015, 423). Comics are often labelled as a medium, but this definition is far from unambiguous, since the essential elements constituting comics, that is, words and images, can equally be defined as basic media in themselves (Rippl & Etter 2015, 194).

The interaction between words and images makes comics intermedial per se (Rippl & Etter 2015, 197). Many of the intertextual references in *Näkymättömät kädet* are intermedial also in a broader sense, as they transform from one medium to another. Irina O. Rajewsky (2005, 47–48) states that "intertextuality in its various narrow or broad conceptions has been a starting point for many attempts to theorize the intermedial". According to her, intermedial references are usually discussed – if discussed at all – as intertextual references (Rajewsky 2005, 54). When the concept of *text* is understood in a narrow sense, intertextuality appears as a subcategory of intermediality. My analysis is guided by an understanding of text in a broader sense: I regard comics as texts in the same way that I regard pictures as texts, as my method of close *reading* implies.

This chapter is constructed so that it moves gradually from one aspect of multilingualism in *Näkymättömät kädet* to another. I start with some of the auditory elements of the storyworld by analysing Spanish song lyrics found on the pages of the graphic novel. After the lyrics, I move to the multilingual diegetic texts, that is, texts that are present as writing in the storyworld. Then I focus on the dialogue and the Spanish and Arabic elements in it. I conclude by returning to lyrics, but this time ones that are in Finnish.

Enhancing the Thematics with Spanish Lyrics

A number of multilingual references to music can be found on the pages of *Näkymättömät kädet*. Representing rhythm or melody in a comic is quite complicated (see, e.g. Cortsen 2015, 170–171), whereas the lyrics of vocal music are easily transformed to the verbal realm of a comic (Schmitz-Emans 2011, 206). Tietäväinen makes use of song lyrics throughout the graphic novel, and through these lyrics the presence of Spanish becomes very visible in the storyworld. In the first part of *Näkymättömät kädet*, Rashid and Nadim, while still in Morocco, have a fleeting encounter with an acquaintance of theirs, a Westernized Moroccan man who is driving around in his convertible car with blonde Scandinavian women. Shakira's "La Tortura" is playing on the car radio. The Spanish lyrics of this song by the Colombian singer are filled with apparent references to sexual frustration, an example being the line: "Man does not live by bread alone"[4] (Tietäväinen 2011, 33). Originally this Biblical reference alludes to the spiritual needs of human beings, but in this context the line can be interpreted also as an expression of sexual lust. This passage reveals the contradictory nature of the desire to leave for Europe; from the vantage point of their culture and faith, the convertible car with its sexually uninhibited passengers appears forbidden to Rashid and Nadim, but at the same time it is also something utterly desirable. This idea is further emphasized by Rashid's father when he says: "[God] created the whole of Europe just to test our faith"[5] (Tietäväinen 2011, 57). Even if Rashid and Nadim despise the driver and his likes, who "fall for everything Western. They'd rather go to Disneyland than Mecca"[6] (Tietäväinen 2011, 35), Europe beckons to them as well.

In the latter part of the comic, Rashid has made his way to Barcelona and arrives in an abandoned house that has been appointed as his lodging by his employer. A young man is singing "Clandestino" by the French-Spanish artist Manu Chao (Figure 12.2). As before, in the case of Shakira's song, this intertextual reference is a direct quotation. Here the music is represented as lyrics but also in a visual form. One of the most common ways to transform music in comics to a visual form is by showing the musician with an instrument (Schmitz-Emans 2011, 199). The young man singing "Clandestino" is pictured just so, with a guitar in his hands. The lyrics stand out from the text in speech bubbles, not just because they differ in their language from the dialogue but also by the slightly wavy font they have been printed in. Tietäväinen has not drawn musical notes or any other signs of notation, which are frequently used in comics as visual representations of music (see Schmitz-Emans 2011, 200). Apart from the instrument pictured in the panels, music in *Näkymättömät kädet* is mainly represented in verbal form, which indicates that the lyrics and their connection to Rashid's story are of greater significance than other qualities of music, such as rhythm, harmony or melody.

According to Julia Tidigs (2014, 81), a foreign language can complement the principal language of a multilingual literary work and strengthen its thematics. This is certainly the case here, since politically and socially critical themes are typical to Manu Chao's lyrics, and "Clandestino" is no exception: besides meaning "secret" or "hidden", in colloquial Spanish the title refers to a so-called illegal migrant. The lyrics depict irregular migration in an unembellished way:

> Lost in the heart of the great Babylon, they call me clandestine for not carrying papers. To a northern city I went to work, my life I left between Ceuta and Gibraltar. I'm a line in the sea, a ghost in the city.[7]
> (Tietäväinen 2011, 157; translation mine)

Figure 12.2 Ville Tietäväinen, *Näkymättömät kädet*, p. 157. © Ville Tietäväinen.

The lyrics function as a prediction of Rashid's time in Barcelona, as the words "a ghost in the city" refer to the invisibility of undocumented migrants. Rashid avoids the police, since getting caught would mean deportation to Morocco and hence giving up the dream of a brighter future. "A line in the sea", besides pointing to the crossing of the Mediterranean made by the migrants, also alludes to the artificiality and impermanence of borders, since a line drawn in the water vanishes rapidly. The line also refers to the thousands of migrants and refugees who don't make the passage successfully but are washed away by the sea.

The lyrics of "Clandestino" contain two locations, both of them referring to a certain kind of geographical ambiguity shaking the idea of natural geographical borders, but also pointing to the colonial past of Europe and Africa. The first, Ceuta, is an autonomous Spanish city in North Africa; even though it is located on African soil, administratively Ceuta is part of the European Union and thus one of the points of entry for refugees and migrants trying to get to Europe. The area is segregated from Morocco with high double fences, which make the crossing tricky and dangerous. In the beginning of *Näkymättömät kädet*, Rashid and his friends have a meeting with a people smuggler in Wafiq's tea room. The smuggler mentions the route to Europe through Ceuta as an unattractive alternative to the sea-crossing: "…or you could try spending years wandering through the hills of Ceuta with coons, eating guard dogs and mountain apes to keep yourselves alive"[8] (Tietäväinen 2011, 37).

The other place name mentioned in the lyrics of "Clandestino" is Gibraltar, a British territory on the southern end of the Iberian Peninsula. The Strait of Gibraltar, which separates Africa and Europe, is only about fifteen kilometres wide. There are multiple references to the strait in *Näkymättömät kädet* (e.g. when Rashid's friend revolts at the price the smuggler charges for the crossing). Twice in the story, both in the prologue as well as near the end of the graphic novel, when Rashid's wife Amina arrives in Spain, Gibraltar is referred to by its Arabic name, Jabal Tariq. Gibraltar is the Spanish version of the Arab phrase, meaning "the mountain of Tariq". The limestone mountain located on the cape of Gibraltar is named after Tariq ibn Ziyad, a Berber commander who was in charge of a successful Muslim expedition to the Iberian Peninsula in 711 (Watt & Cachia 2008, 8–9). On both occasions, the person stating the name of the mountain by saying: "Jabal Tariq, the mountain of the Arab conqueror!"[9] (Tietäväinen 2011, 7, 206) is Wafiq, the only one of the three friends whose dream of a better life on the other side of the sea actually comes true; Nadim's dream gets crushed on the rocks of the Spanish coast, whereas Rashid loses his dream along the way, together with his self-respect and his sanity during the time he spends first working illegally in greenhouses in Andalusia and then as a homeless beggar on the streets of Barcelona. Wafiq, who manages to establish a shop in Valencia, is the exception, the successful Arab conqueror of this story.

Both Shakira's "La Tortura" and Manu Chao's "Clandestino" are songs written and sung in Spanish. The idea that a multilingual text demands a multilingual reader has traditionally prevailed in the scholarship on literary multilingualism (Tidigs 2014, 99–100; Tidigs & Huss 2017, 211–212). Therefore, in the case of *Näkymättömät kädet*, the ideal reader has to understand both Finnish and Spanish in order to be able to connect the meaning of the lyrics of "Clandestino" to the story told in the comic. Understanding the lyrics brings an additional layer to the reading process by enhancing the theme of irregular migration. However, understanding the lyrics is not crucial to the overall comprehension of the story.

Authenticity and References to History through Diegetic Texts

Multilingualism also manifests itself in *Näkymättömät kädet* in the form of diegetic texts. In a way, this kind of code-switching, which takes place outside the representation of the auditory realm of the graphic novel (i.e. the text in speech bubbles or the lyrics of music), might go easily unnoticed. Logos on T-shirts, words on posters or graffiti on the streets are something that we are thoroughly accustomed to in our daily lives. They form a part of a textual mass surrounding us constantly, so much so that we may stop reading them. The panels of *Näkymättömät kädet* contain an abundance of both visual and verbal details, mainly placed in the background of the panels, but what usually catches the eye of the reader are the people pictured in the foreground and the text in the speech bubbles. Noticing all the details can be compared to the question of understanding the Spanish lyrics: readers can peruse the comic without paying attention to, for example, some graffiti appearing on the wall in a panel of the graphic novel, and still comprehend the story; however, an attentive reader will pick up on multiple details which have the power to enrich the story and enhance its thematics. These details also serve the purpose of making the storyworld depicted in the graphic novel more authentic (on creating authenticity through multilingualism, see Tidigs 2014, 81–88). Spanish and Catalan signs place the story in a certain setting, but they also make the Barcelona of the comic more believable to the reader, in addition to binding the events of the story to a specific cultural context.

One important diegetic text in the latter part of the story alludes to two prominent figures in Spanish history. The characters of Queen Isabella I and King Ferdinand II are identified through code-switching, which takes place in the details of a panel: we see two tourist guides who are dressed in robes with the names of these royal figures written on the back (Figure 12.3). This intertextual reference to historical characters binds *Näkymättömät kädet* to the history of Spain, since this couple, also called the Catholic Monarchs, reigned over Spain at the end of the 15th century. The Catholic Monarchs financed Christopher Columbus on his expedition to the Americas, and they started the Spanish Inquisition by ordering the conversion and expulsion of Jews and Muslims (Aronson-Friedman & Kaplan 2012, 8).

In the Middle Ages, Moors (i.e. Muslims) ruled an area that covered most of what is now Spain and Portugal. The Muslim domain of al-Andalus, founded in 711, flourished both culturally and in the field of sciences and philosophy. From the 11th century onwards, the rule of the Islamic caliphates began to crumble, and in 1492 al-Andalus collapsed definitively when Granada, the last emirate, surrendered to Queen Isabella. The period known as Reconquista came to an end, and with it so did tolerance and a rather peaceful co-existence that had prevailed in al-Andalus between three different religious groups: Muslims, Christians

Multilingual Intertextuality 207

Figure 12.3 Ville Tietäväinen, *Näkymättömät kädet*, p. 208, selection. © Ville Tietäväinen.

and Jews (Guzmán 2002, 9, 14–15, 49). Jews were expelled and Muslims were ordered to either convert to Catholicism or leave Spain. The result was that tens of thousands were forced to leave their homes, and the ones who stayed – as converts, in other words – were persecuted by the Inquisition (Benito 2012, 44–45).

According to the historian Ana Benito, the Spanish Inquisition was a powerful means of creating otherness. Benito claims that Moriscos and Conversos (i.e. Muslims and Jews who had converted to Catholicism) became trapped between two religions and two identities, and due to their dual role were seen as the other by both cultures (Benito 2012, 44–45). The Muslim migrants today are in danger of suffering a similar fate of falling between cultures. In Europe they confront prejudice and outright racism, and if they return to their original home countries, the possibility is that they will be met with suspicion and contempt. In *Näkymättömät kädet*, an example of this kind of attitude towards those who return is the aforementioned passage, in which Rashid and his friends despise as well as envy the Moroccan man who has returned from Europe and is now driving Scandinavian women around in his convertible car.

The two continents of Europe and Africa – as well as the distinct worlds of religion and secularity – are also contrasted in *Näkymättömät kädet* through diegetic texts. In Morocco, when Rashid is visiting Wafiq's tea house, there is a soda can pictured in one panel. It is not just any type of soda, as the logo reveals it to be a can of Mecca-Cola. This soft drink, bearing the name of Islam's most sacred place, is a product which is sold worldwide and advertised as an option to American sodas. The slogan of the brand, "Shake Your Conscience", also visible on the can in the comic, is based on the fact that ten per cent of the company's profits are donated to humanitarian work being done in Palestine (Echchaibi 2012, 32). From the point of view of language, the fact that the can has the brand name and slogan in Latin script, not in the Arabic alphabet, suggests that the informational value of this diegetic text is directed towards the Finnish-speaking reader, who presumably is more fluent in English than Arabic. According to Karin Kukkonen (2013, 7, 55), comics contain clues that lead the reader to invoke their cultural knowledge and thus create meaning for the text. The can of Mecca-Cola can be seen as a clue that binds the story to Islamic culture and strengthens the idea of Rashid as a devoted Muslim.

Later in the story, the reader cannot help but observe another beverage, this time a can of Alhambra beer. This Spanish beer, which Rashid drinks in the migrant workers' camp, refers to the period of prosperity of the Muslim domain of al-Andalus, since the beer brand is named after the grandiose Moorish palace of Alhambra in the city of Granada. In *Näkymättömät kädet*, the Muslims working in the greenhouses are forced to drink beer even though alcohol is prohibited by Islam. There is nothing else to drink, since the water container they have been using has been contaminated by the body of a murdered human rights activist. Thus, this can of beer functions as a melancholy allusion to the history of Islamic Iberia. At the same time, the global multilingualism of the beer can – the upper part of the label has the word "beer" written in Italian (*birra*) and German (*Bier*) – points, for instance, to global markets and extensive tourism in Andalusia. These diegetic texts underline the differences between Europe and Africa, but at the same time through their multilingualism they also represent the global world of today, where products cross regional and cultural borders, perhaps more easily than most people. Later on, as Rashid's journey takes him to Barcelona, Catalan becomes visible in the graphic novel in the form of diegetic texts (street signs and signboards), reminding the reader of the multilingualism of present-day Spain.

For the Moroccans, Europe seems like a paradise where food and work is in plenty. The idea of paradise is underlined throughout *Näkymättömät kädet*. For instance, a poster on the wall of the migrants' shack in the

Multilingual Intertextuality 209

greenhouse area shows the emblematic church of La Sagrada Família; a text underneath states that Barcelona is the "Paraíso de Costa Brava", the Paradise of Costa Brava (Tietäväinen 2011, 136). For Rashid, however, Barcelona turns out to be more like hell: it is there that he gradually sinks from the life of a street vendor squatting in an abandoned building to a homeless beggar. The idea of paradise is repeatedly questioned in the graphic novel, a humorous example of this being a sign that the workers have placed outside their greenhouse lodging in Almeria. The word "paradise" has been modified so that instead of garden of Paradise ("El Jardín de Paraíso"), it calls the camp the garden of parasites ("El Jardín de Parasíto") (Tietäväinen 2011, 82).

Another example of meaningful diegetic texts in Tietäväinen's graphic novel can be found in a scene where the workers of the camp try to enter a bar. The wall next to the entrance has been scribbled with graffiti reading "CALORROS FUERA" ("gypsies out") and "RECONQUISTA!!!" (Figure 12.4). The bouncer blocks the migrants from getting in and says:

Figure 12.4 Ville Tietäväinen, *Näkymättömät kädet*, p. 95, selection. © Ville Tietäväinen.

"We didn't order kebab. [...] Fuck off you apes before I start losing customers"[10] (Tietäväinen 2011, 96). The graffiti may refer to history, but accompanied by the bouncer's hostile words these Spanish texts are also revealing in relation to modern-day attitudes towards migrants and the political atmosphere of today. The ideology behind Reconquista, that is, to restore a Spain that never even existed, resonates with present-day perceptions which completely ignore the multicultural history of Europe. Drawing an analogy between the medieval Iberian Peninsula and the thoroughly transnational modern-day Europe may seem far-fetched, but multiculturalism was undeniably an integral part of al-Andalus, and hence this historical context works as an apt background for the present situation (see Corfis 2009, v–vi).

One specific diegetic text included in *Näkymättömät kädet* refers to the most horrific consequence of nationalism in the history of Europe, the Holocaust. When Rashid arrives in Almeria after crossing the Mediterranean, a pickup truck takes the undocumented workers to the greenhouse camps. The first panel on the page in question shows a sign that advertises fresh fruits and vegetables in Spanish (Figure 12.5). This sign, hanging from a barbed-wire fence that surrounds the greenhouse area, has been decorated with graffiti that reads: "TRABAJO LIBERTAR!" (Tietäväinen 2011, 81). This sentence, better known in German as "Arbeit macht frei" ("work makes you free"), was found on the gates of the concentration camps erected by the Germans during the Second World War. Thus, the barbed-wire fence of the greenhouse area is visually equated with the electric fences of concentration camps, and the pickup truck carrying the migrants is reminiscent of the trains transporting Jews to their death. The sentence mocked the victims of the Holocaust (see, e.g. Roth 1980, 75), and the idea of liberation through work is just as untenable in relation to the undocumented greenhouse workers: Rashid is inexorably bound to the inhumane work, since half of what he earns goes directly to the smugglers as payment for the crossing.

The limits that the author's language proficiency – or rather lack thereof – set for the representation of Moroccan culture is perceptible when the first part of *Näkymättömät kädet* taking place in Morocco is compared to the latter part and how Spain is depicted visually. What is most visible is that there are almost no diegetic texts in the panels showing the unnamed Moroccan city, which is represented as barren and ramshackle, without any signboards or other textual references. The whole graphic novel contains only two diegetic texts in Arabic, one in the beginning showing the title of a programme on TV, and the other near the end of the comic in the form of a name of a ferry, written on the side of the ship in Arabic font. The few diegetic texts in the Morocco setting of the graphic novel are mostly in English, such as the aforementioned Mecca-Cola, as well as different slogans on Nadim's shirts – which, judging by their numerous misspellings, appear to be pirated.

Multilingual Intertextuality 211

Figure 12.5 Ville Tietäväinen, *Näkymättömät kädet*, p. 81, selection. © Ville Tietäväinen.

Other Western-influenced textual and visual signs also show up, for example, in a street scene that includes a McDonald's sign and a poster of Mickey Mouse. On the same page, a call to prayers in Arabic can be seen in a speech bubble coming from a minaret. It is the only occasion in the comic where whole sentences of Arabic are represented in the language itself, albeit in Latin script.

Spanish and Arabic in the Finnish Dialogue

An essential aspect of the multilingualism of *Näkymättömät kädet* is that even though there are many languages present in the graphic novel, for the most part other languages are represented in Finnish, in order for Finnish readers to be able to follow the dialogue irrespective of their proficiency in those "foreign" languages. Thus, the reader is left with the task of concluding which language is being spoken in the graphic novel at different occasions. There are certain clues that indicate the actual language, like occasional key words, as in a scene where Rashid has just reached Spain and he calls a number the smuggler has given him. The person he is calling answers: "Dígame? [...] Where are you?"[11] Rashid tries to explain that his Spanish is not very good and says: "Excuse me, please slow... my Spanish..."[12] (Tietäväinen 2011, 75). The reader can detect that Rashid is speaking Spanish when he makes grammatical errors and the speech bubbles are filled with ellipses that function as signs of a pause. "Evening señor... we have celebration... the boy... a man now...",[13] Rashid says to the bouncer at a bar when the group of migrant workers try to get in to celebrate the birthday of the youngest among them. When they are denied access, Rashid faces the bouncer and states that "I see... you fear us... like fear the darkness... the unknown"[14] (Tietäväinen 2011, 96).

Especially in the beginning of the graphic novel when Rashid is still in Morocco, Arabic words are recurrent in the dialogue. Therefore, the reader is constantly aware that the characters in the storyworld are actually speaking in Arabic even though the text is written in Finnish. As was the case with the diegetic texts, the Arabic words here and there create a feeling of authenticity to the speech, since, according to theorists of multilingualism, such as Penelope Gardner-Chloros and Daniel Weston (2015, 186), representing a "foreign" language through code-switching makes it more authentic than trying to convey it through monolingual means. The Arabic words used in the dialogue are mostly ones that have to do quite directly with Moroccan culture, as well as ones that do not have a direct translation in Finnish or in English (e.g. terms such as "harcha",[15] "djellaba",[16] "harraga",[17] "rai",[18] "kif",[19] "fqi"[20] and "haram"[21]). Apart from the aspect of authenticity, questions of inclusion and exclusion in relation to the reader's language proficiency come to the fore here (see Tidigs & Huss 2017, 212). These Arabic terms work inclusively inside the storyworld by connecting the characters using them to Moroccan culture. It would seem that the ideal reader here would be one with knowledge of Moroccan culture and the Arabic language. It can be argued that, for most Finnish readers, many of these terms are likely to be fairly unfamiliar and may therefore function in an excluding manner. At times, the context hints at the meaning of the word, as is the case with "harcha" when Nadim says: "Rashid, we need to keep up your blood sugar levels. Let's get honey harchas, Wafiq's coffee cuts through your stomach"[22] (Tietäväinen 2011, 31). From this line, the reader can detect that "harcha" must be something edible. However, even if their meaning may remain unknown by the reader, these foreign words can still create cultural context by providing the so-called local colour to the dialogue.

There are also examples of intertextual references in *Näkymättömät kädet* that are built into the comic through code-switching in the dialogue. The first reference to Don Quixote, the protagonist of the stories written by Miguel de Cervantes in the beginning of the 17th century, comes in the first part of the graphic novel through a short exchange in Spanish. Rashid and Nadim are buying "harchas" from a food stall in Morocco when the owner of the stall greets a well-dressed man by saying: "Buenas tardes, Señor Quijote". The man answers: "Buenas... the usual, cocoa and churros."[23] When the man has gone, the owner explains to

Figure 12.6 Ville Tietäväinen, *Näkymättömät kädet*, p. 192, selection. © Ville Tietäväinen.

Rashid and Nadim that "Señor Quijote" is actually from Tetouan and that he "got screwed out of all his belongings on the harraga. Thinks he's in Andalusia, although the boat turned back in the dark".[24] The gentleman is thus labelled as a madman – "It's faith, not the flapping of wings, that keeps a bird in the air",[25] states the food stall owner – and madness is represented here as a literary character (Tietäväinen 2011, 32).

In the latter part of the story, the reader recognizes through multiple visual clues – such as armour, a lance and the long and bearded face of an old man – a reference to Don Quixote in visual form. The knight appears to Rashid in a moment of despair, looking as grand as a statue (Figure 12.6). Instead of an actual statue, this Don Quixote is a so-called living statue, a person who is dressed up in a costume and entertains tourists by standing absolutely still for hours on end. Regardless of the immobility of this particular knight, the character of Don Quixote alludes to travelling. In the books by Cervantes, the self-knighted hero roams around Spain in search of adventure with his loyal servant Sancho Panza. Similarly, Rashid travels across Spain and experiences his share of adventures, albeit mostly bleak ones. Another aspect that binds the two men together is madness: like Don Quixote, Rashid has also been displaced both physically and mentally. Don Quixote's journey takes him away not just from his home town and his family but also from the everyday life and domestic routines that define his identity (Boruchoff 2002, 12–13). In like manner, the journey Rashid takes separates him from all that is familiar to him; his family life in Morocco is replaced by day-to-day survival in uncertain and inhumane conditions. In the end, not living up to the great expectations of his family – as well as miserable conditions and constant failure – drives him to despair that gradually makes him delusional. Rashid's journey into madness can be interpreted as a border-crossing of a sort, a consequence or a metaphor of the transnational situation he is caught in. The delusional Rashid tries to earn money as a living statue himself; for this purpose, he makes a shabby superhero outfit out of a towel. The other statues do not appreciate his effort, and the man dressed as Don Quixote calls him a "dressed-up beggar"[26] (Tietäväinen 2011, 200). This confrontation discloses that Rashid might be more insane than one of the most famous madmen in cultural history.

Don Quixote dies in the end with his dream of being a knight dashed (Durán & Rogg 2006, 206), and Rashid similarly faces his end by abandoning all his hopes and dreams. Rashid's journey ends in Barcelona, where he jumps into his death and the empty space of the page from the enormous hand of the Columbus Monument (Figure 12.7). The Europe

Figure 12.7 Ville Tietäväinen, *Näkymättömät kädet*, p. 212, selection. © Ville Tietäväinen.

of his dreams has turned out to be an Eldorado, a paradise that does not actually exist. Through the figure of Christopher Columbus, the idea of travelling is further underlined. Rashid, like Columbus in his time, crossed the sea aiming for an unknown world. The link between the graphic novel and the history of Spain is strengthened with the character of Columbus, since, as earlier mentioned, the Catholic Monarchs paid for his expeditions to the Americas. Columbus set out on his first voyage in 1492, the same year that al-Andalus collapsed for good (Guzmán 2002, 50). The characters of Columbus and the Catholic Monarchs draw a parallel between the events pictured in *Näkymättömät kädet* and the history of colonialism – and its ever-present effects. Colonialism can be seen as a direct consequence of the ideology behind the Reconquista, an ideology that justified the conversion of infidels to Christianity and also the right to conquer the lands of the "new" continent (Guzmán 2002, 11).

The year 1492 has generally been considered a kind of watershed, since that is when Spain definitively switched over from Islamic to Christian culture. Yet the influence of Islamic culture by no means disappeared after 1492, for many of the Iberian cultural forms, such as literature, architecture and costume, were thoroughly hybridized at the end of the Muslim reign (Fuchs 2009, 269–270). The influence of al-Andalus can be seen – and heard – even today, as the Spanish language contains over 4,000 loanwords derived from Arabic (Versteegh 2001, 228). The histories of Spain and Morocco are in many ways entangled: Spain colonized the northern parts of Morocco between 1912 and 1956, and many of the Moroccans born during the colonial period still speak fluent Spanish. Darija, the Arabic variant spoken in Morocco, also includes plenty of loanwords from Spanish (Juntunen 2015, 205).

In addition to the Arabic and Spanish found in the dialogue, there is one more language spoken – or actually sung – in the graphic novel. In the prologue, when Rashid and his friends are in the boat crossing the Mediterranean, there is also a pregnant woman singing to her unborn child (Figure 12.8). The language she is singing is Bambara, called also Bamanankan, a lingua franca spoken in Mali and a few other African countries (see Skattum 2008, 106–109). Here the reader is placed alongside Rashid as the one who does not understand the language being used. The reading experience is thus exclusive, but at the same time the effect is eye-opening in its own way: this is how it feels when you don't understand a single word of the language being spoken. This effect may translate into a feeling of identification with someone (e.g. a migrant) constantly confronted with not being able to understand things in everyday life. Therefore, this lingual exclusion may give rise to identification on the Finnish-speaking reader's behalf with the graphic novel's characters.

There is also another identifying process present in *Näkymättömät kädet* which, instead of exclusion, makes use of inclusion. I mentioned

Figure 12.8 Ville Tietäväinen, *Näkymättömät kädet*, p. 8, selection. © Ville Tietäväinen.

earlier that Finnish is used in Tietäväinen's graphic novel to represent other languages, but also to represent itself. I will conclude this chapter by returning to song lyrics, but this time Finnish ones.

Creating Contact Surface through Finnish Lyrics

Midway through the graphic novel, the focus of the narration temporarily shifts to Ely, a Mauritanian youth also on his way towards northern Spain. Ely has found a Walkman and a cassette on the luggage carousel of an old airport, which has been turned into an immigration detention centre in the Canary Islands (Figure 12.9). On this particular page, the music is present not just in the form of lyrics written on the page but also in a visual manner, as mentioned by Schmitz-Emans (2011, 199), showing the album cover in various panels. The cover, which reveals the cassette to be by the Finnish *schlager*[27] singer Jamppa Tuominen, functions along with the Walkman as an attribute of music in this scene.

Rashid and Ely meet while both are travelling in a truck carrying vegetables from Andalusia to the North. When it is time for their ways to part, Ely gives the Walkman and Tuominen's cassette to Rashid in return for an empty football. In Barcelona, Rashid listens to the cassette repeatedly and in the end also sings along with it. The songs by Tuominen, functioning as subtext in *Näkymättömät kädet*, contain a number of themes that correspond with Rashid's story. Tuominen sings of keeping one's promises, of honour and of leaving and travelling. Tietäväinen has carefully chosen specific songs from Tuominen's wide musical corpus that underline the thematics of Rashid's story. When travelling in the luggage compartment of a bus heading to Barcelona, Rashid listens

Multilingual Intertextuality 217

Figure 12.9 Ville Tietäväinen, *Näkymättömät kädet*, p. 142. © Ville Tietäväinen.

to a song by Tuominen and the lyrics are shown in the lower part of the panels. The lyrics of the song, called *Suureen suureen maailmaan* (To the great wide world),[28] resonate with Rashid's feelings remarkably well: "To the great wide world, wider than I ever thought, I now have to go. It is just destined so"[29] (Tietäväinen 2011, 149). When Ely hands Rashid the cassette, he says: "I don't know what he's singing about, but his comradeship consoles me"[30] (Tietäväinen 2011, 146). It is made clear that neither Ely nor Rashid understands the lyrics of Tuominen's songs. Thus, the extensive use of the lyrics in the graphic novel is primarily directed towards Finnish-speaking readers and their cultural knowledge.

The twofold role of Finnish in the comic, as the procurator of other languages but also as a representation of itself, is noticeable only on rare occasions. One example is a passage in which Rashid is spending time in Barcelona with the other inhabitants of the abandoned building. He is listening to the cassette given to him by Ely and singing along with one of the songs by Tuominen. The others only hear Rashid's singing, which is visible to the reader as strongly accented Finnish. One of the inhabitants asks him: "What are you singing?" and continues by declaring that it "sounds horrible"[31] (Tietäväinen 2011, 164). For the reader of the Finnish-language album, both the singing and the dialogue of the migrants are represented in the same language, in Finnish. If the uses of language were presented in their actual form, in Finnish and Arabic, the typical reader would understand only the former, that is, the song lyrics.

Singing is usually set apart from speech in comics by placing lyrics in so-called singing bubbles, which differ from regular speech bubbles in their form (Schmitz-Emans 2011, 200). This is also the case in *Näkymättömät kädet*, where the singing bubbles have rougher edges than speech bubbles. An example of this is when Rashid listens to Tuominen's cassette for the last time and sings along with the music (Figure 12.10). The original song coming from the headphones is depicted on the left side of the panel, while Rashid's singing is set on the right side. The tails of the bubbles depicting the original song are squiggly, a convention of comics, expressing sound originating from an electronic device (see Cohn 2013, 35–36). By contrast, the tails of the bubbles that contain Rashid's singing are smooth, and the text gives away that Rashid is pronouncing the Finnish lyrics with a thick accent. Rashid might not understand what he is singing about, but the connection of this particular subtext, Tuominen's song *Kaiken teen minkä voin* (I'll do anything I can), with Rashid's sense of honour – but also his failure – is quite obvious to the reader who does understand the lyrics:

> I now want to bear my responsibilities, and give all my love to my family. Even if before I've broken my promises and neglected my dearest. [...] If you just trust me one more time, I'm not going to let you down. I'll do anything I can, and I won't leave.[32]
>
> (Tietäväinen 2011, 205)

Rashid's story also reflects the destiny of Jamppa Tuominen himself. This singer, who was quite popular during the late 1970s and the early 1980s, ended up performing mainly to Finnish tourists in the Canary Islands in the 1990s. In 1998, as a result of a drunken night, the alcoholic singer was jailed for seventy days and suspected of sexually harassing an underage boy. When he was released, his passport was confiscated and he was put under a travel ban to await trial. Tuominen wandered around Playa del Ingles on Gran Canaria until he received some money from friends in Finland and could rent a modest hotel room. While the lawsuit was still pending, Tuominen was found dead there (Tiitto &

Multilingual Intertextuality 219

Figure 12.10 Ville Tietäväinen, *Näkymättömät kädet*, p. 205, selection. © Ville Tietäväinen.

Tuunainen 2008, 196–211, 214–215, 241, 257). Similar to Rashid, Tuominen reached the end of his road in Spain, homeless and alone.

The music of Jamppa Tuominen featured in *Näkymättömät kädet* creates a visible, or even an audible, link to Finnish culture. Through these lyrics, Finnish-speaking readers can find an additional point of entry into the story, a contact surface between themselves and the protagonist of the graphic novel. My own position is thoroughly defined by my own language proficiency – Finnish is my mother tongue – in addition to my cultural knowledge; therefore, in my analysis, which is based on a close reading of the original Finnish version of Tietäväinen's graphic novel, I am not able to study how the references that draw from Finnish language and culture may be interpreted from a different perspective. I can only assume that the songs of Jamppa Tuominen could be perceived quite differently in some other cultural context. When looking at the translations of *Näkymättömät kädet*, it is quite interesting that the lyrics of Tuominen's songs are only translated in the French version. In the Swedish, German and Arabic translations, the lyrics are in Finnish. According to Tietäväinen, the French publisher wanted the lyrics to be in French, so that readers could understand them; the other publishers did not oppose Tietäväinen's wish that the lyrics be in Finnish.[33] This raises interesting questions about the inclusion and exclusion of the reader that I touched on earlier. It is probable that most of the readers of the Swedish, German and Arabic translations of the graphic novel do not understand Tuominen's lyrics, and therefore the lyrics most likely function in a similar manner as Arabic dialogue for Finnish-speaking readers: as cultural peculiarities, or local colour, which in this case serve as a reference to the author's nationality instead of the storyworld.

Conclusions

In the beginning of *Näkymättömät kädet*, just after the title page, there is a white page with a quote in the middle: "Deux rives, un rêve" ("Two shores, one dream"). A short but significant explanation can be found at the bottom of the page, stating that this is

> [t]he slogan of the Boughaz (Gibraltar) ferry connecting Tangiers [in Morocco] and Algeciras [in Spain]. Under its original name of Viking 5, this ferry connected Helsinki and Stockholm in the 1970s, bringing unemployed Finns to Sweden in search of a better life.[34]
> (Tietäväinen 2011, [3])

This French quote – besides adding one more language to the multilingual expression of the graphic novel – links the colonial past and the global present of Europe and Africa, as well as the historical migration of Finns. From the end of the 19th century up to the 1980s, Finland was primarily a country of departure rather than a recipient country. After the Second World War, Sweden became a destination for many Finnish migrants, chiefly uneducated workers and peasantry; a labour shortage, caused by an economic boom, was the primary pull factor. Work and better livelihood were thus the main reasons to cross the Baltic Sea to Sweden (Martikainen et al. 2006, 9, 30–31). In this respect, the Finns that migrated to Sweden did not differ at all from Rashid or the non-fictional migrants trying to get to Europe today.

The French slogan for the ferry crystallizes rather well the idea of the artificiality of borders. "Two shores, one dream" signifies that on both sides of the sea, people dream of work and a decent standard of living, of a good life. This quote sums up the ideology behind *Näkymättömät kädet*, and we are reminded of it near the end of the story when Rashid's wife Amina crosses the Mediterranean on this same ferry while travelling to Europe in hopes of bringing her husband back home. Through the ferry, a parallel is drawn between two seas, two borders, two historical moments, and two different – yet in many aspects similar – migration phenomena.

Näkymättömät kädet tells a tragic story of one individual, a Moroccan migrant, who leaves his home and crosses the Mediterranean hoping to build a better life for himself and his family. Through multilingual intertextuality and other multilingual elements, the graphic novel expands to deal with larger themes which seem all entangled together: national borders and their artificiality, the history of otherness in Europe, colonialism, racism, insanity and the harshly unequal reality behind global markets. Some multilingual elements, such as diegetic texts or foreign words in the dialogue, connect the story to certain locations or cultures and enhance the story's authenticity, while others (e.g. Jamppa Tuominen's lyrics) underline the thematics of the comic. For instance, Finnish migration is placed alongside the global history of migration through multilingual references, such as the song lyrics and the slogan of a ferry that functions as a kind of motto for the whole comic.

The multilingualism of *Näkymättömät kädet* plays a central role in the reading experience of the comic. Depending on the language proficiency of the reader, certain multilingual aspects function in an inclusive manner, while others might – at least seemingly – exclude the reader. My interpretation is that multilingualism plays a significant part in the identification of the reader with the graphic novel. The multilingual elements in the graphic novel – Spanish and Arabic phrases in the dialogue, Spanish and Finnish lyrics and Spanish graffiti, to mention a few – transcend and make visible many kinds of borders: geographical, physical and mental but also the border between the graphic novel and the reader.

Notes

1 The graphic novel has not been published in English, but Tietäväinen has provided me with an unofficial translation of the comic by James O'Connor. This translation was originally made to give an example of Tietäväinen's work when meeting publishers abroad. I have Tietäväinen's permission to use the English translation when quoting the graphic novel's dialogue.

2   "Jumalan, armeliaan armahtajan nimeen".
3   "Eurooppa... näyttää merellä ihan Afrikalta".
4   "No sólo de pan vive el hombre".
5   "[Jumala] on luonut koko Euroopan vain koetellakseen meidän uskoamme".
6   "Imevät kritiikittä kaiken länsimaisen. Matkaavat mieluummin Disneylandiin kuin Mekkaan."
7   "Perdido en el corazón de la grande Babylon. Me dicen el clandestino por no llevar papel. Pa una ciudad del norte yo me fui a trabajar, mi vida la dej entre Ceuta y Gibraltar. Soy una raya en el mar, fantasma en la ciudad."
8   "Kärkkykää kuranaamojen kanssa vuosikaudet Ceutan kukkuloilla, syökää vahtikoiria ja vuoriapinoita henkenne pitimiksi".
9   "Jabal Tariq, arabivalloittajan vuori!"
10 "Ei tilattu kebabia. [...] Painukaa apinatarhaanne, ennen kuin menetän asiakkaat."
11 "Digame? [...] Missä olet?"
12 "Anteeksi, hitaammin... minun espanja..."
13 "Iltaa señor... meillä juhla... poika... tuli mies..."
14 "Minä näen... että te pelkää meitä... kuin pimeää... sitä mistä... ei tiedä."
15 Moroccan semolina flatbread.
16 A long, loose-fitting robe with long sleeves.
17 In the Arabic spoken in North Africa, "harraga" means crossing the Strait of Gibraltar illegally. The term derives from the Arabic word for crossing or piercing (Juntunen 2002, 15).
18 A form of Algerian and Moroccan folk music.
19 A mix of marijuana and tobacco smoked in a long pipe.
20 A religious teacher.
21 Something forbidden, the opposite of "halal".
22 "Rashid, sokeritasapaino. Haetaan hunajahärshät, Wafiqin kahvi polttaa reiän mahaan."
23 "Buenas... se tavallinen: kaakao ja churros".
24 "Siltä kusetettiin omaisuus harragareissulla. Uskoo, että on Andalusiassa, vaikka kuski käänsi pimeällä veneen takaisin."
25 "Se on usko eikä siipien räpyttely, joka pitää linnun ilmassa".
26 "Todellisen taiteilijan ja valepukuisen kerjäläisen välillä on suuri ero".
27 Finnish *iskelmä*, a musical category born in the interwar period and influenced by, for instance, fox trot, polka and tango, is usually translated as popular music or as schlager (Gronow 1973, 60).
28 The lyrics of Jamppa Tuominen's songs included in *Näkymättömät kädet* are also in Finnish in the unofficial English translation. Thus, the translations of the song titles and lyrics in this chapter are mine.
29 "Suuren suureen maailmaan, suurempaan kuin luulinkaan, nyt on mun mentävä. Määrätty niin vain on."
30 "En tiedä mistä mies laulaa, mutta hän lohduttaa minua kuin kohtalotoveri."
31 "Mitä laulat? Kuulostaa kamalalta."
32 "Nyt vastuuni mä toisin tahdon kantaa, ja rakkautta perheelleni antaa. Jos sanani mä ennen oonkin syönyt ja omiani liikaa laiminlyönyt. [...] Jos minuun jaksat kerran vielä luottaa, en aio sulle pettymystä tuottaa. Kaiken teen minkä voin enkä lähde pois."
33 Facebook Messenger chat with Ville Tietäväinen (May 5, 2017).
34 "'Kaksi rantaa, yksi unelma' Tanger–Algeciras-väliä kulkevan lautan mainoslause. Lautta, nykynimeltään *Boughaz (Gibraltar)*, kulki 70-luvulla *Viking 5* -nimisenä välillä Helsinki-Tukholma ja vei kymmeniätuhansia parempaa elämää etsiviä suomalaisia Ruotsiin."

Bibliography

Aronson-Friedman, Amy I. & Kaplan, Gregory B. (2012) Editors' Introduction to Marginal Voices. Studies in Converso Literature of Medieval and Golden Age Spain. In Amy I. Aronson-Friedman & Gregory B. Kaplan (eds): *Marginal Voices: Studies in Converso Literature of Medieval and Golden Age Spain*. Leiden & Boston: Brill, 1–17.

Benito, Ana (2012) Inquisition and the Creation of the Other. In Amy I. Aronson-Friedman & Gregory B. Kaplan (eds): *Marginal Voices: Studies in Converso Literature of Medieval and Golden Age Spain*. Leiden & Boston: Brill, 43–67.

Boruchoff, David A. (2002) On the Place of Madness, Deviance, and Eccentricity in Don Quijote. *Hispanic Review* 70(1), 1–23.

Cohn, Neil (2013) *The Visual Language of Comics: Introduction to the Structure and Cognition of Sequential Images*. London & New York: Bloomsbury.

Corfis, Ivy A. (2009) Introduction: Three Cultures, One World. In Ivy A. Corfis (ed.): *Al-Andalus, Sepharad and Medieval Iberia: Cultural Contact and Diffusion*. Leiden & Boston: Brill, iii–xiv.

Cortsen, Rikke Platz (2015) "By the Cake of the Dark Lord!" Metal Cultures in Three Nordic Comics. In Toni-Matti Karjalainen & Kimi Kärki (eds): *Modern Heavy Metal: Markets, Practices and Cultures*. Helsinki: Aalto University Publication Series, 163–173.

Durán, Manuel & Rogg, Fay R. (2006) *Fighting Windmills: Encounters with Don Quixote*. New Haven: Yale University Press.

Echchaibi, Nabil (2012) Mecca Cola and Burqinis: Muslim Consumption and Religious Identities. In Gordon Lynch & Jolyon Mitchell (eds): *Religion, Media and Culture: A Reader*. New York: Routledge, 31–39.

Fuchs, Barbara (2009) Maurophilia and the Morisco Subject. In Kevin Ingram (ed.): *The Conversos and Moriscos in Late Medieval Spain and Beyond: Departures and Change*. Boston: Brill, 269–285.

Gardner-Chloros, Penelope & Weston, Daniel (2015) Code-switching and Multilingualism in Literature. *Language and Literature* 24(3), 182–193.

Groensteen, Thierry (2007) *The System of Comics*. Translated by Bart Beaty & Nick Nguyen. Jackson: University Press of Mississippi.

Gronow, Pekka (1973) Popular Music in Finland: A Preliminary Survey. *Etnomusicology* 17(1), 52–71.

Guzmán, Roberto Marín (2002) Jihad vs. Cruzada en al-Andalus: La Reconquista española como ideología a partir del siglo XI y sus proyecciones en la colonización de América. *Revista De Historia De América* 131, 9–65.

Juntunen, Marko (2002) *Between Morocco and Spain: Men, Migrant Smuggling and a Dispersed Moroccan Community*. Helsinki: University of Helsinki.

Juntunen, Marko (2015) Marokkolaisen kaupunkiköyhälistön islam. In Joonas Maristo & Andrei Sergejeff (eds): *Aikamme monta islamia*. Helsinki: Gaudeamus, 204–226.

Kukkonen, Karin (2013) *Contemporary Comics Storytelling*. Lincoln: University of Nebraska Press.

Martikainen, Tuomas; Sintonen, Teppo & Pitkänen, Pirkko (2006) Ylirajainen liikkuvuus ja etniset vähemmistöt. In Tuomas Martikainen (ed.): *Ylirajainen kulttuuri: Etnisyys Suomessa 2000-luvulla*. Helsinki: Suomalaisen Kirjallisuuden Seura, 9–41.

Rajewsky, Irina O. (2005) Intermediality, Intertextuality, and Remediation: Literary Perspective on Intermediality. *Intermédialités: Histoire et théorie des arts, des lettres et des techniques* 6, 43–64.

Rippl, Gabriele & Etter, Lukas (2015) Intermediality, Transmediality, and Graphic Narrative. In Daniel Stein, & Jan Noël Thon (eds): *From Comic Strips to Graphic Novels: Contributions to the Theory and History of Graphic Narrative*. Berlin & Boston: De Gruyter, 191–217.

Roth, John K. (1980) Holocaust Business: Some Reflections on Arbeit Macht Frei. *The Annals of the American Academy of Political and Social Science* 450, 68–82.

Schmitz-Emans, Monika (2011) The Languages of Music in Comics, Bande dessinées and Fumetti. In K. Alfons Knauth (ed.): *Translation & Multilingual Literature. Traduction & Littérature Multilingue*. Berlin: LIT Verlag, 195–213.

Skattum, Ingse (2008) Mali: In Defence of Cultural and Linguistic Pluralism. In Andrew Simpson (ed.): *Language and National Identity in Africa*. Oxford & New York: Oxford University Press, 98–121.

Stein, Daniel (2015) Comics and Graphic Narrative. In Gabriele Rippl (ed.): *Handbook of Intermediality: Literature – Image – Sound – Music*. Berlin & Boston: De Gruyter Mouton, 420–438.

Tidigs, Julia (2014) *Att skriva sig över språkgränserna. Flerspråkighet i Jac. Ahrenbergs och Elmer Diktonius prosa*. Åbo: Åbo Akademis förlag.

Tidigs, Julia & Huss, Markus (2017) The Noise of Multilingualism: Reader Diversity, Linguistic Borders and Literary Multimodality. *Critical Multilingualism Studies* 5(1), 208–235.

Tietäväinen, Ville (2011) *Näkymättämät kädet*. Helsinki: WSOY.

Tiitto, Veikko & Tuunainen, Petri (2008) *Jamppa Tuominen: aamu toi, ilta vei. Suomalaisen laulajan tarina*. Helsinki: Minerva.

Versteegh, Kees (2001) *The Arabic Language*. Edinburgh: Edinburgh University Press.

Watt, William Montgomery & Cachia, Pierre (2008) *A History of Islamic Spain*. New Brunswick & London: Aldine Transaction.

13 Multilingualism and the Work of Readers
Processes of Linguistic Bordering in Three Cases of Contemporary Swedish-Language Literature

Julia Tidigs

In this chapter, I work with three examples of contemporary Swedish language literature that are linguistically heterogeneous in order to explore blurred linguistic borders and how the malleable linguistic borders of the texts put their readers to creative work. My examples come from contemporary Swedish-language literature from Finland (Ralf Andtbacka) and Sweden (Alejandro Leiva Wenger and Aase Berg), and from poetry (Andtbacka and Berg) and prose (Leiva Wenger). The examples are not chosen on the basis of cohesion; on the contrary, the texts deal with linguistic diversity in radically different ways, and they likewise engage their readers differently. This, I hope to show, can challenge our conception not only of what constitutes literary multilingualism but also of what a reading of literary multilingualism can look like.

Multilingualism, Readers and Processes of Bordering

From the start, I want to emphasize that it is crucial to speak of readers in the plural, instead of just one reader. Multilingual texts, here understood as texts where more than one "language" is present, make it especially obvious that different readers are targeted – or rather, engaged – in different ways (for a thorough discussion of this, see Tidigs & Huss 2017). This does not imply that a so-called monolingual text addresses or engages all its readers in the same way, but only that multilingual – or, in a broader sense, linguistically heterogeneous – texts tend to do so in a more explicit manner, thereby becoming fruitful objects of study for the scholar concerned with exploring the role of readers vis-à-vis literary effects.

Although linguistically diverse texts make it clear that different readers are treated differently, the focus in the analysis of literary multilingualism has been on a single reader, or rather a group of readers (e.g. Haapamäki & Eriksson 2011; Knauth 2011; Laakso 2012; for a critical discussion, see Tidigs & Huss 2017). In place of the implied monolingual reader of monolingual texts, which has been presupposed these last couple of centuries (see Yildiz 2012, 6–14), literary multilingualism studies has put the multilingual reader of an (identically) multilingual text at the forefront (i.e. the reader with language skills facilitating him or her to *understand* everything, if by "understand" we mean being able to grasp the semantic content of the words, or being able to translate them into another language). According to this view, reading multilingualism has been a question of being able to decode it, being the master of it in the sense that one is not excluded or confused by it.

During the last decade or so, a critique of this conception of the readers of multilingualism has developed, and my examination of contemporary Swedish-language literature is part of this striving towards a more multifaceted view of the readers of multilingual texts. In her seminal *Bilingual Aesthetics*, Doris Sommer turns the question of the reader on its head. With the aid of the Russian formalist Viktor Shklovsky, Sommer convincingly argues for the role of incomprehension, or at least halted or delayed understanding, in the reading of multilingualism: "Ironically", Sommer (2004, 30) states,

> the delays or difficulties that English-only readers may encounter in a multilingual text probably make them better targets for aesthetic effects than readers who don't stop to struggle. […] Roughness can irritate the senses pleasantly enough to notice both the artist at work and a refreshed world that may have grayed from inattention.

Multilingual texts, in Sommer's view, are not "made for" the identically multilingual reader. On the contrary, it might just be that the readers who *struggle* with the languages of the text are the ones getting the most out of their readings. Most significantly, Sommer connects the aesthetic experience of the multilingual text to the *work* the reader has to put in, thereby stressing the active and processual character of reading, in contrast to a conception of reading where a passive reader consumes the finished work. This focus on *the work that readers have to do* is central to my readings of multilingual texts in this chapter, and I will return to it below.

Sommer is, of course, not alone in arguing for a more diverse understanding of readers of multilingualism. In my previous research centred on Finland-Swedish literature from the late 1800s and early 1900s, I have shown that the play between languages, instead of giving multilingual readers a sense of mastery and complete understanding, can highlight the fact that understanding is often partial, temporary or even deceptive (Tidigs 2014). This complication of understanding, however, is not to be viewed as a failure, but instead as something that forces readers to engage and reflect. Furthermore, in *Born Translated: The Contemporary Novel in an Age of World Literature*, Rebecca L. Walkowitz argues that the days of the native reader so cherished since the rise of nationalist language ideology (see Yildiz 2012, 10–14) are long gone. According to Walkowitz (2015, 20–21), the contemporary novel, be it mono- or multilingual, has multiple and heterogeneous audiences from the start, audiences who are often taken into account from the text's inception and who experience the work differently. Walkowitz (2015, 42–44) speaks of *partial fluency* with regard to the reader and how this is far from an impediment to reading, but rather a condition of reading in today's globalized literary arena.

In this chapter, I want to explore partial fluency and the struggle for understanding as a productive motor in the reading of linguistically hybrid texts. The work – or, to put it differently, the active engagement of readers – is not simply the road towards grasping the aesthetic workings of literary multilingualism, but a part of the aesthetic effects of literary multilingualism itself, something that I hope to make tangible with my examples. This necessarily involves a focus on readers not as constructs, but as thinking, feeling beings with language histories. Like Sommer, I argue that the active participation of readers is necessary for the creation of literary effect itself. As Sommer (2004, 63–64) shows, the effect of multilingualism only takes place when readers notice that something happens, that is, when they become aware of their incomprehension, surprise, irritation or whatever affects the multilingual text rouses in them.

In a previous article on the multilingual, multimodal and intermedial works of the poet Cia Rinne (b. 1973), Markus Huss and I have explored how readers are a part of the text coming into being (Huss & Tidigs 2015). With Rinne, we argue, the text can be understood as a musical score, with readers playing the part of vocalists, making the poem come into being with their different readings. This active role of readers becomes especially apparent with the written words of Rinne's poems, which often belong to more than one language, as in the following example (Figure 13.1):

```
*   war was
    was war
    was war?
    war war
    war was?
    war was
    here.
```

Figure 13.1 Cia Rinne, from notes for soloists (2009). © Cia Rinne.

In Rinne's poetry, it is very clear that readers themselves need to draw borders between languages: whether the word "war" belongs to German or English is something decided upon not in the text on the page, but in the mind (and articulated through the voice) of the reader. The drawing of these linguistic borders, in turn, depends to a certain extent on what the readers know and recognize. In the case they comprehend both languages, they also have the possibility of drawing the borders anew with each reading (see Huss & Tidigs 2015, 20–21).

In the case of Rinne it becomes evident that multilingualism not only demands semantic activity on the part of readers, but also the assignation of linguistic identity to words; it is the readers who draw the borders between languages (and, by extension, between language and mere "noise"). Rinne's poetry shows that the border between languages is not necessarily fixed, but rather something that can be understood spatio-temporally as a *process*. The performative character of linguistic borders is one of the central aspects of translation in literary scholar Naoki Sakai's attempt to imagine linguistic difference and unity in an alternative manner. In "How Do We Count a Language? Translation and Discontinuity", Sakai (2009, 71) proposes an "analytic of bordering" that takes "into account simultaneously both the presence of border and the drawing or inscription of it". The view of languages as countable units is central to both modern linguistics and nationalism (see Blommaert 2010; Blommaert et al. 2012); at the same time, Sakai (2009, 73) argues that it is a rather recent invention and a "regulative idea" in the Kantian sense:

> It is not possible to know whether a particular language as a unity exists or not. It is the other way around: by subscribing to the idea of the unity of language, it becomes possible for us to systematically organize knowledge about languages in a modern, scientific manner.

However, Sakai stresses that linguistic difference can indeed be imagined differently than in terms of one and many (countable units/languages). His use of the term "bordering" puts emphasis on the processes by which the idea of linguistic unity is continuously performed and maintained, and how at all times it is dependent on its relation to another unity: "It is never given in and of itself, but in relation to another, transferentially." Here, the act of translation from "one" language to "another" is "not only a border crossing but also and preliminarily an act of drawing a border, of *bordering*" (Sakai 2009, 83). On the one hand, the inscription of a border defines those entities divided by it, and thus even translingual practices such as translation reinforce an artefactualized conception of language (see Blommaert 2010). On the other hand, a conception of border*ing* as process necessarily acknowledges that borders do not just exist, but need to be (repeatedly) drawn, and that they can shift and be dissolved. They are not "natural", but temporary.

It is this thread that I want to follow in my readings of contemporary literature: how are readers active in the bordering of linguistically diverse literary texts? What choices do texts demand that readers make? And what kind of work do readers have to put in?

Multiple Hybridities and Readerly Choice in Alejandro Leiva Wenger's "Borta i tankar"

Alejandro Leiva Wenger's (b. 1976) authorial debut, the collection of short stories *Till vår ära* (In our honour) published in 2001, has been described as the starting point of the new wave of the so-called "immigrant literature" of the early 21 century in Sweden.[1] Like Jonas Hassen Khemiri in his debut novel *Ett öga rött* (2003; One eye red), Leiva Wenger experiments with language that somehow draws on, and has been interpreted as mimicking, the language of the immigrant-inhabited suburbs.[2] While Khemiri's novel is regarded as a modern classic, Leiva Wenger's work has not received the same level of scholarly attention. Most likely, this is partially an effect of it being a collection of short stories instead of a novel, and partly due to the stylistic and narrative diversity of the collection itself.

What should be noted is the multifaceted linguistic and stylistic, as well as narrative, diversity of *Till vår ära*. Although Leiva Wenger was generally treated as a representative of the new generation of immigrant writers by critics (see Dahlstedt 2006, 37–42), it is important to remember that the experimentalism of the collection does not always involve linguistic variation. Instead, most of the stories are written in what can be labelled as "standard Swedish", and their experimental tendencies also regard the use of the second-person singular (*"Song for My Father"* addresses itself to a "you") or first-person plural ("Till vår ära" is written in "we" form). Only two of the six stories in *Till vår ära*, "Borta i tankar" (Lost in thoughts) and "Elixir", put a different kind of Swedish than the standard to artistic use. Of these two, I will focus my attention on the first story of the collection, "Borta i tankar", due to its heterogeneity not only in terms of language but also in terms of style and narrative technique.[3]

"Borta i tankar" is the story of Felipe, called "Fällan" ("The Trap") by his friends, a teenage boy from the suburbs who starts high school in the city where the demographics are very different than in the hoods he grew up in. The story deals with the pressure Felipe is under from his old friends and his brother not to turn into someone different than he used to be, as well as with his relationship with a middle-class girl, Julia, whom he meets in his new school.

As mentioned previously, "Borta i tankar" is experimental on multiple levels – narratively, stylistically and linguistically. The story alternates between two kinds of narration, both of them heterogeneous in several but different ways. On the one hand, we have what would be a more traditional narrative, complete with dialogue, were it not for the instability of the perspective: Leiva Wenger employs first- and third-person perspectives simultaneously. When Felipe says something, Leiva Wenger (2002, 12) writes: "– I – says he says Felipe, says I, says Fällan."[4] The story also involves time jumps, sometimes containing several within a single sentence. These conflicting perspectives and chronologies enact the theme of the novel: the conflict between roles, identities, loyalties and "selves" that Felipe experiences. It also makes the reader a bit dizzy, as well as uncertain of where and by whom the story is being told.

The other kind of narration in "Borta i tankar" consists of two passages where two – or really three – kinds of language are mixed in two parallel narrations, differentiated graphically, alternating line by line:

abo, abo, få kolla len, är det deras andra?, Nico visar och
VÄNTA JULIA, LÄGG INTE PÅ. DU MÅSTE HÖRA FÖRST. JAG VET JAG VAR
dom kollar, sen dom går hem till Nico och lyssnar, eh håll
FALSK MEN DU VAR OCKSÅ. JO, DU VAR. IBLAND ALLA ÄR, JAG MED. MEN
käften, höj, vad säger han, *Dogge och Boastin i den fetaste*
DEN GÅNGEN JAG VAR SUR PÅ DEJ OCH DIN FARSA OCH SKOLAN OCH HELA
kombinationen håller sej till hiphoptraditionen, Bollen höj, ge mej
SKITEN DU VET. FÖRUT DET VAR ANNORLUNDA. JAG FICK INGA SNIGLAR I
en cigg, Fällan tänker, fan vad de knäcker, nästa låt, abo, vad
MAGEN OCH DET. PLUS JAG HADE BRA POLARE, DU VET BOLLEN OCH NICO
säger han, *dags att penetrera, parkera, jag kramar dej som leeeera*,
OCH LATIF OCH DOM. VI HÄNGDE IHOP ALLTID, VÄRSTA STEKARNA VI VAR.
du vill bara baza meera, ha ha ha, höj len, höj, Bollen vafan gör [...]
(Leiva Wenger 2002, 15)

Here, every other line is written in upper-case or lower-case letters. In addition, the lower-case text is interspersed with lyrics from songs by the Swedish hip-hop pioneers The Latin Kings marked with italics. To complicate things even further, the upper-case text consists of Felipe explaining himself to Julia (in an actual or imagined phone call), while Julia's replies are not visible, only hinted at from what Felipe says. The lower-case text, in contrast, involves a narrator and several characters in dialogue, as well as the hip-hop quotes. The narrator's voice and the lines by different characters are not separated visually in any way, forcing the reader to attend to them closely.

It is, therefore, not as simple as standard Swedish appearing in the lower-case text and so-called "immigrant Swedish" in the upper-case text. Rather, following the text line by line (like one usually reads a prose text), readers have to deal with jumping back and forth between narratives *and* taking into account that one of the narratives is interspersed with hip-hop quotes, *as well as* reconciling the syntactical idiosyncrasies of the upper-case text and the heterogeneity of the Swedish of the lower-case text (i.e. transitioning between standard language and slang, from character to character and to the narrator). In this context, the linguistic hybridity is simply one aspect of many aimed at halting an automatized reading, forcing readers to struggle to orientate themselves, leaving them just as disorientated as Felipe feels.

In the second of these passages, the different narratives converge in the last eight lines:

GJORDE DET DÄRA. INNERST INNE JAG VILLE INTE MEN JAG FÖRLORADE
också, här kompis, ta femhundra, nej jag ska inte anmäla er, jag
OCH JAIME OCH DOM PRESSADE DU VET, DOM SA OM DU BANGAR DU ÄR
ska inte säga nåt men det är bra att du byter skola för jag vill
TÖNT, DU ÄR BÖG. OKEJ JAG VET JAG VAR KEFF. JAG VET JAG VAR FALSK MEN
inte se dej mer, okej Julia jag vet jag var keff där, jag vet jag var
DU VAR LITE OCKSÅ. JO JULIA, DU VAR, MEN DET ÄR INTE DITT FEL. ALLA ÄR
falsk men du var lite också, jo Julia du var men det är inte ditt
FALSKA IBLAND, JAG VET NU ALLA ÄR, DOM BLIR TYP TVUNGNA FAST DOM
fel, alla är falska ibland, alla är, dom blir typ tvungna fast dom
INTE VILL. JAG MED, JAG VAR OCKSÅ.
inte vill, jag med, jag var också.

(Leiva Wenger 2002, 25)[5]

The passage ends with the same words repeated in both types of text: Felipe's confession that he had been a phony – and that everyone is, that everyone has to be, even though they do not want to. All of the different ways to tell the story end with the same realization and declaration. However, this passage does not end the story; it returns to a simultaneous depiction of Felipe and Julia's first date and a fight with his brother Jaime.

"Borta i tankar" makes for extremely slow and arduous reading, even though it is a short story written in Swedish. This is a result of narrative, chronological and stylistic heterogeneity, but also language. The Swedish of "Borta i tankar" is seldom stable. The upper-case lines perhaps appear as an exception, since here Felipe uses Swedish marked by syntactical anomalies (e.g. wrong word order). But in the rest of the story, a sentence can follow standard Swedish grammar and then suddenly be interrupted by two words that have been tossed around or by the omission of a preposition. Thus, the reader cannot sort out which parts of the text are standard, and which are not, whether Felipe "knows" standard Swedish word order (sometimes he does, sometimes not, and it cannot be categorized according to whom he is talking to), and so forth. Reading is always halted, the rhythm broken, the Swedish strange – although not in a way that would consequently enable us to label the language of the story as "immigrant Swedish".

On the one hand, the reader simply has to slow down and get to work (or, alternately, close the book). On the other hand, the passages alternating between upper and lower case force readers to choose for themselves, since this style of narration is so radically different from what we are used to. In an article on digital epistemologies in Swedish literature of the 1990s and 2000s, Jonas Ingvarsson discusses Lars Jakobson's novel *Vid den stora floden* (2006; By the great river). Ingvarsson (2015, 52) claims that its parallel narration, where one (part of the) text takes up the upper half of the page and another the lower, frames "the freedom of the reader as an almost *impossible* position". Different parts of the text tell the same story, but in different phases and voices. Ingvarsson highlights how the act of reading is filled with the uncertainty of how to *physically* get through the text and how this forces the reader to make a choice, something that, in turn, establishes a "strong material presence of the book" (Ingvarsson 2015, 52).

Compared to Jakobson's novel, Leiva Wenger's story is still more radical: the narratives are not only competing but also hybrid. With the upper- and lower-case passages, it is almost impossible to read line by line and keep up with both parts of the narrative. What is prompted instead is self-reflection and awareness of the automatization that now has ceased and of the importance of visual markers. If the reader refuses to read in this way, she can follow every other line, choosing visual likeness as the basis for reading instead of the traditional line-by-line method. In turn, this results in her having either to forsake half of the passages or to read and then go back, and start all over again. There are several different reading possibilities; in each, the mix of styles and kinds of language looks different. No reading, however, involves streamlined, continuous and "traditional" understanding. The result is an arduous reading that prompts metacognition of the reading experience itself.

Bilingual Simultaneity in Aase Berg's *Loss*

Swedish poet and critic Aase Berg's (b. 1967) "mommy trilogy", consisting of *Forsla fett* (2002, *Transfer Fat* 2012), *Uppland* (2005, Upland) and *Loss* (2007), is full of words that are inhabited by several other words at once. This cohabitation presents itself in different ways, although mostly monolingually. At times, it is an extra letter that creates a neologism which is a pun on an almost identical word (e.g. when the place name "Arlanda", famously the location of Sweden's largest airport, becomes "Kvarlanda" ("Remainland")), thus creating a whole story around parenthood, liberation and closeness (Berg 2005, 72). Alternatively, an extra letter on the one hand turns a word into no word at all and, on the other, into many different words simultaneously. This is the case with the word *strämja* in *Forsla fett* (Berg 2002, 9). It is a neologism that bears strong connotations of *sträng* ("string, severe"), *sämja* ("harmony"), *tänja* ("strain, stretch"), *tämja* ("to tame") and *stämma*, a word that has multiple meanings (e.g. to tune an instrument, to make sense and in relation to voice, both more generally and as part of a musical piece). In addition to this, Berg's use of *strämja* next to the acoustically similar *stram* ("tight") also connects the two words. These instances bear many of the marks of portmanteau words, so eloquently cultivated, for example, by James Joyce and Lewis Carroll. With Berg, the meanings of the neologisms are often undetermined, making for high intensity.

Interestingly enough, the multilingualism that characterizes many of the poems of *Loss* most often does not function in this manner, although Berg does play with the double meaning of a word in the poem "Stabat mater", where it is declared that "matter / doesn't matter / no more" (Berg 2007, 175). In the poem "Krypskydd",[6] however, something different occurs. The poem begins:

> Smrt,
> smattersalva,
> snart en snärt
> av drömmoservons
> självlänkande
> ödlestjärt
> [...]
>
> (Berg 2007, 194)[7]

The frequency of alliteration and assonance in the passage makes the first line, "Smrt", easy to read as onomatopoetics, as mimicking the noise of the (in itself semi-onomatopoetical) "smattersalva" from a machine gun. "Smrt" can also be read as a cipher, consisting of the consonants of the Swedish word *smärta*, meaning pain. But readers who study the book's endnotes are provided with a definition/translation: "smrt = death (Bosnian)"[8] (Berg 2007, 227). Readers without knowledge of Bosnian are thus given the meaning of the word, which then carries both a sense of death and the onomatopoetically created connotations of violent death.[9]

The most explicit example of multilingual double meanings, however, is the title of the collection itself: *Loss* is a bilingual title. In its double sense, with the Swedish *loss* meaning "loose" (as in "breaking loose") as well as the bereavement of the English "loss", the title encapsulates the themes of the entire book perfectly: the painful and necessary ambiguity of loss and liberation that characterizes the relationship between mother and child as the child grows. In the case of the title, the dual linguistic belonging of *Loss* is not declared explicitly (e.g. via translation or any other commentary). Compared to the Bosnian example of "smrt", however, the English language is a lot more familiar to most readers. Two languages inhabit the word, and readers can read it in English, in Swedish, or in both languages simultaneously, making the word vibrate with both loss and liberation.

In this sense, the "loss" of *Loss* differs from Cia Rinne's "was war" cited in the first section of this chapter, where two languages can inhabit the same words only within a silent reading. With Rinne's bilingual cohabitation of words, when reading aloud the reader has to choose, since the pronunciation of the words differs radically between English and German. With *Loss*, the border between English and Swedish is a lot less clear-cut acoustically.[10] A reader can, to a certain extent, choose to highlight it or not.

With Berg, acoustics play a key role in several, albeit distinct, respects: in her neologisms, the acoustic similarities between a made-up word and several preexisting ones create a force field of connotations, where the reader who has started the search for "hidden words" within the neologism will find more and more. In her use of the Bosnian "smrt", a word is simultaneously affectively loaded noise and, if its linguistic origin and meaning is acknowledged, a semantic unit in line with the rest of the poem. In both capacities, it is effective. And lastly, with *Loss*, a bilingual reading of the title encapsulates the ambiguity of the mother-child bond that the whole collection is concerned with. In Berg's poetry, noise reveals foreign words or multiple words, and several languages inhabit the same word, spilling over into one another. In each case, they result in an intensified poetic tension where the reader finds a door leading to a different word, and then to another, and yet another.

Border Crossings of the Tongue: Ralf Andtbacka's "Tongknoll"

Wunderkammer (2008), a collection by the Finland-Swedish poet Ralf Andtbacka (b. 1963), is indeed a cabinet of curiosities of objects, quotes, jargons and languages: scientific, local, archaic languages, languages chopped into pieces and languages in proliferation. Among many things, *Wunderkammer* is concerned with language and, more specifically, the human voice as an object, as something that it is possible to preserve, reproduce and collect. Some of the poems are also explicitly and practically occupied with the transformation of sound into words and thus, into visual objects. One of them is the erotic poem "Tongknoll" (Tongue fuck):

> Tongknoll
>
> *Beakta ordformen **sku**. Den kan ge ett talspråkligt eller vardagligt intryck i skriven text.*
>
> *Vem ger, vem tar emot.*
>
> HE sku vara naastans ijee,
> fasst he er svårt att verbalisera inom ramen
> för detta knullatiknullspråk.

Tingen som vilar, händernas blånådror,
de, di o ti svällder tongt. Sjölv veitt ja eitt,
men å eitt ana: he finns noo no.

Haa tu tongon i kroppin, haa tu tongon i håli,
i munn, å tzänn ett va du riktit tycker
tå int he finns na ana, tå na ana int finns.

Som regredierar inom ramen för denna
ram som säger sig vara någonting mer än:
oolens sleim, ti er läna. Tzänn.

Du finns här i detta rum och du samlar dig
snart ska du koma fösst, he som komber fösst
komber fösst, he finns alder na ana.

But you who have nothing and no tongue is an island.
Upphääv steedzen ter du gaar. Upphääv
tongon ter jaag slickar. Dzyyft. Säir du.

He smaakar jäärn, sallt, he smakar som yta, textur,
det är svårt att göra någon skillnad, det är vanskligt
att göra någon annan skillnad än:

slickar sååri tett. He er dzyyft, he er som om int
he sku finns na bockn naa aaderstans än just
ijee. He finns ijee. Bockn. Ijee. No. Tzänn.

Ordets salta halka. He fuktas, he er i menn munn,
ja tzender att he finns ter och har textur,
denna lätta kittling mellan apex, clitoris, labia.

Hon er styyv, hon er tong.

Fyll mig. Allt finns.

För att allt finns.
...

(Antbacka, 2008, 76–77)[11]

"Tongknoll" is a poem marked by linguistic variation of several kinds. It is easily recognizable as multilingual, with the English line "*But you who have nothing and no tongue is an island*" marked in italics, as well as Latin words for body parts: "apex, clitoris, labia". The most prominent linguistic tension, however, is "intralinguistic", in that it regards strands of what can be called "Swedish": standard Swedish, on the one hand, and dialectally charged Ostrobothnian Swedish, on the other.

The tension between standard Swedish and spoken language is established right at the beginning with a motto that is actually taken from the computer software Svefix, a resource for the language correction of Finland-Swedish texts. In the context of *Wunderkammer*, the motto reads as the presumptuous voice of a zealous proofreader. It warns against the rather mild marker of the Finnish-Swedish vernacular *sku*, as opposed to the standard Swedish *skulle* ("should"). The motto takes on a ludicrous tone, as it stands in contrast to the much more in-your-face orthographical rendering of dialect that follows, making any caution of *sku* obsolete.

As well as telling of an erotically charged meeting of (different kinds of) corporeal tongues, the poem "Tongknoll" is in itself a meeting of different tongues, tongues that take turns. In fact, the poem oscillates between dialect and standard language in a radical way; at the same time, it becomes difficult to determine what is "the same" and what is "different". The first line "HE sku vara naastans ijee" (in standard Swedish "Det skulle vara någonstans här"; "It should be somewhere here") is dialectal, while the second line switches in the middle: "fasst he er" (standard Swe. "fast det är"; "although it is") gives way to a standard and rather formal "svårt att verbalisera inom ramen" ("difficult to verbalize within the frame"). This undulation between dialect and standard Swedish occurs on several occasions in the poem, right up until it ends.

The dominant variety of Swedish used in "Tongknoll" is not a language that most readers would even recognize as Swedish at first glance. Most Swedish speakers are completely unfamiliar with the Swedish dialects along Finland's western coast; for such readers, this makes for arduous reading. The visual discrepancy between *tzänn* and the standard *känn* ("to feel") is great, and a form such as *ijee* for *här* ("here") is also not easily recognizable to most Swedish speakers. In fact, for many readers this – at least initially – appears as a foreign tongue. In any case, readers must work to connect visual signs to acoustics and to semantics (i.e. to get a clear picture of which words are formed by the sounds that the letters point towards).

Just as the border between different kinds of Swedish is not always clear, neither is the division between readers who "understand" the poem and readers who are shut out. An additional estranging effect of rendering dialect in literature is that even its speakers are unaccustomed to seeing it in print (in written form, it is mostly present in text messages or perhaps in emails). Vernaculars do not have fixed orthographic norms in the way standard language does, so even seemingly "native" or familiar readers have to decipher the poem's orthography in order to create an acoustic image of it. Even they have the possibility of surprise at, and opposition to, the way spoken sounds have been transposed into written letters.

The readers of "Tongknoll" are partially fluent: to a lesser or greater extent, they have to stop in order to struggle (to reference Sommer), to feel their way through the poem in order to grasp the words and imagine what they would sound like. They can dismiss the strange words as senseless noise, or – perhaps trying to read aloud – they can get a new sense of how foreign a variant of Swedish can taste and feel in the mouth. What "Tongknoll" makes obvious is that the border that matters is not between words and expressions that can be counted as Swedish, on the one hand, and those that can be labelled foreign, on the other; on the contrary, English and Latin probably present a much smaller obstacle for most readers. It is not the fixation of the border between inter- and intralinguistic variations that is the crucial issue here. Instead, the vital tension in "Tongknoll" runs between standard and different kinds of deviations, variations or expansions of that standard, regardless of linguistic origin. "Tongknoll" makes it ever so clear that the seemingly familiar entails foreign territories, and that familiar sounds become surprising when transposed into letters.

Not every reader will want to put in the work demanded by the poem of deciphering and sounding things out. It is, of course, entirely possible to dismiss the language of "Tongknoll" as a type of gibberish (even if it is partially comprehensible gibberish) and turn the page. But for the reader who does choose to engage, perhaps by reading aloud, reading is not only a question of cracking the orthographic code to gain access to semantics. The tension between the Swedishes in "Tongknoll" partly regards register – the erotically charged body language of dialect versus a more cerebral language, with words like "verbalize" and "regress" – and partly rhythm and intonation. Reading aloud, the lurches between Ostrobothnian and standard Swedish is a physical, syncopated, tongue-twisting experience.

A recurring theme in *Wunderkammer* is the relationship between reader and poem, a relationship which Andtbacka turns on its head. The collection includes the suite "Personer och föremål" (Persons and objects), where poems are named after pronouns such as "I", "you" and "he/she". Here, the poem "I" starts "Jag skriver dikten" ("I write the poem"). But on the next page, in "You", the circumstances are different: "Nej, dikten skriver dig" ("No, the poem writes you"). With regard to "Tongknoll", both tendencies are present: on the one hand, the reader has work to do, writing/creating the poem when engaging in the bordering process between strains of language, which is necessary for the poem to make some kind of sense. On the other hand, the poem lays out the task for its readers, forcing them to become mouthpieces when trying to sound it out loud. In this way, the readers are made part of the text coming into being.

Conclusion: Text as Physical Labour

The examples by Andtbacka, Berg and Leiva Wenger confront readers with malleable, blurred or confusing linguistic borders. Viewed from one perspective, the very multilingualism of these texts demands readers to come into being: readers who see and hear English and Swedish in *Loss* and readers who search for known sounds in the visual signs of "Tongknoll". From a different perspective, readers can only work with what they are given: Leiva Wenger's short story and Andtbacka's poem simply force them to put in work in order to grasp the texts' meaning, and engagement thus becomes a consequence or direct effect of texts that challenge automatized understanding so blatantly.

In one sense, there is a clear difference between readers drawing and dissolving borders and readers being forced to deal with them. In another sense, however, it is this very process of aesthetic work on the part of the reader that is the point of it all: the work is not an obstacle en route to meaning; it is the most meaningful part of the reading experience. These texts, I would argue, are not so much meant to be understood in the sense of being deciphered, but experienced multisensorially: experiencing the acute sense of disorientation and crisis of perspective in Leiva Wenger's short story; feeling the clatter of a machine-gun resonate in both one's mouth and ears with Berg's "smrt", being forced to take in the corporeality of death through onomatopoetics; and feeling the tongue slip back while trying to follow the rhythm of tongues in Andtbacka's poem.

All of the texts foreground the importance of rhythm and sound. Berg and Andtbacka work with discrepancies between the visual and the acoustic. With Leiva Wenger, the question is more one of rhythm and pace. In addition, all of the examples make clear how fragile, or uncertain, is the border between own and foreign, between Swedish and non-Swedish or other-Swedish. With Andtbacka and Leiva Wenger, the important difference lies not between inter- and intralinguistic variation. Instead, the important borders are the ones coming into place, and dissolving, when the text is read. Whatever freedoms we attribute to readers in this process, it is certain that those readers – as living beings with relationships to different languages and who experience the world through their senses – are an indispensable part of making the languages of these texts happen.

Notes

1 Nilsson (2010, 9) refers to Thomas Mohnike, who marks 2001 as the starting point with reference to Leiva Wenger's debut.
2 For a discussion of the deficiency of the description of the language in Khemiri's novel in terms of authentic Rinkeby-Swedish, see Refsum (2011); Nilsson (2010, 36–40); Källström (2006).

3 "Elixir", written entirely in slang with syntactic deviations from the standard form, has previously received more scholarly attention; see Mohnike (2006).
4 "– Jag – säger han, säger Felipe, säger jag, säger Fällan" (Leiva Wenger 2002, 12).
5 "DID THAT. DEEP INSIDE I DIDN'T WANT TO BUT I LOST / too, here man, take five hundred, no I will not press charges, I / AND JAIME AND THEM PRESSED YOU KNOW, THEY SAID IF YOU BAIL YOU'RE / will not say anything but it is good that you are switching schools because I don't / DORK, YOU'RE A FAGGOT. OK I KNOW I WAS KEFF. I KNOW I WAS PHONY BUT / want to see you again, ok Julia I know I was keff there, I know I was / YOU WERE A LITTLE TOO. YES JULIA, YOU WERE, BUT IT'S NOT YOUR FAULT. EVERYBODY IS / phony but you were a little too, yes Julia you were but it's not your / PHONY SOMETIMES, I KNOW NOW EVERYBODY IS, THEY LIKE HAVE TO EVEN THOUGH THEY / wrong, everybody is phony sometimes, everybody is, they like have to even though they / DON'T WANT TO. ME TOO, I WAS TOO. / don't want to, me too, I was too" (Leiva Wenger 2002, 25. My translation). Here and in the following, English translations of quotes are provided in footnotes, as the materiality of the linguistic variation of the Swedish originals, particularly in the case of Berg and Andtbacka, is central to the chapter's argument and difficult to preserve or signal in translation.
6 The word *krypskydd* plays on *krypskytt* ("sniper") and the acoustic resemblance between *skytt* ("shooter") and *skydd* ("protection, shelter"). In addition, *krypskydd* exists as a name for protective clothing, specifically on the knees of crawling babies (*krypa* = "to crawl").
7 The second part of the poem reads: "Granatgranit / i sluten / gryta gråter // eat" (Berg 2007, 194). English translation by Johannes Göransson, "Kneepad Sniper": "Smrt, / smatter salvo, / soon a lash / of dream serving / self-linking /lizard tail // Garnetgranite / in the ends / pot cries // eat".
8 "smrt = död (bosniska)" (Berg 2007, 227).
9 In the endnotes, Berg lists a suicide bombing as linked to this suite of poems. Overall, many of the suites in *Loss* are about children and violence.
10 Certainly there are differences between how the Swedish *loss* and the English "loss" are pronounced (especially if we go from British to American English), but the differences are in fact smaller than in the example by Rinne. Moreover, if a Swedish reader/speaker were to pronounce the word in Swedish and English, the pronunciation of the two versions would most likely be even closer.
11 In my English translation of the poem, passages that are in dialect in the original are rendered in bold type. I have also made explicit the double meaning of certain homophones in the poem by providing both meanings separated by a backslash.

> Tongue/Heavy fuck / *Take note of the wording sku. It can make an impression of oral / or colloquial language in written text. // Who gives, who receives.* // **IT should be here somewhere,** / although it is difficult to verbalize within the frame / of this fucketifuck language. // The things that rest, the blue veins of hands, / they, **they and/oh they swell heavily. Myself, I know something,** / but also something else: there really is something now. // **Do you have the tongue in your body, do you have the tongue in the hole,** / in the mouth, and try to sense what you really think / when there isn't **anything else, when anything else isn't.** // Which regresses within the frame of this / frame that claims to be something more than: / **the slime of the words, they are slippery. Feel.** // You are here in this room and you

collect yourself / soon you will come first, that which comes first / comes first, there is never anything else. // *But you who have nothing and no tongue is an island.* / Rescind the steps where you walk. Rescind / the tongue where I lick. Deep. You say. // It tastes of iron, salt, it tastes like surface, texture, / it is difficult to make any difference, it is a delicate task / to make any other difference than: // licking your wound. It is deep, it is like there / shouldn't be any bottom anywhere else than just / here. It is here. The bottom. Here. Now. Feel. // The salty slipperiness of the word. It is moistening, it is in my mouth, / I feel that it is there and has texture, / this light tickle between apex, clitoris, labia. // She is stiff, she is heavy/ tongue. // Fill me. Everything is. // Because everything is. /...

Bibliography

Andtbacka, Ralf (2008) *Wunderkammer.* Helsingfors: Söderströms.
Berg, Aase (2002) *Forsla fett.* Stockholm: Albert Bonniers förlag.
Berg, Aase (2005) *Uppland.* Stockholm: Albert Bonniers förlag.
Berg, Aase (2007) *Loss.* Stockholm: Albert Bonniers förlag.
Blommaert, Jan (2010) *The Sociolinguistics of Globalization.* Cambridge: Cambridge University Press.
Blommaert, Jan; Leppänen, Sirpa & Spotti, Massimiliano (2012) Endangering Multilingualism. In Jan Blommaert, Sirpa Leppänen, Päivi Pahta & Tiina Räisänen (eds): *Dangerous Multilingualism.* Houndmills & New York: Palgrave Macmillan, 1–21.
Dahlstedt, Anja (2006) Annorlundahet som kapital. Kategorin invandrarförfattare och annorlundahet på det litterära fältet. Unpublished master's thesis. Biblioteks- och informationsvetenskap, Högskolan i Borås.
Haapamäki, Saara & Eriksson, Harriet (2011) Att analysera litterär flerspråkighet. In Sinikka Niemi & Pirjo Söderholm (eds): *Svenskan i Finland 12.* Joensuu: University of Eastern Finland, 43–52.
Huss, Markus & Tidigs, Julia (2015) The Reader as Multilingual Soloist: Linguistic and Medial Transgressions in the Poetry of Cia Rinne. In Daniel Rellstab & Nestori Siponkoski (eds): *Rajojen dynamiikkaa, Gränsernas dynamik, Borders under Negotiation, Grenzen und ihre Dynamik. VAKKI-symposiumi XXXV 12.–13.2.2015.* Vaasa: VAKKI, 16–24.
Ingvarsson, Jonas (2015) BBB vs. WWW. Digital epistemologi och litterär text från Göran Printz Påhlsson till Ralf Andtbacka. *Tidskrift för litteraturvetenskap* 45(1), 45–60.
Källström, Roger (2006) 'Flygande blattesvenska' – recensenter om språket i *Ett öga rött.* In Per Ledin, Lena Lind Palicki, Christina Melin, Gunvor Nilsson, Karolina Wirdenäs & Håkan Åbrink (eds): *Svenskans beskrivning 28.* Örebro: Örebro universitet, 125–136.
Knauth, K. Alfons (2011) Translation & Multilingual Literature as a New Field of Research in between Translation Studies and Comparative Literature. In K. Alfons Knauth (ed.): *Translation & Multilingual Literature/Traduction & Littérature Multilingue.* Berlin: LIT Verlag, 3–24.
Laakso, Johanna (2012) Linguistic Approaches to Finno-Ugric Literary Multilingualism. In Johanna Laakso & Johanna Domokos (eds): *Multilingualism and Multiculturalism in Finno-Ugric Literatures.* Berlin: LIT Verlag, 26–36.

Leiva Wenger, Alejandro (2002) *Till vår ära*. Stockholm: Bonnierpocket.
Mohnike, Thomas (2006) Doppelte Fremdheit. Zur Verschränkung und Konstitution von poetischer und kultureller Alterität in Alejandro Leiva Wengers *Till vår ära* und seiner Rezeption. In Sven Hakon Rossel (ed.): *Der Norden im Ausland – das Ausland im Norden. Formung und Transformation von Konzepten und Bilden des Anderen vom Mittelalter bis heute*. 25. Tagung der IASS (International Association for Scandinavian Studies) in Wien, 2–7.8.2004. Wiener Studien zur Skandinavistik (WSS) 15. Wien: Praesens Verlag, 150–158.
Nilsson, Magnus (2010) *Den föreställda mångkulturen. Klass och etnicitet i svensk samtidsprosa*. Hedemora: Gidlunds.
Refsum, Christian (2011) Multilingualism in Contemporary Nordic Literature: Jonas Hassen Khemiri. In Bodil Marie Stavning Thomsen & Kristin Ørjasæter (eds): *Globalizing Art: Negotiating Place, Identity and Nation in Contemporary Nordic Art*. Aarhus: Aarhus University Press 2011, 163–181.
Rinne, Cia (2009) *Notes for Soloists*. Göteborg: OEI Editör.
Sakai, Naoki (2009) How Do We Count a Language? Translation and Discontinuity. *Translation Studies* 2(1), 71–88.
Sommer, Doris (2004) *Bilingual Aesthetics: A New Sentimental Education*. Durham & London: Duke University Press.
Tidigs, Julia (2014) *Att skriva sig över språkgränserna. Flerspråkighet i Jac. Ahrenbergs och Elmer Diktonius prosa*. Åbo: Åbo Akademis förlag.
Tidigs, Julia & Huss, Markus (2017) The Noise of Multilingualism: Reader Diversity, Linguistic Borders and Literary Multimodality. *Critical Multilingualism Studies* 5(1), 208–235.
Walkowitz, Rebecka L. (2015) *Born Translated: The Contemporary Novel in an Age of World Literature*. New York: Columbia University Press.
Yildiz, Yasemin (2012) *Beyond the Mother Tongue: The Postmonolingual Condition*. New York: Fordham University Press.

14 "So let me remain a stranger"
Multilingualism and Biscriptalism in the Works of Finland-Swedish Writer Tito Colliander

Helena Bodin

There is an inner, often unimagined affinity between the author, the translator and the stranger – what they all share is the experience of translating. These are the words of Julia Kristeva, who goes so far as to recognize translation and strangeness as the core of creativity. According to Kristeva (2014), we are all translators, being "strangers to ourselves", mediating a continuously recaptured strangeness.[1]

The aim of this chapter is to apply these general thoughts on the affinity between the author, translator and stranger to the singular example of the life and work of the Finland-Swedish writer Tito Colliander (1904–1989), who embodied all of these roles. Although Colliander is one generation older than Kristeva (b. 1941), they share a similar background since they both spent their childhoods in Orthodox Christian societies. Kristeva was born in Bulgaria, as the daughter of an Orthodox church singer, and emigrated to France (Bodin 2014, 206). Colliander was born in Imperial Russia, in Saint Petersburg, to parents whose families had Finland-Swedish and Scottish ancestry, and were of noble military origin. Because of the Russian Revolution, they returned to Finland. As an adult, he lived on the Karelian Isthmus and in the borderlands of Estonia and the Soviet Union before dying in Helsinki. From early childhood, he was a polyglot: he spoke Swedish and Russian at home, while Finnish was encountered only in songs and poems, and his mother taught him English; German was another language present in the family (Colliander 1964, 57–59, 83–89, 93, 100–101).

To readers in Finland and Sweden, Colliander is known both as an author and as a translator. He published short stories and novels, collections of essays and poems, as well as a few biographies, and he was also the author of extensive memoirs, which will be the focus of this chapter. As a translator, he was a groundbreaker in the sense that he translated and introduced Orthodox Christian liturgical texts into Swedish. Due to health reasons, Colliander was unable to become an Orthodox priest, but as a translator and teacher of Swedophone Orthodox pupils at the gymnasium in Helsinki, he became an intermediary of vital importance in the emergence of Swedophone Orthodoxy, not only in Finland but also in Sweden.

Furthermore, Colliander cherished his identity as a stranger. During the harsh and difficult conditions of the interwar period of the 1930s, he deliberately chose to remain in the multilingual borderlands of Finland, the Soviet Union and the Baltic countries around the Gulf of Finland (i.e. on the Karelian Isthmus and in Estonia), together with his wife, the painter and graphic artist Ina Colliander, and their daughters, born in 1931 and 1939. While living in these regions, characterized partly by Orthodox Christian traditions and believers, he decided to become an Orthodox Christian. A case such as his therefore illustrates how religion also needs to be taken into account as an important parameter of cultural diversity, alongside others such as language, gender or class, in the study of literary multilingualism.

Against this background, my intention is to examine issues of multilingualism and the use of biscriptalism in Colliander's Finland-Swedish memoirs, in particular his use of Russian and Church Slavonic and embedded Cyrillic script, in order to discuss what these devices meant for his poetics and identity, not least for his diasporic identity as an Orthodox Christian. After an introductory presentation of Colliander's memoirs and then an explanation of various notions and devices applied in my analysis of Colliander's work – such as literary multilingualism, translingual life writing, allusion, translation, commentary, heterolingual address and translingual paratopia – I shall proceed to discuss the impact of Christian Orthodoxy on his poetics and identity.

Colliander's works, originally written in Swedish, have only exceptionally been translated into English or discussed internationally, for example, in reviews, a few minor articles and a section in *A History of Finland's Literature* (Schoolfield 1998, 515–519). There are many translations, however, from Swedish into Finnish and several studies of his life and work in these languages, such as Hartman (1980, 7–52), Pettersson (1986), Hernberg (1989), Mazzarella (1993, 203–250, 2003) and Andersson Wretmark (2008). Single titles, especially *Asketernas väg* (1951; *The Way of the Ascetics*, 1960) are translated into English, German, French, Spanish, Dutch, Danish, Norwegian and some other languages. The translations from Colliander's works presented in this chapter are my own.

The Memoirs

The seven volumes of Tito Colliander's memoirs were published between 1964 and 1973: *Bevarat* (1964; Saved), *Gripen* (1965; Touched), *Vidare* (1967; Beyond), *Givet* (1968; Granted), *Vaka* (1969; Vigil), *Nära* (1971; Near) and *Måltid* (1973; Meal). They span the whole period from Imperial Russia before the 1917 revolution to Finnish post-war society, and are narrated chronologically but composed in a complex way, as a retrospect of Tito Colliander's life interwoven with his comments as an old man writing down his life story. These two narratives and timelines – one describing his whole life so far and the other only the decade of actual writing – progress at different speeds throughout the memoirs before they finally converge in the last volume. It is clear that the peripeteia in Colliander's memoirs is his decision in the late 1930s to become an Orthodox Christian, as is narrated in the sixth volume, *Nära* (Bodin 2011, 399–401).

In the summer of 1936, when Tito Colliander was living in the part of Estonia bordering on the Soviet Union, close to the Russian Orthodox monastery in Pechory (Estonian: Petseri), he happened to join an Orthodox procession, a so-called *krestnyi khod*. This event, narrated in *Nära* and also in the early novel *Korståget* (1937; The procession), changed his life. Colliander describes the Orthodox services as captivating. He desired to experience not only their beauty or exoticism, as many Western visitors in the interwar period did, but also their *content*, which was more unusual (Ekelund 1956, 80–98; Colliander 1971, 133; Bodin 2008; Bodin 2011, 28–31, 47–51). In order to gain knowledge of the meaning of these complicated and long services, including their many readings, hymns and prayers, Colliander began to study Church Slavonic, the archaic Slavic language used for liturgical purposes – a language that in modern times is not immediately comprehensible even to native Russians but has to be learnt. In the memoirs, Colliander notes the causal relationship between aesthetics and the process of learning in a way that articulates a distinctively Orthodox view: "Beauty enticed knowledge"[2] (Colliander 1971, 133; see further Bodin 2011, 415–419).

As a consequence of his decision to embrace Russian Orthodoxy, Colliander's memoirs portray his life in the linguistic, cultural and religious border zones between Russia (or the Soviet Union), Estonia and Finland from the Orthodox Christian perspective that Colliander acquired as an adult. It follows that the milieus associated with his life story cannot simply be described according to the names of towns in Finland where he spent many years, such as Porvoo (Borgå) or Helsinki (Helsingfors), or by mentioning the rural mansions and manors of noble families in Finland where he stayed periodically, or by referring only to multilingual features, comprising Swedish, Russian and Finnish, and occasionally still more languages, including English, German, French and Italian. From a religious perspective, these milieus taken together may likewise be regarded as an Orthodox Christian diaspora, oriented towards its centres in the different patriarchates (e.g. the Moscow Patriarchate, or, for Russians living in Western exile from the communist regime in the Soviet Union, rather Paris, where there were Orthodox Christian parishes adhering to the Ecumenical Patriarchate in Constantinople, today's Istanbul).

Literary Multilingualism and Translingual Life Writing

Multilingual practices are often thematized in Colliander's memoirs. One example is his vivid description of how his polyglot family relied on several languages during his childhood in Saint Petersburg before the Russian Revolution – English, Italian, German, Russian and French, alongside Swedish and Finnish, of course:

> Man did not exist for the sake of language, but language existed for the sake of man. [...] We lived as if under an umbrella of sayings and proverbs from all over Europe: My home is my castle, Il mondo è nostra casa, Si non è vero è ben trovato, Was willst du denn? Nichts zu machen, Tishe iédesh dál'she búdesh, Nicht sich gehen lassen, Mais c'est la même chose, Utro véchera mudrenéie... And we knew all of them and followed them readily.[3]
>
> (Colliander 1964, 100–101)

According to Colliander's memoirs, neither of his parents spoke or wrote Swedish correctly: "words and expressions in our everyday speech were taken from any language. You chose them according to preference and convenience. [...] / [We] totally lacked respect for the mother tongue, or even love for it"[4] (Colliander 1964, 100). Colliander concludes that the linguistic possibilities brought about by these practices were naturally unlimited. It cannot be stated more clearly. From early childhood, Colliander was a polyglot and the context in which he lived was multilingual. Monolingualism was not even an option. The basis for my analysis and discussion of Colliander's memoirs is therefore not a presupposed normative *mono*lingualism, but a shifting and complex *multi*lingualism. This approach is inspired by Julia Tidigs's dissertation on the prose of Jac. Ahrenberg and Elmer Diktonius – who both wrote in Swedish in Finland – in which she attempts to liberate the study of multilingualism and particularly *literary* multilingualism from the premises of monolingual norms (Tidigs 2014, 308), as well as by Yasemin Yildiz, who has contested the monolingual paradigm as such in *Beyond the Mother Tongue* (2012).

Already in the first volume of his memoirs, Colliander questions the national and linguistic boundaries with which he became acquainted early in life. Instead of borders that keep people, places and generations apart, he imagines a community of floating "mobile points" that are sometimes brought together in order to form various strange and unpredictable patterns, impossible to capture.[5] Although his memoirs are written in Swedish, the foundation on which he writes is multilingual.

Would it be possible to regard Colliander's memoirs as a case of *translingual life writing* (i.e. as an autobiography written in a language which the author has neither learnt at home nor in early childhood, as studied by Alain Ausoni and Fabien Arribert-Narce (2013))? By deciding to write in Swedish, Colliander apparently chose a language other than the Russian of his childhood in order to describe his early years in Saint Petersburg (later Petrograd). But, as mentioned above, Swedish had been equally present in his life all the time, along with Russian and several other languages, and both Swedish and Russian were spoken by his family at home. Therefore, when writing his memoirs, Colliander did not switch languages or learn a new language, but decided which of his available languages to use. Needless to say, he was naturally guided by the linguistic predisposition of his potential audience in Finland and Sweden.

Definitions and discussions of life writing and translingualism are complicated by cases such as that of Colliander, since his memoirs mirror practices of multilingualism experienced from early childhood, as well as his family's non-observance of a particular mother tongue. This raises questions about the significance and purport of the notions of translingualism and translingual authors, as defined by Steven G. Kellman in his influential *Translingual Imagination* (2000). Is translingualism conceivable without a presupposed monolingualism? Does translingualism necessarily imply a transition whereby the author deliberately switches from one language to another within a monolingual paradigm, or may translingualism just as well be a consequence of fundamentally multilingual conditions?

It is from these religiously diasporic and culturally multilingual points of departure that I shall consider Colliander's use of Russian and Church Slavonic within his Swedophone memoirs. Special attention will be paid to phrases rendered in embedded Cyrillic script.

Allusion, Translation and Commentary – Multilingualism and Biscriptalism

In the early 1990s, Rainier Grutman, working in the field of multilingualism and translation studies, published seminal articles on various combinations of linguistic and literary bilingualism (1990, 1993). His premise is rational: it should not be taken for granted that a bilingual author has bilingual readers (Grutman 1990, 202–209). Grutman's model will be applied to my discussion of Colliander's works, but in addition I will also introduce the issue of *biscriptalism*.[6]

Since each of the seven volumes of Colliander's memoirs was published simultaneously in both countries by the renowned Swedophone publishers Schildt (in Finland) and Bonnier (in Sweden), it is clear that they were not intended only for readers who were bilingual in Swedish and Finnish, but also for those ignorant of Finnish. What is more, there cannot have been many readers in the 1960s and 1970s who, like Colliander, were polyglots in Swedish, Finnish and Russian. All the same, this did not prevent him from using phrases and words in Russian and Church Slavonic, or from embedding words in Cyrillic script in his text.

Colliander's memoirs thus match not only one but two of Grutman's categories, since both the author and the text are bilingual (or, in this case, even multilingual), while the intended readers may be either mono-, bi- or multilingual (Grutman 1990, 208–209, types 7 and 8).

According to Grutman, there are certain specific poetic devices available for an author who "wants to suggest bilingualism without exceeding the monolingual competence of his audience" (Grutman 1993, 210). These are allusion, translation and commentary. As we will see, all of them may be found in Colliander's memoirs.

The device of *allusion* applies when the text we read is not affected by the language of the narrated story, that is, when a language other than the one we read is thematized. There are several examples of this device: when Colliander mentions the many languages of his family and childhood (as above); when an unkind nurse at the hospital accuses him of being Russian, because she thinks that his first name (Fritiof, abbreviated to Tito) must be Russian since it ends in "-ov" like Russian names do;[7] when, during a lonely winter stay in Teiskola in Finland, he reflects on the functions of the Finnish, Russian and Swedish languages respectively;[8] when he describes how he was told off by a railway employee who didn't like to be addressed in Russian and maintained that one ought to speak Estonian in that area[9] or when he observes that he and his wife always speak Russian with the cats when staying in Petseri (or Pechory, as the cats would have it).[10]

A particularly interesting example of the device of allusion, where a foreign language is thematized and also rendered without any translation, is the mention of the use of Church Slavonic in the Russian Orthodox monastery in Pechory:

> Why, everything was going on in Church Slavonic, and in the beginning, I did not understand much. Only Gospodi pomilui of course, and some other often repeated phrases. But I listened attentively, and every time I could perceive new words and new contexts.[11]
> (Colliander 1971, 134)

Although Colliander knew Russian, he found the archaic Slavic language initially hard to understand. When he renders this typical phrase in Church Slavonic without translating it as "Lord, have mercy", the reader may therefore experience some of the difficulties he once had himself.[12]

The device of *translation* allows the writer to communicate with readers in the code that they both share, as Grutman explains. The original is replaced by a translation in the reader's mind (Grutman 1993, 210). In my analysis of Colliander's memoirs, reference will be made to examples that use not only bilingualism but also biscriptalism. In almost every volume of Colliander's memoirs, there are single phrases where Cyrillic script is used in order to render expressions in Russian, indicating that the dialogues should be perceived of as conducted in Russian.[13] In most cases, these phrases are immediately translated into Swedish and thus explained to the reader. One such example comes from an episode where an old monk in the New Valamo monastery decides to go to celebrate the Divine Liturgy, despite being in severe pain, a case in which only his decision is rendered in embedded Cyrillic script: "– Пойду́, he said with peculiar composure. I'm going"[14] (Colliander 1973, 229).

In *Gripen*, Colliander describes life on the Karelian Isthmus in the 1930s, which at that time was a part of Finland. He points to the fact that the shops in the multilingual town of Terijoki (Russian Zelenogorsk) were marked by signs in Russian. By inserting a single word in Cyrillic script into the Swedish text he renders visible this practice: "The houses were mostly made of wood and consisted of one or two floors, often in the imaginative Russian style. On every second one, big Russian letters said ТОРГОВЛЯ, which means a store, a shop"[15] (Colliander 1965, 34). Thanks to its immediate translation into Swedish, the word in Cyrillic script is directly comprehensible even to Swedophone readers who know neither Cyrillic letters nor Russian. When it comes to actually reading it and not just grasping its meaning, however, readers are confronted with various possibilities. If they try to assign to the Cyrillic letters the sounds that some of them (T, O, P, B, and the seemingly reversed R) have in the Swedish alphabet, the word may be read aloud, though only in part and mispronounced, as something like *top-ob-r*, that is, as a nonsensical noise. Another possibility is that the word in Cyrillic remains silent to them, like the visual signboard imitating the original Russian sign of the Karelian shop in the Swedish text of the memoirs, though it is rendered exclusively by scriptal means, without any kind of conventional pictorial devices, such as a frame or an assigned space on the page for illustrations. Yet in neither of these cases does the word in Cyrillic script become audible to them as *torgóvlia*, the Russian word for a shop. The reading is therefore affected in different ways, depending on the readers' scriptal competences.[16]

By means of Colliander's use of this device of translation combined with biscriptalism, all readers – whether or not they know Russian and Cyrillic script – are equally invited to experience a piece of multilingual reality in Karelia. Russian culture and the multilingual practices in Finnish Karelia during the interwar period of the 1930s are not only thematized or referred to, but also *made present* by the use of embedded Cyrillic script. Within the text, the word in Cyrillic script functions as a signboard that marks not only the entrance to the shop in Terijoki but also the linguistic and cultural border between, on the one hand, the polyglot and the biscriptal author, and, on the other, monoscriptal Swedophone readers who know neither Russian nor Cyrillic script. Colliander's decision to translate the signboard assists them in overcoming this cultural border of different languages and scripts.[17]

According to Grutman, the device of *commentary* is the one that comes closest to what he calls "true bilingualism", since the text in this case both elucidates the referential meaning of a phrase and comments upon its cultural connotations (Grutman 1993, 211). One example among many potential ones from Colliander's memoirs concerns an important episode that took place in Paris. In a bar far away from home, Colliander happened to listen to a record playing in a jukebox on which a Russian Orthodox choir was singing. When narrating this memory, he renders a few phrases of the chant in Cyrillic script, but this is done without any immediate translation of their meaning:

> A Russian baritone, soft and deep, emphasizing each word:
> – Господи, услыши услыши молитву мою...
> And then the whole choir joined in, both female and male voices:
> И вопль мой Тебе да прибудет...[18]
> (Colliander 1969, 114)

Explication of the chant does not appear until the subsequent pages, where Colliander relates how much this episode meant to him. Totally unprepared, he is overwhelmed by the song, which had reminded him of his childhood in Saint Petersburg and his visits to the Russian cathedral in Helsinki, also as a child. He understands the song as "the cry of all mankind"[19] (Colliander 1969, 115), and he continues to sing its words in Church Slavonic, quietly, to himself:

> when I stepped out into the noisy street, I kept listening to that soft Russian solo voice: Lord, hear o hear my prayer... And no noise could drown out that voice, because it was now inside me. With closed lips, I joined the choir and participated in the singing, insofar as I knew the melody and the words.
> [...] And all the time I sing:
> Господи услыши услыши молитву мою...[20]
> (Colliander 1969, 116–117)

This episode does not actually exemplify a proper case of translation, since the translation of the quotation from the Biblical Psalm 102:1, "Lord, hear o hear my prayer", is not clearly linked to the phrases in Cyrillic script but presented separately.[21] Yet the significance of the song in Church Slavonic is explicated in both culturally and personally revealing ways by Colliander's commentary. This device makes it possible for readers who are neither literate in Cyrillic script nor familiar with the Psalms in the Russian Orthodox tradition to share both Colliander's love for the liturgical language and his experience of bilingualism when he encounters and understands Church Slavonic during a stay in Paris. Thanks to Colliander's commentary, readers may appreciate the cultural and religious connotations mediated by the chant within the context of his memoirs.

However, one complication remains. Although it is a recorded chant that makes such an impression on Colliander by means of its sonic qualities, the sound of the song's words nevertheless remains silent and mute to the majority of readers of Colliander's memoirs who do not know Cyrillic script, since they are never transcribed into Roman script, only translated into Swedish. The devices of translation and commentary, as proposed by Grutman, are therefore not entirely satisfactory in cases like this, when a suggested bilingualism also implies biscriptalism. In the examples mentioned above, the use of embedded Cyrillic script has been seen as affecting the potential sonic qualities of readings of Colliander's memoirs, at least for the majority of the intended Swedophone audience.

But if allusion, according to Grutman, is presented as a device thematizing another *language* than the one we are reading, then the use of biscriptalism seems in these cases rather to thematize another *culture*, in a way similar to that described by Andreas Fischer (1999) in his article on print advertising. Fischer demonstrates that in a context where the writing norm implies the use of a certain script, words or phrases in other scripts may be used "to iconically indicate the presence of the culture identified with that alphabet" (Fischer 1999, 268). In such cases, the aim is not to convey a specific content or meaning but rather to bring about associations between, for example, certain brands and cultures. Though literary texts such as Colliander's memoirs are obviously not the same as print advertising, Fischer's conclusion is still illuminating for my analysis of Colliander's memoirs, where the use of Cyrillic script is made in a text and context where the writing norm certainly implies the use of Roman script. What is accomplished by the embedded words in Cyrillic script in Colliander's memoirs is therefore precisely an iconic indication of the presence of Russian culture and Russian-Orthodox liturgical traditions. For a reader who does not read Cyrillic letters, these words remain mute and are merely presented as visual signboards pointing or alluding to the other, foreign culture.

My conclusion, so far, is that the device of biscriptalism (i.e. the use of Cyrillic script) in Colliander's memoirs not only thematizes or represents the use of Russian and Church Slavonic in his life story, like allusions to the use of Russian or transcriptions of Russian, but his use of embedded Cyrillic script also contributes to making Russian culture and Russian-Orthodox practices present within the Swedophone text where Roman script is the norm.

Heterolingual Address

If we seriously consider, however, that neither Colliander's life nor his memoirs were monolingual or bilingual but essentially multilingual, then Naoki Sakai's notion of *heterolingual address*, as presented in his monograph *Translation and Subjectivity* (1997) may be even more fruitful than the application of Grutman's categories to Colliander's memoirs. Sakai foregrounds the author's address rather than the expected linguistic predisposition of the reader. He argues that it is the phenomenon of translation that makes languages appear distinct from one another. What ultimately constitutes the condition for untranslatability is therefore the possibility of translation: "Untranslatability does not exist before translation: translation is the a priori of the untranslatable" (Sakai 1997, 5).

In accordance with Sakai's argument, the author's address – and not a presumed successful and fulfilled communication – can be regarded as the point of departure for literary analysis. By shifting focus from the readers' linguistic skills to *the attitude of addressing* as articulated by the text, it becomes possible to study Colliander's memoirs in terms of a heterolingual address. This is not based on "any common homogeneity", but the reader is addressed without taking any particular "national, ethnic, or linguistic affiliation for granted". Communicative transparency is not presupposed in heterolingual address; the addressee cannot rely on linguistic reciprocity and must always translate. An author with the attitude of heterolingual address is therefore always "confronted, so to speak, with foreigners" (Sakai 1997, 7–9).

That Colliander ventured to insert words and phrases in Cyrillic script into his Swedophone memoirs suggests such an attitude of heterolingual address: neither the readership's homogeneity, nor any particular affiliation of the readers, nor communicative transparency is presupposed. The text presents itself to readers who – whenever they read – are necessarily involved in a translating process, a procedure that in this particular case is accentuated by the switch of script. By inserting Russian and Church Slavonic expressions, sometimes in Cyrillic script, into the Swedish text, Colliander does not exclusively address either multilingual or Swedophone readers, but makes clear that he considers his readers to be foreigners and strangers like himself. In this way, he becomes able to portray in his memoirs the development of his own multilingual Orthodox diasporic identity and, as will be discussed further below, indicate the movement towards liturgical multilingualism among Swedophone Orthodox believers in the diaspora.

Poetry and Mysticism

In the case of Colliander, the multilingual and biscriptal strategies of the memoirs, as well as their attitude of heterolingual address, may also prompt a profound questioning of language per se and awaken longing for a shortcut that might give direct and mystical access to the meaning and significance that words convey.

Having become an Orthodox Christian in the late 1930s, Tito Colliander experienced a crisis of language that lasted for many years. Before then, he had tried to earn his living as a writer, so it meant a profound change when he more or less abandoned writing fiction and took up studies in theology and patristics (the writings of the Early Church Fathers). For more than a decade, between 1949 and 1961 (i.e. before he began to write his memoirs), Colliander mostly published Swedish translations of Orthodox liturgical texts, such as the Akathistos Hymn (1949), a didactic study of Orthodox faith (1951), prayers and sayings of the Church Fathers (1952) together with notes on his readings of them (1958), and the Divine Liturgy of St John Chrysostom (1958).[22] He was also a frequent guest at the Orthodox New Valamo monastery. After the flight of the monks from their island in Lake Ladoga in 1940, caused by the war between Finland and the Soviet Union, the monastery was relocated on a farmstead in Heinävesi in eastern Finland. As Colliander puts it, "mercy" (as in "Lord, have mercy") was by this time the only word he needed; he could easily live without symphonies, art exhibitions and novels.[23]

In the memoirs, Colliander describes his desire for a new language made up of "completely new words, a new rhythm, a new way to write"[24] (Colliander 1971, 172). But how should it be achieved? He is disappointed and hopeful by turns:

> A richer, more vivid language, embracing infinity while still detached, confident, without any stumbling and fumbling attempts.
> But I do not find it. I am the same as I have been.
> The language we use is quasi-realistic: every word slips past its proper meaning. [...]
> Give me a new language with wordings that last. [...]
> Right now I would like to find a completely new language, a language where each single word carries the golden light of wheat fields and exaltation of larks, where each single word reaches not only heaven as I see it right now, but the heavens of heavens.[25]
> (Colliander 1971, 172–173)

What he is striving for is a language "hidden within words, liberated from words"[26] (Colliander 1971, 175). He considers this to be "the language of prayer, the kind of prayer that leaves words behind" (Colliander 1971, 174); it is "the language beyond letters and sounds" and also "the language of the lighted wax candle" (Colliander 1971, 174), by which he refers to the Orthodox Christian practice of lighting wax candles in church while praying.[27]

Against this background, it is possible to understand Colliander's decision to render certain Church Slavonic phrases in Cyrillic script in his memoirs, not only as a device for making Russian and Orthodox Christian culture present in his texts, or as pointing to a heterolingual address, as discussed above. Furthermore, this practice could have been a device for representing this new language, which to him was – above all – a language of prayer, operating "beyond letters and sounds". Precisely these phrases, introduced in embedded script, may have the effect of signifying the kind of prayer that "leaves words behind". The Swedophone reader cannot decipher them but comes to know their religious meaning through Colliander's mediating commentary.

It is not unusual for a writer to experience such a severe conflict between poetry and mysticism: while mysticism necessarily tries to go beyond words, poetry has to favour them.[28] Sometimes Colliander seems to despair of the possibility of using words at all. In notes in *Glädjes möte* (1957; Joyous encounter), he says that the signs of words are his bonds, and he compares the characters of the alphabet to masquerade attire, a tight carnival costume.[29] His desire for a language without words sometimes comes close to the idea of an Adamic, original language,[30] inspired by Genesis 2:19-20:

> Wordlessly, without assistance from matter, the angels communicate with one another. Adam's conversation with God in the Garden of Eden was free from the shackles and ties of words. The real names of things, the names that Adam gave them, acknowledge neither sound nor letter characters. The presence of reality remains undescribed. [...] O this alienation of mine from original purity: the clothes of skin that tie me to the symbols of words.[31]
>
> (Colliander 1957, 57)

As is evident from the last sentence, however, Colliander realizes that he is inescapably tied to the use of the symbols and signs of words. There comes a certain point when he balances between, on the one hand, rejecting words and, on the other, accepting his alienation "from original purity" and being necessarily reduced to reliance on words. Such an acceptance of the insufficiency of words is also indicated in one of his poems, which opens his book *Samtal med smärtan* (1956; Conversation with pain). It refers specifically to the activity of writing (i.e. the material practice of forming and inscribing letters) as a solution to the problem:

> Letters draw faint outlines of words.
> The words draw faint outlines of a gate.
> The gate itself is indescribably open.[32]
>
> (Colliander 1956, epigraph)

An Orthodox Christian Diasporic Identity

What is peculiar to Colliander's way of handling the conflict between poetry and mysticism is how multilingualism and the identity of the stranger seem to offer him a way out of the dilemma.

When he joined the Orthodox Christian procession in Pechory in the summer of 1936, he experienced something that was completely new to him. This procession was not a political demonstration like those he had watched as a child in Saint Petersburg before the Russian Revolution, nor was it a Scandinavian-German vitalistic "chasing of intense moments" like the wanderings pursued by the eternally rootless man in his early book *En vandrare* (1930, 57; A wanderer), nor a military parade like the ones in Nazi Germany, which he had witnessed a few years earlier while on a writing grant that obliged him to stay in that country. As literary scholar Göran O:son Waltå (1993, 107) has observed, Colliander "apparently often got carried away by Nazi aestheticism" in the early 1930s, as is evident from his book *Glimtar från Tyskland* (1934, 70–71; Glimpses from Germany; see also Colliander 1971, 101–102, and further Waltå 1993 and Bodin 2011, 410–415). But from 1936 onwards, Colliander's inclination for wandering took a new turn and continued under Orthodox Christian banners, combining discipline and rules with humility and a sense of being exiled, since the route of the processions from the Orthodox Pskovo-Pechersky Monastery lay right on the borderland between Estonia and the Soviet Union.

In this case, exile was a concrete political reality, but exile – or alienation – can also be understood as a religious concept, taking on a deeper, existential meaning. In the late 1950s, Colliander reflects on the themes of alienation and the character of the stranger in an essay entitled "Kristendom som dårskap" (in *Nu och alltid*, 1958; Christianity as foolishness, in Now and ever). He quotes sayings by John Chrysostom, one of the Early Church Fathers, who regarded Christians as mere temporary guests on earth, travellers staying overnight at an inn while heading for their final destination. The Early Christian so-called *Epistle to Diognetus* is likewise quoted: "[The Christians] live in their own homelands, but as resident aliens; they participate in all things as citizens, but endure all things as strangers. Every foreign country is their homeland but every homeland is a foreign country"[33] (Colliander 1958, 16; English translation by Dunning 2009, 65). Colliander concludes: "Alienation, as well as foolishness, is an irremovable, ontological quality of all pure Christianity"[34] (Colliander 1958, 20). In an essay entitled "Fosterlandet" (1961; Homeland), he also reflects upon the role of different languages in the shaping of one's identity:

> Minorities and majorities have existed at all times and in countless combinations. You just forget that it is not as important what language you speak and to which people you belong as it is to actually have something to say – or to think, or to do, or just to exist as a human being, to live. Such things are not tied to one or another language or nation. No.
> And those who talk about betraying one's nation or people or language or religion by replacing them with something else, they more often than not have had a grandfather or maybe great-grandfather who did exactly that: they replaced their Russian or German or Finnish with, say, Swedish.[35]
> (Colliander 1961; quoted from Bondestam 1961, 32)

He continues by arguing in favour of the identity of the stranger:

> So let me remain a stranger, an outsider in this my homeland, just as I am in all other countries. Why should my love be enclosed behind some fixed fences? Isn't it more important to learn how to be prepared to depart at any moment? Leaving everything to which you imagine yourself bound. Relinquishing without regret or embitterment what we believed we possessed.[36]
> (Colliander 1961; quoted from Bondestam 1961, 33)

Colliander's homage to the stranger would appear to treat his contemporary life in the multilingual, multicultural Orthodox Christian diaspora in the light of Early Christian ways of defining belonging as *not* belonging: to belong somewhere is equivalent to being on the road, sojourning together. Precisely this paradox – of belonging while not belonging – is the focus of an anthology on contemporary Russian Orthodoxy, *Orthodox Paradoxes*, in which the editor, Katya Tolstaya, discusses it in terms of Russell's paradox (2014, 1–20). From yet another perspective than the religious one, this way of belonging somewhere without being tied to a given place may also, within the field of linguistics and the sociology of literature, activate the notion of *paratopia*, in particular *translingual paratopia*, coined by Julia Őri and defined as "the position of the translingual writer in the literary field of his or her adopted country: a paradoxical location between belonging and at the same time, not belonging" (Őri 2015, 99). Thus, there are both religious and linguistic reasons for the stranger of Colliander to find himself in the particular in-betweenness of bilingual people and translingual writers.

Furthermore, according to Colliander, unity in faith is not threatened by differences in language and nationality, although there is often a strong connection between religious faith, language and nationality in traditionally Orthodox Christian countries where the liturgical languages are similar – or even identical – to the various vernacular languages. Orthodox congregations in the diaspora, such as in the Finland-Swedish parts of Orthodox Christian Finland or in multilingual milieus in Sweden, where the number of Orthodox believers increased a hundredfold from about 500 in the 1930s to 50,000 in 1970, have had to work under other linguistic and national conditions, however, than in their mother countries, such as Greece and Russia (Bodin 2011, 338–339).

In the essay "Ortodoxt, bysantinskt, nationellt" (in *Nu och alltid*, 1958; Orthodox, Byzantine, national), Colliander explains that Byzantium, or the Byzantine heritage, lives on in all parts of the Orthodox Church. But, he continues, each of them is nevertheless characterized by its own language and nationality, and so custom and practice may alter, just like temperaments or history (Colliander 1958, 112–114). From the 1970s and onwards, this standpoint proved to be of vital

256 Helena Bodin

importance in the establishment of multilingual and multicultural Orthodox Christian congregations in the Swedophone Orthodox diaspora where *parallel lingualism* was practised (i.e. the parallel use of different languages without translations in one and the same service, in this context often Swedish, Church Slavonic, Finnish, Estonian, Serbian and Greek in various combinations) (Bodin 2011, 354–371). The first Swedish Orthodox priest, Christopher Klasson, expressed later a similar view to Colliander's: "We cannot in the long run maintain the fiction that faith and nationality are synonymous notions" (Bodin 2011, 362, n. 88).

Needless to say, Colliander's view, dating back to the mid-20th century, still presents a serious challenge to Orthodox Christian nationalism and traditionalism today, as well as to the western parts of Europe, an issue addressed by Irina Paert in her article on Western Europeans as Orthodox Christians. She describes the history of the Orthodox diaspora in Western Europe and refers to an Orthodox statement saying "that Orthodox Christians are not strangers to the West and that Orthodoxy has a legitimate place in modern European culture and identity" (Paert 2003, 121). Particularly in Greece, Orthodox faith has been closely associated with notions of Greekness, purism and authenticity, which the Modern Greek scholar Trine Stauning Willert (2012) has addressed in illuminating studies where she discusses issues of Orthodoxy and national identity, as well as the ethno-religious understanding of Orthodoxy in Greece. Willert has observed and described a new theological current of late modern character in Greek Orthodoxy, which through its emphasis on ecumenism might suggest a religiously based cosmopolitanism. This is an eschatologically oriented theology which is prepared to face the challenges of postmodernity and globalization, as it moves away from ethnicity and nationalism. According to the Greek Orthodox theologian Pantelis Kalaïtzidis, the Orthodox Church accomplishes its mission best in a multicultural environment. The reason is its Byzantine heritage, and Kalaïtzidis explains that Orthodoxy in Byzantium was not ethnocentric but ecumenical (defined as referring to all of the known, inhabited world), and hence multi-ethnic and multicultural (Willert 2012, 195–196). To him, the Christian's identity is an exile-identity. Referring to Zygmunt Bauman's *Postmodern Ethics* (1993), Willert regards Kalaïtzidis's view as "the religious equivalent of late modern identity as the identity of migrants, tourists or wanderers" (Willert 2012, 199).

It is interesting to note that Tito Colliander touched on similar ideas more than fifty years ago. Also, diasporic practices, such as the use of parallel lingualism when celebrating the Divine Liturgy (i.e. the Eucharistic service) in multi-ethnic and multilingual parishes, have preceded Orthodox theological theory in this respect, as is clear from the examples mentioned above. Colliander's idea of alienation as an ontological quality of Christianity, based in the writings of the Church Fathers as well as the multilingual and biscriptal devices employed in his memoirs, therefore looks forward to a vision similar to that of the contemporary discussions of scholars and the progressive Orthodox theologians of today.

Conclusion

In Colliander's memoirs published between 1964 and 1973, religious belief – in this case Orthodox Christianity with its Byzantine heritage conveyed by the Russian and Church Slavonic languages, as well as by Cyrillic script – interacts with multilingualism and biscriptalism in significant ways within a late modern literary context, foreshadowing the emphasis on multi-ethnicity and multiculturalism in the Orthodox theology of the early 21st century, addressing in particular the situation of the Orthodox diaspora in the West.

The memoirs portray the development of Colliander's multilingual and diasporic Orthodox Christian identity as a stranger, formed in-between different nations, languages and cultures around the Gulf of Finland, and across their shifting borders. The multilingual conditions that characterize the Orthodox Christian diaspora are simultaneously represented and made present in his memoirs by means of embedded phrases in Russian, Church Slavonic and Cyrillic script. If, in this case, the attitude of Colliander is regarded as one of heterolingual address, the reader might respond to the text with varying degrees of comprehension since the memoirs do not presuppose that a thorough understanding is accomplished but instead invite participation in translational activity. It might even be that the words in embedded Cyrillic script, incomprehensible to Swedophone readers, imitate or represent the mystical language "beyond letters and sounds" that Colliander longed for. Simultaneously, his in-betweenness can be regarded as located in the translingual paratopia of bilinguals and translingual writers. The idea of alienation as an ontological quality of Christianity is explicitly articulated in his memoirs but also represented by means of the multilingual and biscriptal devices.

By focussing on Colliander's triple roles as author (productive throughout his whole life), translator (of several Orthodox Christian liturgical and didactic texts) and stranger (belonging by means of non-belonging), the experience of translating, mediating and going in-between has been demonstrated to be of fundamental and salient importance to his life and work. Through Colliander's use of multilingual and biscriptal devices in his memoirs, the Swedophone reader is invited to continue this task of the translator and to experience the in-betweenness of Colliander's stranger.

Notes

1 "Je voudrais ici insister sur cette parenté intrinsèque et souvent insoupçonnable entre le traducteur, l'étranger et l'écrivain, pour les réunir tous trois dans une commune et cependant toujours singulière expérience de traduction. [...] 'S'estranger' à soi-même et se faire le passeur de cette étrangeté continûment retrouvée."
2 "Skönheten lockade till kunskap."
3 "Mänskan var inte till för språkets skull, utan språket för mänskans. [...] Vi levde som under ett paraply av talesätt och ordspråk från hela Europa: My home is my castle, Il mondo è nostra casa, Si non è vero è ben trovato, Was willst du denn? Nichts zu machen, Tische jédisch dáljsche búdisch, Nicht sich gehen lassen, Mais c'est la même chose, Utro vétjera mudrenéje... Och vi förstod dem alla och rättade oss gärna efter dem."
4 "För övrigt togs orden och uttrycken i vårt vardagstal ur vilket språk som helst. Man valde dem allt efter tycke och bekvämlighet. [...] / [Vi] saknade varje begrepp om respekt för modersmålet eller ens kärlek till det."
5 "I hela Europa och Gud vet hur långt ser jag rörliga punkter kringkastade... De möts och bildar sällsamma mönster som aldrig kan förutsägas och aldrig infångas" (Colliander 1964, 93).
6 For the issue of embedded alien scripts in literary texts, see the thorough study of Schmitz-Emans (2004). See also Bodin (2018).
7 "– Fritjoff, sa sköterskan. Jasså, du heter Fritjoff – det är ett ryskt namn, alla namn på off ä ryska" (Colliander 1967, 215).
8 "De [tavastländska bönderna] kände till endast ett språk, jag rörde mig med fyra. Mitt främlingsskap för detta folk var alldeles naturligt" (Colliander 1967, 74). Colliander continues: "denna min gräsliga förödmjukelse. Jag kunde varken finska eller ryska. Jag kunde just inget språk. Jag var främmande både här och där och överallt" (Colliander 1967, 79). See further Colliander (1967, 47–85).
9 "– Här talas estniska och inte ryska, nästan skrek han in i mitt ansikte" (Colliander 1971, 195).
10 "Med katterna talade vi för det mesta ryska" (Colliander 1971, 230).
11 "Allt försiggick ju på kyrkslaviska, och till en början begrep jag verkligen inte mycket. Bara Gospodi pomiluj förstås och några andra ofta upprepade ordföljder. Men jag lyssnade uppmärksamt, och för varje gång uppfattade jag nya ord och nya sammanhang."
12 For this device, see also Tidigs (2014, 102) on partial linguistic knowledge (or ignorance) as aesthetically productive and Bodin (2018), on the reader's potential experience of cultural alterity.
13 For more examples (except the ones from *Gripen*, *Vaka* and *Måltid* analysed in this chapter), see Colliander (1969, 29; 1968, 29, 193; 1971, 98).
14 "– Пойду, sade han egendomligt lugnt. Jag går."
15 "Husen var för det mesta av trä i en eller två våningar och ofta i den fantasifulla ryska stilen. På vartannat stod det med stora ryska bokstäver ТОРГОВЛЯ, vilket betyder handel, butik."
16 See Julia Tidigs and Markus Huss' article, which discusses and analyses "how readers with different language skills partake in making literary multilingualism happen". They do not discuss biscriptality but argue that "[r]eaders familiar and unfamiliar with the languages in question will be affected by multilingualism, albeit differently", and conclude that their analyses have demonstrated that "orthography and visual organization suspend an automized understanding of language and sense-making, engaging readers in a productive struggle with the text" (Tidigs & Huss 2017, 208, 217, 230).

17 For this device, see also the analysis of the use of Cyrillic script in Malin Kiveläs' novel *Du eller aldrig* (2006; You or never) in Bodin (2018).
18 "En rysk baryton, mjuk och djup, med varje ord betonat: / – Господи, услыши услыши молитву мою... / Och sedan föll hela kören in, både kvinnliga och manliga stämmor: / И вопль мой Тебе да прибудет..."
19 "Men det var alla mänskors rop, inte bara mitt, det var hela mänsklighetens."
20 "när jag steg ut i gatularmet, så hörde jag allt fortfarande den där mjuka ryska solostämman: Herre, hör, o hör min bön... Och inget buller kunde överrösta den rösten, för den var nu inne i mig. Med slutna läppar föll jag in i kören och deltog i sången, allt som jag bara hade uppfattat av melodin och orden. / [...] Och hela tiden sjunger jag: / Господи, услыши услыши молитву мою..." Phrases in Church Slavonic are in Colliander's memoirs rendered in modern Cyrillic script, without the characteristic letters of the older Church Slavonic alphabet.
21 " – – och låt mitt rop komma inför Dig..." (Colliander 1969, 115). "Herre, hör, o hör min bön..." (Colliander 1969, 116). In English: "Hear my prayer, O Lord, and let my cry come unto thee" (Ps. 102:1).
22 Swedish titles: *Fröjda Dig. Akathisterna till vår högtvälsignade Härskarinna Gudamoder och Eviga Jungfru Maria, och till vår allraljuvaste Herre Jesus Kristus* (translated by Tito Colliander, 1949); Tito Colliander, *Grekisk-ortodox tro och livssyn* (1951); *Asketernas väg* (1952); *Nu och alltid. Studier i ortodox kristendom* (1958); *Vår Helige Faders Johannes Chrysostomos Gudomliga Liturgi*, tolkning av Tito Colliander (1958).
23 "Den som erfarit detta: / att ett enda Herre förbarma Dig! är långt mera innehållsrikt än varje symfonikonsert, varje konstutställning eller roman, vill inte gärna återvända till sådant. Dag och natt håller han fast vid detta 'förbarma Dig'" (Colliander 1956, 49).
24 "helt nya ord, en ny rytm, ett nytt sätt att skriva."
25 "Ett rikare, mera levande språk, ett oändlighetsfamnande och samtidigt sakligt, säkert, helt utan stappel och trevande försök. / Men jag finner det inte. Jag är densamma som jag varit. / Det språk vi använder oss av är kvasirealistiskt: varje ord slinter förbi sin egentliga betydelse. [...] / Ge mig ett nytt språk med ordalydelser som håller. [...] / Men just nu ville jag finna ett helt nytt språk, ett språk där varje enskilt ord bär veteåkrarnas guldgula ljus och lärkornas jubel, där varje enskilt ord når inte bara den himmel som jag nu ser, utan himlarnas himlar."
26 "Det inom orden gömda, från orden befriade språket."
27 "Bönens språk, den bön som lämnar orden bakom sig." "Språket bortom bokstäver och ljud. Den brinnande vaxljuslågans språk." On the language of the lighted wax candle, see further Torsten Kälvemark (2001, 179–198).
28 For another example of the conflict between poetry and mysticism in Swedish 20th-century poetry, see Bodin (2011, 275) on Östen Sjöstrand (1925–2006), with further references.
29 "Framför mig ligger mina bojor: ordens tecken" (Colliander 1957, 52). "ditt eget sinnes grummel iklätt bokstavstecknens trånga karnevalkostym" (Colliander 1957, 37).
30 On Adamic language in linguistic history and translation theory, see, for example, Steiner (1992, 51–114, in particular 60–64). From a semiotic perspective, see Eco (1995, especially 7–24 and 351–353).
31 "Ordlöst, utan tillhjälp av materie, meddelar sig änglarna med varandra. Fritt från ordbundenhetens fängsel var Adams samtal med Gud i lustgården. Tingens verkliga namn, de namn som Adam gav dem, vidkänns varken ljud eller bokstavstecken. Verklighetens närvaro förblir obeskriven. [...] O detta mitt främlingskap till ursprunglig renhet: kläderna av skinn som binder mig vid ordsymbolerna."

32 "Bokstäver drar svaga konturer till ord. / Orden drar svaga konturer till en port. / Porten själv är obeskrivbart öppen."
33 "De (kristna) bo i sina fädernesland, men såsom främlingar, de deltaga i allt såsom medborgare och få lida allt såsom främlingar; varje främmande land är deras, och varje land är dem främmande."
34 "Främlingsskapet och därmed dårskapen är en ofråntagbar, ontologisk egenskap hos all ren kristendom."
35 "Minoriteter och majoriteter har det funnits i alla tider och i otaliga kombinationer. Man bara glömmer, att det inte är lika viktigt vilket språk man talar och till vilket folkslag man hör, som det, att man överhuvudtaget har något att säga – eller tänka, eller göra, eller bara vara till som mänska, att leva. Sånt är inte bundet vid det ena eller andra språket eller landet. Nej. / Och de som talar om att man förråder sitt land eller folk eller språk eller religion om man byter ut dem mot något annat, har inte sällan haft en farfar eller morfar eller kanske farfarsfar som gjorde just detta: de utbytte sin ryska eller tyska eller finska mot svenska t.ex."
36 "Så låt mig förbli en främling, en utböling i detta mitt fosterland, likaväl som jag är det i alla andra länder. Varför skall min kärlek instängas i vissa givna gärdesgårdar? Är det inte viktigare att lära sig konsten att vilket ögonblick som helst vara beredd att bryta upp? Lämna allt det myckna vid vilket man inbillar sig vara bunden. Utan saknad eller grämelse kunna avstå från det vi trodde oss äga."

Bibliography

Andersson Wretmark, Astrid (2008) *Tito Colliander och den ryska heligheten*. Skellefteå: Artos.

Ausoni, Alain & Arribert-Narce, Fabien (2013) *L'autobiographie entre autres: Écrire la vie aujourd'hui*. Peter Lang Publishing Group. (E-book.)

Bodin, Helena (2008) "Gränslandets österländskhet" – om svenskspråkiga reseskildringar från Valamo. In Clas Zilliacus, Heidi Grönstrand & Ulrika Gustafsson (eds): *Gränser i nordisk litteratur: Borders in Nordic Literature, IASS XXVI 2006, Vol. II*. Åbo: Åbo Akademis förlag, 670–677.

Bodin, Helena (2011) *Bruken av Bysans: Studier i svenskspråkig litteratur och kultur 1948–71*. Skellefteå: Norma.

Bodin, Helena (2014) "Into golden dusk": Orthodox Icons as Objects of Modern and Postmodern Desire. In Ingela Nilsson & Paul Stephenson (eds): *Wanted Byzantium: The Desire for a Lost Empire*. Uppsala: Uppsala universitet, 201–216.

Bodin, Helena (2018) Heterographics as a Literary Device: Auditory, Visual, and Cultural Features. *The Journal of World Literature* 3(2), 196–216.

Bondestam, Anna (ed.) (1961) *Jag lever i republiken Finland: tio självdeklarationer av finlandssvenska författare och intellektuella*. Helsingfors: Söderströms.

Colliander, Tito (1930) *En vandrare*. Helsingfors: Söderströms.

Colliander, Tito (1934) *Glimtar från Tyskland: Några antekningar*. Helsingfors: Söderströms.

Colliander, Tito (trans.) (1949) *Fröjda Dig: Akathisterna till vår högtvälsignade Härskarinna Gudamoder och Eviga Jungfru Maria, och till vår allraljuvaste Herre Jesus Kristus*. Helsingfors: Söderström.

Colliander, Tito (1951) *Grekisk-ortodox tro och livssyn*. Studentföreningen Verdandis småskrifter, nr. 513. Stockholm & Helsingfors: Bonnier & Söderströms.

Multilingualism and Biscriptalism 261

Colliander, Tito (1952) *Asketernas väg*. Helsingfors: Söderströms.
Colliander, Tito (1956) *Samtal med smärtan: Anteckningar 1953–1956*. Helsingfors: Söderströms.
Colliander, Tito (1957) *Glädjes möte*. Helsingfors: Söderströms.
Colliander, Tito (1958) *Nu och alltid: Studier i ortodox kristendom*. Helsingfors: Söderströms.
Colliander, Tito (trans.) (1958) *Vår Helige Faders Johannes Chrysostomos Gudomliga Liturgi*. Helsingfors: Söderströms.
Colliander, Tito (1960) *The Way of the Ascetics: The Ancient Tradition of Discipline and Inner Growth*. Translated by Katharine Ferré. Introduction by R. M. French. London: Hodder & Stoughton.
Colliander, Tito (1961) Fosterlandet. *Hufvudstadsbladet*. August 23, 1961.
Colliander, Tito (1964) *Bevarat*. Helsingfors: Schildts.
Colliander, Tito (1965) *Gripen*. Helsingfors: Schildts.
Colliander, Tito (1967) *Vidare*. Helsingfors: Schildts.
Colliander, Tito (1968) *Givet*. Helsingfors: Schildts.
Colliander, Tito (1969) *Vaka*. Helsingfors: Schildts.
Colliander, Tito (1971) *Nära*. Helsingfors: Schildts.
Colliander, Tito (1973) *Måltid*. Helsingfors: Schildts.
Dunning, Benjamin H. (2009) *Aliens and Sojourners: Self as Other in Early Christianity*. Philadelphia: University of Pennsylvania Press.
Eco, Umberto (1995) *The Search for the Perfect Language*. Translated by James Fentress. Oxford: Blackwell.
Ekelund, Erik (1956) *Synvinklar*. Helsingfors: Söderströms.
Fischer, Andreas (1999) Graphological Iconicity in Print Advertising: A Typology. In Max Nänny & Olga Fischer (eds): *Form Miming Meaning: Iconicity in Language and Literature*. Amsterdam & Philadelphia: John Benjamins, 251–283.
Grutman, Rainier (1990) Le bilinguisme littéraire comme relation intersystémique. *Canadian Review of Comparative Literature* 17(3–4), 198–212.
Grutman, Rainier (1993) Mono versus Stereo: Bilingualism's Double Face. *Visible Language* 27(1–2), 207–227.
Hartman, Olov (1980) *Ikon och roman*. Älvsjö: Skeab.
Hernberg, Eira (1989) *Aitoa ihmistä etsimässä: ihmisenä olemisen ongelma Tito Collianderin tuotannossa*. Helsinki: Suomalaisen Kirjallisuuden Seura.
Kälvemark, Torsten (2001) *Låset av ull: utsikter över andliga landskap. Essäer*. Skellefteå: Norma.
Kellman, Steven G. (2000) *The Translingual Imagination*. Lincoln: University of Nebraska Press.
Kristeva, Julia (2014) L'amour de l'autre langue. Sommet du livre à la Bibliothèque nationale de France (International Summit of the book). October 13, 2014. Accessed June 1, 2017, www.kristeva.fr/la-traduction-langue-de-l-europe.html.
Mazzarella, Merete (1993) *Att skriva sin värld: den finlandssvenska memoartraditionen*. Helsingfors: Söderström.
Mazzarella, Merete (2003) Att använda sin erfarenhet – Tito Collianders *Korståget* i självbiografisk belysning. In Pia Forssell & John Strömberg (eds): *Historiska och litteraturhistoriska studier* 78. Helsingfors: Svenska litteratursällskapet i Finland, 149–158.
Őri, Julia (2015) Translingual Paratopia and the Universe of Katalin Molnar. *L2 Journal* 7(1), 84–101.

Paert, Irina (2003) Crossing Confessional Boundaries: Western Europeans as Orthodox Christians. In Jonathan Sutton & Wil van den Bercken (eds): *Orthodox Christianity and Contemporary Europe. Selected Papers of the International Conference Held at the University of Leeds, England in June 2001.* Leuven: Peeters, 121–132.

Pettersson, Torsten (1986) "Att han ingenting förstod": Psyket och ytterbvärlden i Tito Collianders romaner. In Ben Hellman & Clas Zilliacus (eds): *Tio finlandssvenska författare.* Helsingfors: Svenska litteratursällskapet i Finland, 11–20.

Sakai, Naoki (1997) *Translation and Subjectivity: On "Japan" and Cultural Nationalism.* Minneapolis: University of Minnesota Press.

Schoolfield, George C. (ed.) (1998) *A History of Finland's Literature. Vol. 4: A History of Scandinavian Literatures.* Lincoln: University of Nebraska Press in cooperation with the American-Scandinavian Foundation.

Schmitz-Emans, Monika (2004) Geschriebene Fremdkörper – Spielformen und Funktionen der Integration fremder Schriftzeichen in literarische Texte. In Monika Schmitz-Emans (ed.): *Literatur und Vielsprachigkeit.* Heidelberg: Synchron, 111–173.

Steiner, George (1992) *After Babel: Aspects of Language and Translation.* 2nd rev. ed. Oxford & New York: Oxford University Press.

Tidigs, Julia (2014) *Att skriva sig över språkgränserna: Flerspråkighet i Jac. Ahrenbergs och Elmer Diktonius prosa.* Åbo: Åbo Akademis förlag.

Tidigs, Julia & Huss, Markus (2017) The Noise of Multilingualism: Reader Diversity, Linguistic Borders and Literary Multimodality. *Critical Multilingualism Studies* 5(1), 208–235.

Tolstaya, Katya (ed.) (2014) *Orthodox Paradoxes: Heterogeneities and Complexities in Contemporary Russian Orthodoxy.* Leiden & Boston: Brill.

Waltå, Göran O:son (1993) *Poet under Black Banners: The Case of Örnulf Tigerstedt and Extreme Right-Wing Swedish Literature in Finland 1918–1944.* Skrifter utgivna av Litteraturvetenskapliga institutionen vid Uppsala universitet 31. Uppsala: Uppsala universitet.

Willert, Trine Stauning (2012) A New Role for Religion in Greece? Theologians Challenging the Ethno-Religious Understanding of Orthodoxy and Greekness. In Trine Stauning Willert & Lina Molokotos-Liederman (eds): *Innovation in the Orthodox Christian Tradition? The Question of Change in Greek Orthodox Thought and Practice.* Farnham: Ashgate, 183–205.

Yildiz, Yasemin (2012) *Beyond the Mother Tongue: The Postmonolingual Condition.* New York: Fordham University Press.

15 Urbanized Folk Life
Multilingual Slang, Gender and New Voices in Finnish Literature

Kukku Melkas

In this chapter I will focus on the multi-voiced novel *Wenla Männistö* (2014) by Riina Katajavuori (b. 1968). *Wenla Männistö*[1] is based on a Finnish literary classic – Aleksis Kivi's *Seitsemän veljestä* (1870; *Seven Brothers* 1929) – but focusses on the original novel's female minor character, Venla. The modernized version of the classic addresses the same problematics as its predecessor, introducing to the reader the vernacular (folksy) and in many ways improper or vulgar language of the youth of the day. The novel not only presents women as main characters – leaving the seven brothers as a group more in the role of a bystander – but also grants them space to be taken seriously and for their voice to be heard. Adaptations can critique as much as pay tribute to the original work (Hutcheon 2006, 1–26). *Wenla Männistö* does both. The pleasure of adaptations often comes from a repetition of a beloved story with variation. Instead of losing the original work, adaptations often keep and extend it (Hutcheon 2006, 3–5).

Aleksis Kivi (b. Alexis Stenvall) was a Finnish author who wrote the first significant novel in the Finnish language, *Seitsemän veljestä*, in 1870. His work has been noted for its realism; humour; and, most of all, respect for the common people and their language, or manner of speaking. In his own time, Kivi was a controversial character with roots in a Finnish-speaking family and the countryside but education in Swedish-language schools.[2] Swedish-language education was the norm at that time, although the situation was gradually changing as, little by little, Finnish gained an official status in the society. The mixing of languages, or Kivi's multilingual strategy, was a natural consequence of the shifting situation, but it was also revolutionary. We could say that the novel paved the way for the Finnish language, which at that time was held in low regard and had only an unofficial position in both literature and society.

The City and the Social: The Mobility of Language

The seven brothers in *Wenla Männistö* are the Juko Bros or "the Sevens", living in Kumpula, an area of Helsinki previously inhabited mostly by Romani and working-class people. As Wenla's mother puts it: "This area used to be a place for bootleggers and hooch peddlers, but not anymore. Things change"[3] (Katajavuori 2014, 16; trans. David Hackston). Due to gentrification, Kumpula is characterized nowadays as an area of a more hip and politically progressive population. Social change and mobility is thus activated in the novel by choosing this particular area as its setting:

> There is still a sense of good old village spirit in Kumpula. The inhabitants of this gardened suburb all know one another; resident turnover is low. What's more, everyone knows the calibre of the gang of lads living in the red house.[4]
> (Katajavuori 2014, 7; trans. David Hackston)

Like their predecessors, Katajavuori's brothers are "social drop-outs", a bunch of unemployed, parentless adolescents who spend their time watching television and sustaining their PlayStation addiction. Nevertheless, they are warmly depicted – carrying the ethos of the original work – as a tight and loyal group of brothers. Their existence in the novel is based on the same fundamentals as in Kivi's *Seitsemän veljestä*: their lively, wandering, never-ending discussions and dialogue, presented in their own manner of speaking, which in *Wenla Männistö* is the multilingual slang of Helsinki.[5]

Helsinki slang has been considered improper language – or even despicable – in many ways and in different historical contexts (Vaattovaara 2016). Nonetheless, it does have its unique features and it has attracted increasing amounts of both research and appreciation as a unique way of speech. Importantly, it has also been seen as a language variant which brings together people with varying linguistic and cultural backgrounds, and which builds bridges between different social classes. Helsinki slang has also been the language of the youth from early on (see Paunonen 2000). One of the characteristics of Helsinki slang is also its malleability: it is in a constant process of evolution and change due to the addition of new words and their combinations, following the shifting language climate of Helsinki, nowadays borrowing expressions and words from language groups such as Arabic and Somali (Lehtonen 2015). Slang as a language mode always invokes connections to social class and ethnicity, raising questions and concerns about what is considered proper or even pure language (Blommaert et al. 2012, 2–16).

Katajavuori's rewriting of the novel places the brothers in the role of a bystander, while the female characters take over. The novel has four main voices: "Marja Männistö, midwife at the Midwifery Clinic. Wenla's mother, single parent. Alli Jukola, deceased [mother of the seven brothers], spends her time observing from above, thinking, pondering, reminiscing"[6] (Katajavuori 2014, 1). In addition, the reader is acquainted with half-white/half-Roma Kajsa Rajamäki (originally a controversial

Urbanized Folk Life 265

racialized character), who works as a washing woman in a public sauna, and lastly Wenla herself, a "17-year-old fatherless girl in her full bloom"[7] (Katajavuori 2014, 5; trans. David Hackston).

With its multiple voices and intertexts from popular culture, the novel follows its predecessor, which in its own day was accused of being incoherent. The confusion created by incommensurable discourses in the novel was also a source of irritation for one of *Wenla Männistö's* reviewers:

> It is, then, a matter of opinion whether one appreciates the attempt of Katajavuori to transfer this disorder into fiction – or whether one values the novel as the last citadel of order and a world that is at least somehow comprehensible and that merits the kind of narrator who brings order to the story and is appealing to the reader.[8]
> (Harju 2014)

By mixing different language registers and other genres (such as poems, songs and mise en abymes) in the actual storyline, *Wenla Männistö* develops into a mixture that can be said to represent *disorder* or, in Bakhtinian words, polyphony or dialogism. Feminist readings of Bakhtin (see Pearce 1994) remind and emphasize how these concepts are concerned with the question of power in spoken language and in literature. Textual as well as actual voices are "shot through with the registers of nationality, race, class and education" (Pearce 1994, 11).

This disorder – both in narrative strategies and in shifting language registers – is my starting point. How is it connected to the linguistic elements and manners of speaking in the novel? Although there is no traditional narrator in *Wenla Männistö*, in her sections of monologue the voice of the deceased mother of the seven brothers, Alli Jukola, takes the traditional place of the realistic, omniscient narrator. Her reminiscing about her life as a single parent of seven brothers and their everyday life throughout the story has the same kind of gentle and merciful tone as that of the narrator in *Seitsemän veljestä*.

The novel employs the colloquial Finnish and multilingual Helsinki slang of the 2010s. *Wenla Männistö* is not unique in this respect among contemporary urban novels. Julia Tidigs has illuminated the varying levels of present-day multilingualism in fiction in an analysis of two Finland-Swedish novels: Johanna Holmström's *Asfaltsänglar* (2013; Angels of asphalt) and Sara Razai's *Jag har letat efter dig* (2012; I have been looking for you). In Holmström's novel, Muslim girls speak the Finland-Swedish slang of East Helsinki with their friends while using Arabic at home. Through this kind of multilingual representation, the social commitments and power relationships related to languages and the ways in which they are used also become emphasized in Holmström's text (Melkas & Löytty 2016). Consequently, these fictive urban descriptions examined by Tidigs both reflect and dramatize the contemporary situation in which the mixing and moulding of languages is an ongoing quotidian process. She shows how new languages and even new combinations that shake the traditional relationships between languages have surfaced in Finland-Swedish urban novels. The constantly evolving multilingual slang has developed into a local sociolect, and it is usually connected to urban settings and neighbourhoods with social problems. Most of these contemporary urban novels concentrate on the lives of the so-called common people living in the suburbs and, characteristic of this type of literature somehow depict the social problems in these environments. The questions of language and manners of speaking are thus connected to questions of social class and also gender.

Appropriation and Change: What is Accentuated in *Wenla Männistö*?

According to Linda Hutcheon (2006), themes and characters are usually the easiest story elements to adapt. Shifts in the point of view of the adapted story lead naturally to major differences. This is obvious in *Wenla Männistö*. Already the name of the novel tells the reader that a major change involves the person adopting the position of the main character, but there is more to it: namely, the letter "W" in Wenla's name. The original character in Kivi's work was Venla with a "V", emphasizing at that time both the commonness of the young girl and shifts in Finnish language use, differing from the older form of literary Finnish where "W" was used. In *Wenla Männistö*, the "W" underlines an entirely new situation where English is gaining more and more space in young peoples' language repertoire. This minor linguistic change reflects the historical span between Kivi and Katajavuori and draws attention to the movement of language.

Pirjo Lyytikäinen has shown in her study of the transgressive features in *Seitsemän veljestä* how the new and innovative elements operated on various levels of Finnish language and manners of speaking (Lyytikäinen 2004). She lists the following binarisms: a folksy way of speaking vs. old Finnish literary language (used in the Bible and religious texts); secular vs. sacred topics; low (everyday) vs. high; and Finnish folk poetry vs. words from the Swedish language. When mixing these binary elements, *Seitsemän veljestä* is both a polyphonic or multi-voiced novel and, at the same time, a force that shaped new language registers and ways of speaking in the literature of its time.

Katajavuori's novel appears in a very interesting guise: it absorbs its strengths and force from Kivi, but at the same time engages in acts of defiance, aversion and carnival. These same strategies were also important in the original, where Kivi used language and manners of speaking to dismantle the then hegemonic idyllic tradition in literature

(Lyytikäinen 2004; see also Lauerma 2015). *Wenla Männistö* introduces to the literary domain of Finland a rare group of refreshing youths, who, although guilty of launching a linguistic rebellion, are conceived of as serious literary characters.

Playfulness and humorous characterizations are an integral part of *Wenla Männistö*, with most of the scenes consisting of situation comedy as well as the use of slang and colloquial Finnish. In the opening scene of the novel, the girls and the brothers are watching *The Pacific*, an HBO miniseries about the Second World War:

WENLA. (flapping her arms). AARGH! EEK! (laughs) Paper!
JUSA. (dashes here and there, fetches some loo roll, presses it against the soft, open neck of Wenla's romper suit-like outfit). You're such a klutz.
WENLA. (wriggling, giggling, enjoying it). It was an accident! The cappuccino just sloshed between my tits.
ANSKU. How did you manage that?
JUSA. Fine place to pour coffee.
WENLA. (opens her top button and peers down to see how wet everything is, jumps up from the sofa, sniggers. The warm liquid soaks into her turquoise bra, from the bra into her top, then drips down towards her stomach. Wenla shudders). Ugh! It feels just like I've wet myself.
JUSA. (staring at her breasts). Really?
WENLA. (gesticulating by way of explanation). Just a bit higher up.[9]
(Katajavuori 2014, 8; trans. David Hackston)

The two main characters in Katajavuori's novel are the young girls, Wenla Männistö and her friend Ansku Seunala. This accentuation can be interpreted as a statement: it not only rewrites an iconic classic but also brings forth a different kind of character – young girls and their manners of speaking. The use of Helsinki slang and colloquial Finnish with racy language creates both a derogatory and, at the same time, humoristic tone in Wenla's voice. This kind of depiction of characters can also be interpreted as a transgressive gesture. Wenla and her friends are reckless rascals with a carefree attitude towards life, as well as enchanting persons who create reality through their own manner of using language and speech.

We only get to know very little about the Venla of *Seitsemän veljestä*, but in *Wenla Männistö* Wenla's voice sometimes dominates the whole scene. She becomes existent to the readers especially through her special manner of speaking, which creates *the illusion of orality*. The following line of thinking illustrates this:

WENLA. If someone says that he's just gotten out of the joint, I'm not like right away that OMG why were you in. I'm more like what kind of a person are you internally. If it turns out he was in for manslaughter, I'm not going all eek now he's gonna off me, because I'm sure he could think of something better to do with me. If his knife falls next to his chair, I don't get yikes scared but am more like, hey, you dropped some sort of edged weapon thingie.[10]

(Katajavuori 2014, 54; my translation)

Not only does Wenla frequently mix old and new slang vocabulary, she also makes use of utterances and exclamations familiar from comic books ("iik"/"eek", "kääks"/"yikes") to emphasize the important or essential points in her speech. The use of utterances and exclamations also creates movement in her speech. It darts around restlessly, quickly and unpredictably like a pinball. Through this linguistic strategy, speech becomes an integral part of the habitus of the character, which, like her speech, is restless, snappy and unpredictable. At the same time, Wenla's speech conforms to the swift pace and pronunciation characteristic of Helsinki slang.

The way girls – and teenage girls, in particular – talk is often considered trivial, superficial and pointless "prattle" or "babble" accompanied by giggles. There is a direct allusion to this in the novel in the scene where the seven brothers are watching *The Pacific* on television. The boys feel that the presence of the girls, and especially their constant talking, is interfering with their ability to concentrate on the series. When they plead with the pair to be quiet, the girls appeal to the suffrage of women in Finland and continue their babbling. With their way of talking, the girls carnivalize the existing power relations between genders and thereby undermine certain demeaning or denunciatory attitudes directed at them. Through this kind of manner of speaking, they literally take space for themselves in the novel. They have their own voices and language; these make them matter and endow them with an amelioration of status.

An examination of the characters' manners of speaking reveals the hierarchic power relationship between "low" and "high" cultures on a broader level. What is appreciated and why? A male-oriented war series or female prattling? Whose voice becomes heard? And whose speech is considered interesting and important? In this scene, the girls refer to the so-called Bechdel test, a measure of the level of female presence in movies. To pass the test, a movie must have at least two female characters who talk to one another about something else than men. Scenes like this in the novel accentuate the question of the status of different voices. Whose voice is considered interesting and worth listening to?

The manners of speaking and the uses of language that the girls engage in are marked by a hissing "s" sibilant, which has been especially associated with the vernacular of young women of Helsinki, although research into the subject shows that this frontal "s" sibilant can also be found in other areas. Negative connotations have been attached to this sibilant (e.g. by referring to it as a "teenybopper-s") (Vaattovaara & Halonen 2015, 46, cited in Samola 2016). The novel consciously plays with these features, embracing them and turning them into carnivalistic and empowering speech.

In addition to various manners and styles of speech, the gap between generations is ingeniously illuminated by means of changing imageries and song lyrics of popular culture. Marja Männistö sings in a choir, and one of the songs in its repertoire is "Lauantai" (Saturday), a hit song recorded by Laila Kinnunen, a famous Finnish "schlager" singer from the 1960s. When her mother is practising, a verse from the song carries to Wenla's room:

> In secret may blush
> be painted on your cheeks.
> We'll see whatever those young boys
> will whisper in our ee-ears.
> Saturday, that most lovely eve
> may it quickly come to me.[11]
> (Katajavuori 2014, 65; my translation)

The lyrics of the song highlight the intense excitement of waiting and the innocence of the relationship between the sexes, accompanied by a certain kind of "nice" manner of speaking, with which the swift rewording of the song by Wenla creates a stark contrast:

> In secret may cock
> be inserted in your mouth.
> We'll see whatever those young boys
> will squirt in your ee-ears.
> Saturday, that most lovely eve
> come quick or I'll be pissed off.[12]
> (Katajavuori 2014, 65; my translation)

Wenla uses vulgar and straightforward words like "cock" and describes sexual acts, such as a blowjob. The verse ends with the same plea as her mother's, but more demandingly: "come quick or I'll be pissed off". In this scene also, the sounds of the vowels and rhymes in Finnish are of importance, constructing comical effects.

With the original lyrics of the hit song and its "rewording", the novel emphasizes both the gap between generations and the complete discord between their linguistic registers. The pop song from the mother's youth merely hinted at sexuality, with the girl in the original lyrics politely wishing for the exciting and wonderful Saturday evening to arrive soon. In the daughter's version, on the other hand, all manner of innuendo is lost due to the pronounced vulgarity and outrageously straightforward attitude. Vulgar and naughty but easy-going talk about sexuality and bodily organs updates the girl character to this day and age. Consequently, the rewording also signifies the shifting sexual atmosphere, placing mother and daughter in different positions in connection to sexual desire and activity.

Wenla, Ansku and the Sevens move around together in the ecstatic heat of youth. Most of their time is spent in the house of the brothers, where adults cannot supervise the doings of the young people or interfere with their idle way of life. Sexuality is "obsessively on the tip of the tongue" (Saxell 2015) all the time and flashes in the flow of discussion at regular intervals. It is talked about, but not so much allowed to happen, although the drive for that is strong. Girls and boys act as equal participants in the discussions where the matter is addressed.

In literature aimed towards girls and adolescents in general, sexuality and sexual urges are still in many ways linked to the idea of romance, or at least romantic feelings (see Voipio 2015). The lust of adolescent girls is justified by the presumption that there is an underlying desire for an intimate relationship. The characters of Wenla and Ansku are free of such norms of girlishness and sexuality connected to maintaining a good reputation in society, such as decency or modesty, for example. Their lust is just as straightforward and elementary as that of the boys, and it is expressed in that way. For instance, "lustcoyotelust" (*himokojoottihimo*; Katajavuori 2014, 76) uses word play connecting sexual desire to an animal. Especially in literature targeted at adolescents, vernacular language has been socially stigmatized until the 1960s: marginal and minority groups have been differentiated from middle-class adults by forms of language, just as gang members have been from proper youths or naughty girls from those who are nice and decent (Tiittula & Nuolijärvi 2013, 192, 233). In Katajavuori's rewriting, the girl characters are free of moral judgement. In this way, her work also rewrites the tradition of youth literature to justify the way girl characters speak and behave. This becomes clear in one scene of the novel which includes an intertextual allusion to the work of the Finland-Swedish author Monika Fagerholm.

One of the chapters in *Wenla Männistö* is called "In *The American Girl* there are seven girls on the stage".[13] It refers to Monika Fagerholm's novel *Den amerikanska flickan* (2004; *The American Girl*, 2009) where the friendship and play between the two main girl characters are underscored. Fagerholm is known for her empowerment of female characters and innovative play with novel forms, structure and language.[14] Wenla and Ansku go to the theatre to see a play that is based on *The American Girl*. Wenla admiringly watches the seven actresses. Noting that without "any taboos, they were emancipated and innocent rascals at the same time" [15] (Katajavuori 2014, 153; my translation), she experiences a moment of awakening. This epiphany concerns an unexpected pregnancy and her decision not to have the baby she is carrying.

Wenla does not conceive of the situation as a moral or social problem, but instead adopts a more pragmatic attitude towards it: "This time I won't give birth, but tomorrow is another day. [...] Scarlett will always survive, says Mum too"[16] (Katajavuori 2014, 157; my translation). In

Wenla's musings, pragmatism and straightforward thinking form the bedrock, but so does self-determination in relation to one's own body. Seeking consolation around an unwanted situation, her thoughts go to one of the classics in women's literature, *Gone with the Wind* (1936). The main protagonist and heroine of the novel, Scarlett O'Hara, has in her relentlessness and complexity fascinated generations of readers. Her famous last words in the novel, "After all, tomorrow is another day", underline hope and faith in the future.

By not featuring an omnipotent girl character but a mundane one, *Wenla Männistö* promotes the ethos of communality, not individuality. In *Wenla Männistö*, this is achieved linguistically as well. Katajavuori's novel reproduces working-class idiolect, values it and, most of all, plays with it by placing it in opposition to normative language. The "lightness" of language and expressions is often in contradiction with the serious themes of the novel – poverty, social problems, abortion – thereby creating an interesting contradiction. As a critic of Finland's largest newspaper *Helsingin Sanomat* encapsulated it in his review:

> Instead of a cheap topsy-turvy movement, Katajavuori makes Kivi's epic equal. This means that from now on, women, too, have the right to make their own mistakes. It also means that the hustles and bustles of women are at least as interesting as the undertakings of the men.[17]
> (Majander 2014)

Gender and Class in Urbanized Folklife

"Folk" and the tradition of folk description have primarily been conceived of as a male affair. In Finland, among the most obvious and famous representatives of this tradition are, for instance, *Ryysyrannan Jooseppi* by Ilmari Kianto (1924; Joseph of Ryysyranta) or Juutas Käkriäinen in *Putkinotko*[18] by Joel Lehtonen (1920). Although Maria Jotuni's *Arkielämää* (1909; Everyday life) is included in the same tradition of folk depiction, its female characters have not reached the level of culturally significant icons or become representative of Finnish "folk" in the same way as the above-mentioned male characters. Placing *Wenla Männistö* in the tradition of folk description is justified by the fact that it features a variety of plain, common "women of the people". Its main protagonist is an ordinary young woman whose voice is allowed to become heard. The description in the novel conveys a benevolent and compassionate touch without value judgements or moralizing in its examination of people. The quaint humour gives its own flavour to the narration, but with appreciation of its subjects.

The mundane and practical aspects of motherhood become emphasized through Wenla's mother Marja Männistö and their mutually warm-hearted relationship. Within the society of Kumpula in the novel, children living in a nuclear family are considered freaks: almost every child in Kumpula is the fatherless offspring of a poor single mother. Katajavuori's work relates the quotidian survival of single mothers in a manner that does not underline problems or incriminate anyone. Everyday challenges do surface now and then, but as a part of the normal state of affairs – as, for instance, in the conversation where Marja expresses her wish that Wenla would get a job, because the salary of a midwife is not big enough to pay the rent and all the bills.

Kajsa Rajamäki, the half-white/half-Roma washer woman of Harju's Sauna, has in her profession[19] the opportunity to observe people without their clothes. In the sauna, people seem to be all alike with their joys and sorrows. To Kajsa they are all equal in their need for human and bodily touch. In her statements, as she reminisces on the poor history of the Romas and her own life story as a kind of forgotten or silenced piece of history, social and cultural inequalities are blatantly clear. Her character reveals attitudes towards a minority and how a whole group of people have been demoted to a marginal and disregarded role: "Forgotten is also my mother, who moved to Sweden and left me in my father's white relatives' care..."[20] (Katajavuori 2014, 225; my translation). Forgetting refers here to a broader cultural amnesia of an oppressed group of people. Through Kajsa's voice, the novel opens to the reader yet another area of social reality, within which the practices and structures that increase inequality imperceptibly function.

When considering Romas as the Other in the history of Finnish literature, Viola Parente-Čapková has stated in her analysis of *Seitsemän veljestä* that Kivi's characters are more than stereotypes due to the mixture of romanticism and realism, as well as polyphony and irony, in the novel. Although the representation of Romas is based on both negative and positive stereotypes, and it functions as an element of constructing Finnishness, "the foregrounding of the Roma's role in the interpretation of the novel shows another aspect of the rich picture which *Seven Brothers* offers concerning the construction of national identity and of social order in the modernizing Finland" (Parente-Čapková 2011, 13).

Taken together, all of the voices in *Wenla Männistö* open up a spectrum where the adverse and even fierce features of life are thrown in the face of the reader, very much in the manner of *Seitsemän veljestä*. While bowing to the literary tradition and its predecessor, the novel rewrites these to fit the life circles of contemporary "common" people. It does this with poignancy derived from description of life in the suburban areas in the Helsinki region.

The Power of Language

Wenla Männistö reforms the literary tradition of the depiction of common people. It values the ways of speaking ("the voice") of young, suburban girl characters. It underlines the ways in which language moves and changes in different social and cultural contexts. And it shows how language and manners of speaking intertwine with power and gender in numerous ways. Overall, the novel foregrounds the change of sociolinguistic norms in the contemporary world.

Language is power, and through language it is possible either to deny or to allow the self-representation of certain social groups and communities. Language can enable as well as silence certain voices in society. The ethos of *Wenla Männistö* could be summed up as an attempt to treasure the idea of communality: nobody has to try to make it through life alone. "The Sevens", a group of siblings loyal to one another and loved by their mother, convey this warm undercurrent to the reader in the epilogue to the novel. The brothers are spending a peaceful evening together. Their leisurely gathering to play a word game leads them into a realm of verbal joy and inventiveness. The epilogue bows to *Seitsemän veljestä* as the brothers mix nouns that normally do not go together and invent whole new words and meanings – both absurd and humorous – in Finnish:

(Pondering, playing).
EPPU. RETROAFRO. Goddamn what a word!
AAPO. SLEEPCOTTON.
EPPU. The dude's going soft. Not accepted.
AAPO. GOFOOD is a real word for sure.
JUSA. Okay. But Eppu's TRICKDUST is clearly cloudy.
TOMMI. Yup. Disqualified.
JUSA. What about HILLFOREST?
TOMMI. STUMPHILL?
AAPO. Not an established concept.
JUSA. HILLPONY. A pony that is used in hills. A mountain pony specialized in climbing.
AAPO. Or PONYPIECE?
SIMPPA (FROM THE COUCH). Oh please. What are you guys on?
EPPU. Woohoo. Look at this: NOONTIDE.[21]
(Katajavuori 2014, 268; my translation)

Wenla Männistö ends with the word "NOONTIDE" being shouted by the youngest of the brothers, Eppu. This contains a reference and appreciative wink to a great classic, whose narrative ends as follows:

And I have now told of seven brothers in the backwoods of Finland; and what could I relate of the day of their life and its fortunes here on earth? It rose steadily to its noontide height and sank steadily downward to evening rest amidst the passing of many thousands of golden suns.[22]
(Kivi [1870] 1929, 336; trans. Alex Matson)

274   Kukku Melkas

The lives of Katajavuori's brothers are still at noonday in all their hopefulness – and in the form of a word game, their lives emphasize the malleability and mobility of language. Language moulds and shapes us. Enabling and limiting at the same time, it offers old and new possibilities for imagining ourselves.

Notes

1 The novel has been adapted for the stage as *Alli Jukolan tarina* (The story of Alli Jukola) for the National Theatre of Finland in 2015 and further scripted as a radio play. The theatre play focusses on the mother of the seven brothers, whereas the radio play underlines the gap between generations by concentrating on the multiple types of speech and expressions in the mother-daughter relationships.
2 The author's language history and his position between Finnish-speaking common people and Swedish-speaking educated people have been illuminated in the critical edition of Kivi's correspondence by Mirja Saari in her article on Kivi as user of the Swedish language.
3 "Joskus tämä oli lestinheittäjien ja trokarien seutua, mutta eipä ole enää. Suhdanteet muuttuu."
4 "Kumpulassa on vielä hyvää vanhan ajan kylähenkeä. Puutarhakaupunginosan asukkaan tuntevat toisensa, vaihtuvuus on vähäistä. Myös punaisen talon poikajoukkion laatu on kaikkien tiedossa."
5 Helsinki slang, or "stadin slangi" ("Helsinki's slang"; from the Swedish word for city, *stad*), is a local dialect and sociolect of the Finnish language used in the capital city of Finland. It is characterized by its abundance of foreign loan words not found in other Finnish dialects. Helsinki slang first evolved in the late 19th century as a sociolect of the multilingual Helsinki working-class communities, where Swedish- and Finnish-speaking youth lived together with Russian, German and various other language minorities (See more in Paunonen 2000).
6 "Marja Männistö, kätilö Kätilöopistolla. Wenlan äiti, yksinhuoltaja. Alli Jukola, vainaa, joka ylhäältä käsin tarkkailee, miettii, muistelee ja pohdiskelee."
7 Namely, an "isätön tyttö kukkeimmassa iässään".
8 "Onkin mielipidekysymys, arvostaako Katajavuoren pyrkimystä siirtää tämä epäjärjestys romaanikirjallisuuteen vai arvostaako enemmän romaania järjestyksen ja edes jotenkin rajatun maailman viimeisenä linnakkeena, jonka ansioihin kuuluu lukijaa puhutteleva ja tarinaa järjestävä kertoja."
9 "WENLA. (vispaa käsiään sivuilla). ÄÄÄK! IIIK! (nauraa) Paperia!
    JUSA. (ryntäilee ja säntäilee, tuo vessapaperia, painelee Wenlan avokaulaisen potkupukumaisen sortsitoppiasun pehmeää, kukkeaa kaula-aukkoa). Sä oot yks söhelö.
    WENLA. (kiemurtelee, hekottelee, nauttii). Se oli vahinko! Cappucinot hulahti tissien väliin.
    ANSKU. Miten sä onnistutkin.
    JUSA. Sinne lorautit sumpit.
    WENLA. (avaa ylimmän napin ja kurkistaa miten märkää kaikki on, puokkaa ylös sohvalta, hihittää. Lämmin neste imeytyy turkooseihin rintaliiveihin, rintaliiveistä miehustaan ja valuu edelleen mahalle. Wenla ravistelee hartioitaan). Uuu! Tuntuu samalta ku olis pissanu housuun.
    JUSA. (Tuijottaa rintoja). Ai?
    WENLA. (selittää käsillään). Mut vaan vähän ylempänä."

10 "WENLA. Jos joku sanoo että se on just päässyt posesta niin ei mun eka veto ole että ai hui miksi istuit. Vaan niinku millanen ihminen sä oot sisäisesti? Jos käy ilmi että taposta esim. niin en mä heti kelaa että iik nyt se murdaa mut, koska kai se nyt mun kanssa parempaa tekemistä keksis. Jos sen mora putoaa tuolinjalan viereen niin en kääks pelästy, sanon vaan että hei sulta putosi joku tommonen teräasekapine."
11   "Myös salaa voi punaa
      nyt poskiin huiskuttaa.
      Saa nähdä mitä pojat nuo
      taas korvaan kuiskuttaa-aa.
      Lauantai, ilta ihanin
      tulla piankin jo saa."

12   "Myös salaa voi munaa
      nyt poskiin humpsuttaa.
      Saa nähdä mitä pojat nuo
      taas korvaan ruiskuttaa-aaa.
      Lauantai, ilta ihanin
      tule pian tai vituttaa."

13 "*Amerikkalaisessa tytössä* on seitsemän tyttöä lavalla".
14 About the significance of Fagerholm's oeuvre in the Finnish literary tradition, see (Malmio & Österlund 2016).
15 "Niillä ei ollut tabuja, ne oli vapautuneita ja viattomia kelmejä yhtaikaa."
16 "Nyt tällä kertaa en synnytä, mutta huomenna on uusi päivä. ... Scarlett pärjää aina, sanoo Mamikin."
17 "Huokean ylösalaisin kääntämisen sijaan Katajavuori tasa-arvoistaa Kiven eepoksen. Se tarkoittaa sitä, että nyt naisillakin on oikeus omiin virheisiinsä. Sekä sitä, että naisten kohkaamiset ovat vähintään yhtä kiintoisia kuin urosten vaiheet."
18 An invented, onomatopoetic place called Hogweed Hollow.
19 Women who belonged to this traditional Finnish profession would wash people's bodies in public saunas.
20 "Unohdettu on äitinikin, joka muutti Ruotsiin ja jätti minut isäni valkolaissuvun hoteisiin, valtaväestön vaikutuspiiriin."
21 "(Pohtivat, pelaavat).
      EPPU. RETROAFRO. Jumalauta mikä sana!
      AAPO. UNIVANU.
      EPPU. Jätkä pehmoilee. Ei hyväksytä.
      AAPO. MENOEVÄS on kyllä ihan oikea sana.
      JUSA. Okei. Mutta Epun KUJETOMU on ohutta yläpilveä.
      TOMMI. Jep. Diskataan.
      JUSA. Onko semmonen kuin MÄKIMETSÄ?
      TOMMI. KANTOMÄKI?
      AAPO. Ei ole mikään vakiintunut käsite.
      JUSA. MÄKIPONI? Semmoinen poni, jota käytetään mäessä? Kiipeämiseen
         erikoistunut vuoristoponi?
      AAPO. Tai PONITEOS?
      SIMPPA. Hei haloo. Mitä te ootte vetäny.
      EPPU. Wouhou. Katsokaas tätä: PUOLIPÄIVÄ."

22 "Ja niin olen kertonut seitsemästä veljeksestä Suomen saloissa; ja mitäpä kertoisin enään heidän elämänsä päivästä ja sen vaiheista täällä? Se kulki rauhaisesti puolipäivän korkeudelle ylös ja kallistui rauhaisesti alas illan lepoon monen tuhannen, kultaisen auringon kiertoessa."

Bibliography

Blommaert, Jan & Leppänen, Sirpa & Spotti, Massimilian (2012) Endangering Multilingualism. In Jan Blommaert, Sirpa Leppänen, Päivi Pahta & Tiina Räisänen (eds): *Dangereous Multilingualism. Northern Perspectives on Order, Purity and Normality.* Basingstoke: Palgrave Macmillan, 1–21.
Harju, Saara (2014) Riina Katajavuoren *Wenla Männistö. Keskisuomalainen* (August 27, 2014).
Hutcheon, Linda (2006) *A Theory of Adaptation.* New York & London: Routledge.
Kåreland, Lena (2016) Re-imagining Girlhood: The Revisioning of Girls' Books Tradition in Monika Fagerholm's DIVA and the American Girl. In Kristina Malmio & Mia Österlund (eds): *Novel Districts. Critical Readings of Monika Fagerholm.* Studia Fennica Litteraria 9. Helsinki: Finnish Literary Society, 25–37.
Katajavuori, Riina (2014) *Wenla Männistö.* Helsinki: Otava.
Kivi, Aleksis ([1870] 1929) *Seven Brothers.* Translated by Alex Matson. London: Coward-McCann Inc.
Lauerma, Petri (2015) Kiven komedioiden kieli: herrasväen puhetta ja kyökkisuomea. In Pentti Paavolainen, Sakari Katajamäki et al (eds): *Aleksis Kivi: Kihlaus, Leo ja Liina, Selman juonet. Kriittinen editio.* Helsinki: Suomalaisen Kirjallisuuden Seura, 127–139.
Lehtonen, Heini (2015) *Tyylitellen. Nuorten kielelliset resurssit ja kielen sosiaalinen indeksisyys monietnisessä Helsingissä.* Helsinki: Helsinki University Press.
Lyytikäinen, Pirjo (2004) *Vimman villityt pojat. Aleksis Kiven Seitsemän veljeksen laji.* Helsinki: Suomalaisen Kirjallisuuden Seura.
Majander, Antti (2014) Herkullinen päivitys *Seitsemästä veljeksestä. Helsingin Sanomat* (August 26, 2014).
Malmio, Kristina & Österlund, Mia (eds) (2016) *Novel Districts: Critical Readings of Monika Fagerholm.* Studia Fennica Litteraria 9. Helsinki: Finnish Literary Society.
Melkas, Kukku & Löytty, Olli (2016) Liikkuvat lukemiskontekstit. In Heidi Grönstrand, Ralf Kauranen, Olli Löytty, Kukku Melkas, Hanna-Leena Nissilä & Mikko (eds): *Pollari: Kansallisen katveesta. Suomen kirjallisuuden ylirajaisuudesta.* Helsinki: Suomalaisen Kirjallisuuden Seura, 118–138.
Parente-Čapková, Viola (2011) A Domestic Other: The Role of the Roma Literary Characters in the Process of Constructing Finnishness. *Multiethnica* 33, 8–21.
Paunonen, Heikki (2000) Stadin slangi historiallisena, kielellisenä ja sosiaalisena ilmiönä. In *Tsennaaks Stadii, bonjaaks slangii. Stadin slangin suursanakirja.* Helsinki: WSOY, 14–44.
Pearce, Lynne (1994) *Reading Dialogics.* London & New York: Routledge.
Saari, Mirja (2012) Kivi ruotsin kielen käyttäjänä. In Juhani Niemi, Sakari Katajamäki, Ossi Kokko, Petri Lauerma & Jyrki Nummi (eds): *Kirjeet. Aleksis Kiven kriittiset editiot.* Helsinki: Suomalaisen Kirjallisuuden Seura, 114–131.
Samola, Hanna (2016) *Siniparran bordelli. Dystopian ja sadun lajiyhdistelmät romaaneissa Berenikes hår, Huorasatu ja Auringon ydin.* Tampere: Tampere University Press.

Saxell, Jani (2015) Rikkaruohot Kumpulan puutarhaonnelassa. *Kiiltomato* March 30, 2015.
Tidigs, Julia (2016) Språk i rörelse. Flerspråkighet och urbana rum i Sara Razais *Jag har letat efter dig* och Johanna Holmströms *Asfaltsänglar*. *AVAIN – Kirjallisuudentutkimuksen aikakauslehti – Finsk tidskrift för litteraturforskning* 2(2016), 41–56.
Tiittula, Liisa & Nuolijärvi, Pirkko (2013) *Puheen illuusio suomenkielisessä kaunokirjallisuudessa*. Helsinki: Suomalaisen Kirjallisuuden Seura.
Vaattovaara, Johanna (2016) Helsinki sylkykuppina – miksi stadilaista puhetyyliä vihataan? In Irina Piippo, Johanna Vaattovaara, & Eero Voutilainen (eds): *Kielen taju. Vuorovaikutus, asenteet ja ideologiat*. Helsinki: Art House, 40–83.
Vaattovaara, Johanna & Halonen, Mia (2015) Missä on ässä? "Stadilaisen s:n" helsinkiläisyydestä. In Marja-Leena Sorjonen, Anu Rouhikoski & Heini Lehtonen (eds): *Helsingissä puhuttavat suomet. Kielen indeksisyys ja sosiaaliset identiteetit*. Helsinki: Suomalaisen Kirjallisuuden Seura, 40–83.
Voipio, Myry (2015) *Emansipaation ja ohjailun ristivedossa. Suomalaisen tyttökirjallisuuden kehitys 1889–2011*. Jyväskylä Studies in Humanities 263. Jyväskylä: Jyväskylä University Press.

16 The Permeable Border
Anxieties of the Mother Tongue in Contemporary Nordic Poetry

Elisabeth Friis

This chapter investigates the locution *mother tongue* and what the seemingly organic link between the tongue and the mother that this locution establishes really means – or rather *might come to mean* if we take a closer look at its configurations in contemporary Nordic poetry, where a conspicuous interest in this very link is detectable. The locution or metaphor of the *mother tongue*, when interrogated by contemporary poetry, turns out to be a far cry from the safe container of linguistic identity that its first propagators imagined. Rather, it is inhabited by a deep ambivalence, just as the act of breastfeeding is inhabited by a deep ambivalence as breastfeeding triggers feelings of aggression as well as feelings of satisfaction or love. This inherent ambivalence of lactation will come as no surprise to readers of Melanie Klein, who is an important reference here; her groundbreaking clinical description of the infant's ambivalent experiences of breastfeeding to a certain degree informs the readings of the three poets that are presented here: Jessie Kleemann (Greenland), Athena Farrokhzad (Sweden) and Ursula Andkjær Olsen (Denmark). I will suggest that their specific, poetic dealings with the *mother tongue* is rooted in the inherent ambivalence of the corporeal reality of the locution and that this in fact allows the motif of the *mother tongue* to function as a overdetermined nodal point: a point from which contemporary Nordic poetry can engage in a nuanced and inclusive critique of colonialism, racism, linguistic homogenization and cultural (re)production in the broadest sense. As turns out, this critique is based on a negotiation of the nature of linguistic borders as it questions the very conceptualization of such borders. Is the border between two different languages a barrier? Or is it a permeable line, a line that can be crossed?

Where Did the Mother Come From?

The first question that needs to be addressed is when and how we came to understand our first language in terms of the corporeal metaphors of nativity and maternity. In fact, it is a relatively recent phenomenon. Classical Antiquity offers no examples of a naturalized link between mother and language, neither from Greece nor from Rome, where Latin is referred to as *sermo patrius*, often translated as "mother tongue" or "native language", but which literally means "father-speech" or the "speech of the fathers/the fatherland". No maternal body is indicated and thus no organic bond between lactation and language acquisition is established.

It is well known how the mother figure enters the stage along with Christianity. The Church is the mother of all children, and its exaltation of the Virgin Mary is therefore accompanied by a mise-en-scène of itself as a breastfeeding mother, while *ecclesia lactans*, the milk that Mary/the mother/the Church gives to her children, is a double infusion of nourishing food and Christian spirit. Establishing a direct, intimate connection between the mother and learning, however, is not a matter for the Church. The language of the Church is Latin, and that cannot be learned through the breast of one's mother, but in grammar school, where there are, of course, no mothers. The organic and intimate connection between the mother and language does not primarily originate with the Church, even though the Church promotes itself as a breastfeeding mother on every occasion imaginable. Rather, it originates from the development of written literatures in the vernacular, as heralded by Dante (Bonfiglio 2010, 73). The *mother tongue* is quite simply an invention of the Renaissance and Dante is, in *De vulgari eloquentia*,[1] the first to make an unmistakable connection between the vernacular, the female body and lactation. The defenders of the vernacular from here on continued to advocate the vernacular as a "natural", personal and intimate language: a language that was a prolongation of the mother's body: a *lingua materna*, a *mother tongue*, *die Muttersprache* or, in the Scandinavian languages, *Modersmålet*.

From the late medieval period, the locution gained popularity, first in the Germanic languages and later on in France, Italy and Spain. When we reach the Enlightenment, the link between mother and tongue seems to be solidly established and therefore ready to be put to use, for instance, by Johann Gottfried Herder and Friedrich Schleiermacher.

As has often been pointed out, most recently and poignantly by Yasemin Yildiz, the notion of the *mother tongue* is of particular importance in the 19th century's development of the conception and establishment of the nation state. One nation, one people and one language comprise the parole, not least, as Yildiz emphasizes, for the German idealists Herder and Schleiermacher (Yildiz 2012, 7).

Yildiz claims that in this way is instilled a *monolingual paradigm*, according to which "individuals and social formations are imagined to possess one 'true' language only, their 'mother tongue,' and through this possession to be organically linked to an exclusive, clearly demarcated ethnicity, culture, and nation" (Yildiz 2012, 2). Yildiz (and others with her) makes a convincing case. Surely the idea of a monolithic *Muttersprache* is defining for the ideological discourse Thomas Bonfiglio has described as *ethnolinguistic nationalism* (Bonfiglio 2010, 122–142). The locution "mother tongue" is, of course, meant to call forth the nation's warm, caring and nourishing embrace of the individual subject – the status of the latter not being a question of mere citizenship but of the linguistic identity of the "native" speaker – where "native" also refers to the mother as it derives from the Latin *nascor* ("to be born").

This is exactly the idea that seems to have paved the way for the notion (the metaphor) of the mother tongue to take ever since such a prominent place in the general description of language, a place that it, in spite of the efforts in modern linguistics to drive out the maternal connotations by referring instead to first and respectively second (third, etc.) languages, not terming the first language the mother tongue, to a large degree occupies to this day. For instance, UNESCO celebrates *International Mother Language Day* once a year.

There are many reasons why it may be sensible to cease to refer to a first language as a mother tongue, but it is not the discussion of those principles that is of interest to us here. What we shall be examining is the resistance which the notion of a mother tongue, of receiving language and culture along with one's mother's milk, produces in the poetry that deals with exactly that notion: that is, poetry which explicitly mentions and relates to the mother tongue. A resistance articulated by poetry in various interesting ways, which, it seems to me, is already present in the very construction "mother tongue", making it an obvious phenomenon to unfold, work through and challenge when poets use precisely the construction "mother tongue" as their subject matter.

If we look to negotiations of the notion of the mother tongue in contemporary Nordic poetry, we soon find that all of the repressed anxieties implied by the assumed organic link between the maternal body and language present themselves. Consequently, the Romantic Nationalist attempts to establish the metaphor as what Roland Barthes would call a natural sign, therefore backfires in ways that the patriarchs of German idealism certainly did not anticipate. The identity that the link between mother (the female body/lactation) and tongue (The First Language) constructs is inherently unstable, even rebellious. The idea of the *mother tongue* in itself carries a potential for resistance or conflict, a conflict whose dynamics and whose bodily grounding has been described best of all by Melanie Klein. Before we turn to the highly intensive poetic material, a rough outline of the Kleinian perspective on breastfeeding is necessary.

The Good and the Bad Breast

Melanie Klein is the theoretician of object-relations. Klein, who unlike Freud and Lacan takes an interest in the child from the moment it is born, claims that the human being's first relation after the trauma of birth (which creates the *anxiety of persecution* – a fear of dying) is the relation to a partial object, the mother's breasts. The infant has no idea of the maternal body as a separate entity, as there is no discrete border between part and whole or inner and outer, and yet this *dyad* is already determined by an experience of division and ambivalence. Klein considers this to be the case on the basis of, among other things, the observation of infants biting the breast they are sucking. The sucking impulse is an expression of the oral libido (life drive), while the biting impulse is an oral-destructive impulse, thus representing the death drive, which in this case takes a cannibalistic form. Klein's explanation of the oral-destructive impulse is as logical as it is sensational: aggression is simply grounded in greed, and greed is thus established as an *oral* emotion.

Of course, the double emotion prompted by breastfeeding is connected to the infant's varying experiences of hunger (frustration) and fullness (satisfaction): "powerful stimuli for libidinal and destructive impulses – love and hatred" (Klein 1952, 199), something which is connected to the inherent duality of breasts: "The breast, inasmuch as it is gratifying, is loved and felt to be 'good'; in so far as it is a source of frustration, it is hated and felt to be 'bad'" (Klein 1952, 199–200). These contradictory impulses are "not wholly distinct" (Klein 1952, 200), and so they form what we might call the infant's double-sided relation to the first (partial) object. Another important point made by Klein is that the good/bad breast is experienced as both an internal and an external object because of the infant's supposed ontological situation in the first three to four months of its life, lacking the ability to distinguish between internal and external objects, a state which Klein incidentally terms the paranoid-schizoid position. By virtue of a distinction lacking between internal and external, the good and the bad breast become both introjected (internalized) objects *and* projected ones – that is, they are transferred onto the mother's body or other external objects. The good breast becomes a defence against anxiety; however, since the bad breast simply aims to kill the infant (denying it food), it creates anxiety, setting the stage for possible later states like hypochondria and eating disorders by and large.[2]

This strong ambivalence, this: "synthesis between feelings of love and destructive impulses towards one and the same object – the breast – gives rise to depressive anxiety, guilt and the urge to make reparation to the injured love object, the good breast" (Klein 1952, 203) is a depressive state leading towards the healing possibility of the Oedipal phase (here Klein is entirely in line with Freud), but what is of decisive importance in this connection is that the impulses in question are simultaneous. They exist side by side, and if a psychically "healthy" adult existence is to come out of the object-relational process, it is critical that the *floating* border between the good and the bad breast (the introjected as well as the projected one) does not change into a *barrier*, but remains floating, that is, permeable (Klein 1952, 229); an observation that leads us directly to a specific post-colonial aesthetics.

Jessie Kleemann's *Eskimothertongue*

My first two examples of poetry that attempt to *cross*, *stay at* or *work with* the border between "the good breast" and "the bad breast" originate in poetic practices that protest the linguistic mode Yildiz defines as monolithic. They are – perhaps not surprisingly – conducted by poets who, because of colonialism or because of migration, share the experience of living in and between several languages.

As Rosi Braidotti (2011) and Doris Sommer (2004) have asserted, among others, people who live with several languages (for pleasure or out of necessity) have a strong awareness of the fact that the relationship between language and identity formation is a construction. As Braidotti (2011, 39) says, "being in-between languages constitutes a vantage point in deconstructing identity." In other words, the polyglot has an embodied experience of the arbitrariness of the relation between expression and content. This embodied experience is surely the point of departure for the Greenlandic poet and performance artist Jessie Kleemann.

Kleemann works with and within at least three languages: Kalaallisut, Danish and English – a logical constellation if we consider the political and geographical situation of Greenland. Greenland has self-governance, but enjoys strong political and economic relations with Denmark. Approximately 50,000 people live in Greenland, while almost 20,000 Greenlanders live in Copenhagen. The predominant languages in Greenland are Greenlandic (Kalaallisut) and Danish. Not all Greenlandic people speak one of the three relatively different main dialects that Greenlandic contains: East Greenlandic (Tunumiutut), West Greenlandic (Kitaamiutut) and North Greenlandic (Avanersuarmiutut/Thule language). West Greenlandic is the dominant language (according to UNESCO it is a "vulnerable" dialect), while the other two are "definitely endangered". English is everybody's lingua franca, of course – not least because the country is located in the middle of the Atlantic, bordering on Canada.

Greenland's post-colonial period began in 1953, the year in which Greenland was raised from the status of colony to autonomous province, and the great Greenlandic founder of a Greenland-based, post-colonial aesthetics, an artistic stance which Kleemann prolongs, is the artist Pia Arke (1958–2007). Arke worked in many different media, but the common denominator of most of her art is the incorporation of an assumed "ethnographic" look in her representation of Greenlandic material.[3] She explains why this device is necessary in her seminal booklet *Ethno-aesthetics/Etnoæstetik* ([1995] 2010).

As is the case with many other indigenous groups, Greenlanders have also suffered from an ethnographic worship of their "original" culture – a "cult" which sometimes may well have been motivated by the best of intentions, but which has nonetheless changed or destroyed the Inuits' relation to their own traditions through the Western ethnographer's *ethnoaestheticzation* of these traditions' values and artefacts. For the young Greenlandic artist of today, according to Pia Arke, the conditions "[...] are no longer those of the unspoiled Eskimo life, but rather the making of it into a cult" (Arke 2012, 21). Paradoxically enough, this means that young Greenlandic artists have no way around relating to the Western *ethnoaesthetics*. Indeed, they are bound to work *with* it if they want to work from an "authentic" Greenlandic perspective, and Arke continues: "The ethnics intensify their ethno-aesthetics, expose it to itself, take control of it in a confusing operation of reproductions, thematizations and loving suppression" (Arke 2012, 21).

One of the young artists that Pia Arke mentions in *Ethno-Aesthetics* is none other than Jessie Kleemann. We shall now see exactly how the *confusing operation of reproductions, thematizations and loving suppression* is articulated in her double poem "Eskimuuara/Eskimother".[4] Here it is in its English version (the other version is in Greenlandic):

> My eskimother
> Is like the baby I
> Carry on my back
> Head held high
> Proud
> Like a real orsoq-Inuit
> I smell good and
> Strong as my lovely eskimother
> My eskimothertongue
> Is written in Danish through and through
> Orville's learning it in English
> Because it's almost Alive
> So alive that it's seen as
> One of the endangered species
> As the DNA you cannot read
> Yourself into
> My eskibaby
> Smells and tastes good
> Like orsoqbacon on top
> Of the roast of seal
> That is not in danger of extinction
> Eeri is written in Greenlandic here
> Just as you know it
> My eskimothertongue says what there's to read.
>
> (Kleemann 2012)

This is a compact text which needs some unfolding and contextualization, but as the reader may have noticed, Jessie Kleemann's poem thematizes a phenomenon that I have already specified as ambivalent: the link between the mother tongue and identity. When the poem speaks of an "eskimothertongue", this is an intrinsically hybrid (and ironic) construction. The word "Eskimo" is a derivation of the Jesuits' word for Inuit, as the Jesuits referred to Inuits as "the excommunicated", a people located completely outside the Christian church; the word "excommuniqué" quickly became worn down or garbled into "Eskimo". Thus, "Eskimo" is both a foreign word to the Inuits themselves and a name that has been extensively used as a tool of negative categorization.

What the poem's composite "eskimothertongue" points to is that the Greenlandic language, or Inuit languages, is a language deeply influenced by colonial categorizations – not least because it was Danish colonizers who codified Greenlandic so that it could become a written language: "My eskimothertongue / Is written in Danish through and through."

The poem stages the tradition originating from "the mother" (a tradition that is oral, and therefore different from the Danish (written) language) as something which has an almost physiological or intimate quality. The poem compares the lyrical subject's relation to the mother tongue to "carrying a baby on her back", which is the traditional Inuit way of taking care of small infants. The traditional Greenlandic costume-for-mothers, the *ammat*, has a device on the back so that the child can sit against the mother's naked skin; thus, the *ammat* delivers contact and warmth to the baby.

What Kleemann's poem does is to effect a reversal of tradition, as it places the "eskimothertongue" (i.e. both the ancestral Inuit culture and the legacy of the colonial power) on the back of the post-colonial "I", who can then proudly carry both her mother's language and the Jesuit word for inuit, *eski*, "Like a real orsoq-Inuit".

Even though there is no "original" language in this text, since the "eskimothertongue" "is written in Danish through and through", there is an "original" inuit.

The "Orville" mentioned here is most likely the puppet of a famous (English) ventriloquist, and this might be a sarcastic reference to the colonized voice as a kind of puppet speech, since it really comes from the puppeteer/ventriloquist and not from the puppet itself. In addition to the right-handed, post-colonial criticism implied by this reference, it might also be interesting that the ventriloquist's speech is somehow derived from the belly: the seat of the unborn child.

The poem's final stanzas speak of "my eskibaby / which smells and tastes / good like orsoqbacon on top of / roasted seal". The word "orsoq" means blubber and the smell of blubber is wonderful if you are accustomed to it, but it might also be experienced as a rather crude food that is difficult to digest if one is not a native eater. Food is a strong component in the building of national identities, of course. In Greenland, there is a word for food prepared from Greenlandic ingredients, *kalaaliminiq*, which can be loosely translated as "a piece of Greenlander".

However, "orsoqbacon" is also a hybrid and ambivalent construction. In the fashionable "New Nordic" cuisine, imagine blubber being served exactly as "blubber-bacon" in tiny portions on top of a less "intimidating" dish. Furthermore, bacon is perhaps the most famous export item originating from Denmark (with the exception of porn possibly).

Blubber-bacon is therefore also an "eeri[e]" food, just as "eeri[e]" as the situation which the poem describes: the relationship between Greenlandic tradition, the mother tongue on the back which is also a burden to carry, and the post-colonial situation, which transforms this tradition into something fine and edible like a delicious baby with a little bacon on top that will hide the strong taste of blubber.

But "eeri", most importantly, is also a letter. It is a notation of how the letter "r" has to be pronounced in Greenlandic so the letter "r" is actually written in Greenlandic here.

The Greenlandic language is written with the Latin alphabet and the transcription system used was, as I mentioned, invented by Danish linguists. This is not always logical, as Greenlandic phonetics have very little in common with Danish phonetics. "R" is an important letter in Danish – and for that matter in Swedish, Norwegian, English and so on. One cannot, however, pronounce a single "r" in Greenlandic, since it is a hiatus – a tongue-breaker – which is why there must always be an "i" or "u" attached to it. Thus, "eeri" is therefore *really* "r" in Greenlandic, which means that the poem ends with an ambivalent and complex, yet nevertheless affirmative, gesture or statement: "my eskimothertongue *says* what there is to read".

Thus, the ambivalence of the Inuit experience, which is spoken out by the poem's "eskimothertongue" which represents both oral Inuit tradition *and* the language of the colonizers, is stressed. The post-colonial work consists, as Pia Arke asserted, not just of reconstructing a lost precolonial state, however important that might be. The Greenlandic artist must be as courageous as this poem is courageous. She, the Greenlandic artist, must dare to expose the anthropological gaze to itself in order to take control of it. Ambiguity – in this case, linguistic ambiguity – is her very field of investigation. The border between the internalized ethnographic gaze and the external object of this gaze is permeable and so it stays with the trouble, as prescribed by Klein (and Donna Haraway), by creating a "synthesis between feelings of love and destructive impulses towards one and the same object", as Klein puts it: an external object which in this case is the colonized Inuit tradition incarnated by the transformation of the mother tongue into a hybrid "eskimothertongue".

The good breast is the nourishing "orsoq", and the bad breast is the destructive "bacon" – but it is a bacon which is also "delicious". The inuit tradition is a "mother", but it is *also* a burden to be carried on the back. The poem operates exactly as the ethnoaesthetics described by Pia Arke: It calls forth *"a confusing operation of reproductions, thematizations and loving suppression"*. The border between the "orsoq" and the "bacon" is not a barrier. It is – as strong poetry should be – as permeable as naked skin.

White Milk from the Bad Breast[5] – Athena Farrokhzad's *White Blight (Vitsvit)*

Athena Farrokhzad's collection of poems, *Vitsvit* (2013; *White Blight*, 2015), also questions the relation between language and breastfeeding. *Vitsvit* takes its point of departure in a refugee experience. A family has fled from Iran to Sweden and the mother's milk becomes an almost violently ambivalent symbol of the family's readiness towards acculturation and adaptation. This is a process described in the terms of "a mother feeding a child with the whiteness[6] of (Swedish) language":

>My family arrived here in a Marxist tradition
>
>My mother immediately filled the house with Santa knick-knacks
>Weighed the pros and cons of the plastic Christmas tree
>as if the problem were hers
>
>During the day she distinguished between long and short vowels
>as if the sounds that came out of her mouth
>could wash the olive oil from her skin
>
>My mother let the bleach run through her syntax
>On the other side of punctuation her syllables became whiter
>than a winter in Norrland
>
>My mother built us a future consisting of quantity of life
>In the suburban basement she lined up canned goods
>as if preparing for a war
>
>In the evenings she searched for recipes and peeled potatoes
>as if it were her history inscribed
>in the Jansson's temptation casserole
>
>To think that I sucked at those breasts
>To think that she put her barbarism in my mouth.[7]
>
>(Farrokhzad [2013] 2015; trans. Jennifer Hayashida)

The poem's articulation of the relation between mother, child and language is complex, but the first thing to note is that the unifying, yet unnamed, referent for the poem is the *mother tongue*. By contrast, the expression, very much connected to this, of "receiving something along with one's mother's milk" – an idiomatic expression in the Scandinavian language which is meant to suggest that a relationship to a language, or indeed to anything else, is the deepest one possible – is quite explicitly present ("Tänk att jag sög på de brösten" / "To think that I sucked at those breasts").

The "mother" of the poem is above all described as a place of accumulated *nutrition*: the mother "fyllde huset" ("filled the house"), hoarded food ("canned goods") and cooked ("peeling potatoes") – and further breastfed and nourished the child with her milk. The milk must be the Swedish language, which shares with the mother's milk the feature of being "white", and so, in this connection it is the "tongue" which the child receives from its mother. But the milk of the "white" language is not nourishing milk. On the contrary, it has a corrosive influence on the first language (which must here be supposed to be the mother's first language, an Iranian language), which the child precisely does not seem to receive in any satisfactory manner since the mother has decided to teach herself and the child the new language, the second language.

The mother's personal acquisition of the language is described as a cleansing process: she has to learn how to differentiate between short and long vowels, as well as a new syntactical pattern, in order to speak properly (or, in the corresponding Scandinavian idiomatic expression, "to speak purely"; compare the German: *ein reines Deutsch sprechen*).

The mother's attempt at linguistic assimilation separates the child from the properly nourishing ascendance ("olivoljan"/"the olive oil"), thereby establishing a border between what is nourishing and what is corrosive ("blekmedlet"/"the bleach"), which seems quite *fixed* ("På dagarna skiljde hon" / "During the day she distinguished"; "på andra sidan skiljetecknet" / "On the other side of punctuation").

The mother's language-milk, then, does not nourish the child. Quite the contrary, it is life-threatening to the child and thus has to stem from the "bad" breast, the breast which (according to Klein) is "the persecuting breast", present in the poem both as an external object and as an internalized object: "Tänk att jag sög på de brösten" / "To think that I sucked at those breasts" (external object), "Tänk att hon stoppade sitt barbari i min mun" / "To think that she put her barbarism in my mouth" (internal object).

The fact that the poem uses the verb "att stoppa" (which is much stronger than "to put" – "to stuff" would have been closer to the Swedish original) is interesting, and so is the presence of the loanword (or to use the corresponding Scandinavian term, "the foreign word"; compare the

German: *Fremdwort*) "barbari". To stuff something into somebody or something is an action connected with coercion. In this case it even connotes forced feeding, an action that consequently fosters aggression in the poem's "I" – compare with the aggressive repetition of "Tänk att" / "To think that". Aggression, according to Klein, is an integral component to the paranoid-schizoid position, making the child bite its mother's breast: bite the hand that feeds it – one might add – since the father-voice in *Vitsvit* on a later occasion gives his daughter the following piece of advice: "tala det språk som betalar ditt bröd" / "Speak the language that pays for your bread" (Farrokhzad 2013, 59). The logic of this image (also economical) resembles the metaphors traditionally surrounding breastfeeding, since it is possible, as is well known, to "nurture a snake by one's bosom". Furthermore, Farrokhzad here seems to quote Billie Holliday, a point to which we shall return in a little while.

The breastfed snake, unlike the *mother tongue*, is an image which is very much traceable to classical antiquity. In Aeschylus' *Oresteia*, Clytemnestra dreams that a snake is sucking blood at her breast, which, of course, portends Orestes' murder of his own mother. We have seen Farrokhzad's poem's "I" (symbolically) biting her mother's breast through the aggressive repetition of "Tänk att", and the snappish relationship to the breast is also evident in the poem's generally aggressive valorization of the mother's milk as the carrier of a destructive, corrosive, language.

The strain of images established in the poem thus seems closely connected to the ambivalent workings of primary object-relations. It comes only a little short of landing squarely on its "bad" side, that is, in pure, negative death drive, due to the final line which may offer a reopening of the border: "To think that she put [*stoppade*] her barbarism in my mouth." At first glance, this line could be read as fury culminating, but Farrokhzad's texts are by and large more complex than that. "Barbari" is a loan from the Greek βαρβαρος, an onomatopoetic word designating every other tongue than the Greek one, the speech of strangers being heard as a *bar-bar* ("blah blah"), whereby the word "barbarian" came to signify all peoples who were not Hellenic. This was the case with the Persians, the Greeks' arch-enemy. In *The Persians* of Aeschylus, which depicts the Greek naval victory over the Persians at the battle of Salamis (480 BCE), we have, according to Edward Said, an early example of Western Orientalism in the rendering of the greedy, immensely rich and effeminate Persian "barbarians". A reference to this locus classicus by Said is not at all improbable in a volume of poetry dedicated to racism, which quotes among others Frantz Fanon and Audre Lorde.

The "barbarian" language, which the I's mother stuffs into her mouth, according to this ironic logic, ends up representing *both* the first language (which we may assume is an Iranian language) as a language that has been the object of Orientalization *and* the second language (which is Swedish). The fact that we are told later on that the I is named after "the cradle of civilization" does not make things any more univocal, to put it mildly.

Poetically speaking, the linguistic status of barbarian stays in an open field; language is other, but it is also the same, in a gesture by which the poem cannot be said to definitely land on the side of the bad breast (the side of pure aggression). The border between what is corrosive and what is nourishing, articulated here in relation to "the mother", is not (just) a barrier – it may be crossed. Staying in the complex pain spot is, however, neither without cost nor without pain: "Min morbror sa: Om du inte darrar när du korsar en gräns / är det inte gränsen du har korsat" / "My uncle said: If you do not tremble when you cross a border / it is not the border you have crossed" (Farrokhzad 2013, 52).

The motive of the mother's milk returns on several occasions throughout the text, first and foremost in a chain of sentences culminating in a quotation of Paul Celan's "Todesfuge" (Death fugue), which mentions "Black milk of dawn" (Schwarze Milch der Frühe / Svarta gryningsmjölk):

My father said: To those who have more will be given
and from those who lack even more will be taken
My mother said: Take some more milk before it turns

My mother said: Wouldn't it be strange to feel
a single night like this one
my language in your mouth
[...]
My mother handed the glass to her mother and said: Now we
 are even
Here is the milk back
[...]
My mother said: If we meet again we will not let on that we
 knew each other
when you were hungry and it was I who carried the milk
[...]
My brother said: Black milk of dawn, we drink you at night.[8]
 (Farrokhzad [2013] 2015, 22, 24, 26, 27)

Here, too, the milk is laden with a strong ambivalence, which is further strengthened through the passage's pronounced polyphony, a polyphony which is the general mode of the volume *Vitsvit*.[9]

The father appears to quote Matthew 13:12, where Jesus answers the disciples' question why he is speaking in similes: "For whosoever hath, to him shall be given, and he shall have more abundance: but whosoever hath not, from him shall be taken away even that he hath." Jesus's dictum is susceptible to a radical interpretation, of course, since it accords well with Marx's analysis of the exploitative logic of capitalism (on several occasions the book's father is given to Marxist reasoning), but another voice seems to resound here, namely that of Billie Holiday, thus changing the significance of this utterance.

Holiday's signature song "God Bless the Child" quotes Matthew 13:12. While it dates from 1939, the text is older and was written by Holliday herself, supposedly after a quarrel over money with her mother. Holiday's interpretation of the Gospel is chilling: "Yes, the strong gets more / While the weak ones fade / Empty pockets don't ever make the grade." The song (desperately) stresses the futility of trusting in biological relatedness to necessarily lead to intrafamilial economic solidarity, something that can be seen in the song's familiar refrain: "Mama may have, Papa may have / But God bless the child that's got his own." Holiday, also the singer of "Strange Fruit", seems (like Said) a likely reference in a volume of poetry which is about racism. Holiday's song moreover depicts a relationship that is exactly resemblant of the relationship in which the poetry volume's "I" is placed: family ties are no guarantee of survival, as one must become one's own origin(ator) and go beyond the compelling structure of an unequal exchange. *Vitsvit* gives the paradoxical formulation of a wish to return the mother's milk to its source. Its libidinal economics are described in the following way in Holiday's song: "You can help yourself / but don't take too much", a phrase with as threatening a sound as that of the pressing mother's voice in *Vitsvit*: "Ta lite mer mjölk innan den härsknar" / "Take some more milk before it turns".

The chain of images quoted above also contains a reference to another poem, Edith Södergran's "Dagen svalnar" (The day cools), which says:

> It would be strange to feel
> a single night like this one
> your heavy head against my breast.[10]

And the corresponding rewriting in *Vitsvit*:

> My mother said: Wouldn't it be strange to feel
> a single night like this one
> my language in your mouth.[11]
>
> (Farrokhzad [2013] 2015)

Södergran's love poem is transformed into a poem about the language transfer of breastfeeding, which is a logical change for several reasons. First, Södergran's line "ditt tunga huvud mot mitt bröst" / "your heavy head against my breast" depicts a situation in which the loved one is in a sense placed in the role of a child. Secondly, Södergran's mother tongue is Swedish, but she grew up in Saint Petersburg, where she went to a German school. This gives one explanation why she wrote her first poems in German – a language seemingly less alien to her than the Swedish in which she would later write the bulk of her poetry. Södergran's bilingual experience is shared by the lyrical "I" of *Vitsvit*, of course. In *Vitsvit*, those lines are also about a "strange" experience of love – "mitt språk i din mun" / "my language in your mouth" – which stresses both the physical closeness (orality) of the relation between mother and daughter ("mun" / "mouth") and the logic of exchange that is likewise expressed by this relation, once more an ambiguous construction, to put it mildly.

The milk passage, then, ends by quoting Celan, who is a poet of exile *par excellence*, since he felt compelled to write his poems in a language that was also "die Sprache der Täter", the language of the perpetrators. Celan's famous metaphor, the black milk of dawn,[12] might even be what occasions *Vitsvit* to frame a reckoning in terms of "milk". In the notes to his famous Meridian text, Celan describes his image as an anti-metaphor: "das ist keine Redefigur und kein Oxymoron mehr, das ist Wirklichkeit" (Celan 1999, 158, underscore in original). A similarly anti-metaphorical feeling also emerges when reading *Vitsvit*. This might be the case because of the fact that this volume, like Celan's "Todesfuge", is very much directed by what might nowadays be termed post-productive principles. *Vitsvit* is not a piece of literary confessionalism. The text gathers bits and pieces (quotations, expressions, experiences) into a mirror image of the reality of racism – just like Celan's poem gathers bits and pieces of the real components of the Holocaust into a memorial (he calls the poem his mother's tombstone in a letter to Ingeborg Bachmann) for all the victims of Nazism (Friis 2017). I see no reason to question the fact that Celan regards his image as a piece of reality. But it is also evident that, technically speaking, "black milk" *is* an oxymoron. Precisely that figure of speech is characterized by a certain form of productivity.[13] The border between the two elements in the figuration is permeable. The point of tension in an oxymoron is irresolvable, and the lack of solvability exemplifies *Vitsvit*'s treatment of its subject matter, which is just as it should be, if we were to ask Melanie Klein, Pia Arke or Jessie Kleemann. Being in and between two languages and two cultures (or more) is not a situation that is given a dichotomical formulation, if it has to be formulated truthfully. It *is* oxymoronical, it is a black sun – and so must the poetry be that tries to give it a form.

Jessie Kleemann's and Athena Farrokhzad's renegotiations of the *mother tongue* are obviously very different, but they are united by a courageous readiness to rearticulate the link between mother and tongue as an ambivalent and yet – or at least so it seems – unavoidable figure: the mother tongue is at the same time a good and a bad breast. What these poets do is expose that idea to itself by finding alternative – sometimes disturbing – routes through the pain of that experience, all the while insisting on the bodily and intimate quality of the matter. Their poetry can be read as (non-linear) works of mourning, but also as pointing to possible ways of grasping/dealing with/analysing specific post-colonial and migratory experiences in the Nordic region of today.

I Am a Wall, and My Breasts Like Towers – Ursula Andkjær Olsen's *Third-Millenium Heart*

The ambivalence of the mother tongue is not just an issue for the poets that in practice live in and between several languages. It also finds more univocally feminist expressions, as in Ursula Andkjær Olsen's *Det 3. årtusinds hjerte* (2012), translated into English as *Third-Millenium Heart* (2017). Here, the transfer of language from mother to child, the "gift" of language which the child receives, is largely described in terms of a bodily anchored process: "Alt er som grebet ud af min krop" (Olsen 2012, 79) / "Everything seems to have been snatched out of my body" (Olsen [2012] 2017, 73). Moreover, the body from which language is formed is a specific body, namely that of pregnancy.

Pregnancy as a cultural sign or a cultural unit is interpreted through the bodily experience, here of course the female bodily experience connected to fertilization, pregnancy, labour and breastfeeding. In Andkjær Olsen's volume of poetry, breastfeeding is written in such a manner that it comes to include the notion that culture enters along with mother's milk; this naturally depends on the notion that one's first language is a *mother* tongue. Another strain of images that runs through *Det 3. årtusindes hjerte* is based on a quote from Song of Solomon 8:10: "I am a wall, and my breasts like towers." Here follows an example from a suite of poems in the volume, "Darling Gloria" (Olsen [2012] 2017), which is tender in every sense of the word. What is said is spoken from a mother to a child:

> I am everything
> you are
> I am warmth, shelter, food.
>
> You ascend
> to drink from sun and moon.
>
> Before, I would have dreamt of a weapon
> to kill the enemy; now I need a gun to shoot
> you, before anyone harms a hair on your head
>
> The way
>
> I am the house, you are inside me
> as if I were a house.
> The way
>
> I am the castle, yes, I am
> sinking into rubble, I won't be doing that
> I just gained my towers, after all.

I am. God is the lifting of differences between part and whole.
The structure of breastfeeding is divine, we are God, every day

GLORIA.

Every hour there's milk that
hasn't seen the light of day
like the babel and ivory

that it is.[14]
(Olsen [2012] 2017, 91–92; trans by Katrine Øgård Jensen)

Here we find the Kleinian ambivalence of breastfeeding in a concentrated form. On the one hand, it is recreating a dyadic pre-natal state, in which the difference between mother and child has been abolished: "Gud er ophævelsen af forskellen på del og helhed" / "God is the lifting of differences between part and whole." On the other hand, the breasts are two towers – one an ivory tower, the other the Tower of Babel – thus pointing to two cultural topoi: the ivory tower as the bastion of high culture (and of poetry) and the Tower of Babel as a monument to cultural arrogance, an arrogance paradoxically punished with multilingualism. Both towers are pulled down and crushed elsewhere in the text, but in this passage they are intact. To give the child language, language which in the book is repeatedly called "structure", is made to parallel breastfeeding. The acquisition of a language is an instrument of cultivation – to speak a language is to take on a world, a culture, Fanon says – giving rise to what Freud calls "das Unbehagen in der Kultur" ("the discontent of civilization"). The following passage in *Det 3.årtusindes hjerte* (Olsen [2012] 2017) states:

> The towers are there already; you need to
> build the bridges, stairs. Remember, the towers are the cradle,
>   cradle
> of culture. Warm towers. Proud. You need to build a
> complex being with bridges and passages
> transporting bodies around
> increasingly fleeting and flexible patterns
> around the overflow of means, of social control
> to be a society-suckling, political mammal.[15]
> (Olsen [2012] 2017, 102)

To become a "society-suckling, political mammal" is what the nexus-mother's milk (acculturation) implies here. We can be confident in labelling this a political statement about what also forms part of the symbolic connection between language acquisition and breastfeeding.

A "society-suckling, political mammal" is a figure that points precisely to the implications of "societality" for the individual. Society is not the entire world, but a set of regulations to which the individual adapts. This adaptation Freud considered necessary, but he nevertheless was wary of its possible aggression-provoking effects – its repression of the individual's libido. If we connect this concern with the symbolization of the purported transfer of "culture" to the child by the maternal body, and we read Andkjær Olsen's text as informed by a feminist stance, it is clear that when the *Muttersprache* of romantic nationalism "genders" the acquisition of language, this is not only a question of conferring upon this acquisition a positive, comforting quality. This particular "gendering" of learning has the further consequence of making it possible to direct any aggression, triggered by limitations placed upon the libido's enactments, against women.

Of course, the breasts as "two towers" also points to Klein's theory that the breastfed infant imaginarily divides the mother's breasts into the good breast (the breast that gives satisfaction) and the bad breast (the breast that withdraws from the child), here finding a parallel in the "good" ivory breast, which stimulates culture, and the "bad" Babel breast, which is destructive of culture.

As already mentioned, the infant at a later state discovers that the good and the bad breast are not separate objects, but both belong to the actual body of the mother, something that creates a dividedness or ambivalence with respect to the child's perception of real bodies: the real, actual mother-body is both good and bad. This fundamental dividedness or ambivalence is present in *Det 3. årtusindes hjerte* in a form that in a most palpable manner can be deciphered from Klein's theorization of the imaginary value of the breasts, something which is not least visible in the aggressively feminist battle suite: "Forestillingen om RED" / "The Idea of RED":

> You all dream of freedom
> it's simple
> liberate your cocks in me
> You search my name and get 20,000 tits
> Good tits
> and bad tits.
> 20,000.
> I want to be more.
> Only an unfertilized egg can stay whole.
> Every split kingdom is a wasteland.
> I want to be every split kingdom:
> gain twice the towers.[16]
>
> (Olsen [2012] 2017, 123–124)

Quite apart from the rather funny juxtaposition of "tits" and "[Google] hits", which seems like a sarcastic comment on what most people are actually googling on the internet (porn and their own name), we also get a feminist affirmation of the right to let the pregnant body be "a split kingdom" – a kingdom divided – a right which is not a given in a biopolitical society busy categorizing and streamlining its citizens.

Jessie Kleemann, Athena Farrokhzad and Ursula Andkjær Olsen use experiences rooted in the female body and the heavy symbolicity that it has prompted – the mother tongue – as the point of departure for a critique of society and of civilization. This is also a critique of language when they poetically explore what this notion of the mother tongue actually carries with it in terms of division, confusion, pain and profound ambivalence. It is possible that, as Yildiz suggests, we have to move "beyond the idea of the Mother Tongue", but as one can see in the poetical works treated here, which address and explore the idea of the mother tongue in different ways, the relation between the mother and language is not one to unproblematically be left behind, neither from post-colonial, migratory nor gender perspectives. In these texts the relation between the mother and language/culture, a relation grounded in the ambivalence of breastfeeding, is configured as a crossing of borders that actually makes you shiver, or, in Arke's words, as "a confusing operation of reproductions, thematizations and loving suppression". This is exactly the place in which it is necessary to have the courage to tarry and whence exploration has to set out, if we are to move away from the monolingual and monocultural ideal that marks (and mars) the self-images of the Nordic countries.

Notes

1 See also Cestaro (2003). The quote in *De Vulgari Eloquentia* (1.1) goes like this in English:

> I declare that vernacular language is that which we learn without any formal instruction, by imitating our nurses. There also exists another kind of language, at one remove from us, which the Romans called *gramatica*. The Greeks and some – but not all – other peoples also have this secondary kind of language. Few, however, achieve complete fluency in it, since knowledge of its rules and theory can only be developed through dedication to a lengthy course of study. Of these two kinds of language, the more noble is the vernacular: first, because it was the language originally used by the human race; second, because the whole world employs it, though with different pronunciations and using different words; and third because it is natural to us, while the other is, in contrast, artificial. And this more noble kind of language is what I intend to discuss.

2 For an interesting take on Klein's view on eating disorders as connected to fear of internal persecution, see Elizabeth A. Wilson's book *Gut Feminism* (2015).

3 The best summary of Pia Arke's work is *TUPILAKOSAURUS: An Incomplete(able) Survey of Pia Arke's Artistic Work and Research* (2012). My textual references are to the booklet *Ethno-Aesthetics/Etnoæstetik* ([1995] 2010), where the text is printed in English, Greenlandic and Danish.
4 Both the Greenlandic and the English version of Kleemann's poem can be found in *Jessie Kleemann – Qivittoq* (2012).
5 "White milk from the bad breast" is a line borrowed from Danish poet Mette Moestrup's 2012 volume *Dø løgn, dø* (Die, lie, die). The first, long suite is simply called "White milk from the evil breast". The volume's central theme is whiteness, not in the sense of the great, white, Modernist nothingness, but in the sense of white skin colour and its past and current implications of a historical, social and symbolic nature. Whiteness is not only a skin colour, since "whiteness" as a concept forms an entire mindset, reflecting the "racial" division of people in master/slave categories in imperialism and colonialism, forming the basis of the well-known distinction between "us", who are the norm, and "them", who remain outside of this norm. The white milk from the evil breast in Moestrup's book becomes a metaphor for the violence of colonization: the experience of drinking white milk, that is, "whiteness" (language acquisition/acculturation) from a breast in whose formative power one is. This is exactly as seen in the example in Athena Farrokhzad's work.
6 Quite a lot has been written about the significance of the book's graphic appearance, namely, its being printed in white letters on black bars. See, for instance, Friis (2014) and Stenbeck (2017).
7 "Min familj anlände hit i en marxistisk idétradition

    Min mor fyllde genast huset med prydnadstomtar
    Vägde plastgranens för-och nackdelar mot varandra
    som om problemet vore hennes

    På dagarna skiljde hon mellan långa och korta vokaler
    som om ljuden som kom ur hennes mun
    kunde tvätta olivoljan ur huden

    Min mor lät blekmedlet rinna genom syntaxen
    på andra sidan skiljetecknet blev hennes stavelser vitare
    än en norrländsk vinter

    Min mor byggde oss en framtid av livskvantitet
    I förortsvillans källarförråd radade hon upp konservburkar
    som inför ett krig

    På kvällarna letade hon recept och skalade potatis
    som om det var hennes historia som fanns chiffrerad
    i Janssons frestelse

    Tänk att jag sög på de brösten
    Tänk att hon stoppade sitt barbari i min mun" (Farrokhzad 2013)

8 "Min far sa: Åt de som har ska vara givet
   och från de som saknar- ska ännu mer tas
   Min mor sa: Ta lite mer mjölk innan den härsknar

Min mor sa: Visst vore det underligt att känna
en enda natt som denna
mitt språk i din mun" (Farrokhzad 2013, 22)
"Min mor räckte glaset till sin mor och sa: Nu är vi kvitt"
Här har du mjölken tillbaka" (Farrokhzad 2013, 24)
"Min mor sa: Om vi mötes igen ska vi låtsas att vi inte kände varandra"
när du var hungrig och det var jag som bar på mjölken" (Farrokhzad 2013, 26)
"Min bror sa: Svarta gryningsmjölk, vi dricker dig om natten"
(Farrokhzad 2013, 27)

9 For instance, *Vitsvit* quotes Frantz Fanon, Audre Lorde, Beyoncé, Lady Gaga, Edith Södergran, Paul Celan and Forough Farrokzhad.
10 My translation. "Det vore underligt att känna, / en enda natt, en natt som denna, / ditt tunga huvud mot mitt bröst" (Södergran 1916).
11 "Min mor sa: Visst vore det underligt att känna
en enda natt som denna
mitt språk i din mun."
(Farrokhzad 2013, 22)

12 The "black milk" is in fact a Rose Ausländer quote. See my reading of *Todesfuge* as an intertextual machine in Friis (2017).
13 On the oxymoron as endless productivity, see Jakobson & Stegagno's "Les oxymores dialéctiques de Fernando Pessoa".
14 "Jeg er alt
du er
jeg er varme, beskyttelse, mad."
"Du letter
sol og måne, dem drikker du af
Før drømte jeg om et våben for at
dræbe fjenden, nu må jeg have en
gun for at kunne skyde dig, før nogen krummer
et hår på dit hoved.
Som
Jeg er huset, du er i mig
som i et hus.
Som
Jeg er det slot, ja, det er jeg,
der synker i grus, det gør jeg ikke,
jeg har jo lige fået tårne.
Jeg er. Gud er ophævelsen af forskel på del og helhed.
Amningens struktur er guddommelig, vi er Gud, hver dag.
GLORIA.
Hver time mælk som
ikke har set dagens lys, som det
babel og elfen
ben den er."
(Olsen 2012, 97–98)

15 "Tårnene står der, du skal
bygge broerne, trapper. Tårnene er jo kulturens
vugge, vugge. Varme tårne. Stolte. Du skal bygge et
kompliceret væsen med broer og passager til at
transportere legemer rundt i

stigende flygtige og fleksible mønstre
rundt i beherskelsesmidlernes
overflod, at være samfundspatte- og politisk dyr."

(Olsen 2012, 108)

16   "I drømmer om frihed, det er enkelt,
befri jeres pikke i mig
I søger mit navn, det giver 20.000 tits
Good tits
og bad tits.
20.000.
Jeg vil være mere
Kun et ubefrugtet æg kan forblive helt.
Ethvert rige i splid med sig selv lægges øde.
Jeg vil være ethvert rige i splid med sig
selv,
får tårne."

(Olsen 2012, 123-124)

Bibliography

Arke, Pia ([1995] 2010) *Ethno-Aesthetics/Etnoæstetik*. Copenhagen: Pia Arke Selskabet & Kuratorisk Aktion.
Arke, Pia (2012) *Tupilakosaurus: An Incomplete(able) Survey of Pia Arke's Artistic Work and Research*. Edited by Kuratorisk Aktion. Copenhagen: Kuratorisk Aktion.
Bonfiglio, Thomas (2010) *Mother Tongues and Nations: The Invention of the Native Speaker*. New York: De Gruyter Mouton.
Braidotti, Rosi (2011) *Nomadic Subjects*. New York: Columbia University Press.
Celan, Paul (1999) *Der Meridian. Endfassung, Vorstufen, Materialen*. Edited by Bernhard Böschenstein & Heino Schmull. Frankfurt: Suhrkamp.
Cestaro, Gary P. (2003) *Dante and the Grammar of the Nursing Body*. Notre Dame, IND: University of Notre Dame Press.
Farrokhzad, Athena (2013) *Vitsvit*. Stockholm: Albert Bonniers Förlag.
Farrokhzad, Athena ([2013] 2015) *White Blight*. Translated by Jennifer Hayashida. Brooklyn, NY: Argos Books.
Friis, Elisabeth (2014) Mörka Platser. *Lyrikvännen* 4, 9-18.
Friis, Elisabeth (2017) Intertextuality. In Mads Rosendahl Thomsen, Lasse Horne Kjældgaard, Lis Møller, Lilian Munk Rösing, Peter Simonsen & Dan Ringgaard (eds): *Literature: An Introduction to Theory and Analysis*. London: Bloomsbury Academic, 131-147.
Jakobson, Roman & Stegagno Picchio, Luciana (1968) Les oxymores dialectiques de Fernando Pessoa. *Langages* 12(3), 9-27.
Kleemann, Jessie (2012) Eskimuuara/Eskimother. In R. Broberg & Iben Mondrup (eds): *Jessie Kleeman – qivittoq, eqqarsaatersuutnik naatsumik allakkat, essays*. Vejby: Hurricane, 87-88.
Klein, Melanie (1952) Some Theoretical Conclusions Regarding the Emotional Life of the Infant. In Joan Riviere (ed.): *Developments in Psycho-Analysis*. London: The Hogarth Press, 198-237.
Moestrup, Mette (2012) *Dø løgn, dø*. Copenhagen: Gyldendal.

Olsen, Ursula Andkjær (2012) *Det 3. årtusindes hjerte.* Copenhagen: Gyldendal.
Olsen, Ursula Andkjær ([2012] 2017) *Third-Millenium Heart.* Translated by Katrine Øgård Jensen. Berlin & New York: Broken Dimanche Press & Action Books.
Said, Edward (1978) *Orientalism.* New York: Pantheon Books.
Södergran, Edith (1916): "Dagen svalnar...". Accessed January 14, 2019, http://runeberg.org/sodrgran/.
Sommer, Doris (2004) *Bilingual Aesthetics: A New Sentimental Education.* Durham, NC: Duke University Press.
Stenbeck, Evelina (2017) *Poesi som politik: Aktivistisk poetik hos Johannes Anyuru och Athena Farrokhzad.* Lund: Ellerströms.
Wilson, Elizabeth A. (2015) *Gut Feminism.* Durham, NC: Duke University Press.
Yildiz, Yasemin (2012) *Beyond the Mother Tongue: The Postmonolingual Condition.* New York: Fordham University Press.

17 The Small Mysteries of Code-switching

A Practitioner's Views on Comics and Multilingualism

Interview with Mika Lietzén by Ralf Kauranen

Mika Lietzén is a comics artist based in Turku, Finland. In addition to creating comics, Lietzén is also an illustrator, comics publisher, translator and letterer of comics. He has published multiple comics albums in Finnish as well as many shorter comics in various anthologies. His album *Elegia. Yksinäytöksinen uninäytelmä* (2008; Elegy: A dream play in one act) was published in French by Actes sud – l'An 2 in 2009. Lietzén and Pauli Kallio's *Kukkakauppiaan onnenpäivä* (2005) was published in English in *Finnish Comics Annual 2012* (Kallio & Lietzén 2012). Lietzén has been awarded three times in the Nordic Comics Competition in Kemi, and in 2016 he received a three-year artist grant from the Arts Promotion Centre Finland.

RK: Let's begin by shortly summarizing your career in the field of comics in more general terms and then move to the issue of multilingualism and comics, along with your views on that issue. *Lohikäärmeen varvas* (Lietzén 2003; The dragon's toe), published in 2003 by your own publishing moniker Asema Kustannus, which you run with Ville Ranta [another renowned Finnish comics artist], is your first book publication. What brought you to that point in comics artistry and business?

ML: I have always made comics, although I stopped doing them at the beginning of my high school years. I somehow lost interest. The break lasted until some point in my university studies, when I discovered Pauli Kallio and Christer Nuutinen's comic strip "Kramppeja ja nyrjähdyksiä" (Cramps and sprains), which showed me that comics don't need to be funny. Saying that is probably a bit cruel, but I mean that that comic showed that comics can be genuine and can tell about real things, rather than just tell jokes. Then, when I finished university and started working and moved from Turku to Helsinki, I suddenly had more spare time and ended up hanging out with the comics people there. The company of like-minded peers fed my renewed interest in comics. There were meetings for comics people in a café in Helsinki. That's where I met Ville Ranta for the first time, among others, as well as probably most of the comics folks that were active at the end of the 1990s and the beginning of the 2000s. In 2000, we started Asema Kustannus.

My first published comics were probably in the anthologies from the Arctic Comics Competition arranged in Kemi. Those publications, by the way, also included translations into Swedish (see also Kauranen's chapter in this volume). In 2000, I got second prize in the short story competition, and two years later I won first prize. Before the *Lohikäärmeen varvas* book, we – meaning Asema – had also published two issues, if I remember correctly, of the *Laikku* ("spot" in English) anthology. Yes, the first two issues were published in 2001 and 2002. The third and fourth issues were published at the same time in 2004. The third was delayed due to one person, who was supposed to do a story for the book, but never did it. The book was finally published without that story.

RK: Were you possibly this one person?

ML: No, no, by no means. I deny everything! But, yes, in fact I was to make a comics adaptation of the well-known Finland-Swedish author Kjell Westö's short story "Moster Elsie" (Aunt Elsie), or "Elsie-täti" in Finnish, published in the collection *Utslag och andra noveller* (1989; Rash and other short stories). I had even acquired permission for that, but it was just left undone. It's actually a really good short story. I think that it in fact had an effect on the story in *Lohikäärmeen varvas*. The short story, as well as my comic, is set in the archipelago. The Westö story is very different, but both have young main characters. That must have affected me, and I'm sure the Swedish-speaking milieu in Westö's story also inspired me. But the fact that *Lohikäärmeen varvas* takes place in the Swedish-speaking archipelago on the south-western coast of Finland also has a background in my spending a summer holiday as a child on the island of Korpo/Korppoo. The scenery is the same. Perhaps the bilingualism and the presence of the Swedish language in the otherwise Finnish-language comic comes from reading and working on the Westö short story. It would be wrong to say that it's only because of that, but it certainly was an inspiration.

The short story evoked my memories of those childhood summer vacations at the summer cottage of a friend of my father's. We fetched drinking water from the main island, and by the well there was an older woman, just like in *Lohikäärmeen varvas*, who spoke only Swedish. My parents didn't speak Swedish at all. I can remember the language difference, and that was perhaps the first time that I realized that there are people who speak different languages. I must have been four or five years old then. Much younger than the main character in my comic.

302 *Interview with Mika Lietzén by Ralf Kauranen*

Figure 17.1 Mika Lietzén, spread from *Lohikäärmeen varvas* (2003, np.). © Mika Lietzén.

RK: That incident is quite straightforwardly represented in the comic, with the little boy fetching water and meeting this woman, who not only speaks a foreign language but also has an extra thumb, making her a rather frightening figure in the boy's eyes (Figure 17.1).

ML: Yes, and the foot callus thing then is based on my grandmother. Everything is more or less based on experiences from my own life. The cat in the story, Benjamin, had been in a one-page story I'd made before; it was borrowed from my previous work. And the incident with the cat tipping the bucket of water also happened for real. We had our cat with us at the cottage. But of course the real cat didn't die like the cat in the story. There's a difference.

RK: I think the multilingualism of *Lohikäärmeen varvas* actually anticipates your later work. Thinking of your production, I find it striking that, compared to most other comics in the Finnish field, multilingualism, language contact or code-switching, and the fact that the characters often speak different languages are a bit of a trademark for you. It's not ever-present, in all stories, but still it's very common.

ML: No, not in all stories. It does not fit into everything. I suppose it basically comes from some kind of "childhood trauma", but I guess it's also inspired by movies, for example. It's an attempt to be realistic, I think, to display the fact that people actually do speak different languages, and that multiple cultures and languages are present in different situations. Simply not everyone always communicates with each other in the same language. It's a way of pursuing realism. Also, it adds some flavour to or spices up a story. I detest Finnish culture. I don't want to make comics about going to the sauna. Actually the whole sauna culture is exotic to me since I don't use the sauna. It happens perhaps when visiting my parents or occasionally in connection with parties or things like that. But it's not part of everyday life. And if you look at the books I have at home, they are all in English or some other language. I haven't read Finnish literature for a long time, or at least very little.

RK: What did you mean by the "childhood trauma" that you mentioned? Was that in reference to the incident in the archipelago?

ML: Well, it's not really a trauma, but more of an observation that must have stayed with me.

RK: Literary multilingualism has often been interpreted as a form of realism, a means of presenting real-life language use authentically in stories, simply because people very often do speak different languages.

ML: But there's also something else to it. I used the expression "spicing up", but you could also say it gives some kind of colour to a story. The language switch somehow enriches a story and breaks a calm surface. I think authors and comics artists want to mix things up and create some confusion, perhaps – if nothing else, at least – for their own excitement or inspiration. I know I think that stories become more interesting if there is someone who looks outside their own circle or reaches out a bit further to other cultures or other countries. It means that something doesn't happen "just here", but that there's a jump a bit further away, at least on the level of ideas.

Language switches are helpful when you want to share with the reader the confusion or disorientation that you can feel when, for example, on a holiday trip somewhere abroad where you don't speak the local language you suddenly realize that you don't even understand the most simple phrases or words of what is being said around you. Sharing with the reader the feeling about not understanding Russian, for example, can be acquired by the use of Russian text and Cyrillic letters in an otherwise Finnish comic. The reader is able to tell that the characters are communicating with each other, but what they say remains a mystery. I think that is interesting, that everything doesn't add up or is comprehensible. There needs to be some mysteries, small mysteries in the everyday, riddles which possibly remain without answers. The reader perhaps has some kind of understanding, perhaps based on the gestures of the characters or on the context, but the reader is forced into some kind of interpretative mode; she needs to think a little bit more or in various ways, rather than just reading and reading and reading further. The code-switching is a place where the reader needs to stop for a bit and study a bit more carefully. It's also a means of changing the pace of reading.

RK: I like the description of them as "small mysteries". Having read your comics and having paid attention to the language switches, I wouldn't say that those places are very dramatic or high points in

304 *Interview with Mika Lietzén by Ralf Kauranen*

Figure 17.2 Mika Lietzén, page from "Alkoholi" / "Alcohol" (in *Kaksi ja puoli novellia (Two and a Half Stories)* 2015, np.). © Mika Lietzén.

the stories. They aren't central driving forces in the stories, but really minor occurrences rather than turning points.

ML: I think I'm basically trying to make those spots as intelligible as possible. The switches occur rather naturally, I think. They resemble natural communication as much as it is rather easy to anticipate what is being said in exchanges in a dialogue. If someone says "hi!", it is possible to guess what kind of reply that gets. It's possible for the reader to know, based on the context, what the parts of dialogue in a "foreign" language – be it Russian, for example –mean. I'm thinking of the short story "Alkoholi" / "Alcohol" in the book *Kaksi ja puoli novellia (Two and a Half Stories)* (Lietzén 2015), in which there's a Russian character who at one point speaks Russian; he speaks Russian to his Russian pal (Figure 17.2). The reader who doesn't know Russian has possibly some kind of understanding of what he is saying, some idea that he is asking the other guy to bring something. The phrase in Russian is a likely continuation of what has been said in the preceding dialogue and not at all surprising in the context of the actions of the characters. But for the reader who isn't able to read Russian, a small mystery remains.

RK: A different kind of mystery is offered by your collection of short stories *Tarinoita lännestä. Neljä novellia* (Lietzén 2007; Stories from the West: Four short stories). The first three stories are in Finnish, and suddenly the fourth story ("Tarina Ruissalosta" (A story from Ruissalo)) begins – and mainly continues – in English, which may baffle the reader. Reading the story, of course, explains why English is used.

ML: Yes, I didn't want to add English translations to that book, but I wanted the book to have a part in English. Some Finnish artists were already then publishing comics entirely in English, but I didn't want to do that, at least not at that point. The fact is, I do work in English when writing my comics. Then I thought, why not keep the English in one story instead of translating it into Finnish? Also, there is some Finnish in that story as well, as the two English speakers, who are Canadian tourists in Finland, meet some Finnish-speaking characters (Figure 17.3). I also wanted to have some fun with the languages and the language contact, as one of the Finnish-speaking characters doesn't know English and the other one needs to translate, and something is left untranslated. But I guess I was trying for some kind of realism here as well.

RK: So, in *Lohikäärmeen varvas* we have Swedish, Russian is spoken in the short story "Alkoholi" / "Alcohol", and English is present in one of the stories from the West. Is that all, or is the linguistic scope even broader?

ML: I use some German in my latest book published both in Finnish and Swedish, *Jääkärit. Viisi tarinaa* or *Jägarna. Fem berättelser* (Lietzén 2017a; 2017b; The Finnish Jägers: Five stories), for example, in the story "Libau" [also published in English in this volume]. There are at least two lines in German in the book. In one case in "Libau", I wanted to accentuate the point that a German officer is cold and callous. I didn't want to use foul language in Finnish or Swedish, and therefore he speaks German when addressing the girl in the story. Even if the reader doesn't know German, I think the whole demeanour of the officer makes his standpoint clear. The second example is a German officer saying that the Finnish soldiers are to be removed from the frontline. In that book, I also use some gibberish.

RK: In the "Libau" story, you also thematize language and language contact, the themes of understanding and misunderstanding.

ML: The two main characters do not speak a common language, and German is a foreign language for both of them. The woman probably speaks Yiddish or Latvian, I'm not sure, perhaps Russian. Still,

Figure 17.3 Mika Lietzén, spread from "Tarina Ruissalosta" (in *Tarinoita lännestä. Neljä novellia*, 2007, np.). © Mika Lietzén.

although they speak different languages, they belong together and to the same group of people, whereas the German officer clearly is an "Other". He's cold, but he's also distant, and the switch in code and his speaking German perhaps accentuate this distance. While the other two characters possibly also have spoken German together, their speech is represented in Finnish. That the German officer's line isn't translated has the effect of disentangling him from the others. The German language perhaps also has this particular sound to it; it appears brusque.

RK: A stereotypical view of the Finnish (male) comics reader is, perhaps, that he's familiar with the German language from the British war comics in the *Korkeajännitys* (High voltage) comic books.

ML: Achtung, achtung! Scheisse! What do they say?

RK: Zum Teufel! Schweinhunde! Anyway, in your book *Minä olen saari* (Lietzén 2016; I am an island) we have a nice detail: on the final page of the comic we have small birds chirping in...

ML: In Sanskrit, yes. That's based on the last line of T. S. Eliot's "The Waste Land", which is "Shantih shantih shantih", repeating the word for peace three times, and I used Sanskrit for that. [See also Ahvenjärvi's chapter in this volume on Sigurd Skåden's play with the same phrase.] A reader might recognize that that book of mine is

Small Mysteries of Code-switching 307

faithful to the structure of "The Waste Land". There are five headings in the poem which are also to be found in my book. One heading is "A Game of Chess", which in the album is depicted in the form of a game of chess. And the book also starts with a motto from "The Waste Land", in English. At the end of the book you find the same lines in the comic, in my own free translation into Finnish. The idea with this motto is to give the reader the idea that the story follows the structure of "The Waste Land". It's not necessary to see this connection to be able to read the book; it's perhaps a remark that is a little bit elitist. If someone is interested in this connection, it is to be found there, but it's not necessary. It shares a lot of features with Eliot's poem: for example, some Arthurian themes and the legend of the Fisher King, who also appears in *Minä olen saari*. He offers a drink to the main protagonist, who declines, which is directly from the Arthurian legends. But from the point of view of the reader it's not necessary to get these intertextual references. It's an old idea I've had that it would be nice to re-interpret an old story in the vein of James Joyce's *Ulysses*, for instance. But it's perhaps a bit superficial. Anyway, I need to finish that work, as the publication shows a work in progress with some pages only in sketch form.

RK: Another work where you use a motto in another language than the book's main language is *Elegia. Yksinäytöksinen uninäytelmä*, which also includes an English translation of the dialogue at the end of the book.

ML: It's a quote from the poet Edith Södergran, in Swedish, yes. And a little Swedish is used in the comic as well. The story is again set somewhere in the archipelago. That explains why there's some Swedish. Another reason perhaps is the inspiration from August Strindberg.

RK: That comic seems very "Nordic", perhaps due to the use of Swedish, but also because of the importance of Nordic summer light and the visual references to Scandinavian artworks by Peder Severin Krøyer and Edvard Munch.

ML: Maybe I had a Nordic period at that point. My interests vary over time. If that's a Nordic work, then maybe *Minä olen saari* is a bit more American or Anglo-Saxon, not just because of the reference to Eliot, but visible in the protagonist's American muscle car and the American flag on his jacket sleeve. Also, the album *1986* (Lietzén 2014), I think, was a very American comic. A book called *Moje* that I'm working on at the moment, on film director Mauritz Stiller, again is a very Swedish thing. But Stiller was very mobile: he was in Helsinki, St. Petersburg, Stockholm and Hollywood, which I think is a very attractive thing to work with. Another thing I'm working on involves a Romanian beggar girl in a city that perhaps could be described as a somewhat futuristic Turku. Here my intention is to avoid the language issue, because I am unable to use Romanian, by presenting the main protagonist as mute. She won't be speaking at all in the story. But the story itself also has traits of a fantasy story from the silent movie era. I think silent movies have some kind of universal or multilingual quality to them, due to the lack of spoken language. With sound, movies became more attached to places and localities.

RK: You already said something about your working language being English. I'd like you to elaborate on that. Your first language and school language is Finnish, but you have studied English and have a degree in English language and literature from the University of Turku.

ML: Practically all literature that I read is in English, and I watch a lot of movies and television shows, and they all are – or at least 90 per cent is – in English. So, my literary language is English rather than Finnish. When writing dialogue for a comic, for example, it's much easier in English than in Finnish. If I work in Finnish I get fixated on details, but in English I'm able to work more with rhythm and the flow of the text. I think it also has a dimension of estrangement or detachment, that it feels more natural to write in English. When you read and hear a lot of dialogue in English, it seems easier to write it as well. Finnish is also perhaps a bit hard to use in small talk or dialogue. When seldom reading Finnish literature, parts of the dialogue often jar on the ears. The language doesn't feel familiar or like something I would use in everyday communication or hear around me. For instance, youth language seems fake. But in English I don't have the same problem. Maybe I'm not able to differentiate between all the nuances in English.

RK: This last work of yours on the Finnish Jägers, who were Finnish soldiers trained in Germany at the beginning of the 20th century and were, for example, involved in the Finnish Civil War in 1918, was published in Finnish and Swedish. But you originally wrote it in English, didn't you?

ML: Yes, I wrote it in English and then translated it into Finnish. The English language never ended up in the finished comic, but in my notebooks the stories are in English.

RK: So, what does a comic look like in your notebook?

ML: I write all the textual elements, narrative captions, dialogue, etc. non-stop, line for line, working out the rhythm of the text, but without any kinds of divisions vis-à-vis the visual layout. After that I divide the text into pages, what parts go into one page and what on the next, and what goes in each panel on the pages.

I usually also write the whole text in one sitting. Strangely perhaps, that also ends up being the final text in the completed comic. The first draft of the text ends up being the final version. Very seldom do I change something. Sometimes I may change the place of something or minor details, but overall the draft is the final version as well. That's how I work: I sit on things for a long time, and when I'm ready to put something to paper it is almost completed. I've thought about the rhythm and everything at that point.

RK: And the verbal elements always come to you before the visual aspects of the comic?

ML: Yes, the verbal is there first. I may add some comments to the text, such as remarks about a character doing something when uttering the words. Of course, those are references to the visual world of the comic. And if a character is silent or the goings-on in the comic aren't commented upon in words at some point of the story, I may add comments about what is happening while the silence lasts. I may imagine in my mind what the pages or individual panels may look like and what kinds of actions are depicted, but I don't write it down in the first draft of the story. I first try to create a rhythm for the verbal elements. Only after that do I think of panel separations and page layouts and what the comics pages are to look like. I do have some kind of, at least subconscious, idea of the whole and of the visual aspects, but I dissemble the ideas I have in the form of the verbal elements first.

RK: And the visual ideas, are they concerned with what is to be depicted in the panels as well as with page layouts?

ML: I think most often those come as a package. To use an example from the *Jääkärit* album, while writing I knew, for example, where I wanted to place a large image of a cat. I had an idea that at this point in the story the cat is to show its face to the reader. It's not so much that I think first in the form of verbal elements, but rather that that's my method: I draw out the textual elements first when breaking down the story.

Sometimes when writing a story there is a gap in my ideas concerning the visual execution; I have the verbal elements but no visual imagery. I know that this is something I need to tell, but there's a break in the visual sequence that needs to be filled. At that point, I may have to mull it over some more and think of what to show. It might end up a bit boring if the images show some action too straightforwardly. Instead of only having two characters talking to each other, which could be boring, what if I put a moving cat here in the foreground for the reader to follow on the page? There has to be some visual action as well. Those are the kinds of gaps that could exist in my drafts. On the other hand, at times I have really strong feelings about how to depict something, ideas that seem to come very easily.

RK: When you first write the story in English, are the language shifts already there in that version? And what about silent or wordless parts of the comic, which could be multiple pages? Are they also in place in the draft?

ML: Yes, the "foreign" language elements are already there. It's only that what ends up in Finnish in the comic is in English in the draft. An exception, of course, is if somebody is using English in the comic, then I've made a remark about that in the draft. The silent parts I mention in brackets in the draft. And at times the silent parts are the result of me deleting some verbal elements when I start drawing. If words aren't necessary, there is no point in using them.

RK: Since English comes so naturally to you when writing comics and you surround yourself with English-language literature, cinema and television, why do you not publish your comics in English, but in Finnish?

ML: I think I have to, living in Finland and all. I've been playing around with the idea of making comic books of the more fanzine type and that those perhaps could be in English. I think, however, that comics albums published here need to be in Finnish because of library sales, for example. And I'm not very keen on translations in subtitles. I'm not interested in them and they simply are visually ugly.

RK: Comics scholar Neil Cohn (2013) has suggested that there are different visual languages, and that comics are made in different visual languages. For instance, he separates "American visual language" and "Japanese visual language", which are furthermore divided into different dialects. We are in that sense involved with another kind of multilingualism of the comics field, in addition to different so-called natural, verbal languages being used in comics. Is this an idea you can identify with?

ML: Yes, for example, my book *1986*, containing a short horror and coming-of-age story, was an attempt to make an American comic or to use American visual language through the breaking of panel frames and working with page layout in the same way that is often done in DC or Marvel comics. It was a conscious attempt to use the gutters and let characters invade the empty spaces between panels and to adapt to an American visual language (Figure 17.4). On the other hand, *Elegia* is a very Nordic comic, perhaps a bit claustrophobic or closed, and an attempt to use the visual language of the theatre. That's also the case with *Tarinoita lännestä*. And in the *Moje* project I wish to cross the borders between comics and silent film. Different media have their own grammars, and comics can be told using languages with somewhat different grammars. Each comics project needs its own grammar and language, which delimits the storytelling but is also formed in that very same process. A comic needs to be stylistically coherent. It would be really hard to read and comprehend a story in which the grammar and style are changing, such as from those I use in *Elegia* to the ones in use in *1986*. There needs to be some rules that the storytelling is adapted to. A mixing of styles or grammars can, of course, be used as a device similar to language shifts, where the change in language – be it a natural,

Small Mysteries of Code-switching 311

Figure 17.4 Mika Lietzén, page from *1986* (2014, np.). © Mika Lietzén.

verbal language or a visual language – calls for the reader's attention. I think, however, that changes in the visual language are more radical than changes in verbal language.

Many comics artists change style from one project to another. Consider, for example, the Finnish comics artist Terhi Ekebom, whose visual style and visual grammar change in every book. I might not be as radical as she is, as the visual aspects in my comics perhaps aren't as emphasized as in hers. At least the changes between my projects aren't as easily detectable, but certainly the execution follows different logics to a certain degree. *Moje* is quite a radical shift from my recent comics, while also perhaps a return to the reduced or minimalistic language of *Elegia* and *Tarinoita lännestä*. But I enjoy that project, as the images are completely silent and I get to focus on the visual storytelling. The verbal elements are limited to a few in-between panels, to "intertitles" (to use the term from silent movies). I think the effect is really funny. In the imagery, for example, you get to accentuate the characters' facial expressions to create proper drama. And the text panels are bilingual in Finnish and Swedish, just like silent movies in Finland have traditionally been represented. The bilingualism comes very naturally, at least to those who are familiar with this tradition. Translation of the work would also be much simpler than that of many other comics, as it would be enough to digitally typeset the text frames.

RK: In addition to creating comics, you have been active as an editor and publisher of comics for quite a number of years. Asema Kustannus has published more than fifty books during its existence since 2000. You have published albums by individual artists as well as anthologies. Most works are by Finnish artists but you've also put out some translations of books by artists such as Lewis Trondheim, Gipi and, more recently, Berliac. More than a few of the Finnish-language books by Finnish artists have been published with added English translations. In all cases, I think, the translations are there as "subtitles" with the English language running in the bottom margins of the pages.

ML: Yes, but I'm not really sure if the translations have much value in the albums by individual artists, as our books don't travel that much outside of Finland. I think, for example, books by the now defunct Finnish publisher Huuda Huuda spread abroad much more and were better served by English translations. The publisher-artist Tommi Musturi of Huuda Huuda was much more active in taking books abroad – for example, in connection to exhibitions and festivals – than we have been. I really don't know what significance the added translations have in the books, since we don't sell that much outside Finland. Of course, when artists go somewhere, for example, in connection to an exhibition, they have the possibility of handing out books to non-Finnish readers as well. But I don't know anything about the amount of readers that would be dependent on and would be reading those translations. Perhaps someone into comics who was visiting Finland might happen to bring a book home if it had English subtitles. But it would be interesting to know how much the subtitle translations are read.

RK: Did you consider different means of presenting a comic multilingually or were the subtitles a self-evident option?

ML: I think that's something we learned from the Finnish *Napa* anthology and used right away in our *Laikku* anthology. I think the use of translations in anthologies is clearly motivated, since they have the function of presenting the work of multiple artists to new readers, perhaps also outside the local market. But in individual artists' albums, it's up to the artist to say whether he or she wants translations in the book. I have done some translations for our books, but I try to avoid that nowadays to lessen my workload. As editors, we obviously check the translations, perhaps made by the artists themselves, to see that they are okay. I've been playing with the idea that the translations would differ from the originals, a bit like Samuel Beckett did when writing in both English and French. It would be a bit in the vein of Monty Python to go against the expected and alter things. For example, instead of a translation you could present some kind of commentary on what's happening in the story. It could be a bit interesting to play around with these conventions on a metalevel.

Subtitles have also been used in more specific cases, such as when providing a translation of a single line in the dialogue. I'm thinking of Manuele Fior's *5,000 km Per Second*, published by Fantagraphics in 2016. There's a part in it that takes place in Norway, and the translation of a line in Norwegian is then provided below the panel. But I haven't felt the need to do this in my books when I've used a "foreign" language. Why not use Norwegian if a character is Norwegian-speaking? And why not leave it untranslated if the other characters do not know Norwegian? But it's obviously a question of whether you want the reader to be able to understand or if you want to provide the reader with the sensation of hearing a foreign language.

RK: And in your books you instead want to provide the reader with a feeling of estrangement, or non-comprehension before comprehension, through encounters with different languages and language shifts.

I'm wondering whether, on the one hand, the fact that the English language plays a significant role in your work process and, on the other hand, your approach to code-switching in your comics could be thought of as breaches in the traditionally very tight-knit connections between language, culture and nation. Your comics reach outside this totality with their multilingualism, and your own multilingual practices are a convincing affirmation of comics culture being post-national – although we might also ask whether comics culture ever was national. At least comics in Finland haven't been as significant a national symbol as prose fiction written in the one or two national languages.

Anyway, in your short story "Fia" (in *Kaksi pientä novellia* (Two small short stories); Lietzén 2012), there's a beautiful passage in which multilingualism is connected to a longing beyond national borders. The young woman Fia, working as a cashier in a supermarket, tries to get an older woman out of the shop because she thinks she's a bum and a nuisance (Figure 17.5). The older woman doesn't reply to any of Fia's ushering, prompting Fia to use multiple languages (Finnish, English and Swedish): "Etkö sä ymmärtänyt mitä mä sanoin? Ala vetää. / Understand? Get lost. Ulos, ut, out." ("Didn't you understand what I said? Get lost. / Understand? Get lost. Out, out, out.") Later on in the story, we find out that the older

Figure 17.5 Mika Lietzén, "Fia" (in *Kaksi pientä novellia* 2011), p. 8. © Mika Lietzén.

woman used to work in the supermarket. Through a flashback, we get to know her frustration with working there and her wish to leave: "Mä kyllä häivyn täältä. Pois. Amerikkaan tai edes Ruotsiin. Uusi elämä." ("I'll get out of here, I will. Away. To America or at least to Sweden. / A new life.") Here Fia's choice of languages is echoed in her predecessor's dreams of escaping the tediousness of her situation, which is also framed in terms of the national.

ML: There's a lot of reaching out outside of the Finnish borders in my comics and the language shifts are related to that. Among other things, they serve the function of creating a vision of far-away places or another place than the one where the characters actually are situated. There's quite a lot of longing for somewhere else in the stories. It could be related to my childhood experiences, growing up in a small place (Mynämäki), next to a field where there was nothing else. My childhood and teenage reading were a gateway from the countryside to more interesting worlds. That shows in my comics as well. But I don't know if I'm breaking the connections between language and nation. It seems such a self-evident fact that many languages are in use in a country. And certainly characters in my comics do not represent "their" national cultures, and language use is not necessarily tied to national belonging. Somebody speaking Italian doesn't necessarily represent Italy or Italian culture. I also think that national belonging or identity is a rather odd concept. Metalheads or manga fans in different locations around the globe may share much more with each other than they share with their national fellows or language groups. There are so many cultures based on anything else than belonging to a nation or a language group. Or at least these different cultures and forms of belonging are parallel. People have so many other interests than traditional national symbols, such as a flag or national hymn. In my album on the Jägers, I deal with nationalism to an extent. There are a lot of cats in the book, in every story, and in the end characters are gazing at the Finnish flag, which at that point, when Finland had gained independence, was a red flag with the yellow heraldic lion, a yellow feline. The nationalism of the period and the characters is represented by the small cats.

Bibliography

Cohn, Neil (2013) *The Visual Language of Comics: Introduction to the Structure and Cognition of Sequential Images*. London: Bloomsbury.
Kallio, Pauli & Lietzén, Mika (2005) *Kramppeja ja nyrjähdyksiä: Kukkakauppiaan onnenpäivä*. Helsinki: Arktinen Banaani.
Kallio, Pauli & Lietzén, Mika (2012) The Florist's Lucky Day. Trans. Viljami Jauhiainen. In Reija Sann (ed.): *Finnish Comics Annual 2012*. Helsinki: Huuda Huuda & Finnish Comics Society, 134–56.
Lietzén, Mika (2003) *Lohikäärmeen varvas*. Oulu: Asema.
Lietzén, Mika (2007) *Tarinoita lännestä. Neljä novellia*. Oulu: Asema.
Lietzén, Mika (2008) *Elegia. Yksinäytöksinen uninäytelmä. / Elegy. A Dream Play in One Act*. Oulu: Asema.
Lietzén, Mika (2009) *Élégie. Un songe en un acte*. Translated by Thierry Groensteen. Actes sud – l'An 2.
Lietzén, Mika (2012) *Kaksi pientä novellia*. Oulu: Asema.
Lietzén, Mika (2014) *1986*. Oulu: Asema.
Lietzén, Mika (2015) *Kaksi ja puoli novellia (Two and a Half Stories)*. Oulu: Asema.
Lietzén, Mika (2016) *Minä olen saari*. Turku: Mika Lietzén.
Lietzén, Mika (2017a) *Jägarna. Fem berättelser*. Translation by Semantix Finland. Vasa: Österbottens museum.
Lietzén, Mika (2017b) *Jääkärit. Viisi kertomusta*. Vaasa: Pohjanmaan museo.
Westö, Kjell (1989) *Utslag och andra noveller*. Lovisa: Alba.

18 1917 – Libau (Comics Short Story)

Mika Lietzén

Index

Note: *Italic* page numbers refer to figures and page numbers followed by "n" denote endnotes.

Abidin, Adel 40
Abu-Hanna, Umayya 16, 114; see also *Sinut*
acoustics of language 17, 180, 184, 187, 193
actor-network theory 5
adaptations 263
Aeschylus: *Oresteia* 288; *The Persians* 288
affiliation, Said's concept of 58, 59
Ahrenberg, Jac. 245
Ahvenjärvi, Kaisa 15
"Aicha" (Lundin's song) 172
Aikio, Inger-Mari 91, 97n3
Ala-Ojala, Sanna: *Ättä ääriolosuhteissa / Mama to the Max* 78–9, 79
Alexis, Petter 161
"Alkoholi" (in Lietzén's *Kaksi ja puoli novellia*) 304, *304*
Alli Jukolan tarina (The story of Alli Jukola) 274n1
alliterations 136, 233
allusion 246–50
Al-Nawas, Ahmed 29, 32, 34, 44n10
Amoc (Sámi rapper) 90
Andersson, Claes 132
Andersson Wretmark, Astrid 243
Andtbacka, Ralf 234–8
Anglophone novels 36
"Annie Lööf" (Lundin's song) 165
Anyuru, Johannes 161
appendices and subtitling 69
Arabic literature 14, 28–30, 37
Arabic-Nordic literature 34
Arke, Pia 282–3, 286, 295, 296n3; *Ethno-aesthetics* 282, 283

Arkielämää (Jotuni) 271
Asema Kustannus 300, 301
Asfaltsänglar (Holmström) 265
Ashcroft, Bill 111n2
Ash Wednesday (Eliot) 58
Asketernas väg (Colliander) 243
assemblages 11
Ättä ääriolosuhteissa / Mama to the Max (Ala-Ojala) 78–9, 79
Auerbach, Erich 57
Auringon asema (El Ramly) 115

"Backstage, Sámi Grand Prix" (Skåden's poem) 94–6
Bakhtiari, Marjaneh 115
Bakhtin, Mikhail 6–7, 110, 156, 265
Baltics see *Östersjöar. En dikt* (Tranströmer)
bambara language, in *Näkymättömät kädet* 215
Bankier, Joanna 179
Bara gudarna är nya (Anyuru) 161
barbarian language 288, 289
Barthes, Roland 280
Bassnet, Susan 41, 43
Bauman, Zygmunt 256
Beaty, Bart 66, 67
Bechdel test 268
Behschnitt, Wolfgang 9, 41
Benito, Ana 207
Berg, Aase 233–4, 238
Bergman, Ingmar 131
Bhabha, Homi K. 166
bilingualism 250, 312; in comics culture 68, 80–3; parallel 91; true 248–9

324 Index

bilingual simultaneity, in *Loss* (Berg) 233–4
biscriptalism 246–50
Blasim, Hassan 14, 27–8; awards 31, 37; "born translated" 33–7; and Comma Press 30–3; *Corpse Exhibition and Other Stories of Iraq* 31; *Digital Hats Game* 32; *The Iraqi Christ* 31, 32, 34, 37; *Iraq + 100* 31–2, 44n12; *The Madman of Freedom Square* 30–3; "New Finnish Literature" 38; "The Reality and the Record" 31; "A Refugee in the Paradise that is Europe" 29–30, 44n6; *The Shia's Poisoned Child* 32; "The Truck to Berlin" 34–5
Bonfiglio, Thomas 279–80
border(ing) 4, 48, 228; in Estonian literary field 49–52; multilingual comics publishing and 82–3; orders and 5; processes and practices of 11–20; Sakai's discussion of 176, 193; travel literature 111
"Borta i tankar" (Leiva Wenger) 229–32
Bourdieu, Pierre 27; symbolic capital 30
Boyaciaglu, Daniel 161
Bradley, Adam 153, 161
Braidotti, Rosi 282
Brennan, Timothy 60
Bronze Soldier conflict 50

Canto General (Neruda) 107
Carroll, Lewis 233
Casanova, Pascale 31; international literary space 27; literariness 36
Celan, Paul: "Todesfuge" 289, 291
censorship 32
Cervantes, Miguel de 212, 213
Chao, Manu: "Clandestino" 203–5
Ch'ien, Evelyn Nien-Ming 167, 169, 172
Chrysostom, John 254
code-switching 19–20, 90, 92, 115, 154, 155, 212, 200–315; concept of 6; Fix's definition of 188; multilingualism and 65, 90, 158; research on 108; in Skaden's poems 92–6
Coetzee, J. M. 8, 33
Cohn, Neil 310
Colliander, Tito 242–3; allusion, translation and commentary

246–50; heterolingual address 250–1; literary multilingualism and translingual life writing 245–6; memoirs 243–4; Orthodox Christian diasporic identity 253–7; poetry and mysticism 251–3
Columbus, Christopher 206, 215
Comma Press 30–3, 44n7
Comment tu tchatches! (How you talk!) 158
Connor, Stephen 180
consecration 27, 31, 36
contemporary Nordic poetry, mother tongue in 19, 280, 282–95; Farrokhzad's *Vitsvit* 286–91, 297n9; Kleemann's *Eskimothertongue* 282–6; Olsen's *Third-Millenium Heart* 292–5
contemporary Swedish language literature 18; "Borta i tankar" (Leiva Wenger) 229–32; *Loss* (Berg) 233–4; meanings separated by backslash 240n11; multilingualism, readers and processes of bordering 225–9; "Tongknoll" (Andtbacka) 234–8
Corpse Exhibition and Other Stories of Iraq (Blasim) 31
cosmopolitanism 59–61
creativity 115, 122, 123
Cronin, Michael 102, 108–9; *Across the Lines* 107–8
cross-border/transnational studies 9
cross-cultural autobiographies 114
culture, Said's definition of 57
Cyrillic script 243, 246–9, 251

"Dagen svalnar" (Södergran) 290
Damrosch, David 42
Deleuze, Gilles 7, 11, 156
Demidov, Ivan 134
Den hemmelege jubel (Fløgstad) 101
Derrida, Jacques 41, 124
Det 3. årtusinds hjerte see *Third-Millenium Heart* (Olsen)
deterritorialization 7, 13, 156
De Vulgari Eloquentia (Dante) 279, 295n1
Diakité, Jason 162, 164
dialogism 265
Díaz, Junot 167
Digital Hats Game (Blasim) 32
Diktonius, Elmer 245

Index 325

diversity of speech 6
Divine Liturgy 248, 256
Dogge Doggelito (Douglas Léon) 158, 161
dominant language 87, 117; stabilization of 13
Dostoyevsky's *Notes from Underground* 55
doubling 67, 68, 69
Do You Miss Your Country (Szydłowska) 84n7

Ekebom, Terhi 311
Elegia. Yksinäytöksinen uninäytelmä (Lietzén) 300, 307, 310, 311
Eliot, T. S. 49, 58, 163; *Ash Wednesday* 58; "The Waste Land" 55, 94, 96, 306–7
"Elixir" 229, 239n3
Ellerström, Lars 190
El Ramly, Ranya 115
Enckell, Martin 132
En vandrare (Colliander) 254
Epistle to Diognetus 254
Eskimothertongue (Kleemann) 282–6
Espmark, Kjell 179, 182, 184, 186–8, 190
Estonian literary field 14; Ivanov's position in 49–52
Estonia, Russian-language literature in 51
ethno-aesthetics 282–3, 286
Ethno-aesthetics (Arke) 282, 283
ethnolinguistic nationalism 280
Et øyeblikk noen tusen år (Siri) 89
Ett öga rött (Hassen-Khemiri) 163, 229
Eurocomics 80–1
extrinsic multilingualism 155

"Fabulas Panicas" (Jodorowsky) 84n10
Fagerholm, Monika 132, 270, 275n14
Fanon, Frantz 293
Farrokhzad, Athena 19, 278, 291, 295; *White Blight (Vitsvit)* 286–91
Feven (Swedish rap artist) 154, 158–60
"Fia" (in Lietzén's *Kaksi pientä novellia*) 313–14, *314*
Finland-Swedish novels 265–6
Finnish comics, multilingual publishing in 15, 66–8; bordering process 82–3; doubling 67, 68,

69; English-language original publications 67, 84n5; integration 67, 76–82; subtitling 67, 69, 72–6, 84n4; supplementing 67, 69–71
Finnish-English combination 64, 67, 82
Finnish *iskelmä* 222n27
Finnish literary field, Blasim in 32–3, 37–41, 44n18
first language 280, 288, 292
Fischer, Andreas 250
Fix, Ulla 188
Fløgstad, Kjartan 15–16, 112n6; *Den hemmelege jubel* 101; *Pampa Unión* 101–11; *Seremoniar* 101; *Valfart* 101
För många länder sedan (Lindén) 135
Forsla fett (Berg) 233
Foster, Jodie 136
"Fosterlandet" (Colliander) 254
Freud 280, 293, 294
Friis, Elisabeth 19
Frith, Simon 154
Fulton, Robert: *Baltics (Östersjöar* translation) 177, 182, 186, 194n2

Gardenia (Blasim's short film) 43n1
Gardner-Chloros, Penelope 212
Gilroy, Paul 156, 163
Girls und Panzer 80
Glädjes möte (Colliander) 253
Glimtar från Tyskland (Colliander) 254
"God Bless the Child" (Holiday's song) 290
Gomix 69–70, *70*
Gone with the Wind, Scarlett O'Hara in 271
Gordon, Elizabeth 155
Goudaillier, Jean-Pierre 158
Greenland: hip-hop culture in 171; predominant languages in 282
Greenlandic literature 88
Griffiths, Gareth 111n2
Gripen (Colliander) 248
Groensteen, Thierry 81, 202
Gröndahl, Satu 9
Grönstrand, Heidi 16
Grutman, Rainier 246–8, 250–1
Guattari, Félix 7, 11, 156

Haavisto, Camilla 37, 40, 44n19
Haddad, Joumana 31, 44n8
Hagelberg, Matti 69

326   Index

Hamann, Johann Georg 178
Hamlet (Shakespeare) 96,
    99n13
Hannerz, Ulf 66
Harlahti, Satu 32
Hartman, Olov 243
Hassen-Khemiri, Jonas 163
Helsingin Sanomat (Finnish
    newspaper) 38, 271
Helsinki slang 264, 274n5
Henry V (Shakespeare) 94
Herder, Johann Gottfried 279
Hernberg, Eira 243
Hetekivi-Olsson, Eija 118, 126n2
heteroglossia 110, 154, 156, 158, 161
heterolingual address 250–1
hip-hop 17; aesthetics of 157; artists
    154, 162; in Denmark 171–2;
    "dialect rap" 172; glocal genre
    of 156–7; in Greenland 171; in
    Norway 172; scholarship 153;
    in Sweden (see Swedish hip-hop
    culture); see also multilingual hip-
    hop lyrics
Hirvonen, Vuokko 89, 90
Hoffman, Eva 117
Högl, Stefan 134
Holiday, Billie 288; "God Bless the
    Child" 290
Holmberg, Niillas 91
Holmström, Johanna 265
Horsti, Karina 44n19
humor 122; in Sinut 16, 115, 122,
    126; Sommer's idea of 115; in
    Wenla Männistö 267
Huss, Markus 17, 155, 170, 227
Hutcheon, Linda 266
Hvostov, Andrei 51
hysterical realism 60

Ibsen, Henrik 97
idioms, difficulty of translating
    135–6
Ilf, Ilya 135
Imam, Silvana 160
"immigrant Swedish" 231, 232
Imperial Eyes (Pratt) 102
incomprehension 177, 184, 226
Ingenbarnsland (Hetekivi-Olsson)
    118, 126n2
Ingvarsson, Jonas 232
integration of translation 67, 76–82
intertextuality 199, 202
intratextual multilingualism 6–8

Invisible Forces / Näkymättömiä
    voimia (Juliacks) 77, 77–8
The Iraqi Christ (Blasim) 31, 32,
    34, 37
Iraq + 100 (Blasim) 31–2, 44n12
Istället för hip hop (Boyaciaglu) 161
Ivanov, Andrei 14, 48; in Estonian
    literary field 49–52; individualism
    48; institutional position of 49–52,
    61n3; man in-between 48; "Moi
    datskii diadiushka" 49, 61n4; non-
    belonger 48; Peotäis põrmu 48, 50,
    52, 54–6, 61n4; publication history
    49; Puteshestvie Hanumana na
    Lolland 48, 49, 60; "Zola" 48, 49,
    52–4, 61n4
I väntan på en jordbävning
    (Lindén) 134

Jag har letat efter dig (Razai) 265
Jakobson, Lars 232
Jameson, Fredric 102, 111n2
JanMohamed, Abdul R. 102
Jannok, Sofia 90
Jodorowsky, Alejandro 84n10
Joffe, Eleonora 132
Jonsson, Carla 90, 108
Jotuni, Maria 271
Joyce, James 233; Ulysses 307
Juliacks: Invisible Forces /
    Näkymättömiä voimia 77, 77–8

Kafka, Franz 7
Kahn, Douglas 180
Kaksi ja puoli novellia (Lietzén) 304
Kalaitzidis, Pantelis 256
Kallio, Pauli 300
Kankare, Wolf: Miska Pähkinä
    72–5, 74
Karpinsky, Eva C. 118
Katajavuori, Riina 263
Kaurala, Saana 67
Kauranen, Ralf 15
Kellman, Steven G. 8, 246
Khaled: "Aicha" song 172
Khemiri, Jonas Hassen 115
Kianto, Ilmari 271
Kincaid, Jamaica 33
Kinnunen, Laila 269
Kirjeitä / Letters (Rantanen) 69
Kis, Danilo 36
Kivi, Aleksis 19, 263, 264, 266,
    274n2
Klasson, Christopher 256

Kleemann, Jessie 19, 278, 291, 295, 295n2; *Eskimothertongue* 282–6
Klein, Melanie 278; perspective on breastfeeding 280–1; theory of good and bad breast 281, 285, 294
Kleveland, Anne Karine 15
Knauth, Alfons 8
"Kom igen" (Outlandish's song) 172
Korhonen, Outi 39–40
Korståget (Mazzarella) 244
Kotsinas, Ulla-Britt 158
krestnyi khod 244
Kristeva, Julia 242
Kroyer, Peder Severin 307
"Krypskydd" (Berg) 233, 239n6
Kukkonen, Karin 208
Kuti (magazine) 67, 84n3, 84n10

Laanes, Eneken 14
Laestadius, Ann-Helén 89–90
Laikku 84n2
language: Bakhtin's framework for 6–7; dominance 13; heterogeneity of 12; and migration 8; of minor literature 7; mother tongue 10; rhizomatic framework 11–13
language games 115, 122
Larsen, Irene 90
Läskimooses (Hagelberg) 69
Latin Kings 154, 158, 159; *The Latin Kings: Texter* 161
"La Tortura" (Shakira's song) 203, 205
"Lauantai" (Kinnunen's song) 269
Lehtinen, Anita 68, *69*
Lehtonen, Joel 271
Leiva Wenger, Alejandro 115, 229–32, 238
Leonidov, Maxim 136
Leskinen, Juice 123
lexical multilingualism 6, 177, 189
Lietzén, Mika 19–20, 75, 300; "Alkoholi" / "Alcohol" 304, *304*; *Elegia* 300, 307, 310, 311; "Fia," in *Kaksi pientä novellia* 313–14, *314*; interest in comics 300–1; *Jääkärit* album 309; *Lohikäärmeen varvas* 300–2, *302*; *Minä olen saari* 306–7; *1986* 307, 310, *311*; "1917 - Libau" 20, 305; *Tarinoita lännestä. Neljä novellia* 305, *306*, 310
Lindanserskan (Lindén) 135, 138

Lindén, Zinaida 16; alliterations 136; difficulty of translating idioms 135–6; early childhood 130–1; *Finlands historia/ История Финляндии* 132; *Finland 1944/ Финляндия 1944 год* 132; *För manga länder sedan* 135; "I bergakungens sal" 136; *I väntan på en jordbävning* 134; and Joffe, Eleonora 132; *Lindanserskan* 135, 138; "lost in translation" 16, 138; multilingualism 130–1; *Överstinnan och syntetisatorn* 130; The Pilot's Son 16–17; Scandinavian readers 135; *Scheherazades sanna historier* 130; *Takakirves – Tokyo* 134, 136, 137; as translator 132, 133; *Valenciana* 17; writing in Swedish and Russian 134–5, 137; *Голос женщины* (The woman's voice) 132
Lindgren, Astrid 158
linguistic revitalization projects 91
literary multilingualism 3–4, 18, 176, 180, 193, 225–7, 243, 245–6; multimodal approach to 12; processes and practices of border-making 11–20; research on 5–11; *see also* contemporary Swedish language literature
Lohikäärmeen varvas (Lietzén) 300–2, *302*
Loss (Berg) 233–4, 238
Löytty, Olli 19
Lukkari, Rauni Magga 97
Lundin, Erik 154, 160–2, 172; "Välkommen hem" 164–5, 167; "weird Swedish" 167, 168, 172; *see also Suedi* (Lundin)
Lyytikäinen, Pirjo 266

Madinah: City Stories from the Middle East (Haddad) 31
The Madman of Freedom Square (Blasim) 30–3; "The Truck to Berlin" 34–5
Madsen, Claus K. 179
"Malmbyen" (Ore city) 105–7
"Manichean allegory" 102, 111n2
Manuele Fior: *5,000 km Per Second* 313
"Maskinen" (The machine) 103–5, 111, 111n3
Mazzarella, Merete 243

Index 327

Index

Meinander, Henrik 132
Melberg, Arne 103, 104
Melkas, Kukku 19
Mestari / Maestro (Vähämäki) 70–1, 71
Micheva, Neva 32
Miira (Hetekivi-Olsson) 127n2
Mimesis (Auerbach) 57–8
Minä olen saari (Lietzén) 306–7
minor literature 7
Miska Pähkinä (Kankare) 72–5, 74
Mitchell, Toni 172
Moestrup, Mette: *Dø løgn, dø* 296n5
Mohnike, Thomas 239n1
"Moi datskii diadiushka" (Ivanov) 49, 61n6
monolingualism 3, 10, 245
monolingual literature 176
monolingual paradigm 3, 154, 279, 282
monolingual text 225
Moomintroll and the End of the World (Jansson) 84n8
"Moster Elsie" (Westö) 301
mother tongue 10, 19, 122–6; in contemporary Nordic poetry 19, 280, 282–95; in Farrokhzad's *Vitsvit* 286–91, 297n9; in Kleemann's *Eskimothertongue* 282–6; locution/metaphor of 278; in Olsen's *Third-Millenium Heart* 292–5; Yildiz's notion of 279
Mufti, Aamir R. 59, 62n9
Mu gonagasa gollebiktasat – Min konges gylne klær (Lukkari) 97
multiculturalism 9
multilingual comics publishing 67–8; and bordering 82–3; doubling 67, 68, 69; integration 67, 76–82; subtitling 67, 69, 72–6, 84n4; supplementing 67, 69–71
multilingual hip-hop lyrics 154; construction of national identity 156; extrinsic multilingualism 155; organic multilingualism 155; political multilingualism 155, 160–4; Swedish 154–5
multilingualism 3, 6, 13, 14, 90, 246–50; of bordering 225–9; in comics culture 64–6; political 96–7; of Sámi authors 88, 91; in Sámi literature (*see* Sámi literature, multilingualism in); in Sámi music culture 90; stylistic 94–6

multilingual landscape, Hirvonen's notion of 89
multilingual publishing strategy, Sámi literature 91
multiple readerships 13
"Mumintrollet och jordens undergang" *see Moomintroll and the End of the World* (Jansson)
"Mu Muhammad Ali" (Skåden) 92
Munch, Edvard 307
Musset, Alfred de 131
Muttersprache 279, 294
Myers-Scotton, Carol 111n1
"My Grand Prix Song" (Skåden) 96

Nabokov, Vladimir 8, 167
Näkymättömät kädet (Tietäväinen) 17–18, 199, 222n1; bambara language in 215; Chao's "Clandestino" lyrics 203–5; diegetic texts in 206–11; intertextual references in 199, 202, 212; multilingual combination of words and images 200–2; multilingualism of 199, 206, 211, 221;
Napa 69, 72, 84n2
Neruda, Pablo 107
The Nightmare of Carlos Fuentes (Razaq) 45n20
Nikkilä, Aura 17–18
Nilsson, Magnus 9, 41, 239n1
1986 (Lietzén) 75, 307, 310, *311*
"1917 – Libau" (Lietzén) 20, 305
Nissilä, Hanna-Leena 88
noise, in multilingual literature 180
Norway, hip-hop culture in 172
Notes from Underground (Dostoyevsky) 55
Novyi Zhurnal, "Zola" in 48, 49
Nurinkurin 114
Nuuk Posse 171
Nuutinen, Christer 72, 300
Nykvist, Karin 17

Ogbar, Jeffrey 162
Olmi Kolmonen (comics anthology) 72, 75
Olsen, Ursula Andkjær 19, 278, 295; *Third-Millenium Heart* 292–5
Olsson, Jesper 8
Orbita group 61
Orda – This Is my Land (Jannok's album) 90
Oresteia (Aeschylus) 288

organic multilingualism 155
Öri, Julia 255
Orthodox liturgical texts, Swedish translations of 252
Orthodox Paradoxes (Tolstaya) 255
Orthodox theological theory 256–7
Östersjöar. En dikt (Tranströmer) 17, 177, 179, 196n8; acoustic sphere of language 180, 184, 187; Fulton's translation 177, 182, 186; lexical multilingualism 177, 189; listening to language borders in 184–9; materiality of block letter 189–93; metaphors of reading and writing 180–4; misspelled conversations 182–3; partial comprehension 179, 184, 193
Ottosson, Robert 72
Øverås, Asbjørn 32
Överstinnan och syntetisatorn (Lindén) 130

Paert, Irina 256
Page, Ra 30, 31, 44n10
Palandt, Ralf 84n9
Palmer, Marion 90
Pampa Unión (Fløgstad) 15–16, 101–2; alienating the matrix language 108–9, 111n1; "Barnet til hesten" (The horse's child) 107–9; code-switching 108; losing letters 103–5, 111; "Løyndemålet" (Secret language) 109–10; "Malmbyen" (Ore city) 105–7; "Maskinen" (The machine) 103–5, 111, 111n3; multilingualism 102, 108; otherness 105–8
parallel bilingualism 91
parallel lingualism 256
paratopia 255
Parente-Čapková, Viola 272
partial fluency 226; and aesthetic effects 177–8
Peotäis põrmu (Ivanov) 14, 48, 50, 52, 54–6, 61n4
Perloff, Marjorie 8
The Persians (Aeschylus) 288
Petrov, Yevgeniy 135
Pettersson, Torsten 243
The Pilot's Son (Lindén) 16–17
Platt, Kevin M. F. 61
political multilingualism 96–7, 155, 160–4
polyphony 265

Postmodern Ethics (Bauman) 256
Pratt, Mary Louise 102
Prekariáhta lávlla (Skåden) 91, 92, 97
Pullapoika / Doughboy (Rapi) 72, 75–6, 76
Puteshestvie Hanumana na Lolland (Ivanov) 48, 49, 60
Putkinotko (Lehtonen) 271

Rajewsky, Irina O. 202
Rakkautta viimeisellä silmäyksellä (Turunen) 70
Rantanen, Miissa 69
Ranta, Ville 300, 301
Rapi, Aapo: *Pullapoika / Doughboy* 72, 75–6, 76
Razai, Sara 265
Razaq, Rashid 45n20
Reconquista 206, 209–10
"Reflections on Exile" (Said) 56
"A Refugee in the Paradise that is Europe" (Blasim) 29–30, 44n6
reterritorialization 7
Ringgren, Magnus 179
Rinne, Cia 227, 227–8, 234
Roađđi – Rosa Boreal – Boreal Rose 91
Rönnerstrand, Torsten 182, 186
Rose, Tricia 156
Roy, Arundhati 167
Rushdie, Salman 39, 48, 49, 60–1
Russian Estonian literature 51
Ryysyrannan Jooseppi (Kianto) 271

Sahlin, Mona 159
Said, Edward 14, 62n9, 288; affiliation 58, 59; condition of exile 56–7, 59; crisis of natural filiation 58; definition of culture 57; filiation 58, 59; "Reflections on Exile" 56; secular criticism 58, 59; *The World, the Text and the Critics* 56
Sakai, Naoki 4, 12, 48, 176, 193, 228, 250–1
Sámi authors, multilingualism of 88, 91
Sámi languages 87
Sámi literature, multilingualism in 15, 87–8; children's books 91; code-switching 90; lost language 89; parallel bilingualism 91; Sámi authors 88, 91; self-translation 89; in Skåden's work (*see* Skåden, Sigbjørn)

Sámi music culture, multilingualism in 90
Samtal med smärtan (Colliander) 253
Sandström, Daniel 32
Sanmagumo 80
Scandinavian languages 82
Scarlett O'Hara, in Gone with the Wind 271
Scheherazades sanna historier (Lindén) 130
Schleiermacher, Friedrich 279
Schmitz-Emans, Monika 178, 199, 216
second language 288
Seitsemän veljestä (Kivi) 19, 263–5, 266, 267, 272, 273
self-translation 89
semiotic modality 190
Seremoniar (Fløgstad) 101
Shakespeare, William: Hamlet 96, 99n13; Henry V 94; Skaden's "stylistic multilingualism" 94–6
Shakira's "La Tortura" 203, 205
The Shia's Poisoned Child (Blasim) 32
Shklovsky, Victor 115, 226
The Silence of the Lambs (film) 136
Simmel, Georg 37
Sinut (Abu-Hanna) 16, 114, 125–6, 126n1; Arabic and Finnish elements 118–19; Arabic words and expressions in 119; autofiction 116; book's layout 117; collisions with language borders 120–2; English language 119–21, 126; language learning 114–16; "migration story" 116; mother tongue 122–6; playful and humoristic style 16, 115, 122, 126
Siri, Hege 89, 90
Skåden, Sigbjorn 15, 88; "Backstage, Sámi Grand Prix" 94–6; double allusion 94; and Ibsen's poem 97; Ihpil: Láhppon mánáid bestejeaddji 91; "Mu Muhammad Ali" 92; "My Grand Prix Song" 96; political multilingualism 96–7; Prekariáhta lávlla 91, 92, 97; Skomakernes konge 92; Skuovvadeddjiid gonagas 91–4, 96–7; stylistic multilingualism 94–6
Skomakernes konge (Skåden) 92
Skulskaya, Elena 51

Skuovvadeddjiid gonagas (Skåden) 91–4, 96–7
"Slajka" 72–3, 73
Sms från Soppero (Laestadius) 89–90
Södergran, Edith 290–1, 307; "Dagen svalnar" 290
Sommer, Doris 10, 13, 115, 122, 155, 177, 226, 227, 282
"Stabat mater" 233
Sternberg, Meir 108, 109, 112n8
Stiller, Mauritz 307
Strindberg, August 307
stylistic multilingualism 94–6
subtitling 67, 69, 84n4; appendices and 69; Kankare's Miska Pähkinä 72–5, 74; Olmi kolmonen 72; Rapi's Pullapoika / Doughboy 72, 75–6, 76
Suedi (Lundin's album) 154, 162, 164; "Annie Lööf" 165; cover photo of 165; "Haffla" 170–1; "Haram" 168–70; "Suedi" 165–8; "Västerort" 165
"Suedi" (Lundin's song) 165–8
Sugarhill Gang's "Rapper's Delight" 157
Suomusume (Maro & Nieal) 80–1
surprise effect 115–16
Swedish-Finnish literature 68, 118
Swedish hip-hop culture 17, 172; demand for authenticity 162–3; Dogge Doggelito (Douglas Léon) 158, 161; Feven 154, 158–60; Imam, Silvana 160; Just D 157–8; Latin Kings 154, 158, 159; Lundin, Erik 154, 160–2, 172 (see also Suedi (Lundin)); lyrics 157–60; political multilingualism 160–4
Szydłowska, Monika 84n7

Tagore, Rabindranath 36
Takakirves – Tokyo (Lindén) 134, 136, 137
Tarinoita lännestä. Neljä novellia (Lietzén) 305, 306, 310
Tarkovsky, Andrei 131
Thiong'o, Ngũgĩ wa 8
Third-Millenium Heart (Olsen) 292–5
Tidigs, Julia 6, 7, 155, 170, 177, 190, 203, 245, 265, 266
Tietäväinen, Ville 17–18, 199, 202, 216, 220, 221n1; see also Näkymättömät kädet (Tietäväinen)

Tiffin, Helen 111n2
Till vår ära (Leiva Wenger) 229
"Todesfuge" (Celan) 289, 291
"Tongknoll" (Andtbacka) 234–8
translation(s) 4–5, 27, 246–50; of Blasim's texts 29, 36–7, 43, 44n4; as bordering process 176, 193; in Finnish comics 65, 67 (*see also* multilingual comics publishing); idioms 135–6; as one-way process 41–2; transformations 42
translational mimesis 108
translingualism 8, 246
translingual life writing 245–6
translingual literature 8
translingual paratopia (Ori) 255
transnational/cross-border studies 9
transnationalism 28; in comics culture 64–7
Tranströmer, Tomas 177–84, 189–93; see also *Östersjöar. En dikt* (Tranströmer)
travel literature: bordering 111; and otherness 102–3
"true bilingualism" 248–9
Tuominen, Jamppa 216–20
Turunen, Marko 70
Two and a Half Stories see *Kaksi ja puoli novellia* (Lietzén)

Ulysses (Joyce) 307
Undusk, Jaan 50
Uppland (Berg) 233
US hip-hop 153; aesthetics 157; artists 162; Mobb Deep 161; Sugarhill Gang's "Rapper's Delight" 157
Uthaug, Maren 92

Vähämäki, Amanda: *Mestari / Maestro* 70–1, 71
Valenciana (Lindén) 17
Valfart (Fløgstad) 101
Valkeapää, Nils-Aslak 88
"Välkommen hem" (Lundin's song) 164–5, 167

"Västerort" (Lundin's song) 165
Venuti, Lawrence 42
Vertovec, Steven 28
Vid den stora floden (Jakobson) 232
Vilkkumaa, Maija 44n6
Virtual Baltic Sea Library 179
Vitsvit (Farrokhzad) 286–91, 297n9

Walkowitz, Rebecca L. 33, 65, 178, 226–7
Waltå, Göran O:son 254
"The Waste Land" (Eliot) 55, 94, 96, 306–7
"was war" (Rinne) 234
Weird English (Ch'ien) 167, 172
Welsh, Irvine 167
Wenla Männistö (Katajavuori) 19, 263, 274n1; accentuation 267; "The American Girl" 270; appropriation and change 266–71; Helsinki slang 264, 265, 274n5; illusion of orality 267; mobility of language 263–6; multiple voices and intertexts 264–5; power of language 272–4; Wenla's speech/voice 267–8
Westö, Kjell 132, 301
Weston, Daniel 212
White Clay (Blasim's short film) 43n1
Willert, Trine Stauning 256
Williams, Mark 155
Wood, James 60
world literature 42, 176
Wunderkammer (Andtbacka) 234–8

Yassin-Kassab, Robin 34
Yildiz, Yasemin 124, 154, 156, 158, 177, 245, 295; monolingual paradigm 3, 279, 282; mother tongue 10; notion of mother tongue 279

Zakharov, Alexander 137
Zaldua, Iban 91
"Zola" (Ivanov) 14, 48, 49, 52–4, 60, 61, 61n6

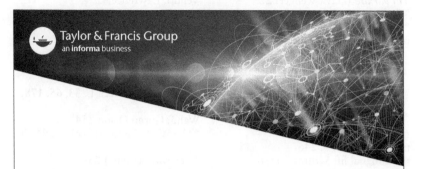